Governing Cyberspace

Digital Technologies and Global Politics

Series Editors: Andrea Calderaro and Madeline Carr

While other disciplines like law, sociology, and computer science have engaged closely with the Information Age, international relations scholars have yet to bring the full analytic power of their discipline to developing our understanding of what new digital technologies mean for concepts like war, peace, security, cooperation, human rights, equity, and power. This series brings together the latest research from international relations scholars—particularly those working across disciplines—to challenge and extend our understanding of world politics in the Information Age.

Governing Cyberspace: Behavior, Power, and Diplomacy, edited by Dennis Broeders and Bibi van den Berg

Governing Cyberspace

Behavior, Power, and Diplomacy

Edited by
Dennis Broeders
Bibi van den Berg

ROWMAN & LITTLEFIELD
Lanham • Boulder • New York • London

Published by Rowman & Littlefield
An imprint of The Rowman & Littlefield Publishing Group, Inc.
4501 Forbes Boulevard, Suite 200, Lanham, Maryland 20706
www.rowman.com

6 Tinworth Street, London, SE11 5AL, United Kingdom

Copyright © 2020 by Dennis Broeders and Bibi van den Berg

British Library Cataloguing in Publication Information Available

Library of Congress Cataloging-in-Publication Data

Names: Broeders, D. (Dennis), editor. | Berg, Bibi van den, editor.
Title: Governing cyberspace : behavior, power, and diplomacy / edited by Dennis
    Broeders, Bibi van den Berg.
Description: Lanham : Rowman & Littlefield, [2020] | Series: Digital technologies
    and global politics | Includes bibliographical references and index. | Summary:
    "Contributes to the discussion of growing insecurity and the unpredictable and often
    authoritarian use of the digital ecosystem"—Provided by publisher.
Identifiers: LCCN 2020004795 (print) | LCCN 2020004796 (ebook) |
    ISBN 9781786614940 (cloth) | ISBN 9781786614957 (paperback) |
    ISBN 9781786614964 (epub)
Subjects: LCSH: Computer networks—Law and legislation. | Internet—Law and
    legislation. | Cyberspace.
Classification: LCC K564.C6 G685 2020 (print) | LCC K564.C6 (ebook) |
    DDC 343.09/944—dc23
LC record available at https://lccn.loc.gov/2020004795
LC ebook record available at https://lccn.loc.gov/2020004796

Contents

Acknowledgments

This book resulted from the inaugural conference of the Hague Program for Cyber Norms, titled "Novel Horizons: Responsible Behaviour in Cyberspace," which was held in the Hague on November 5–7, 2018. The editors thank the participants for a great conference and especially those that submitted their work for this edited volume.

A first round of editorial comments was done for the conference itself, and we thank Liisi Adamson, Els de Busser, Ilina Georgieva, and Zine Homburger, who were at the time all affiliated to the program, for their editorial contribution. We also thank Corianne Oosterbaan for all her hard work organizing the conference and her invaluable help with the editorial process.

Lastly, we would like to thank the Dutch Ministry of Foreign Affairs who generously fund the Hague Program for Cyber Norms and all of its activities and publications.

The Hague, 2.12.2019
Dennis Broeders and Bibi van den Berg

Chapter 1

Governing Cyberspace

Behavior, Power, and Diplomacy

Dennis Broeders and Bibi van den Berg

WELCOME TO CYBERSPACE

When states look at cyberspace, they do not necessarily see the same as most end users do. Sure, they see the massive added value in terms of the digital economy and, like their citizens, they have difficulties imagining life without the constant interactions and communication that is the bedrock of modern digital society. However, many parts of the government see cyberspace increasingly as a source of threat, insecurity, and instability. Where states looked at the early stages of the development of cyberspace with a certain degree of "benign neglect," it became much more of a government interest when the digital economy started off in earnest. Now, states increasingly view cyberspace through a lens of security. Not just in terms of cybercrime but more and more in terms of the high politics of international security (Klimburg 2017; Segal 2016; DeNardis 2014; Deibert 2013; Betz and Stevens 2011). Many states have formally declared the cyber domain to be the fifth domain of warfare—after land, sea, air, and space—and increasingly states conduct intelligence and pseudo-military operations in the cyber domain that fall short of "cyber war" but do create a permanent state of "unpeace" (Kello 2017; see also Boeke and Broeders 2018). The increase in cyber-attacks among states, or at least those that come out into the open, seem to be intensifying in terms of damage and impact, and provoke reactions from states and corporations. Cyber operations like WannaCry and NotPetya, politically attributed to North Korea and Russia, respectively, were both damaging and indiscriminate, which added to the feeling of vulnerability in the digital domain. However, even with NotPetya, of which the global damages have been estimated at roughly $10 billion (Greenberg 2018), no state was willing to say this operation was in violation of international law. More in general, all public attributions of cyberattacks to states have not invoked international law other than in the most general terms possible (Efrony and Shany 2018).

In cyberspace, a state of unpeace is heating up and although most states agree in principle that international law applies in cyberspace as it does in the analogue world, they do not seem to be able to agree on specifics. Furthermore, "the" regulation of "the" Internet does not exist. Nye (2014) has shown that the Internet is regulated through an elaborate cyber regime complex that has pockets of dense regulation in some subject areas as well as patches that are largely unregulated. Moreover, there are many aspects on which states are still struggling to find an effective governance structure to address the issues at hand (see also Klimburg and Faesen 2020 in this volume). Moreover, some elements of governance are firmly in the hands of private parties (companies, the technical community), whereas others—for example, military, intelligence, and diplomatic—are firmly in the hands of states. The mix between public and private actors in Internet governance is called "multistakeholder governance," a concept that is embraced by Western liberal states (at least in theory) but is disputed by states that favor a much stronger role for sovereign states in the regulation and governance of cyberspace. States like Russia and China would like to bring "Internet governance" into a multilateral setting where sovereign states, rather than a wide array of stakeholders, steer the direction of cyberspace. This archetypical divide between multistakeholderism and multilateralism when talking about cybersecurity and Internet governance structures is connecting with rising geopolitical tensions between the major global powers. The global strife between the United States and China and Russia—with the European Union somewhere in the middle of the mix—works as a force multiplier for tensions in both interstate behavior—cyber operations among states— and positions in diplomatic negotiations on "responsible state behavior" in cyberspace (Broeders, Adamson, and Creemers 2019). In this volume, Klimburg and Faesen (2020) search for ways to square the circle the between classic balance of power politics and the complicated governance structures that are needed to regulate cyberspace.

OF LAWS AND NORMS

The possible negative effects of the use of ICTs for international peace and security were flagged by Russia in 1998 when it submitted a resolution on "Developments in the field of Information and Telecommunications in the context of International Security" to the UN's First Committee, which deals with disarmament and international security (UNGA 1999). While recognizing that the Internet brought many good things, Moscow feared an arms race in this new domain and aimed for the negotiation of a treaty that would ban the use of information weapons in order to prevent information wars. To some extent, Russia feared in 1998 what many now consider Moscow to be the best at: information operations and the spread of disinformation. Russia was aiming for a new treaty specifically for cyberspace but ran into Western resistance to the notion that cyberspace needed *lex specialis*. Western states, in this field often loosely assembled under the heading of the "like-minded" states, depart from the notion that international law, including International Humanitarian Law, applies in the digital domain as it does in the "real world." The UN Group of Governmental Experts (UN GGE) process was started in 2004 to create a venue at the UN level for deliberation of the issue without going down the road of a treaty. Out of five iterations of the process the group of experts produced a consensus report three times, with as main yields the principle that international law applies in cyberspace in 2013 and the formulation of a number of nonbinding norms for responsible state behavior in the 2015 consensus report (UN General Assembly 2010, 2013, 2015). After the 2017 round of the UN GGE failed to achieve consensus, there were many reports of the "death of the norms process" (see, e.g., Grigsby 2017), but in November 2018, the UN General Assembly voted on two parallel and competing resolutions. The first was submitted by the United States and supported by the "like-minded" states calling for a new round of the GGE. The second was submitted by Russia and called for an Open-Ended Working Group (OEWG) to discuss roughly the same issues. Both were voted through by the General Assembly in substantial and significantly overlapping numbers, and the twin processes have started in 2019.

In a parallel trajectory to the diplomatic processes at the UN and regional organizations, international legal scholars embarked on a project to flesh out how exactly international law applies in cyberspace. This project under the sponsorship of the NATO CCDCOE—which does not make it a NATO project—resulted in the Tallinn Manual (2013) and the Tallinn Manual 2.0 in 2017 (Schmitt et al. 2013, 2017). Both are academic, nonbinding studies on how international law applies to cyber conflicts and cyber warfare and on many issues contain majority and minority opinions. The first manual focuses on the *jus ad bellum* and International Humanitarian Law and the second focuses on cyber operations that are "below the threshold" of armed conflict, or "peacetime operations." The Tallinn manuals are the most comprehensive analyses of International Humanitarian Law and cyberspace available and serve as an important reference point. However, and as indicated before, states are reluctant to refer to (specific principles of) international law when they publicly address cyber operations and conflict, leading Efrony and

Shany (2018) to refer to the manual as "a rulebook on the shelf." Many legal scholars in this fieldwork on different aspects of international law and how these relate to state operations in the cyber domain. In this volume, Roguski (2020) analyses the principle of territorial sovereignty in cyberspace through a lens of an "intrusion-based approach" and Tsagourias (2020) looks at cyber interference with election processes in light of the legal principle of non-intervention. Principle-by-principle and case-by-case legal scholars are adding to the growing literature on the application of international law to state behavior in cyberspace.

The limited diplomatic progress on the application of international law to cyberspace also led to what is called the cyber-norms process, both in diplomatic practice as in academia. The 2015 UN GGE consensus report included a section on "general non-binding, voluntary norms, rules and principles for responsible behaviour of states." This section contained eleven "new" recommendations for norms and gave an impetus to the international debate about cyber norms. These norms are often juxtaposed with international law. The states that participate in the GGE process went the route of norms, in part because achieving agreement on the question of *how* exactly international law applies to cyberspace proved a size too big for the negotiations. However, it is also misleading to set norms and international law totally apart from each other in this domain. In this volume, Adamson (2020) highlights the fact that many of the norms in the 2015 UN GGE report actually reflect existing international law. Norms and international law can and do mutually reinforce each other and should not be seen as two completely different and parallel discourses.

International law and international norms—as well as Confidence Building Measures (CBMs), which are also part of the GGE process—all serve the same basic function in the context of cyberspace. They are all meant to make state behavior more predictable—especially in times of conflict—when operating in a context that is unpredictable and where actions are easy to obfuscate and misinterpret. Norms and international law serve to set benchmarks against which we can measure and evaluate state behavior and call actors out on bad behavior. International law would be the gold standard for this but is problematic for two reasons. Firstly, because it has proven hard to get substantial agreement on the question of how specific principles of international law apply in cyberspace. Secondly, because many of the cyber operations that have states worried are below-the-threshold operations and, moreover, they are usually executed by intelligence agencies and proxy actors, which are not meaningfully regulated by international law in the first place (Boeke and Broeders 2018; Maurer 2018). In order to make some progress, academics and states have gone down the route of norms.

THE CYBER-NORMS DISCOURSE

Norms have been a part of the academic debate for far longer than the rise to fame of the cyber-prefix. In international relations theory, Peter Katzenstein's definition of a norm is often the point of departure. According to him, a norm in international politics is "a collective expectation for the proper behaviour of actors with a given identity" (Katzenstein 1996, 5). This implies that there is some sort of community that has—or develops—an idea of what appropriate behavior is. And even though there is no enforcement mechanism in place, the community expects its members to behave a certain, appropriate, way. In the cyber-norms discourse that community is often equated with states, especially in the diplomatic, state-led norms debate, even though many other public and private actors populate the cyber domain and even dominate important aspects of Internet governance. Finnemore and Sikkink (1998) argue that norms are often championed by a norms entrepreneur and when successful the norm they champion goes through a norms cycle. This cycle starts with "norms emergence," in which the role of the norms entrepreneur(s) to propagate the norm is vital. If their advocacy for the norm is successful, the community to which the norm should apply may reach a tipping point which leads to the second stage, labeled the "norms cascade." During this phase, the pioneering work of the norms entrepreneur gets taken over by many other actors within the community who see the norms as central to their identity and propagate its spread. In the last stage, actors "internalize" the norm into their everyday behavior and the norms effectively come to serve as a benchmark for appropriate behavior. Finnemore and Hollis (2016) have taken this classic approach to norms creation into the cyber domain and highlighted the dynamic and interdependent character of cyber norms. They also found that much of the debate about norms in this domain was (too) centered on norms as an end goal and not enough on the value of the process itself. Kurowska (2019) takes that argument further and emphasizes that the classic model of the norms cycle—perhaps especially in the cyber-norms debate—often has a teleological character and does not take norms contestation into account as an important part of the model. This blind spot has consequences not only for the empirical analysis of the norms process but also for the legitimacy of the norms process as a political and a policy process: "a norm that cannot be contested, cannot be legitimate" (Kurowska 2019, 8).

Cyber norms as they stand today are highly contested among governments, despite the efforts of diplomats over the last decades. Moreover, the community to which the norms apply—and who feel part of it as norm entrepreneurs—is by no means convincingly demarcated. States consider themselves to be the core community, but civil society and corporations are increasingly vocal about their place and role in this normative and regulatory domain and engage with the norms debate on their own accord. In this volume, Eggenschwiler and Kulesza (2020) analyze the role of a number of civil society and corporate initiatives that engage with, and shape the norms debate. Gorwa and Peez (2020) and Hurel and Lobato (2020), both also in this volume, analyze the role, goals, and strategies of Microsoft that has put itself forward as a major actor in the international cyber-norms debate.

However, the diplomatic track does not easily open up to "outside" actors even when it has failed to make much substantial progress on the issue. The 2015 UN GGE norms may be agreed upon but are in the words of Maurer (2019) "considered voluntary, defined vaguely, and internalized weakly." After the attacks on the Ukrainian grid in December 2015, many wondered why this was not called out as a violation of the norm that states do not attack critical infrastructures in peacetime as formulated in the 2015 UN GGE consensus report.[1] Now that the stalemate that came into being after the 2017 round of the UN GGE failed to produce consensus has been replaced with the political surprise of the creation of two UN processes in 2018, states bear a great responsibility for moving the process forward. If they do not, the UN is unlikely to remain the focal point for discussion. And while the United States is heavily invested in the GGE as a format and Russia is heavily invested in the OEWG, and more generally in the idea of a multilateral approach, the differences of opinion remain substantial.

Meanwhile, cyber norms are also emerging through state practice rather than diplomatic agreement. States engage in certain behavior in cyberspace: they conduct cyber operations, develop (military) cyber doctrine, change cybersecurity policies and thus create new facts on the digital ground. States also draw red lines that are either respected or violated. When violated, some are met with consequences and some are not. All of this is norm-setting behavior. Actual state behavior shapes normative behavior but is "implicit, poorly understood, and cloaked in secrecy" (Maurer 2019). A good example of that is the norm-setting behavior of intelligence agencies that is analyzed by Georgieva (2020b) in this volume (see also Georgieva 2020a). Power relations and actual state behavior go a long way in explaining how state relations in cyberspace develop.

POWER AND NORMS

One complicating factor of state relations is the Orwellian notion that all states are equal, but some are more equal than others. Even the UN, an organization founded on the principle of the equality of sovereign states, acknowledges this through the mechanism of the five permanent members of the Security Council that hold a veto. As "cyber" rose to the top of the international and national security agenda, geopolitics and strategic considerations became more prominent in the debate about responsible state behavior in cyberspace. States may agree that cyberspace is a source of threats to national security, but simultaneously it is also a possible strategic military advantage, especially to the top-tier cyber powers. Powerful states are usually reluctant to give up capabilities, especially when it is uncertain that others will do the same (Broeders 2017). Countries like the United States, China, Russia, the United Kingdom and Israel, but also Iran and North Korea, have invested heavily in military and foreign intelligence capacity to operate in cyberspace. Other countries have followed suit in different degrees creating a landscape in which operational cyber capacity and cyber power are unequally divided among states.

Moreover, in recent years, the global balance of power has been shifting. American global dominance is challenged by the rising star of China. While China's cyber power is still mostly focused on (economic) espionage and control on the domestic information sphere, rather than all-out military cyber power, China is also asserting itself as a tech developer and vendor at the global level as one of the underpinnings of its status as an economic superpower (Inkster 2016). Russia is trying to reassert itself in terms of being a key player in international cyber peace and security. In cyberspace it does so by—allegedly—being one of the most active cyber powers operating below the threshold of armed conflict in the networks of a great number of countries, as well as by being one of the leading countries in the diplomatic processes on responsible state behavior in cyberspace (see Kurowska 2020 in this volume). China and Russia are also formally and informally aligned on a number of foreign policy objectives, including in the cyber domain. They present a seemingly united front to the world, largely aimed at countering US hegemony, but underneath the façade of unity there are also structural differences that may put cracks into Sino-Russian cooperation in the longer run (Broeders, Adamson, and Creemers 2019).

As a general principle, all states want other states to be bound by a framework of rules while retaining as much room to maneuver for themselves. Great powers like strategic ambiguity in military affairs (Taddeo 2017) and exceptionalism in political affairs. To global powers, like the United States, China, and Russia, the latter is almost an informal doctrine: they all apply a sense of exceptionalism to themselves. China and Russia have clear, explicit, and extensive rules and regulations with regard to cyberspace for their own territories, and (global) companies wishing to do business there must comply or else face the consequences. In this volume, Hoffman (2020) analyses the ways in which China has dealt with US pushback on freedom of expression surrounding Google's entry into the Chinese market.

Russia and China both rally around the idea of "cyber sovereignty" as one of the main organizing principles for interstate relations in cyberspace (see Creemers 2020 and Kurowksa 2020 in this volume). To these countries, cyber sovereignty means control over the domestic information sphere internally, and strict adherence to the principle of non-intervention and self-determination externally. Both China and Russia see information operations in their nation's information sphere as the greatest ICT-related threat. Ironically, what Moscow fears most is what it is generally considered to be best at: information operations and the spread of mis- and disinformation. More in general, "sovereignty" is a bone of contention between Western states and authoritarian states. In this volume, Creemers (2020) highlights that tension in the Chinese case: "China's definition of sovereignty primarily concerns the integrity of its political structure, while Western states consider this a defence of exactly those abuses that the more conditional, post-Cold War reading of sovereignty sought to curtail" (Creemers 2020, 112). Moreover, for countries like China and Russia, sovereignty is not the same for all states: the sovereignty of great states is of a different order than those of smaller states. Great power status is paired with exceptionalism. In the eyes of both Russia and China, the *Pax Americana* was built on American exceptionalism—"do as I say, don't do as I do." Their (rise to) great power status will likewise be built on the idea of exceptionalism, which in turn will influence their views and role in disrupting, reforming, and building the future world order (Broeders, Adamson, and Creemers 2019). The cyber order will be shaped by great power politics, which is currently and for the foreseeable future in flux.

It is also interesting to see how less powerful states seek to navigate the power divides in cyberspace, aligning themselves with one power block on some issues, while choosing to align themselves with a competing power block on others. In this volume, Shires (2020) looks at states in the Middle East—a complex region with multiple allegiances on different issues—and shows how "their regulations, laws, and participation in international institutions places them with Russia, China, and other proponents of cyber sovereignty; on the other, their private sector cybersecurity collaborations, intelligence relationships, and offensive cyber operations are closely aligned with the USA and Europe" (Shires 2020, 205–206). For many countries then determining their position on security, international law, and norms is often an undertaking characterized by a degree of ambiguity.

In the practice of everyday cyber diplomacy, the inequality between sovereign states often means that smaller states favor and support the development of a rules-based order, engaging, for example, in cyber-norms entrepreneurship (Adamson and Homburger 2019), while larger states engage with these processes but allow themselves at least a certain degree of strategic ambiguity. Russia and the United States may be the primary instigators of the UN processes that seek to define how international law applies in cyberspace and which cyber norms could help shape state behavior, they are also the states that shift the posts on these issues through their actual behavior and advances in national (military) doctrine and operations. In terms of espionage (NSA mass surveillance, Chinese economic espionage, Russian digital sabotage), the "militarization" of cyberspace (building up military cyber commands) and the return of information operations (Russian influence operations, most notably interference with the 2016 US presidential election) it has been state practice, not laws and rules, that set the tone. Development in military cyber doctrine in some of the top-tier countries also points in the direction of a more aggressive posture in cyberspace. For example, the US Department of Defence (DoD) cyber strategy states that US cyber forces are in "persistent engagement" with their adversaries and, therefore, need to "defend forward" and "continuously contest" those adversaries, creating more possibilities for escalation of cyber conflict, even though the intention may be the opposite (Healey 2019). States interpreting the actions and intentions of other states erroneously is a classic source of instability as it can lead to the unintended escalation of conflict, a dynamic captured by the idea of the classic security dilemma (Jervis 1978). As Buchanan (2016) has shown, cyberspace provides an excellent context for what he calls a cybersecurity dilemma, highlighting how misinterpretation and escalation of conflict in cyberspace may emerge easily. Therefore, stability in cyberspace may be best served by consciously preparing for the moment that states wrongly interpret the actions of their adversaries. In addition to international law and cyber norms, the world also needs Confidence Building Measures (CBMs) as the third part of the triptych to avoid (unwanted) escalation of conflict in cyberspace (Kavanagh and Crespo 2019). Even though they are widely considered to be vital, CBMs mainly play a useful role when the escalation of (cyber) conflict is *un*-intentional (Pawlak 2016, 135). When states intentionally seek to escalate a conflict, CBMs are useless: in that case the red phone may ring, but will not be picked up. In spite of the realities of power politics, a rules-based order—international law foremost and to certain degree norms—is still the most promising route to stability in cyberspace. International law does not always prevent hostilities; however, states but it does provide a benchmark by which to judge and call out state behavior that is in breach of laws and norms.

NEGOTIATING CHANGE

Finding a framework that applies to the problems at hand in cyberspace is not easy, however. Even though cyberspace does not change the world beyond recognition, it does present severe challenges for international governance.

The regional level has gained in importance when it comes to issues of international peace and security in relation to cyberspace. The ASEAN Regional Forum (ASF) has been an active player in the international debate about cyber stability and norms (Heinl 2018) and announced in November 2019 the start of an ASEAN working group on the implementation of the UN cyber norms. Likewise, the work done in the Organisation for Security and Co-operation in Europe (OSCE)—especially in the field of CBMs—and the Organisation of American States (OAS) has been valuable in and of itself, but also as a means to continue the conversation about international cyber stability when the UN GGE process ground to a temporary halt in 2017 (Ott and Osula 2019). As a military alliance that spans the Atlantic, NATO's role in the cyber domain is more complicated. There is no clear mandate for the organization itself on the operational level, even though the alliance does recognize the importance of cyberspace as an operational domain of warfare. Operational cyber power rests with the member states and the differences within the alliance in terms of operational capacity are vast. NATO houses both top-tier cyber powers like the United States and the United Kingdom as well as states that have hardly developed any military or foreign intelligence capacity to operate in cyberspace. At the Wales summit in 2014, NATO declared cyber defense a core part of collective defense, meaning that a cyberattack could trigger Article 5, the collective defense clause, of the treaty. In this volume, Hill and Marsan (2020) sketch how NATO as a multilateral organization is charting a course to help its member states build their cyber defense capabilities, both individually and collectively, and also seeks to contribute to building a legal and normative framework in which cyber capabilities can be deployed and contested.

Cyberspace may have been named the fifth domain of warfare by states but the actual day-to-day operation of that domain is only to a very limited amount a state affair. Cyberspace's rise to global dominance was to a very large extent a private affair driven by businesses and the technical community laying the groundwork of the logical and technical infrastructure. Most states regarded its development with a benign neglect until cyberspace also became a foundational value for the national economy and society (Mueller 2010; DeNardis 2014; Broeders 2015). With the growth of cyberspace, the stakes of states have risen, but so did the stakes of the private sector and the technical community. Both "communities"—whose interests sometimes overlap and align but who also frequently find themselves at opposite ends of Internet governance debates—have massive interests in how cyberspace develops both in a technical sense as well as in a socioeconomic and political sense. Whether cyberspace is seen as a domain of warfare, whether notions of sovereignty are overlaid on a global system of information exchange, whether privacy regulations have extraterritorial effects, and whether governments are going to expect, request, and/or direct Internet companies and ISPs to enforce national policies matters a great deal to globally operating tech companies. Both in terms of their business models and opportunities and in terms of their (corporate) identities. Some companies have been seeking ways to insert themselves into the political debates about global Internet governance, especially into the field of international security which is traditionally closed to all actors other than states.

In this volume, Eggenschwiler and Kulesza (2020) analyze a number of corporate and multistakeholder initiatives that aim to influence the global debate about responsible behavior of states in cyberspace. Private initiatives coming from, for example, Microsoft and Siemens and global fora such as the Global Commission on the Stability of Cyberspace, which recently published its final report (GCSC 2019), aim to influence state and corporate behavior in cyberspace. Two chapters in this volume, Hurel and Lobato (2020) and Gorwa and Peez (2020), dive deeper into Microsoft's role as a norms entrepreneur. Microsoft has been at the forefront of corporate involved in the cyber-norms process which has for now culminated in its (informal) co-authorship of the French government initiative of the *Paris Call for Trust and Security in Cyberspace* which was launched in November 2018 and its sponsorship of the recently founded Cyber Peace Institute.[2] Hurel and Lobato (2020) analyze Microsoft's internal structures and complexities to gain insight in the how and why of Microsoft's engagement with the international norms processes. They also raise an interesting question with regard to where a global corporation's allegiance lies (in addition to its shareholders). How does Microsoft balance the interest of its global user base with the interest of the United States, its home country? When push comes to shove—and it might very well in these times of geopolitical strife—what will carry more weight: its global user base or the interest of its home government? Gorwa and Peez (2020) make an in-depth analysis of the Microsoft-led initiative of the Cyber Security Tech Accord (CTA). The CTA is focused on corporate self-regulation—partly in response to government pushback to Microsoft's earlier high-profile "Digital Geneva Convention" initiative—and has been backed by over 120 companies. They argue that Microsoft's CTA initiative served to brush up their reputation on data protection after the damage done by the Snowden revelations about their involvement with the NSA surveillance. The success of the accord in terms of the growing body of signatories is at least partially explained by their assessment that "the Accord offers all the PR potential and heavyweight legitimacy and very little of the normative obligation of the international legal language" (Gorwa and Peez 2020, 277). However, their characterization of Microsoft as a "quasi-diplomatic entity" (based on Hurel and Lobato 2018) ultimately points back into the direction of the diplomatic tables where the seats are taken by states.

The reports of the GGE's death in 2017 seem to have been greatly exaggerated given that the sixth round of the process has started in December

2019. The fact that twenty-five UN member states will again meet to discuss the application of international law to the cyber domain and cyber norms is in itself not a guarantee for success, although sources say that the 2017 round found quite a lot of common ground, in addition to the disputes that eventually blocked consensus. As the General Assembly of the UN thickened the diplomatic cyber plot by also voting through the Russian resolution that called for the installation of an Open-Ended Working Group (OEWG), the revival of the UN GGE is in no way "business as usual." Russia has claimed the moral high ground and played the card of international political legitimacy. The Russian delegation built its case for the OEWG on the principle that it is open to the participation of all states and renounced the UN GGE as "the practice of club agreements that should be sent into the annals of history" (cited in Kurowska 2019). As one of the permanent members of the Security Council, Russia is assured of a seat in that club, but given their sponsorship of the OEWG resolution the stakes are high. The parallel tracks have ushered in a state of Mutually Assured Diplomacy: it is more than likely that either both processes yield a result or that both will fail (Broeders 2019). If one fails on account of one political camp, the other camp is likely to respond in kind and derail the other process. This will complicate an already difficult process. Getting agreement on how existing international law applies to cyberspace—generally agreed to be the stumbling block of the 2017 GGE round—now has to be navigated in two processes that are at once separate and joined at the hip. Add in the new geopolitics of technical Internet governance and rising tensions about the permanent state of "unpeace" in cyberspace and those working on the diplomatic challenges of cyberspace stability and Internet governance have their work cut out for them.

NOTES

1. Article 13 F of UNGA 2015: "A State should not conduct or knowingly support ICT activity contrary to its obligations under international law that intentionally damages critical infrastructure or otherwise impairs the use and operation of critical infrastructure to provide services to the public."
2. See also: https://cyberpeaceinstitute.org/

BIBLIOGRAPHY

Adamson, L. 2020. "International Law and International Cyber Norms: A Continuum?" In *Governing Cyberspace: Behaviour, Power and Diplomacy*, edited by D. Broeders and B. van den Berg. London: Rowman & Littlefield.

Adamson, L. and Z. Homburger. 2019. "Let Them Roar: Small States as Cyber Norm Entrepreneurs." *European Foreign Affairs Review* 24 (2): 217–234.

Betz, D. and T. Stevens. 2011. *Cyberspace and the State. Towards a Strategy for Cyber-Power*. Abingdon: Routledge for the IISS.

Boeke, S. and D. Broeders. 2018. "The Demilitarisation of Cyber Conflict." *Survival* 60 (6): 73–90.

Broeders, D. 2015. *The Public Core of the Internet. An International Agenda for Internet Governance*. Amsterdam: Amsterdam University Press.

Broeders, D. 2017. "Aligning the International Protection of "The Public Core of the Internet" with State Sovereignty and National Security." *Journal of Cyber Policy* 2 (3): 366–376.

Broeders, D. 2019. "Mutually Assured Diplomacy: Governance, 'unpeace' and Diplomacy in Cyberspace." *Global Policy—Digital Debates 2019* 6: 26–29.

Broeders, D., L. Adamson and R. Creemers. 2019. *Coalition of the Unwilling? Chinese and Russian Perspectives on Cyberspace*. The Hague Program for Cyber Norms Policy Brief. November 2019.

Broeders, D., S. Boeke and I. Georgieva. 2019. *Foreign Intelligence in the Digital Age. Navigating a State of "unpeace."* The Hague Program for Cyber Norms Policy Brief. September 2019.

Buchanan, B. 2016. *The Cybersecurity Dilemma: Hacking, Trust and Fear Between Nations*. Oxford: Oxford University Press.

Creemers, R. 2020. "China's Conception of Cyber Sovereignty: Rhetoric and Realization." In *Governing Cyberspace: Behaviour, Power and Diplomacy*, edited by D. Broeders and B. van den Berg. London: Rowman & Littlefield.

Deibert, R. 2013. *Black Code. Inside the Battle for Cyberspace*. Toronto: Signal.

DeNardis, L. 2014. *The Global War for Internet Governance*. New Haven and London: Yale University Press.

Efrony, D. and Y. Shany. 2018. "A Rule Book on the Shelf? Tallinn Manual 2.0 on Cyber Operations and Subsequent State Practice." *American Journal of International Law* 112 (4): 583–657.

Eggenschwiler, J. and J. Kulesza. 2020. "Non-State Actors as Shapers of Customary Standards of Responsible Behaviour in Cyberspace." In *Governing Cyberspace: Behaviour, Power and Diplomacy*, edited by D. Broeders and B. van den Berg. London: Rowman & Littlefield.

Finnemore, M. and D. Hollis. 2016. "Constructing Norms for Global Cybersecurity." *The American Journal of International Law* 110: 425–479.

Finnemore, M. and K. Sikkink. 1998. "International Norm Dynamics and Political Change." *International Organization* 52: 887–917.

GCSC. 2019. *Advancing Cyberstability*. Final Report of the Global Commission on the Stability of Cyberspace, November 2019.

Georgieva, I. 2020a. "The Unexpected Norm-Setters: Intelligence Agencies in Cyberspace." *Contemporary Security Policy* 41 (1): 33–54.

Georgieva, I. 2020b. "The Power of Norms Meets Normative Power: On the International Cyber Norm of Bulk Collection, the Normative Power of Intelligence Agencies and How These Meet." In *Governing Cyberspace: Behaviour, Power and Diplomacy*, edited by D. Broeders and B. van den Berg. London: Rowman & Littlefield.

Gorwa, R. and A. Peez. 2020. "Big Tech Hits the Diplomatic Circuit: Norm Entrepreneurship, Policy Advocacy, and Microsoft's Cybersecurity Tech Accord." In *Governing Cyberspace: Behaviour, Power and Diplomacy*, edited by D. Broeders and B. van den Berg. London: Rowman & Littlefield.

Greenberg, A. 2018. "The Code That Crashed the World." *Wired*, September 2018: 53–63.

Grigsby, A. 2017. "The End of Cyber Norms." *Survival* 59 (6): 109–122.

Healey, J. 2019. "The Implications of Persistent (and Permanent) Engagement in Cyberspace." *Journal of Cybersecurity* 5 (1): 1–15.

Heinl, C. 2018. "Cyber Dynamics and World Order: Enhancing International Cyber Stability." *Irish Studies in International Affairs* 29: 53–72.

Hill, S. and N. Marsan. 2020. "International Law in Cyber Space: Leveraging NATO's Multilateralism, Adaptation and Commitment to Cooperative Security." In *Governing Cyberspace: Behaviour, Power and Diplomacy*, edited by D. Broeders and B. van den Berg. London: Rowman & Littlefield.

Hoffman, G. 2020. "Cybersecurity Norm-Building and Signaling with China." In *Governing Cyberspace: Behaviour, Power and Diplomacy*, edited by D. Broeders and B. van den Berg. London: Rowman & Littlefield.

Hurel, L.M. and L.C. Lobato. 2020. *"Cyber-Norms Entrepreneurship?* Understanding Microsoft's Advocacy on Cybersecurity." In *Governing Cyberspace: Behaviour, Power and Diplomacy*, edited by D. Broeders and B. van den Berg. London: Rowman & Littlefield.

Inkster, N. 2016. *China's Cyber Power*, Adelphi 456. Abingdon: Routledge for the IISS.

Jervis, R. 1978. "Cooperation under the Security Dilemma". *World Politics* 30 (2): 167–214.

Katzenstein, P., ed. 1996. *The Culture of National Security: Norms and Identity in World Politics*. New York: Columbia University Press.

Kavanagh, C. and L. Crespo. 2019. "Confidence Building Measures and ICT." *European Foreign Affairs Review* 24 (2): 187–202.

Kello, L. 2017. *The Virtual Weapon and International Order*. New Haven and London: Yale University Press.

Klimburg, A. 2017. *The Darkening Web. The War for Cyberspace*. New York: Penguin Press.

Klimburg, A. and L. Faesen. 2020. "A Balance of Power in Cyberspace." In *Governing Cyberspace: Behaviour, Power and Diplomacy*, edited by D. Broeders and B. van den Berg. London: Rowman & Littlefield.

Kurowska, X. 2019. *The Politics of Cyber Norms: Beyond Norm Construction Towards Strategic Narrative Contestation*. EU Cyber Direct: Research in Focus.

Kurowska, X. 2020. "What Does Russia Want in Cyber Diplomacy? A Primer." In *Governing Cyberspace: Behaviour, Power and Diplomacy*, edited by D. Broeders and B. van den Berg. London: Rowman & Littlefield.

Maurer, T. 2018. *Cyber Mercenaries. The State, Hackers and Power*. Cambridge: Cambridge University Press.

Maurer, T. 2019. "A Dose of Realism: The Contestation and Politics of Cyber Norms." *Hague Journal on the Rule of Law*, First Online: September 17, 2019.

Mueller, M. 2010. *Networks and States. The Global Politics of Internet Governance.* Cambridge, MA: MIT Press.

Nye, J. 2014. *The Regime Complex for Managing Global Cyber Activities.* Global Commission on Internet Governance Paper Series, Paper No. 1.

Ott, N. and A. Osula. 2019. "The Rise of the Regionals: How Regional Organisations Contribute to International Cyber Stability Negotiations at the United Nations Level." In *2019 11th International Conference on Cyber Conflict: Silent Battle*, edited by T. Minarik et al., 321–346. Tallinn: CCDCOE.

Pawlak, P. 2016. "Confidence-Building Measures in Cyberspace: Current Debates and Rrends." In *International Cyber Norms. Legal, Policy & Industry Perspectives*, edited by A. Osula and H. Rõigas, 129–153. Tallinn: CCDCOE.

Roguski, P. 2020. "Violations of Territorial Sovereignty in Cyberspace—An Intrusion-based Approach." In *Governing Cyberspace: Behaviour, Power and Diplomacy*, edited by D. Broeders and B. van den Berg. London: Rowman & Littlefield.

Schmitt, M., ed. 2013. *Tallinn Manual on the International Law Applicable to Cyber Warfare.* Cambridge: Cambridge University Press.

Schmitt, M., ed. 2017. *Tallinn Manual 2.0 on the International Law Applicable to Cyber Operations.* Cambridge: Cambridge University Press.

Segal, A. 2016. *The Hacked World Order. How Nations Fight, Trade, Maneuver, and Manipulate in the Digital Age.* New York: Public Affairs.

Shires, J. 2020. "Ambiguity and Appropriation: Cybersecurity and Cybercrime in Egypt and the Gulf." In *Governing Cyberspace: Behaviour, Power and Diplomacy*, edited by D. Broeders and B. van den Berg. London: Rowman & Littlefield.

Taddeo, M. 2017. "Deterrence by Norms to Stop Interstate Cyber Attacks." *Minds & Machines* 27: 387-292.

Tsagourias, N. 2020. "Electorial Cyber Interference, Self-Determination and the Principle of Non-Intervention in Cyberspace." In *Governing Cyberspace: Behaviour, Power and Diplomacy*, edited by D. Broeders and B. van den Berg. London: Rowman & Littlefield.

UNGA. 1999. A/RES/53/70 *Developments in the Field of Information and Telecommunications in the Context of International Security.* New York: UN.

UNGA. 2010. A/65/201 *Report of the Group of Governmental Experts on Developments in the Field of Information and Telecommunications in the Context of International Security.* New York: UN.

UNGA. 2013. A/68/98 *Report of the Group of Governmental Experts on Developments in the Field of Information and Telecommunications in the Context of International Security.* New York: UN.

UNGA. 2015. A/70/174 *Report of the Group of Governmental Experts on Developments in the Field of Information and Telecommunications in the Context of International Security.* New York: UN.

Part I

INTERNATIONAL LEGAL AND DIPLOMATIC APPROACHES

Chapter 2

International Law and International Cyber Norms

A Continuum?

Liisi Adamson

The international community has recognized the need for "rules of the road" in cyberspace not only for individuals and private sector actors but also for states. The issue of responsible state behavior in the context of international peace and security was raised by the Russian Federation already in 1998 when it called for an international dialogue under the auspices of the United Nations (UN) (UNGA 1998; UNGA 1999). Over the past two decades that regulatory discussion pertaining to cyberspace has evolved from a possible multilateral treaty to application of existing international law, and to the development and application of cyber norms.

Norms of responsible state behavior in cyberspace, or more commonly noted as *cyber norms*, have developed into a very broad research focus that can be part of various different discourses in the realm of cybersecurity. Norms, in general, can be found everywhere, from everyday interactions to norms that have been codified as law. Yet, in the interactions between states as well as in the academic discourse cyber norms and international law are often perceived as two different tracks of regulatory approaches. Mainly inspired by the work of the United Nations Group of Governmental Experts on Developments in the Field of Information and Telecommunications in the Context of International Security (hereinafter UN GGE), norms in cyberspace are increasingly approached as nonbinding and voluntary in nature. The latter aspect is often interpreted as being a pathway to easier consensus in a challenging realm. At the same time, international law is portrayed as a binding source of normative behavior, application of which often leads to contestation among states.[1]

This chapter argues that norms and international law are not detached from each other. Instead, they are mutually reinforcing and ought to not be seen as two completely different parallel discourses. At the same time, not all norms are to be seen as international laws. Instead, norms of responsible state behavior ought to be seen in terms of continuums. A first continuum focuses on the spectrum from nonbinding norms to hard law. A second continuum emphasizes the specificity of norms.

Thus, the article first elaborates on the move to international law in the cybersecurity and state behavior discourse from a historical perspective. Second, the article then explains the origins of the cyber-norms discourse and how the norms discourse was and is seen as an easier avenue to achieve consensus on after the contesting approaches to application of international law. However, the opaque nature of the concept of nonbinding, voluntary norms in the context of cybersecurity can hamper the implementation of said norms. Furthermore, one could argue that cyber norms now mean everything and nothing at all. Last, the article argues that the binary dialogue of international law *versus* norms could be undermining the whole discourse. Instead, norms and international law ought to be seen as building on each other.

RULES OF THE ROAD: THE MOVE FROM INTERNATIONAL LAW TO CYBER NORMS

The origins of the *cyber-norms* discourse can be found in a proposal for an United Nations General Assembly (UNGA) resolution by Russian Federation to the UN First Committee—the Disarmament and Security Committee, which later was adopted as the first resolution in the series pertaining to "Developments in the field of information and telecommunications in the context of international security" (UNGA 1999). In 1998, Russia claimed that the world had entered through the development and application of new information technologies and means of telecommunication qualitatively a new stage of scientific and technological revolution. While this revolution had brought about many positive developments, it was essential to consider, even if at the time only potential in nature, the threats that such rapid growth of dependency on information and telecommunications technologies (hereinafter ICTs) could present. Russia put forth that ICTs could be used for purposes incompatible with the objectives of maintaining international peace and security and such technologies could breach several established international law principles, such as nonuse of force, non-intervention, and respect for human rights and freedoms. Thus, Russian foreign minister Igor Ivanov concluded that "such a threat requires that preventive measures be taken today" (UNGA 1998). The international community could not permit the emergence of a "fundamentally new area of international confrontation, which may lead to an escalation of the arms race based on the latest developments of the scientific and technological revolution" (UNGA 1998). Carried by the possible arms race and conflict mind-set, the proposal called for a ban on information weapons to prevent information wars, as information weapons could have the destructive effect comparable to weapons of mass destruction (UNGA 1998). Hence, the issue of international regulation of ICTs was raised in the context of possible future conflicts among states,[2] and Russia was the first country to link international law and information security in the context of international peace and security.

Even though the 1998 Russian proposal to discuss information security-related issues in an international setting had merit, the rest of the international community was not immediately drawn to the idea to deliberate the regulation of ICTs. The Russian proposal was perceived as an invitation to negotiate a potential multilateral treaty to stop the proliferation of information weapons and prevent information wars.[3] The United States, a historically technologically powerful country, entered the republican Bush administration era in 2001. Due to different policy priorities in the early 2000s and the skepticism toward Russian proposals, considerations for responsible state behavior were deadlocked. The West was not interested in discussing a possible treaty to regulate behavior or curtailing developments in cyberspace. It was only six years later, in 2004, when the resolution served as a basis for convening the first session of the UN GGE under the chair of Russia. The task for the expert group was to consider existing and potential threats in the sphere of information security and possible cooperative measures to address them. Even though it was the first UN GGE convened under the aegis of the 1998 "Russian" resolution, it yielded no real outcome (UNGA 2005).

The Catalyst

A broader discussion on the regulation of cyberspace started a little over a decade ago. The catalyst for a deeper regulatory discussion was the denial-of-service (hereinafter DoS) and distributed-denial-of-service (hereinafter DDoS) attacks against the Estonian government, e-services and financial sector in April–May 2007 (Tikk et al. 2010, 14–35). This incident made it visible to the international community how vulnerable ICT-reliant states can be (Aaviksoo 2010). Although there was no physical damage to the servers, systems, and X-road infrastructure,[4] the DoS and DDoS attacks halted the functioning of several governmental vital services, which at the very least caused financial damage, but more importantly showed where digital states are vulnerable. Moreover, due to the supposed involvement of a neighboring government, this was also the first time tensions between states moved to a completely new realm of actions.[5] If the attacks had been attributed to Russia as a state, it would have been a clear indication that cyber operations have moved qualitatively to a different level and have become politicized. The 2007 Estonia attacks showed that there is a new possible domain for interstate conflict, which was promptly proven during the 2008 Georgia–Russia war. A rise in state-sponsored offensive activity in cyberspace led to calls for a secure and stable cyberspace in multiple avenues.[6]

Besides the diplomatic process among states under the aegis of the UN, the Estonian incident in 2007 and Iranian Stuxnet incident in 2010 also led to the start of the *Tallinn Manual* process.[7] It was one of the first academic initiatives and focused on putting forth an interpretation of existing international law pertaining to conflict and laws of war (*jus ad bellum* and *jus in bello*). The focus on conflict was understandable due to the catastrophic picture that was painted by policy makers and academics alike of the effects that cyber incidents could have.[8] Stuxnet had after all signified another qualitative leap from politically motivated operations to offensive state-sponsored cyber operations. It also raised questions of low-intensity conflict (Buchan 2012; O'Connell 2012) and assured the academics working on the normative framework for cyber operations and laws of armed conflict. Even though Stuxnet was never attributed to a state, the technical analysis left no doubt that at the very least, the offensive operation was backed by a nation-state (De Falco 2012), which once again emphasized the necessity to address the application of international law in cyberspace. The *Tallinn Manual* project was spearheaded by then newly created NATO Cooperative Cyber Defence Centre of Excellence, a NATO-accredited cyber defence hub, established in Tallinn, Estonia, in 2008. Ever since, the NATO CCD COE has become one of the strongest academic voices in the discussion revolving around the application of international law to cyberspace and operations.

After 2007, the conflict-focused regulatory discourse rebooted the UN GGE process, which convened after a five-year hiatus for their 2009–2010 session under the chair of Russia. Even though the United States, Russia's strategic contestant and another cyber power, still did not want to discuss the negotiation of a cybersecurity treaty, the new Obama administration broke the deadlock in discussions and shifted conversation from a possible multilateral treaty to responsible state behavior. Since 2009, the Obama administration advocated a general approach that favored the development of multilateral norms for responsible state behavior in cyberspace. The Cyberspace Policy adopted in 2009 emphasized that the "United States cannot succeed in securing cyberspace if it works in isolation" (The White House 2009, iv), which was a contrast to the policy of Obama's predecessor. The policy continued stating that "international norms are critical to establishing a secure and thriving digital infrastructure" (The White House 2009, 20). The Obama administration adopted an outward-looking and "norms-based" approach to international regulation of cyberspace, which paved the way for a cyber-norms discourse, including in the framework of the UN GGE.

The UN GGE has been a high-level diplomatic avenue for the discussion of responsible state behavior in cyberspace, where the strategic contestants United States and Russia among others are pushing forward their views and value systems. More than half of the world's countries—115 as of 2018—have sponsored the 1998 Russian resolution,[9] which indicates their support for and prioritization of the issue. However, the original resolution also asks states to provide the committee with their views pertaining to the developments in the field of ICTs in the context of international security. This call is reiterated annually. Here, less than half of the world's countries—seventy states as of 2018 have replied to this call.[10] In the face of criticism pertaining to the representation issues and the fact that the UN GGE is a closed process with limited outcome,[11] the UN GGE has adopted three reports, in 2010, 2013, and 2015, which are considered cumulative in their recommendations.

The Progress

The task for the 2009/2010 UN GGE was identical to the previous UN GGE in 2004/2005: to study both the threats in the sphere of information security as well as suggest cooperative measures to strengthen the security of global information and communication systems. This time the UN GGE identified several motives for disruption, sources of threats as well as objectives. The 2009/2010 session resulted in a consensus report outlining the main threats stemming from the development and use of ICTs to international peace and security, such as the terrorist use of ICTs, ICTs as instruments of warfare and intelligence, attribution issues, use of proxies, protection of critical infrastructures, ICT supply chain security, and ICT capacity and security differences among states (UNGA 2010). Ever since, the UN GGE has become one of the most important avenues for regulatory discussion pertaining to the maintenance of international peace and security and the development and use of ICTs.[12] Bringing together strategic contestants, agile tech adopters and developing countries, the UN GGE has offered a venue to discuss which threats result from the development and the use of ICTs to international peace and security and how to prevent and mitigate such threats through the application of norms, international law, confidence-building measures[13] and capacity-building measures.[14]

During the hiatus year of the UN GGE, Russian Federation attempted to propose another opportunity for a negotiation of a cybersecurity treaty. Namely, in 2011, the Russian Ministry of Foreign Affairs put forth a Draft Convention on International Information Security (The Ministry of Foreign Affairs of the Russian Federation 2011). The general values and ideas of the convention were the same as in the original 1998 resolution proposal. The overall aim of the convention was to prevent "possible uses of information and communication technology for purposes not compatible with ensuring international stability and security" (The Ministry of Foreign Affairs of the Russian Federation 2011). With a heavy focus on sovereignty and the governance of a "sovereign information space," the convention did not find support among the like-minded Western allies. The Obama administration was still focusing on international norms and application of international law for responsible state behavior in cyberspace.

The following 2013 UN GGE report was heralded as a qualitative leap forward in regulating state behavior in cyberspace (Wolter 2013). Its major contribution lies in the fact that the group was able to conclude that international law, and in particular the UN Charter, applies to cyberspace and the activities therein (UNGA 2013, para. 19). The year 2013 was also the first time when the UN GGE included a section in its report on "Recommendations on norms, rules and principles of responsible behavior by States," which were seen as norms deriving from existing international law. Even though the report concluded that unique attributes of ICTs might warrant the development of additional norms over time, the main focus lied still with international law (UNGA 2013, para. 16). The report named a number of international law norms and principles that states ought to abide by ranging from sovereignty, including the international norms and principles that flow from sovereignty, to human rights and state responsibility (UNGA 2013, para. 19–23). This was a big step in the thus far binary discussion on whether international law applies or not. Together with the *Tallinn Manual on the International Law Applicable to Cyber Warfare* published in 2013 (Schmitt 2013), high hopes were put on international law to provide the normative framework applicable to states' cyberspace activities. The norms discussion continued in connection to international law. To keep the momentum, the UNGA decided to gather another UN GGE as soon as possible.

The Turn

The 2015 iteration of the UN GGE was tasked with analyzing the specific application of international law principles elaborated in the 2013 report. However, this turned out to be a contested area of study, as states' understanding and interpretations of international law in general already vary greatly,[15] let alone in the context of cyberspace and responsible state behavior. The application and interpretation of international law reflect different value systems that states have. These fundamental differences necessitated an approach that would allow the group to not address the disputed issues regarding international law. In an effort to make progress on previous groups' work, the UN

GGE turned to a new construct to get past the contestation: general nonbinding, voluntary norms, rules, and principles for the responsible behavior of states. The latter, that is, norms as a concept, which had been in 2013 report deriving from international law and thus, deeply connected to it, was now presented as a different source for guidance regarding responsible state behavior than international law. This was reflected in the fact that international law and norms, rules and principles were now two different sections in the UN GGE report (UNGA 2015b, sec. III and VI). Moreover, the new norms, rules, and principles section reflected to a great extent (with some exceptions) already existing international law (for further elaboration, see UNODA 2017). The UN GGE, however, did not put forth any conceptualization regarding the relationship between the proposed recommendations of norms and international law. Yet, this conceptual opaqueness seemed to not be a concern. The U.S.-led voluntary, nonbinding norms approach, as argued by some, was a way sidestep the question of a possible cybersecurity treaty amid conflicting views on the application of international law, and at the same time allowed states to articulate issues that require more normative guidance than international law currently offers (Tikk et al. 2018b, 20–21). Outside the UN GGE, despite the fact that norms were seen as voluntary and nonbinding in the context and framework of the UN GGE, the following academic (Crandall et al. 2015; Finnemore 2017, 2011; Finnemore et al. 2016) as well as policy[16] discussion saw *cyber norms* the same way as the UN GGE. Thus, the narrative created by the UN GGE of norms as an alternative to binding international law had carried over to the wider cyber-norms debate.

However, the eleven recommendations for cyber norms (UNGA 2015, para. 13) proposed by the UN GGE in 2015 reflect to a great extent already existing international law. The implementation guide for said norms was left as a task for the following UN GGE that commenced its work in 2016. In 2017, however, the UN GGE failed to reach consensus. For the first time, two countries—the United States and Cuba—explained their views as to the failure of the closed and nontransparent process. The United States argued that the process failed over states' unwillingness to clarify how specific aspects of international law, such as law of the armed conflict or state responsibility, apply to cyberspace. Furthermore, the United States saw the lesser extent of the agreement in the 2017 UN GGE as backtracking the progress that had been made with previous reports (Markoff 2017). Cuba, on the other hand, argued that reinterpreting law of armed conflict would legitimize cyberspace as a domain for military conflict, giving thereby state-sponsored cyber operations a green light (Cuba's Representative Office Abroad 2017).

While the progress at the UN GGE stalled due to strategic, value, and interpretation differences, the international dialogue outside of the UN GGE continued. The year 2017 also marked the publication of *Tallinn Manual*

2.0 on International Law Applicable to Cyber Operations, which this time focused on peacetime operations as well as provided a revised look at the law applicable during conflict (NATO CCD COE 2017). The second iteration of creating the interpretative guidelines attracted over fifty states in the Hague Process. This was, however, in a merely consultative, not substantively contributing role.[17] The states participating in the Hague Process did not put forth their official positions on the interpretation of international law.[18] Thus, the *Tallinn Manual* represents an academic process focusing solely on the application of international law. The policy action in the parallel track has moved from application of international law and norms deriving therefrom to a dialogue focusing on international law and *cyber norms* without a clear understanding what the status and meaning of the latter vis-à-vis the former is. This has led to methodological and conceptual opaqueness.

INTERNATIONAL NORMS

The political, as well as academic focus on *international cyber norms,* aims at reconciling the contestation among different views. Even though the vision and characteristics, how peace and security ought to be achieved in cyberspace have divided the discourse into multiple views[19] they still share the understanding that cyberspace and activities therein need regulation. Yet, the focus on cyber norms that the international community has seen since 2013 and especially after the 2015 UN GGE session is no silver bullet for fundamental differences among stakeholders. Different understandings of the development, role, and form of norms have created diverging views as to the necessity and utility of norms for cyberspace and norms for responsible state behavior. At the same time, the initiatives for creating or developing the norms discourse have not been able to unequivocally explain what norms are, why norms are needed, what type of norms are considered and how this discourse is or is not different from the international law discourse that has been going on for the past decade.[20] The Western approach highlights regulation through existing legal and other regulative frameworks. Yet, they fail at providing an understanding of the application and context-specific interpretation of said frameworks. At the same time, latching on to the novelty argument surrounding cyberspace activity, the Sino-Russian coalition is lobbying for a new multilateral cyber-specific legislation. Different approaches to the regulation to cyberspace reflect that the inherent differences in the state approaches pertain not only to norms, laws, and cyberspace, but toward a legal, strategic, and regulatory culture, as well as the understanding of the existing world order in a wider sense (Roberts 2017).

The definition of what an international cyber norm is depends on the disciplinary perspective of the person who poses the question. Those firmly believing in the adequacy and sufficiency of existing international law do not necessarily comprehend the utility of norms in a more general sense, especially in their nonbinding, voluntary form (Grigsby 2017) and at times conflate norms and cyber norms automatically with international law (Schmitt et al. 2014; Schmitt 2018). Defining a norm from the legal perspective entails mostly a strict view of norms as laws established by treaties or customary international law. From a more philosophical perspective, norms could be understood, for example, as social norms or ethical norms. From the international relations and especially constructivist perspective, international norms are defined as shared expectations or standards of appropriate behavior accepted by and applied in a certain community of actors with a given identity (Martinsson 2011, 2; Khagram et al. 2002, 4; Klotz 1995, para. 14; Katzenstein 1996, para. 5).

Norms can take different forms, as there is no single definition or one particular form of norms. According to one categorization, norms can be either constitutive or regulative. Some norms can have a constitutive effect, which means that they will specify what actions will cause others to recognize a particular entity (Katzenstein 1996, 5). For example, the Montevideo Convention establishes what entities can be considered states (Seventh International Conference of American States 1933). Its criteria have come to be accepted as the international norm on what constitutes a state. Regulative norms, on the other hand, are standards for the proper behavior for an entity with particular identity (Jepperson et al. 1996, 54). This entails in the context of responsible behavior of states in cyberspace, for example, standards defining what a properly conforming state would do in particular circumstances. Thus, regulative norms can prescribe or proscribe behavior for already constituted entities. These norms establish expectations how those defined entities will behave in varying circumstances (Jepperson et al. 1996, 54). This article focuses on responsible behavior of states. According to this categorization, the article would look into states and the regulative norms that prescribe, regulate, and constrain states' behavior in cyberspace.

Continuums of Norms

Yet, instead of binary approaches, this article proposes to address norms in terms of continuums.[21] The first continuum ranges from norms that have been codified into hard laws to soft law to voluntary, nonbinding norms. Generally, laws are expressions of norms that the international community accepts. States conform their behavior to laws because of the wide acceptance of the underlying norms (Sloss 2006, 170). Moreover, international law often also serves an expressive function. States become a party to a treaty or engage in discussions to express their support for the emerging norm (Sloss 2006, 187).[22] International law provides a baseline to evaluate behavior—whether it conforms to the expectation of appropriate behavior in the international community or not—and threatens consequences for noncompliance. The aim of international law norms, as well as other regulative norms, is to induce a certain behavior. International law facilitates this behavior by delivering the framework and vocabulary that enables international politics among the international community (Klabbers 2017, 18).

International law is to a large extent comprised of hard norms. Treaty law and customary international law are the most binding forms of international law that also means that upon breaching the obligations therein state responsibility and sanctions mechanisms could apply. However, international law increasingly encompasses a substantive body of soft norms as well (Terpan 2015; Chinkin 1989). The body of international law is increasingly seen as a continuum between law and non-law, as formal law ascertainment has not managed to offer solutions to various legal phenomena in the international arena or offer them fast enough. Thereby, norms enshrined in soft instruments, as opposed to hard instruments such as treaties, belong to the continuum between hard and soft norms (D'Aspremont 2011, 128–29). On the other end of the bindingness spectrum[23] are completely legally nonbinding, voluntary norms, which does not mean that they might not be binding socially or morally and call for corresponding consequences once breached. The recommendations for norms made by the UN GGE in 2015 were from the outset framed as being nonbinding, voluntary norms. The Code of Conduct proposed by the Shanghai Cooperation Organization similarly frames the norms in the document in voluntary terms (UNGA 2011, 2015a). At the same time, the UN Charter, the applicability of which was confirmed by UN GGE in 2013 in the norms, rules, and principles section of the report comprises solely of hard norms as accepted by the international community (UNGA 2013, para. 19).

The second continuum that needs to be considered moves on the scale from general standards to specific rules. Norms can be understood as general standards, which are often goal-oriented and allow discretion for interpretation and do not prescribe specific action, which is needed to conform by the standard. Specific rules, however, allow for very limited discretion and set red lines in order to convey an obligation to achieve a certain outcome through certain means and measures (Wolfrum 2010, para. 65 ff). Thus, rules work well in circumstances when there is no solidarity or there is limited trust among the community. At the same time, the issue to be regulated occurs often. On the other hand, standards fulfill their intended outcome in opposite circumstances. Since standards are open-ended and allow for discretion, they require trust and solidarity among the community. When the issue to be regulated occurs rarely, that is, single isolated incidents, standards alongside trust ensure that given the circumstances, the actors will balance all relevant interests while making the decision on how to act (Koskenniemi 2019).

When it comes to the UN GGE norms, majority of them seem from the outset to be rather specific, that is, they have been cast in ICT-specific terms. Even though they pertain to specific "siloed" categories, such as cooperation (UNGA 2015b, para. A, D, H, J), due diligence of transit states (UNGA 2015b, para. C), critical infrastructure protection (UNGA 2015b, para. F, G), human rights protection (UNGA 2015b, para. E), and protection of CERTs (UNGA 2015b, para. K), they are essentially cast in the form of standards, providing no further guidance than the basic goal-oriented obligation set forth in the norm.

For example, the UN GGE 2015 report put forth a norm that state should not knowingly allow their territory to be used for internationally wrongful acts using ICTs (UNGA 2015b, para. 13[C]). Even though it is made ICT specific through the addition of "using ICTs," it still puts forth a general obligation of due diligence in cyberspace. The latter is a standard in itself, which means that the ICT specificity of it has created marginal additional value. The use of general standards applies to norms in the SCO's Code of Conduct's as well. Even content wise specific norms' proposals for the protection of the public core of the Internet[24] or the norm against the manipulation of the integrity of financial data[25] are inherently standards. Thus, considering the uncertainty and the novelty of activities in cyberspace, the push for standards instead of rules makes somewhat sense. Standards are useful when stakes and the cost for errors are high. This has been inherently the case in cyberspace. However, considering the state of the regulatory debate surrounding cyberspace, political contestation, and the lack of trust and solidarity among the international community, the likelihood of implementation and purposeful functioning of these standards is small.

Thus, even though the concept of norms has grown to be used in the cybersecurity discourse as indicating only voluntary and nonbinding nature, the view of norms ought to be much wider. Yet, even when options are abundant and clarity would help with reducing uncertainty, participants in different norms discussions are reluctant to define what they mean by norms. They are often conjoined with the notion of responsible state behavior. Norms are seen as a tool to limit the malicious or negligent behavior of actors and incentivize desired behavior, thereby defining and explaining acceptable and unacceptable behavior.[26] If binding international law is not clear or its application is contested due to grave political differences, norms of different nature may offer an avenue for striving toward predictable behavior of states, creating trust and stability.

Hence, the article sees cyber norms for responsible state behavior in the broadest sense as legally relevant expectations, in the form of rules or standards, regarding appropriate behavior in cyberspace among the international community. Yet, norms in and of themselves do not guarantee compliance. All emergent norms must compete with existing or even countervailing ones, as norms are not created in a vacuum. Whereas new norms do not guarantee action nor do they determinate the results of said norm, they can legitimize new types of action (Jepperson et al. 1996, 56). At the same time, if complied with, norms also channel, constrain, and constitute action. As such, norms are "a fundamental component of both the international system and actors' definitions of their interests" (Klotz 1995, 15). Cyber norms regulate or the very least guide, depending on their nature, the behavior of states in cyberspace (Iasiello 2016, 31–32).

Different Shades of Norms

Norms are not all equal, nor are they created, implemented, or interpreted equally. Norms may be different in terms of the sphere that they are established in. For example, the UN GGE has proposed global norms applicable to all. At the same time, norms agreed upon in the SCO (e.g., see Shanghai Cooperation Organization 2019), OSCE, ASEAN Regional Forum (hereinafter ARF) are regional norms. Additionally, there can be a wide variety of domestic norms that each state can enact. Norms vary also in terms of their content. As shown above, norms can be specific, for example, pertain to a particular part of critical infrastructure such as the submarine cables or they can be general and address the whole cyberspace and activities therein. One of such norms is the cooperation norm in the UN GGE 2015 report. It establishes that "States should cooperate in developing and applying measures to increase stability and security in the use of ICTs and prevent ICT practices that are acknowledged to be harmful or that may pose threats to international peace and security" (UNGA 2015b, para. 13(a)). This norm is a blanket suggestion for states to cooperate, leaving a wide room for interpretation.

The interpretation of norms adds another layer of complexity. As norms are expectations of behavior in a certain community, there might be differences of opinion with respect to the existence of the norms, that is, whether there exists a norm at all. For example, for some countries reporting of ICT incidents might be a norm, for others it might not. There might also be difference of opinion, when it comes to applicability of a norm. In this instance, there is an agreement that there is a norm, but disagreement about its application. For example, some characterized the Stuxnet attack on Iranian nuclear facility as an armed attack, which would have allowed Iran to use self-defence measures under UN Charter Article 51. At the same time, there were also those, who asserted that the attack did not reach the level of use of force in order to be considered an armed attack. As such, it remained a below-the-threshold operation which would have prevented Iran from acting in self-defence. In this case, there is an agreement that states have the right to act in self-defence, if there is an armed attack. However, there is disagreement whether the cyber-attack reached the threshold of an armed attack or not. Third, there might be variations of application of the norm, that is, interpretation of how to apply the norm in a particular case. This would be the case, for example, with the UN GGE 2015 report recommended norms, as there is no uniform interpretation guidance, all states can interpret them as they wish.

What connects this fragmented picture of norms is that they are all created through interaction among different actors in the international community. This is especially true when it comes to international norms. As the international level does not have a single authority who could prescribe or proscribe norms upon the international community, it is generally understood that most international norms for states are created through the interaction of states.[27] This does not mean that all international norms are created by states. Yet, considering that states are still the main subjects of international law, creating binding norms regulating their behavior still belongs to the purview of states. However, norm-creation in a broad sense is not just the prerogative of states or powerful states for that matter. Non-state actors and states alike can act as norm entrepreneurs. This has been particularly evident in the cybersecurity discourse.[28] It is then up to states to decide whether these norms, created or championed by non-state actors or nonbinding and voluntary, are legally relevant for them or not. As a result, some of those soft or voluntary, nonbinding norms created in the interaction among states or put forth by non-state actors can harden and become binding treaty or customary law, backed by responsibility and liability mechanisms in occurrence of noncompliance.

THE FUTURE

The policy action regarding "the rules of the road" has not dealt with norms in such detail, rather the calls for promoting voluntary, nonbinding norms have become ubiquitous and opaque without clear understanding of what are the norms that are being promoted, how they should be implemented and what is the impact of such calls. The intricacies and different "shades" of norms are not always apparent.

On the one hand, the conceptual opaqueness created by the UN GGE and carried forward by states allows for room of manoeuvre. The conceptual and terminological opaqueness serves the interest of those who want to maintain the regulatory grey areas. States not agreeing on the binding rules of the road and instead focusing on developing voluntary, nonbinding cyber norms make use of the permissive system of international law. When the rule is what is not prohibited is permitted, states can make use of the grey areas with no direct violations of international law.[29] Legal uncertainty and ambiguity surrounding the existence, content, and interpretation of a normative framework for activities in cyberspace is thus instrumentalized by states for their own benefit (Mačak 2017, 887).

In addition, cyber norms, as put forth by the UN GGE and promoted by states, have been framed as voluntary, nonbinding, and thus qualitatively different from international law norms. This means that there is no framework for implementing and enforcing them, which often leads to calls for the end of cyber norms (Grigsby 2017; Tikk et al. 2018a; van de Velde 2018; Soesanto et al. 2017) and for getting "past" cyber norms (Hampson et al. 2017; Segal 2017). Thus, norms, which were and are seen as a way out of the contestation regarding international law, are seen by many in rather grim tones due to their voluntary nature. Regardless of enforceability and their binding or nonbinding nature, norms establish expectations in the international community and delineate what is acceptable and unacceptable behavior. Norms influence state behavior (Sloss 2006; for an opposite view, see Goldsmith and Posner 2005). Even though cyber norms that are considered voluntary, nonbinding do not allow for legal consequences, such as countermeasures or self-defence, there are several other more political responses (such as retorsion, naming, and shaming that leads to reputation loss [Sloss 2006, 194], economic and diplomatic consequences) that can be more effective than legal consequences the use of which is highly regulated (Adamson et al. 2017).

The conceptual opaqueness regarding norms, international law, and their relationship is reflected in the cyber norms discourse by the fact that cyber norms now have come to mean everything and at the same time nothing at all. From the UN GGE interpretation, the previously existing connection between international law and norms has been significantly downplayed, indicating that norms are something different than international law. At first, states and academics alike were enthusiastic of the flexibility and vagueness of the concept of norms of responsible state behavior framing it as generally a good thing that promises progress for the establishment of rules of the road in cyberspace. Norms were perceived as being more malleable than hard laws. Yet, increasingly the concept of *cyber norms* acts as a "sponge for meaning, soaking up whatever content is nearby."[30]

Moreover, putting forth cyber norms as standards, implementation of which relies on overall solidarity and trust among the international community, might turn out to be a futile effort. Considering the contestation and strategic behavior surrounding regulatory efforts, the continued increase of offensive cyber activities, and the rise of political attributions instead of legal ones, it is clear that there is significant lack of trust in the international community. Without trust, however, there is no meaningful way to apply the agreed-upon standards or hope for reciprocated behavior on others' part. At the same time, there is no space nor political will to create red lines rules, as cyberspace activity is largely unpredictable due to exponential technological development. Thus, the challenge here is to create actionable norms, whether standards or rules, in and for a highly unpredictable, contested, and strategic environment.

While there is a push forward on the progress regarding international legal norms applicable in cyberspace, states do not necessarily interpret cyber norms as legal norms, emphasizing often separately the adherence to international law and the support for norms for responsible state behavior in cyberspace. The latest *National Cyber Strategy of the United States of America*, for example, states that "International law and voluntary non-binding norms of responsible state behavior in cyberspace provide stabilizing, security-enhancing standards that define acceptable behavior to all states and promote greater predictability and stability in cyberspace" (The White House 2018, 20). This clearly shows that for the United States, norms and international law are as regulatory frameworks two complementary, yet conceptually separate things. Without defining the relationship between international law and international norms of behavior that have been created and are created, the opaqueness might lead to fragmentation and eventually unclear guidance for state behavior. This runs contrary to the object and purpose of cyber norms and norms in general, as norms are supposed to provide clarity, stability, and predictability.

It is apt to recall that norms and international law influence, condition, and develop dependent on each other. Voluntary, nonbinding norms do not undermine existing binding hard norms. On the contrary, laws yield a deeper support for the ideas reflected by norms. Cyber norms, even if seen in a voluntary, nonbinding form, are grounded in international law and at the same time, eventually, norms are going to have an impact on the interpretation and development of international law as well. There is no regulatory vacuum or norm vacuum when it comes to cyberspace. New norms build on already existing regulatory order. Thus, as norms build on and influence other norms, it is a fallacy to depict the norms and international law as being detached from each other, as is a fallacy to equate international law and cyber norms.

The UN GGE-proposed recommendations of future norms are clearly grounded in existing international law (see further, UNODA 2017). It is often used as a point of criticism, yet the norms could also be seen as ICT-specific iteration of standards known and accepted in general international law. Existing international law provides the new norms legitimacy and might thus invite a normative pull toward the norms. Denying then the applicability of norms, which are informed by existing international law, means indirectly denying the applicability of international law to cyberspace activities. This contravenes then the accepted and endorsed view that existing international law applies in cyberspace (UNGA 2013). Similarly, relying only on binding international law and denying the impact of other norms, which are not characterized by their binding nature, means denying the ethos and underlying fundamental values carried by those norms. Thus, norms and international law need to be grounded in each other.

In October 2018, both the United States and Russia put forward their vision for the next UN GGE in the UN 1st Committee in the form of draft resolutions. Russia and allies were emphasizing the need for a more open-ended UN GGE process and pushed the international community to accept a draft resolution containing a Code of Conduct 3.0 that integrated the content of previous reports of the UN GGE and the Code of Conduct previously presented by the Shanghai Cooperation Organization (UNGA 2018a). This was a clear move toward politically binding norms.[31] The United States and like-minded states continued with the known format of UN GGE and the dual logic of international law and norms, rules and principles of responsible behavior of states. As a novelty, the US draft resolution emphasized the need for UN GGE-participating states to clarify through national contributions how international law applies in cyberspace.[32] Thus far, a few countries, such as the United Kingdom, Estonia, and France, have put forth such declarations. While the progress of regulation for responsible state behavior is welcomed, the conceptual ambiguity continues, hampering the understanding and implementation of already agreed-upon norms and leading to the question whether the norms, in the eyes of the states, are legally relevant or not. If the answer would be no, then it is questionable, what would be the utility and possible impact of such standards. If the norms are considered legally relevant, it would mean that even if they are framed as voluntary, nonbinding, they are still to be considered as connected to international law, informing the cyberspace-specific application thereof. However, if the UN GGE, as a pioneer in the cyber-norms debate continues to promote the conceptual opaqueness, it might lead states to turn inward[33] and look at domestic solutions to international cybersecurity issues instead of embracing the international normative toolbox. Nevertheless, there is hope that the two parallel and hopefully complementary processes—the UN GGE and the Open-Ended Working Group—in the UN manage to make progress and stride toward further clarity regarding responsible behavior in cyberspace in the years to come.

CONCLUSION

Calls for responsible behavior of states in cyberspace and rules of the road in said space have become ubiquitous. Out of the work of the UN GGE a distinct discourse on cyber norms has emerged. First developed as a response to contestation regarding international law, cyber norms have gradually obtained a rather opaque meaning.

This chapter argued that even though the UN GGE has moved from discussing international law norms to discussing international law and norms, rules and principles, the two are not detached from each other. Norms in general ought to be seen in several continuums, where norms have the potential to move and change when it comes to their binding nature and specificity. Having a "siloed" understanding of norms, meaning considering one type of norms detached from others is detrimental to the international community's understanding of what shapes state behavior. For example, hard norms in the form of international law might not always be the most effective forms of regulating behavior, as they are often accompanied by grave political differences. All norms pertaining to an issue-area ought to be seen as an ecosystem, where norms are mutually reinforcing, sometimes contesting, yet in general inform and influence the application of each other. Thus, when it comes to cyber norms, norms and application of international law to cyberspace cannot be seen as two parallel tracks of regulatory interventions. Norms are not necessarily an easier avenue to achieve consensus amid disagreement on the application of international law. Norms, even in voluntary, nonbinding form, are a powerful tool to change and regulate behavior, but not when they mean everything and nothing at all.

NOTES

1. Most notably, international law was also a point of contestation in the 2016/2017 iteration of the UN GGE, which did not adopt a consensus report (Markoff 2017; Cuba's Representative Office Abroad 2017).

2. Interestingly, Russia raised the issue of regulation of ICTs in the Disarmament and Security Committee, but not in the UN Sixth Committee, which addresses the development of international law and other legal issues. Especially because the issues that Russia wanted to discuss among states pertained not only to international conflict and sovereignty, but also to terrorist and criminal use of such technologies.

3. The perception was created by point 3(c) in the draft resolution proposal, which called for "advisability of developing legal regimes to prohibit the development, production or use of particularly dangerous forms of information weapons, and of taking measures to combat information terrorism and crime, including the establishment of an international system (centre) for monitoring threats to the security of

global information and telecommunications systems." The Russians defined information weapon in their proposal as a weapon "the destructive effect of which may be comparable to that of weapons of mass destruction." Information war was understood as "actions taken by one country to damage the information resources and systems of another country while at the same time protecting its own infrastructure" (UNGA 1998).

4. The X-road is the data exchange layer for information systems. It is a technological and organizational environment enabling a secure Internet-based data exchange between information systems. X-road is the backbone of all Estonian e-services (Estonian Information System Authority 2018).

5. In his foreword, President Toomas Hendrik Ilves noted that the 2007 attacks in Estonia, even though mild in retrospect, considering our current capacity and capabilities, were the first time "one could apply the Clausewitzean dictum: War is the continuation of policy by other means" (NATO CCD COE 2017, xxiii).

6. For example, UN GGE process, Shanghai Cooperation Organization Code of Conduct process and Organization for Security and Co-Operation's proposals for stabilizing confidence-building measures to be applied among adversaries.

7. The first edition of the Tallinn Manual was published in 2013 with the second iteration published in 2017 (NATO CCD COE 2017; Schmitt 2013).

8. These ranged mostly from nuclear disasters to Cyber Pearl Harbor. Leon E. Panetta stated that "[t]he collective result of these kinds of attacks could be a cyber Pearl Harbor; an attack that would cause physical destruction and the loss of life. In fact, it would paralyze and shock the nation and create a new, profound sense of vulnerability" (Panetta 2012; Clarke and Knake 2012; Farwell and Rohozinski 2012, 2011).

9. Table of sponsorship of the UN I Committee Resolution 2006–2018 (compiled by the author, available upon request).

10. Table of replies from governments 1999–2017 (compiled by the author, available upon request). Of the cyber powers, Russia has never presented their views on the matter after putting forth the first proposal. The United States has presented their views three times and China four times.

11. Only thirty-eight countries in the world have been part of this process over fourteen years of having UN GGE's. Six countries have been part of all five UN GGE's (China, France, Germany, Russia, United Kingdom, and United States). (Table of membership of the UN GGE 2004–2017, compiled by the author, available upon request.)

12. UN GGE has had five iterations and three of them had a substantial outcome in the form of a consensus report. UN GGE is increasingly also perceived as an avenue of diplomatic negotiations in an issue which lends itself to increasingly contested views on how cyberspace ought to be regulated.

13. Confidence-building measures (CBMs) are a set of practical measures aimed at enhancing interstate cooperation, transparency, predictability, and stability in order to reduce the risks of misperception, escalation, and conflict that may stem from the use of ICTs. This entails for example exchanging white papers, strategy documents and national views on cyber matters, sharing information and implementing legislation that would allow to do so, encouraging responsible disclosure of ICT vulnerabilities,

and nominating a national point of contact to facilitate dialogue between states on cyber matters. CBMs are often employed among adversaries to increase transparency and thereby maintain peace and security (UNGA 2015b, 9; OSCE 2013, 2016).

14. UN GGE understands capacity-building measures as measures that "provide technical or other assistance to build capacity in security ICTs in countries requiring and requesting assistance" (UNGA 2015b, paras 19–23).

15. For an overview of different approaches to International Law, see Roberts (2017).

16. The language on international law and voluntary, nonbinding norms for responsible state behavior in cyberspace has been increasingly adopted in several multilateral settings (see G7 2017, 2016; US Department of State 2016; NATO 2016a, 2016b; Australian Minister for Foreign Affairs 2017).

17. The Netherlands facilitated the consultation process between the States and NATO CCD COE (NATO CCD COE 2016).

18. Thus far, only United Kingdom, Estonia, and France have officially explained how principles and rules of international law apply in cyberspace according to their understanding (Wright 2019; Kaljulaid 2019; Ministère des Armées 2019).

19. Most notably the like-minded Western view and the Sino-Russo vision of the future of cyberspace.

20. For a solid effort in understanding the different aspects and forms of cyber norms, see Osula and Rõigas (2016).

21. This chapter addresses only the two most pertinent continuums for cyber norms' purpose. For more specific general categorizations of norms, see Bodansky (2004).

22. A good example here is Sweden's actions during the negotiation of the nuclear nonproliferation treaty. It had nothing to gain security wise in signing the Treaty on the Non-Proliferation of Nuclear Weapons; however, it primarily ratified it to express its support for the emerging nonproliferation norm.

23. Bindingness spectrum then ranges from hard laws, which are norms codified in written form and noncompliance with said norms is backed by sanctions, to voluntary, nonbinding norms.

24. The norm pertains to the protection of core logical and physical ICT infrastructure from unwarranted state interventions (Broeders 2015, 2017).

25. The norm is a specific norm for the protection of a specific critical infrastructure component (Maurer, Levite, and Perkovich 2017).

26. On the explanatory power of norms, see Björkdahl (2002, 11 ff).

27. As only states have the formal authority to craft new international legal regimes and authoritatively interpret existing international law (Shaw 2017, 155 ff).

28. This has been particularly visible for example regarding the norm entrepreneurship of Microsoft and Siemens, but also in the work of the Global Commission on the Stability of Cyberspace (see further McKay et al. 2014; Charney et al. 2016; Smith 2017; Microsoft et al. 2018; Airbus et al. 2018; GCSC 2018a, 2018b).

29. PCIJ, SS Lotus, 1927, Publ. PCIJ, Series A, no. 10. (Klabbers 2017, 25).

30. The problematique is inspired by James Shires and Max Smeets' analysis of similar tendencies when it comes to the word "cyber" (Shires and Smeets 2017; see also Futter 2018).

31. UNGA resolutions are not legally binding on states.

32. The draft resolution envisages an annex to the report containing "national contributions of participating governmental experts on the subject of how international law applies to the use of information and communications technologies by States" (UNGA 2018b, para. 3).

33. After the non-report outcome of the 2016/2017 UN GGE, US put forth that violations of norms need to be responded to and violators need to be held accountable. It recognized that this may not be achievable through the UN framework, which is why the United States is focusing on imposing consequences, also with like-minded partners and "call out bad behavior and impose costs on our adversaries." The same was echoed by the latest US national cybersecurity strategy (The White House 2017, 2018).

BIBLIOGRAPHY

Aaviksoo, Jaak. 2010. "Cyberattacks Against Estonia Raised Awareness of Cyberthreats." *Defence Against Terrorism Review* 3 (2): 13–22.

Adamson, Liisi, and Eneken Tikk. 2017. "The International Law Playbook of Consequences: From Acts of Retorsion to Countermeasures." Background Paper for the workshop "Writing the International Playbook of Cyber-Consequences." The Hague.

Airbus, IBM, Siemens, Allianz, Munich Security Conference, SGS, Daimler, NXP, and T-Mobile. 2018. "Charter of Trust: For a Secure Digital World."

Australian Minister for Foreign Affairs. 2017. "Joint Statement: Australia-Japan-United States Trilateral Strategic Dialogue." August 7, 2017.

Björkdahl, Annika. 2002. "Norms in International Relations: Some Conceptual and Methodological Reflections." *Cambridge Review of International Affairs* 15 (1): 9–23.

Bodansky, Daniel. 2004. "Rules vs. Standards in International Environmental Law." *Proceedings of the ASIL Annual Meeting* 98: 275–280.

Broeders, Dennis. 2015. *The Public Core of the Internet, An International Agenda for Internet Governance.* 1st ed. Amsterdam: Amsterdam University Press.

Broeders, Dennis. 2017. "Defining the Protection of 'the Public Core of the Internet' as a National Interest." 190. ORF Issue Brief. https://doi.org/10.1080/23738871.20 17.1403640.

Buchan, Russell. 2012. "Cyber Attacks: Unlawful Uses of Force or Prohibited Interventions?" *Journal of Conflict & Security Law* 17 (2): 211–227.

Charney, Scott, Erin English, Aaron Kleiner, Nemanja Malisevic, Angela McKay, Jan Neutze, and Paul Nicholas. 2016. "From Articulation to Implementation: Enabling Progress on Cybersecurity Norms," June: 1–20. https://mscorpmedia. azureedge.net/mscorpmedia/2016/06/Microsoft-Cybersecurity-Norms%7B_%7D vFinal.pdf.

Chinkin, Christine M. 1989. "The Challenge of Soft Law: Development and Change in International Law." *International and Comparative Law Quarterly* 38: 850–866.

Clarke, Richard A., and Robert K. Knake. 2012. *Cyber War: The Next Threat to National Security and What to Do About It*. Ecco.

Crandall, Matthew, and Collin Allan. 2015. "Small States and Big Ideas: Estonia's Battle for Cybersecurity Norms." *Contemporary Security Policy* 36 (2): 346–368.

Cuba's Representative Office Abroad. 2017. "71 UNGA: Cuba at the Final Session of Group of Governmental Experts on Developments in the Field of Information and Telecommunications in the Context of International Security." June 23, 2017. http://misiones.minrex.gob.cu/en/un/statements/71-unga-cuba-final-session-group-governmental-experts-developments-field-information.

D'Aspremont, Jean. 2011. *Formalism and the Sources of International Law: A Theory of the Ascertainment of Legal Rules*. Oxford: Oxford University Press.

Estonian Information System Authority. 2018. "Data Exchange Layer X-Tee." https://www.ria.ee/en/state-information-system/x-tee.html.

Falco, Marco De. 2012. "Stuxnet Facts Report. A Technical and Strategic Analysis." Tallinn.

Farwell, James P., and Rafal Rohozinski. 2011. "Stuxnet and the Future of Cyber War." *Survival* 53 (1): 23–40.

Farwell, James P., and Rafal Rohozinski. 2012. "The New Reality of Cyber War." *Survival* 54 (4): 107–120.

Finnemore, Martha, and Duncan B. Hollis. 2016. "Constructing Norms for Global Cybersecurity." *American Journal of International Law* 110 (3): 425–479.

Finnemore, Martha. 2011. "Cultivating International Cyber Norms." *America's Cyber Future Security and Prosperity in the Information Age* II: 87–102.

Finnemore, Martha. 2017. "Cybersecurity and the Concept of Norms." *Carnegie Endowment for International Peace*. http://carnegieendowment.org/files/Finnemore_web_final.pdf.

Futter, Andrew. 2018. "'Cyber' Semantics: Why We Should Retire the Latest Buzzword in Security Studies." *Journal of Cyber Policy* 3 (2): 201–216.

G7. 2016. "Principles and Action on Cyber." May 27, 2016.

G7. 2017. "Declaration on Responsible States Behaviour in Cyberspace." Lucca, April 11, 2017.

GCSC (Global Commission on the Stability of Cyberspace). 2018a. "Global Commission Urges Protecting Electoral Infrastructure." May 24, 2018. https://cyberstability.org/research/global-commission-urges-protecting-electoral-infrastructure/.

GCSC (Global Commission on the Stability of Cyberspace). 2018b. "Global Commission Proposes a Definition of the Public Core of the Internet." June 27, 2018. https://cyberstability.org/research/global-commission-proposes-definition-of-the-public-core-of-the-internet/.

Goldsmith, Jack L., and Eric A. Posner. 2005. *The Limits of International Law*. New York: Oxford University Press.

Grigsby, Alex. 2017. "The End of Cyber Norms." *Survival* 59 (6): 109–122. https://doi.org/10.1080/00396338.2017.1399730.

Hampson, Fen Osler, and Michael Sulmeyer. 2017. *Getting Beyond Norms: New Approaches to International Cyber Security Challenges*. Centre for International Governance Innovation.

Iasiello, Emilio. 2016. "What Happens If Cyber Norms Are Agreed To?" *Georgetown Journal of International Affairs: International Engagement on Cyber VI, Assessing Cyber Strategy* 18 (3): 30–37.

Jepperson, Ronald L., Alexander Wendt, and Peter J. Katzenstein. 1996. "Norms, Identity, and Culture in National Security." In *The Culture of National Security: Norms and Identity in World Politics*, edited by Peter J. Katzenstein, 33–75. New York: Columbia University Press.

Kaljulaid, Kersti. 2019. "President of Estonia: International Law Applies Also in Cyber Space." Keynote speech CyCon 2019, May 29, 2019. https://www.presiden t.ee/en/meedia/press-releases/15243-president-of-estonia-international-law-appli es-also-in-cyber-space/index.html.

Katzenstein, Peter J. 1996. *The Culture of National Security: Norms and Identity in World Politics*. Edited by Peter J. Katzenstein. New York: Columbia University Press.

Khagram, Sanjeev, James V. Riker, and Kathryn Sikkink. 2002. *Restructuring World Politics: Transnational Social Movements, Networks and Norms*. Minneapolis: University of Minnesota Press.

Klabbers, Jan. 2017. *International Law*. 2nd ed. Cambridge: Cambridge University Press.

Klotz, Audie. 1995. *Norms in International Relations: The Struggle Against Apartheid*. Ithaca: Cornell University Press.

Koskenniemi, Martti. 2019. "International Cyber Law: Does It Exist and Do We Need It?" European Cyber Diplomacy Dialogue, EU Cyber Direct.

Mačak, Kubo. 2017. "From Cyber Norms to Cyber Rules: Re-Engaging States as Law-Makers." *Leiden Journal of International Law*, September 2016: 1–23. https ://doi.org/10.1017/S0922156517000358.

Markoff, Michele G. 2017. "Explanation of Position at the Conclusion of the 2016–2017 UN Group of Governmental Experts (GGE) on Developments in the Field of Information and Telecommunications in the Context of International Security." US Department of State Releases and Remarks. June 23, 2017.

Martinsson, Johanna. 2011. "Global Norms: Creation, Diffusion, and Limits." CommGAP Discussion Papers. Washington, DC.

Maurer, Tim, Ariel Levite, and George Perkovich. 2017. "Toward a Global Norm Against Manipulating the Integrity of Financial Data." White Paper. Carnegie Endowment for International Peace.

Mckay, Angela, Jan Neutze, Paul Nicholas, and Kevin Sullivan. 2014. "International Cybersecurity Norms," 24. https://blogs.microsoft.com/cybertrust/2014/12/03/ proposed-cybersecurity-norms/.

Microsoft et al. 2018. "Cybersecurity Tech Accord." 2018. https://cybertechaccord. org/accord/.

Ministère des Armées (French Ministry of Defense). 2019. "Communiqué_La France s'engage à promouvoir un cyberespace stable, fondé sur la confiance et le respect du droit international." September 9, 2019. https://www.defense.gouv.fr/salle-d e-presse/communiques/communiques-du-ministere-des-armees/communique_la -france-s-engage-a-promouvoir-un-cyberespace-stable-fonde-sur-la-confiance-et-le-respect-du-droit-international.

NATO CCD COE. 2016. "Over 50 States Consult Tallinn Manual 2.0." 2016. https://ccdcoe.org/over-50-states-consult-tallinn-manual-20.html.

NATO CCD COE. 2017. "Tallinn Manual 2.0 on the International Law Applicable to Cyber Operations." In *Tallinn Manual 2.0 on the International Law Applicable to Cyber Warfare*, edited by Michael N. Schmitt. Cambridge: Cambridge University Press.

NATO. 2016a. "Cyber Defence Pledge." July 8, 2016.

NATO. 2016b. "Warsaw Summit Communiqué." July 9, 2016.

O'Connell, Mary Ellen. 2012. "Cyber Security Without Cyber War." *Journal of Conflict & Security Law* 17 (2): 187–209.

OSCE. 2013. *Decision No. 1106 Initial Set of OSCE Confidence-Building Measures to Reduce the Risks of Conflict Stemming from the Use of Information and Communication Technologies*.

OSCE. 2016. *Decision No. 1202 OSCE Confidence-Building Measures to Reduce the Risks of Conflict Stemming from the Use of Information and Communication Technologies*.

Osula, Anna-Maria, and Henry Rõigas. 2016. *International Cyber Norms*. https://ccdcoe.org/sites/default/files/multimedia/pdf/InternationalCyberNorms_full_book.pdf.

Panetta, Leon E. 2012. "Remarks by Secretary Panetta on Cybersecurity to the Business Executives for National Security." US Department of Defense. 2012. http://archive.defense.gov/transcripts/transcript.aspx?transcriptid=5136.

Roberts, Anthea. 2017. *Is International Law International?* Oxford: Oxford University Press.

Schmitt, Michael N. 2013. *Tallinn Manual on the International Law Applicable to Cyber Warfare*. Edited by Michael N. Schmitt. Cambridge: Cambridge University Press.

Schmitt, Michael N. 2018. "International Cyber Norms: Reflections on the Path Ahead." *Netherlands Military Law Review*. https://puc.overheid.nl/mrt/doc/PUC_248171_11/1/

Schmitt, Michael N., and Liis Vihul. 2014. "The Nature of International Law Cyber Norms." 5. The Tallinn Papers. Tallinn. https://ccdcoe.org/sites/default/files/multimedia/pdf/Tallinn Paper No 5 Schmitt and Vihul.pdf.

Segal, Adam. 2017. "The Development of Cyber Norms at the United Nations Ends in Deadlock. Now What?" Council on Foreign Relations. https://www.cfr.org/blog/development-cyber-norms-united-nations-ends-deadlock-now-what.

Seventh International Conference of American States. 1933. *Montevideo Convention on the Rights and Duties of States*. https://doi.org/10.1007/s13398-014-0173-7.2.

Shanghai Cooperation Organization. 2009. *Agreement Between the Governments of the Member States of the Shanghai Cooperation Organization on Cooperation in the Field of International Information Security*. https://ccdcoe.org/sites/default/files/documents/SCO-090616-IISAgreement.pdf.

Shaw, Malcolm N. 2017. *International Law*. 8th ed. Cambridge: Cambridge University Press.

Shires, James, and Max Smeets. 2017. "The Word Cyber Now Means Everything—And Nothing At All." *Future Tense*, 2017. http://www.slate.com/blogs/future_tense/2017/12/01/the_word_cyber_has_lost_all_meaning.html.

Sloss, David. 2006. "Do International Norms Influence State Behavior?" *George Washington International Law Review* 159: 159–207.

Smith, Brad. 2017. "The Need for a Digital Geneva Convention." Microsoft on the Issues. https://blogs.microsoft.com/on-the-issues/2017/02/14/need-digital-geneva-convention/.

Soesanto, Stefan, and D'Incau Fosca. 2017. "The UN GGE Is Dead: Time to Fall Forward." European Council on Foreign Relations. https://www.ecfr.eu/article/commentary_time_to_fall_forward_on_cyber_governance.

Terpan, Fabien. 2015. "Soft Law in the European Union—The Changing Nature of EU Law." *European Law Journal* 21 (1): 68–96.

The Ministry of Foreign Affairs of the Russian Federation. 2011. *Convention on International Information Security (Concept).* http://www.mid.ru/en/foreign_policy/official_documents/-/asset_publish.

The White House. 2009. "Cyberspace Policy Review: Assuring a Trusted and Resilient Information and Communications Infrastructure." https://www.energy.gov/sites/prod/files/cioprod/documents/Cyberspace_Policy_Review_final.pdf.

The White House. 2017. "Remarks by Homeland Security Advisor Thomas P. Bossert at Cyber Week 2017." 2017. https://www.whitehouse.gov/briefings-statements/remarks-homeland-security-advisor-thomas-p-bossert-cyber-week-2017/.

The White House. 2018. "National Cyber Strategy of the United States of America." Washington. https://www.whitehouse.gov/wp-content/uploads/2018/09/National-Cyber-Strategy.pdf.

Tikk, Eneken, and Mika Kerttunen. 2018a. "Cyber Treaty Is Coming : Что Делать ?" Tartu.

Tikk, Eneken, and Mika Kerttunen. 2018b. "Parabasis: Cyber-Diplomacy in Stalemate." Oslo.

Tikk, Eneken, Kadri Kaska, and Liis Vihul. 2010. *International Cyber Incidents—Legal Considerations.* Tallinn: NATO CCD COE Publications.

UNGA (United Nations General Assembly). 1998. "Letter Dated 23 September 1998 from the Permanent Representative of the Russian Federation to the United Nations Addressed to the Secretary- General." A/C.1/53/3. 1998.

UNGA (United Nations General Assembly). 1999. *A/RES/53/70 Developments in the Field of Information and Telecommunications in the Context of International Security.*

UNGA (United Nations General Assembly). 2005. *A/60/202 Group of Governmental Experts on Developments in the Field of Information and Telecommunications in the Context of International Security Report of the Secretary-General.*

UNGA (United Nations General Assembly). 2010. *A/65/201 Report of the Group of Governmental Experts on Developments in the Field of Information and Telecommunications in the Context of International Security.*

UNGA (United Nations General Assembly). 2011. *A/66/359 49656 Letter Dated 12 September 2011 from the Permanent Representatives of China, the Russian Federation, Tajikistan and Uzbekistan to the United Nations Addressed to the Secretary-General.*

UNGA (United Nations General Assembly). 2013. *A/68/98 Report of the Group of Governmental Experts on Developments in the Field of Information and Telecommunications in the Context of International Security.*

UNGA (United Nations General Assembly). 2015a. *A/69/723 Letter Dated 9 January 2015 from the Permanent Representatives of China, Kazakhstan, Kyrgyzstan, the Russian Federation, Tajikistan and Uzbekistan to the United Nations Addressed to the Secretary General.*

UNGA (United Nations General Assembly). 2015b. *A/70/174 Report of the Group of Governmental Experts on Developments in the Field of Information and Telecommunications n the Context of International Security.*

UNGA (United Nations General Assembly). 2018a. *A/C.1/73/L.27, Developments in the Field of Information and Telecommunications in the Context of International Security: Draft Resolution*, October 22, 2018.

UNGA (United Nations General Assembly). 2018b. *A/C.1./73/L.37, Advancing Responsible State Behaviour in Cyberspace in the Context of International Security*, October 18, 2018.

UNODA. 2017. *Voluntary, Non-Binding Norms for Responsible State Behaviour in the Use of Information and Communications Technology: A Commentary.* New York: UNODA.

US Department of State. 2016. "Joint Statement on Third Annual Nordic-Baltic + U.S. Cyber Consultations." September 16, 2016.

Velde, James van de. 2018. "Why Cyber Norms Are Dumb and Serve Russian Interests." *The Cipher Brief*, June 6, 2018.

Wolfrum, Rüdiger. 2010. "General International Law (Principles, Rules, and Standards)." *Max Planck Encyclopedia of Public International Law.* https://opil.ou plaw.com/view/10.1093/law:epil/9780199231690/law-9780199231690-e1408

Wolter, Detlev. 2013. "The UN Takes a Big Step Forward on Cybersecurity." *Arms Control Today* 43 (7): 25–29.

Wright, Jeremy. 2019. "Cyber and International Law in the 21st Century." Speech on May 23, 2019. https://www.gov.uk/government/speeches/cyber-and-internation al-law-in-the-21st-century.

Chapter 3

Electoral Cyber Interference, Self-Determination, and the Principle of Non-intervention in Cyberspace

Nicholas Tsagourias

It is by now accepted that international law applies to cyberspace. The 2013 Report of the United Nations Group of Governmental Experts (GGE) on developments in the field of information and telecommunications in the context of international security affirmed that international law, especially the UN Charter, applies to cyberspace and that state sovereignty and international norms and principles that flow from sovereignty apply to state conduct of Information and Communication Technology (ICT)-related activities, and to jurisdiction over ICT infrastructure within a state's territory (U.N. General Assembly 2013, paras 19–20). The 2015 GGE Report went a step further by spelling out specific international norms and principles that apply, or should apply, to cyberspace. Among the international law principles that apply to cyberspace are the principle of state sovereignty and the principle of non-intervention in the internal affairs of other States (U.N. General Assembly 2015, para. 26). In the same vein, states have affirmed the application of international law and of the principle of non-intervention to cyberspace. According to China, "[c]ountries shouldn't use ICTs to interfere in other countries' internal affairs and undermine other countries' political, economic, and social stability as well as cultural environment" (P. R. C. Permanent Mission to the U.N. 2013).

Notwithstanding such strong assertions, how international law or, more specifically, how the principle of non-intervention applies to cyberspace and to cyber operations is beset by uncertainty. According to the former legal adviser to the State Department, Brian Egan, "States need to do more work to clarify how the international law on non-intervention applies to States' activities in cyberspace" (Egan 2017, 175).[1] This state of affairs came to a head with regard to the Russian cyber interference in the 2016 US presidential election. Russia's toolkit of electoral interference consisted of disinformation and "hack and leak" operations (U.S. ODNI 2017, 1; EU vs Disinfo 2019). Views concerning the legal characterization of Russia's actions vary and although commentators invoked the principle of non-intervention, the majority concluded that Russia's actions did not fulfill its conditions in particular that of coercion (Hollis 2016; Ohlin 2016; Watts 2016). The US incident is not the only example of electoral cyber interference; other incidents involve elections in the Netherlands, the United Kingdom, France, and Germany to name just a few (Brattberg and Maurer 2018; Galante and Ee 2018; Bay and Šnore 2019).[2] Although electoral interference is not a new phenomenon, cyberspace increases the scalability, reach, and effects of such interference and poses a serious threat to a state's sovereign authority.

Against this background, this chapter examines the question of how the principle of non-intervention can be contextualized and reconceptualized in cyberspace in order to attain its purpose of protecting a state's sovereign authority in cases of electoral cyber interference. I will do this by aligning the principle of non-intervention with the principle of self-determination and by identifying the baseline of intervention and the pathways intervention can take in cyberspace. By reassessing the concept of intervention, its regulatory scope and effectiveness in cyberspace will be enhanced since cyberspace is linked to the political, economic, military, diplomatic, social, and cultural functions of a state and is a domain within which, or through which, states operate, interact, and exert power.

The chapter proceeds in the following manner. In the next section, I explain the content and meaning of the principle of non-intervention as traditionally interpreted in international law and in the third section I will apply this definition to Russia's interference in the 2016 US election. Because of the identified normative and regulatory gaps, in the fourth section I expose the relationship between the principle of non-intervention and that of self-determination, define the baseline of intervention as control, and explain the different pathways intervention can take in cyberspace. In the fifth section, I apply this concept to electoral cyber interference such as the interference in the 2016 US election. The conclusion sets out the chapter's overall findings and explains the importance of reassessing the meaning of intervention in the cyber context and more generally.

THE PRINCIPLE OF NON-INTERVENTION

Non-intervention is a fundamental principle of international law that has acquired customary law status even if it is not mentioned in the UN Charter (*Nicaragua Case* 1986, para 202; Jamnejad and Wood 2009, 347–367).[3] According to the 1965 General Assembly Declaration on the Inadmissibility of Intervention in the Domestic Affairs of States and the Protection of Their Independence and Sovereignty, which was repeated almost verbatim in the 1970 General Assembly Declaration on Friendly Relations: "No State has the right to intervene, directly or indirectly, for any reason whatever, in the internal or external affairs of any other State. Consequently, armed intervention and all other forms of interference or attempted threats against the personality of the State or against its political, economic and cultural elements, are condemned" (U.N. General Assembly Res. 1965, Annex, para. 1).[4] In the *Nicaragua Case*, the ICJ defined non-intervention as "the right of every sovereign State to conduct its [external or internal] affairs without outside interference."[5]

The importance of the principle of non-intervention derives from the fact that it emanates from and protects essential aspects of the principle of state sovereignty (Jennings and Watts 1992, 428; Vincent 1974, 14; U.N. General Assembly 1964, para. 216). Sovereignty as the foundational principle of the modern international system is an all-embracing principle and can be dissected into more specific principles or rules that protect specific aspects of state sovereignty. The principle of non-intervention protects the integrity and autonomy of a state's authority and will in the sense of its capacity to internal and external self-governance.[6] Understood in this way, the principle of non-intervention creates a juridical space where the government, as the holder of authority and will, can exercise its will freely and make free choices in view of the fact that in international law the state is represented by the government. Because it protects an essential aspect of state sovereignty, the principle of non-intervention acquired independent legal status and it is critical in an international system defined by sovereignty and by interactions between sovereign States. Its alignment, however, with the principle of sovereignty has important normative and operational implications in that the scope and content of the principle of non-intervention is molded by the meaning and content of the principle of sovereignty as developed in international law and relations.

In order to define the content and meaning of the principle of non-intervention in international law, we need to explain the meaning of its opposite, that is, intervention. According to Oppenheim's definition, intervention is interference "forcible or dictatorial, or otherwise coercive, in effect depriving the state intervened against of control over the matter in question" (Jennings and Watts 1992, 428).[7] The ICJ in the *Nicaragua Case* defined prohibited intervention as "one bearing on matters in which each State is permitted, by the principle of State sovereignty, to decide freely . . . and uses methods of coercion in regard to such choices, which must remain free ones."[8] From the above definitions, it transpires that in order for interference to constitute intervention, it should satisfy two conditions: first, it should impinge on matters that fall within a state's sovereign affairs and, second, it should be coercive.

The first condition describes the domain within which interference should take place as well as the object of such interference. In this respect, the ICJ mentioned the choice of political, economic, social, and cultural systems and the formulation of foreign policy.[9] It thus transpires that the protected domain is a state's political, economic, social, and cultural system whereas the object of intervention is the ability to make free choices in this domain. That said, the aforementioned list is not exhaustive and can change in light of related developments concerning the meaning and scope of state sovereignty (Jennings and Watts 1992, 428). As a result, the domain protected from intervention may expand or decrease, something that will affect the scope of the non-intervention principle.

The second condition—coercion—refers to the nature of the interference and is what differentiates intervention from pure interference or influence. As the ICJ said, "the element of coercion . . . defines, and indeed forms the very essence of, [a] prohibited intervention."[10] Traditionally, coercion in international law has been taken to imply compulsion whereby one state compels or attempts to compel another state to take a particular course of action against its will thus obtaining, in the words of the 1970 Friendly Relations Declaration, "the subordination of the exercise of its sovereign rights" (U.N. General Assembly Friendly Relations Declaration 1970).[11]

Such a construction of intervention can very well apply to cyberspace. For instance, if a state's governmental services are targeted by a Distributed Denial of Service (DDoS) attack in order to compel its government to change its policies or decisions, this would amount to prohibited intervention. The 2007 DDoS attacks against Estonia come immediately to mind. They were launched after the Estonian government decided to relocate a Soviet-era statue, a decision that was resisted by the country's Russian-speaking minority and was frowned upon by Moscow. To the extent that they were intended to put such pressure on Estonia to change its decision and provided that they were attributed to Russia,[12] in my opinion, they would constitute prohibited intervention (Tsagourias 2012, 35; Buchan 2012). In contrast, the 2014 Sony attack (Zetter 2014) does not amount to intervention because the target of the attack was a private company not connected to the US government and it did not involve a matter that falls within the sovereign prerogatives of the United States nor was there any attempt to coerce the US government to take a particular course of action.

INTERFERENCE IN THE 2016 US ELECTION AND THE PRINCIPLE OF NON-INTERVENTION

How would the abovementioned construction of intervention apply to Russia's interference in the 2016 US presidential election? Russian operations included hacking into the Democratic National Committee e-mails and the release of confidential information as well as disinformation operations (U.S. ODNI 2017, 2-5). The former is referred to as doxing (Kilovaty 2018, 152) whose objective is to "expose, disgrace, or otherwise undermine a particular individual, campaign, or organisation in order to influence public opinion during an election cycle" (EU vs Disinfo 2019) whereas disinformation is the dissemination of "false, inaccurate, or misleading information designed, presented and promoted to intentionally cause public harm or for profit" and can threaten the "democratic political processes and value" (European Commission 2018, 10).[13] The Department of Homeland Security (DHS) and the Office of the Director of National Intelligence (ODNI) issued a joint statement claiming that the Russian government was responsible for the hack and the publication of the materials in an attempt to "interfere with the US election process" (U.S. DHS and ODNI 2016) and, according to ODNI, the intention of the leaks was to "undermine public faith in the US democratic process, denigrate Secretary Clinton and harm her electability and potential presidency" (U.S. ODNI 2017, ii). Following investigations, a number of Russian operatives were indicted. According to the Mueller indictment, "[t]he conspiracy had as its object impairing, obstructing, and defeating the lawful governmental functions of the United States by dishonest means in order to enable the Defendants to interfere with U.S. political and electoral processes, including the 2016 U.S. presidential election" (Mueller Indictments 2018).[14]

One can plausibly say that Russia's actions satisfied the first condition of unlawful intervention by targeting the conduct of elections. As the ICJ opined in the *Nicaragua Case*, the "choice of political system" is a matter falling within a state's sovereign prerogatives which should remain "free from external intervention"[15] and went on to say that holding elections is a domestic matter.[16] There are problems, however, with the second condition namely that of coercion. According to Brian Egan, "a cyber operation by a State that interferes with another State's ability to hold an election or that manipulates a State's election results would be a clear violation of the rule of non-intervention" (Egan 2017, 175). Likewise, according to the former UK attorney general, "the use by a hostile state of cyber operations to manipulate the electoral system to alter the results of an election in another state . . . must surely be a breach of the prohibition on intervention in the domestic affairs of states" (U.K. Attorney General's Office 2018). These statements refer to interference with the electoral administration, for example, interference with electoral registers to delete voters' names as well as on interference with the electoral infrastructure, for example, interference with the recording or counting of votes or the blocking of voting machines thus cancelling an election. Since Russia's operations, according to the aforementioned reports (U.S.

ODNI 2017, 3), did not amount to such interference, they do not breach the non-intervention norm.

That said, many states since then have designated their electoral infra-structure (registration, casting and counting votes, submitting and tallying results) as critical national infrastructure (U.S. DHS "Election Security").[17] In the same vein, the Global Commission on the Stability of Cyberspace (GCSC) proposed a norm prohibiting the disruption of elections through cyberattacks on the technical infrastructure that supports elections (GCSC 2018).[18] Although these are important developments, they only address one aspect of the phenomenon of electoral cyber interference, that is, meddling with the electoral infrastructure but do not extend to the process according to which the will of the people is formed and how intervention can impact on them. Yet, outcomes can be affected not only by interfering with the electoral infrastructure but also by interfering with the process of will formation. This is an issue that will be discussed in the next section.

CONTEXTUALIZING AND RECONCEPTUALIZING INTERVENTION IN CYBERSPACE

In this section, I revisit the phenomenon of intervention in order to contextualize and reconceptualize the principle of non-intervention for cyber purposes. This is necessary for many reasons. In the first place and as was said earlier, cyberspace is a new domain but one that is embedded in the political and legal environment where states operate. States thus use cyberspace as a conduit of power and indeed as a conduit of intervention by employing not only the traditional diplomatic, political, military, or economic tools of coercion but also new tools suitable to cyberspace. Second, because of the particular features of cyberspace such as its interconnectedness and anonymity, the pathways of coercion can diversify whereas the scalability, reach, and effects of intervention enhanced.[19] Third, the very nature of the concept of intervention invites such reassessment. Intervention is not a static concept but a concept that is constantly contextualized in time or domain and whose meaning, scope, and practice changes accordingly. What intervention signified in the nineteenth century is not the same today, neither is the meaning of military, diplomatic, political, or legal intervention. It is for these reasons that the concept of intervention needs to be contextualized and reconceptualized for cyber purposes and in what follows I will do this by first explaining the intimate relationship between non-intervention and self-determination, hence repositioning the domain and object of intervention and, secondly, by reassessing the baseline of coercion and by explaining the pathways coercion can take in cyberspace and how they impact on self-determination and consequently on the principle of non-intervention.

Non-intervention and Self-Determination

With regard to the first issue, it was said in the first section that intervention acquires meaning within a configuration of sovereign relations by protecting the integrity and autonomy of a state's authority and will against external interference. As was also explained, the domain protected from intervention consists of the state's sovereign prerogatives whereas the object of intervention is the ability to make free choices on these matters. This traditional reading of intervention focuses on the internal and/or external manifestation of authority and will by the state represented by the government; it vests, in other words, all sovereign authority and will in the government which is then protected from intervention but does not take into account how this authority and will are formed and how intervention can impact on the process of their formation. Instead, it treats the state and its government as if they were cut off from the prior process of authority and will formation. However, that process of authority and will formation is connected with the internal and external manifestation of such authority and will by the government. To explain, a government's authority and will remain free only when its sourcing is also free. This immediately brings to light the relationship between non-intervention and self-determination (Ohlin 2016; U.N. General Assembly 1964, para. 216), another principle that derives from and protects the principle of state sovereignty. Self-determination refers to the right of peoples to determine freely and without external interference their political status and to pursue freely their economic, social, and cultural development (U.N. General Assembly ICCPR 1966, article 1(1); U.N. General Assembly 1970).

From this definition, it transpires that the scope of the right to self-determination is broader and is not exclusively linked to the right of peoples to form their own state. Moreover, it does not cease once a state has been created but thereafter self-determination refers to the "right to authentic self-government, that is, the right of a people really and freely to choose its own political and economic regime" (Cassese 1995, 137).[20] It follows from this that the principle of non-intervention protects against external interference the expression of authority and will by the people and also protects the conditions that enable the people to form authority and will freely and make free choices.[21] External interference through disinformation combined with identity falsification, for example, distorts, undermines, or inverses this process and nullifies the genuine expression of authority and will by the people (Ohlin 2018). It also taints the internal or external manifestation or expression of authority and will by the government that emerges. For this reason, in the words of Crawford, "the principle of self-determination is represented by the rule against intervention in the internal affairs of that state" (Crawford 2007, 127).

By aligning the principles of non-intervention and self-determination, the normative and operational scope of the principle of non-intervention shifts. More specifically, the domain and object of intervention shifts from the government to the actual power holder, the people, and to the process of forming authority and will through which the goal of free choice is also attained. Whereas the government as the depository of such authority and will is protected by the principle of non-intervention, it is not the primary object of protection as the traditional reading holds, but a derivative one; the primary object of protection are the people and the process of authority and will formation.

Control as the Baseline of Coercion and the Pathways of Coercion

Having identified the domain and object of protection by the principle of non-intervention, I will now consider its second element, that of coercion. In international law, there has been little consideration of the threshold or the baseline of coercion above which intervention takes place. Oppenheim's definition is, however, quite instructive. According to him, the essence of coercion is the fact that a state intervened against is, in effect, deprived of control over a matter. Control means one state's intentional direction *over* another state's authority and will, which prevents the latter from discharging its authority and will freely and making free choices. When a state assumes control over a matter at the expense of the state, which has a legitimate claim of authority and will over that matter because it falls within its sovereign prerogatives, it effectively curtails the latter's capacity to self-determination as self-governance, which, as was said, are protected by the principle of non-intervention. It inverses these values by forcing the state to act counterintuitively to what its free authority and will would advocate.[22]

Regarding the pathways to coercion, or the means and methods through which coercion can be actualized, the ICJ spoke of "methods" of coercion in the plural and also spoke of direct and indirect methods. This means that there is a spectrum of coercion which can manifest itself through various means and methods. In the first place, coercion, as Oppenheim noted, can be forcible. In the *Nicaragua Case*, the ICJ said that one of the most obvious forms of coercion is the one that uses force either in the direct form of military action or in the indirect form of support for subversive or terrorist armed activities within another state.[23] In this case, the intervened against state loses control over a matter, for example, over parts of its territory, through the use of armed force. Forcible coercion is direct and perhaps the most dramatic and serious form of coercion and, for this reason, it acquired its own legal meaning and status in the rule prohibiting the use of force contained in Article 2(4) of the UN Charter and in customary law.

Another pathway to coercion mentioned by Oppenheim is that of dictatorial interference. Dictatorial interference is when a state prescribes a course of action in imperative terms and usually by threatening negative consequences, forcing thus the will of the recipient state. This is again a direct form of coercion and describes a situation where two sovereign "wills" clash over a matter and one state loses control over a matter by subordinating its will.

In addition to these direct pathways, there are also other more subtle or indirect pathways to coercion where one state extends its will over another and thus assumes control even if the latter State appears to behave freely. This can happen when the intervening state arranges the targeted state's choices in such a way that it has no effective choice. Another instance is when the intervenor, through manipulation, arranges the other state's preferences in such a way that the state acts in accordance with the intervenor's preferred choices. In these cases, coercion as control does not appear to be conflictual since the victim state apparently acts voluntarily but the intervenor exerts control over the other and extends its will by rearranging the available choices or by rearranging preferences to align them with its own. For example, if a state assumes control over another state's governmental systems (or systems supporting critical national infrastructure) and manipulates their operation, this would amount to coercion to the extent that the systems operate counterintuitively to how they were programed to operate by the victim state and produce actions and effects desired by the intervener. Also, when a state, through cyber espionage, acquires information on another state's policies which is then used to direct the choices of the victim state, it controls the latter's choices against its wishes.[24]

Electoral Cyber Interference and Intervention

Where coercion as control can manifest itself more acutely is when a state's authority and will are manipulated at its source; in the process of their formation. To explain, when a state interferes with the structures and the environment that condition and facilitate the formation of authority and will by the people, and substitutes the legitimate process of self-determination with an artificially constructed process in order to generate particular attitudes and results to serve its particular interests,[25] the intervening state controls not only the attitudes, will, and choices of the people, but also the will of the government that emerges. Consequently, the right to self-determination as self-governance which is protected by the non-intervention principle is essentially curtailed. Take, for example, the case of deep fakes when, during an electoral campaign, imageries, voices, or videos of politicians are simulated in order to discredit them. To the extent that such operations are designed and executed in such a way as to manipulate the cognitive process where authority and will are formed and to take control over peoples' choices of government, they would constitute intervention.

As the aforementioned example shows, cyberspace provides a facilitative ecosystem where electoral interference can take place and as was said, it can also enhance its scalability, reach, and effects of coercion. To explain, cyberspace has made it easier to produce, disseminate, and share disinformation, enhances its accessibility by amplifying the circle of targeted audiences or by micro-targeting, increases the immediacy and speed of such operations, complicates attribution, and allows for remotely conducted operations.

The interference in the 2016 US elections is a case in point. As was said, Russian operations included the hacking and release of confidential information and social media-enabled disinformation. The primary target of such operations was the cognitive environment which enables the making of choices that are subsequently reflected in the type of government that emerges from the process (Hollis 2018, 36; Lin and Kerr 2017). As James Comey, the former FBI director, said before the Senate Intelligence Committee: "[t]his is such a big deal, . . . we have this big, messy, wonderful country where . . . nobody tells us what to think, what to fight about, what to vote for, except other Americans . . . . But we're talking about a foreign government that, using technical intrusion, lots of other methods, tried to shape the way we think, we vote, we act" (New York Times 2017). In a similar vein, the 2017 US National Security Strategy opined that "[a] democracy is only as resilient as its people. An informed and engaged citizenry is the fundamental requirement for a free and resilient nation. . . . Today, actors such as Russia are using information tools in an attempt to undermine the legitimacy of democracies. Adversaries target media, political processes, financial networks, and personal data" (U.S. White House 2017, p. 14).

From the preceding discussion, it can be said that Russia's interference met the two conditions of unlawful intervention. Although one could have stopped here, it is important to consider a number of other issues which should be present although their status has not been firmly settled in legal doctrine.

The first is intention and more specifically whether coercion should be intentional. The *Tallinn Manual* treats intent as a constitutive element of the principle of non-intervention (Schmitt 2017, Rule 66, para. 27), but there are also dissenting voices who treat intervention as an objective state of affairs (Watts 2015, 249, 268–269). If, as was said previously, intervention is relational and contextual, it can never be an objective state of affairs. It seems that the ICJ in the *Nicaragua Case* required intent when it said that "in international law, if one State, *with a view to* the coercion of another State, supports and assists armed bands in that State whose purpose is to overthrow the government of that State, that amounts to an intervention by the one State in the internal affairs of the other, whether or not the political objective of the State giving such support and assistance is equally far-reaching."[26] What the court meant is that a state should have the intention to coerce another state by using proxies although it may not share the particular objective of the proxies it is supporting.

In the opinion of the present writer, intent is critical, particularly in cyberspace, where operations are often factually indistinguishable, and their effects permeate borders unintentionally. Moreover, intent distinguishes influence operations or in general propaganda from operations that are purposively designed to exert control over a sovereign matter (self-determination) through false, fabricated, misleading, or generally through disinformation.

That having been said, it should be acknowledged that it is difficult to establish intent. There may exist some factual and demonstrable evidence to prove intent in the form of statements or the involvement of state operatives (U.S. ODNI 2017; Mueller Indictments 2018), otherwise intent can be constructed from circumstantial evidence and from surrounding circumstances. For example, the target of the operation[27] and the means used (disinformation) are important indicators (U.S. ODNI 2017, 3; Mueller Indictments, para. 2). With regard to the latter, one can look into whether the confidentiality, integrity, or availability of information has been breached (Herpig, Schuetze and Jones 2018, 14ff). For example, in the case of deep fakes or leaked e-mails, it is the authenticity, integrity, and confidentiality of the disseminated information that is breached but even in the case of true information, it is its integrity and authenticity that is encroached if it is mixed with false information or is presented in a false or fabricated context or if it relates to partial truths. Other factors to take into account to establish intent are the political and ideological competition that exists between states, the strategic or other interests served by the operation, the timing of the operation, the intensity and widespread nature of the operation. With regard to the latter, the Mueller indictment demonstrated the widespread and systematic nature of Russia's interference. [28]

The second condition is that of knowledge in the sense of whether the victim state should be aware of the coercion. Certain commentators contend that knowledge is not required whereas others claim that it is required because a state cannot be coerced when it is unaware of the act of coercion (Schmitt 2017, Rule 66, para. 25). In international relations theory, which views coercion as an instrument of power and usually identifies it with threats, knowledge of the threat and of its author is important because it relates to the persuasiveness and credibility of the threat. For this reason, some international relations commentators view cyber coercion as inconsequential because of the covert nature of cyber operations (Lindsay and Gartzke [2014] 2018, 179).

The difference, however, between international law and international relations is that the latter takes a functional approach to intervention whereas international law takes a normative approach. It is thus submitted that knowledge is not a constitutive element of intervention, but knowledge is required in order to trigger a claim that intervention has taken place. This also means that the fact that intervention may be covert, or that it was attempted without actually succeeding, will not affect the qualification of the impugned behavior as intervention for international law purposes when the intervened against state becomes aware of the situation, provided of course that the criteria of intervention have been satisfied. To put it differently, the intervening state cannot claim that there was no intervention or that there is no breach of the non-intervention rule because at the time intervention happened the victim state was not aware of the intervention. This also means that the victim state is not prevented from taking countermeasures after acquiring knowledge of the intervention even if the act of intervention occurred much earlier because there will be temporal proximity between the countermeasures and the claim of wrongfulness. In the US case, the fact that subsequent reports established the facts will not prevent the United States from claiming that it was victim of unlawful intervention although whether it will do so is a matter of politics.

Finally, such interference needs to reach a certain level of severity to amount to intervention. Severity can be assessed against the importance of the values affected which in this case is the value of self-determination; the consequences of intervention which in this case is the control of a state's authority and will and, according to McDougal and Feliciano, the extent to which values are affected and the number of participants whose values are so affected.[29] Although no analytical tool exists to measure the real impact of electoral interference on people or how their voting preferences were affected, however, analysis of social networks can reveal the number of viewers or artificial movements and to some extent measure the number of affected individuals (Howard et al. 2018).[30]

CONCLUSION

This chapter has shown that cyberspace is a new domain where the principle of non-intervention can apply. However, deciphering its content and understanding how it applies to cyberspace are a difficult exercise that can impact its effectiveness to regulate cyber activities. Consequently, reassessing the meaning of intervention in the cyber domain is critical because cyberspace is a domain where states compete and exert power and it is an environment which increases the scalability, reach, and effects of intervention.

For this reason, in this chapter I contextualized and reassessed the principle of non-intervention for cyber purposes. More specifically, I aligned the principle of non-intervention with that of self-determination and argued that non-intervention protects not just the integrity and autonomy of a state's authority and will as it manifests itself internally and externally through the government, but primarily it protects its source, the people, and the process according to which authority and will are formed. I then identified the baseline of coercion as control over a matter that falls within a state's sovereign prerogatives and applied this definition to cyberspace by looking into the different ways control and, therefore, coercion manifests itself. In relation to electoral interference, it manifests itself as control over the conditions that enable the exercise of self-determination by the people in the sense of freely forming authority and will that subsequently extends to control over the manifestation and expression of such authority and will by the government.

By reassessing what the principle of non-intervention entails in the cyber era, international law will be able to fill many normative and operational gaps that currently exist when it is called upon to apply to cyber operations. The implications of such reconceptualization are not limited to cyber intervention but extend to the concept of intervention in general which, as was said, is a dynamic concept that requires constant reevaluation. However, it should be admitted that this is not the end of the road because it is for states to take up the mantle and provide normative and operational clarity as to the meaning of intervention in cyberspace and, more broadly, in the physical world. Yet, even if agreement on the meaning of cyber intervention is attained, intervention will still be a controversial concept because there is disagreement as to which interventions are lawful or unlawful but justified. For example, is electoral cyber interference in democracies unlawful whereas a cyber campaign to overthrow a dictatorial regime lawful or at least justified? To the extent that these issues have not been settled in international law, intervention and non-intervention will remain a Jekyll and Hyde concept even in the cyber context. That having been said, this is a second-order enquiry because the first-order enquiry is ontological; it is about the meaning of intervention to which this chapter attempted to provide an answer.

NOTES

1. In the same vein, the UK attorney general said: "The precise boundaries of this principle are the subject of ongoing debate between states, and not just in the context of cyber space" (U.K. Attorney General's Office 2018).

2. For similar activities during the 2018 elections in Cambodia, see Henderson et al. (2018).

3. Military and Paramilitary Activities in and against Nicaragua (*Nicaragua v United States of America*) (Merits) [1986] ICJ Rep 14 para 202 (hereinafter referred to as *Nicaragua Case*); See: Maziar Jamnejad and Michael Wood, "The Principle of Non-Intervention in International Law" *Leiden Journal of International Law* 22 (2009): 345, 347–367.

4. See also: U.N. General Assembly Res., *Declaration on Principles of International Law Concerning Friendly Relations and Co-Operation Among States in Accordance with the United Nations*, October 24, 1970, U. N. Doc. A/RES/2625 (XXV), Annex: "No State or group of States has the right to intervene, directly or indirectly, for any reason whatever, in the internal or external affairs of any other State. Consequently, armed intervention and all other forms of interference or attempted threats against the personality of the State or against its political, economic and cultural elements, are in violation of international law."

5. *Nicaragua Case*, para 202.

6. Ibid., para 202.

7. See also: Philip Kunig, "Prohibition of Intervention" *Max Planck Encyclopedia of Public International Law* (2012) para 1.

8. *Nicaragua Case*, para 205.

9. Ibid.

10. Ibid.

11. See also: Christopher C. Joyner, "Coercion" *Max Planck Encyclopedia of Public International Law* (2006): "Coercion in inter-State relations involves the government of one State compelling the government of another State to think or act in a certain way by applying various kinds of pressure, threats, intimidation or the use of force."

12. For attribution see: Nicholas Tsagourias, "Cyber Attacks, Self-Defence and the Problem of Attribution," *Journal of Conflict Security Law* 17, no. 2 (2012): 229.

13. According to *EU vs Disinfo*, disinformation is "the fabrication or deliberate distortion of news content aimed at deceiving an audience, polluting the information space to obscure fact-based reality, and manufacturing misleading narratives about key events or issues to manipulate public opinion. Disinformation is the most persistent and widespread form of the Kremlin's interference efforts. Importantly, it is not limited only to election cycles, but has now become a viral feature of our information ecosystem" and its objective is "to paralyse the democratic process by fuelling social fragmentation and polarisation, sowing confusion and uncertainty about fact-based reality, and undermining trust in the integrity of democratic politics and institutions": *EU vs Disinfo*, "Methods of Foreign Electoral Interference," April 2, 2019, https://euvsdisinfo.eu/methods-of-foreign-electoral-interference/. Others speak of "information manipulation" encompassing three criteria: a coordinated campaign, the diffusion of false information or information that is consciously distorted, and the political intention to cause harm," see: Jean-Baptise Jeangène Vilmer, Alexandre Escorcia, Marine Guillaume, and Janaina Herrera, "Information Manipulation: A Challenge for Our Democracies, Report by the Policy Planning Staff (CAPS) of the Ministry for

Europe and Foreign Affairs and the Institute for Strategic Research (IRSEM) of the Ministry for the Armed Forces" (Paris, August 2018), 21.

14. U.S. District Court, District of Columbia, United States v. Internet Research Agency LLC et al. (Indictment, 16 February 2018), Criminal Action No. 100032 (DLF), para 25 and United States v. Victor Borisovich Netyksho et al. (Indictment, 13 July 2018), Criminal Action No. 00215 (ABJ), para. 28 (The Mueller Indictments), https://d3i6fh83elv35t.cloudfront.net/static/2018/07/Muellerindictment.pdf.

15. *Nicaragua Case*, para 205.

16. Ibid., paras 257–259.

17. U.S. Department of Homeland Security, *"Election Security,"* https://www.dhs .gov/topic/election-security.

18. See also: U.K. Cabinet Office, National Security Capability Review, March 28, 2018, 34 https://assets.publishing.service.gov.uk/government/uploads/system/upl oads/attachment_data/file/705347/6.4391_CO_National-Security-Review_web.pdf; For Sweden see: Government Offices of Sweden, Ministry of Justice, "National Strategy for Society Information and Cyber Security," June 2018, 6–7. https://ww w.government.se/4ac8ff/contentassets/d87287e088834d9e8c08f28d0b9dda5b/a-nat ional-cyber-security-strategy-skr.-201617213; Sean Kanuck, Global Commission on the Stability of Cyberspace, "Protecting the Electoral Process and its Institutions," January 2018, https://cyberstability.org/research/.

19. For example, the U.S. ODNI Report 2017, says that Russia's actions "repre- sented a significant escalation in directness, level of activity and scope of effort."

20. See also: Patrick Thornberry, "The Democratic or Internal Aspect of Self- Determination with Some Remarks on Federalism" in *Modern Law of Self-Deter- mination*, edited by Christian Tomuschat (Dordrecht, Boston and London: Martinus Nijhoff, 1992), 101.

21. According to Universal Declaration of Human Rights, Article 21(3): "[t]he will of the people shall be the basis of the authority of government." See: U.N. Gen- eral Assembly Res., *Universal Declaration of Human Rights*, December 10, 1948, 183rd Plenary Meeting, U.N. Doc. 217A (III).

22. Rosenau, for example, speaks about a sharp break with conventional patterns of behavior. See: James N. Rosenau, "Intervention as a Scientific Concept," *Journal of Conflict Resolution* 13, no. 2 (1969): 149–171, 162–163.

23. Nicaragua Case, para 205.

24. For cyber espionage, see also: Russell Buchan, *Cyber Espionage and Interna- tional Law* (Hart, 2018), 48–69.

25. According to Rosenau, intervention is addressed to "the authority structure of the target society-that is, to the identity of those who make the decisions that are binding for the entire society and/or to the processes through which such deci- sions are made. New foreign policy initiatives designed to modify the behavior of voters abroad are thus likely to be regarded as interventionary even though equally extensive efforts to modify the behavior of tourists in the same country are not": Rosenau, "Intervention as a Scientific Concept," 149–171, 163; Myres S. McDougal and Florentino P. Feliciano, "International Coercion and World Public Order: The General Principles of the Law of War," *The Yale Law Journal* 67 (1957): 771, 793:

"The use of the ideological instrument commonly involves the selective manipulation and circulation of symbols, verbal or nonverbal, calculated to alter the patterns
of identifications, demands and expectations of mass audiences in the target-state and
thereby to induce or stimulate politically significant attitudes and behavior favorable
to the initiator-state"; Contra see: Duncan Hollis, "The Influence of War; The War for
Influence," *Temple International and Comparative Law Journal* 32 (2018): 31, 41.

26. *Nicaragua Case*, para 241.

27. According to the ODNI Report 2017, the target was the Democratic candidate.
Also, "Russia collected on some Republican-affiliated targets but did not conduct a
comparable disclosure campaign"; Mueller Indictments.

28. Mueller's indictments, for example, reveal the systematic and widespread
nature of Russian activities.

29. McDougal and Feliciano, supra note 25, 782–783.

30. Philip N. Howard, Bharath Ganesh, Dimitra Liotsiou, John Kelly and Camille
François, "The IRA, Social Media and Political Polarization in the United States,
2012–2018." Working Paper 2018 (University of Oxford), which provides data about
the activities of the Russia's Internet Research Agency.

BIBLIOGRAPHY

Bay, Sebastian, and Guna Šnore. 2019. "Protecting Elections: A Strategic Communications Approach." *NATO Strategic Communications Centre of Excellence*, June
2019. https://www.stratcomcoe.org/download/file/fid/80396.

Brattberg, Erik, and Tim Maurer. 2018. "Russian Election Interference: Europe's
Counter to Fake News and Cyber Attacks." *Carnegie Endowment for International
Peace*, May 23, 2018. https://carnegieendowment.org/2018/05/23/russian-electi
on-interference-europe-s-counter-to-fake-news-and-cyber-attacks-pub-76435.

Buchan, Russell. 2012. "Cyber Attacks: Unlawful Uses of Force or Prohibited Interventions?" *Journal of Conflict and Security Law*, 17(2): 212–227.

Buchan, Russell. 2018. *Cyber Espionage and International Law*. Bloomsbury: Hart
Publishing.

Cassese, Antonio. 1995. *Self-Determination of Peoples: A Legal Reappraisal*. Cambridge: Cambridge University Press.

Crawford, James. 2007. *The Creation of States in International Law*. Oxford: Oxford
University Press.

Egan, Brian J. 2017. "International Law and Stability in Cyberspace." *Berkeley Journal of International Law*, 35(1): 169.

EU vs Disinfo. 2019. "Methods of Foreign Electoral Interference." April 2, 2019.
https://euvsdisinfo.eu/methods-of-foreign-electoral-interference/.

European Commission. 2018. "A Multi-Dimensional Approach to Disinformation:
Report of the Independent High Level Group on Fake News and Online Disinformation." Publications Office of the European Union.

Galante, Laura, and Shaun Ee. 2018. "Defining Russian Election Interference: An
Analysis of Select 2014 to 2018 Cyber Enabled Incidents." *Atlantic Council,*

Scowcroft Center for Strategy and Security, September 2018. https://www.atlantic council.org/images/publications/Defining_Russian_Election_Interference_web.pdf.

Global Commission on the Stability of Cyberspace. 2018. "Global Commission Urges Protecting Electoral Infrastructure." May 24, 2018. https://cyberstability.or g/research/global-commission-urges-protecting-electoral-infrastructure/.

Henderson, Scott, Steve Miller, Dan Perez, Marcin Siedlarz, Ben Wilson, Ben Read. 2018. "Chinese Espionage Group TEMP. Periscope Targets Cambodia Ahead of July 2018 Elections and Reveals Broad Operations Globally". *FireEye*, July 10, 2018. https://www.fireeye.com/blog/threat-research/2018/07/chinese-espionage -group-targets-cambodia-ahead-of-elections.html.

Herpig, Sven, Julia Schuetze and Jonathan Jones. 2018. "Securing Democracy in Cyberspace, an Approach to Protecting Data-Driven Elections." October 2018. https ://www.stiftung-nv.de/sites/default/files/securing_democracy_in_cyberspace.pdf.

Hollis, Duncan B. 2016. "Russia and the DNC Hack: What Future for a Duty of Non Intervention?" *Opinio Juris*, July 25, 2016. http://opiniojuris.org/2016/07/25/russia -and-the-dnc-hack-a-violation-of-the-duty-of-non-intervention/.

Hollis, Duncan. 2018. "The Influence of War; The War for Influence." *Temple International and Comparative Law Journal*, 32(1): 31.

Howard, Philip N., Bharath Ganesh, Dimitra Liotsiou, John Kelly and Camille François. 2018. "The IRA, Social Media and Political Polarization in the United States, 2012–2018." Working Paper 2018. University of Oxford.

I. C. J., Military and Paramilitary Activities in and against Nicaragua (Nicaragua v United States of America) (Merits) [1986] ICJ Rep 14.

Jamnejad, Maziar, and Michael Wood. 2009. "The Principle of Non-Intervention." *Leiden Journal of International Law*, 22(2): 345–381.

Jennings, Robert Y., and Arthur D. Watts. 1992. *Oppenheim's International Law*, 9th edn. Oxford: Oxford University Press.

Joyner, Christopher C. 2006. "Coercion." *Max Planck Encyclopedia of Public International Law*. https://opil.ouplaw.com/home/mpil.

Kanuck, Sean, Global Commission on the Stability of Cyberspace. 2018. "Protecting the Electoral Process and Its Institutions." January 2018. https://cyberstability.org/research/.

Kilovaty, Ido. 2018. "Doxfare: Politically Motivated Leaks and the Future of the Norm on Non Intervention in the Era of Weaponized Information." *Harvard National Security Journal*, 9:146.

Kunig, Philip. 2012. "Prohibition of Intervention." *Max Planck Encyclopedia of Public International Law*. https://opil.ouplaw.com/home/mpil.

Lin, Herbert., and Jaclyn Kerr. 2017. "On Cyber-Enabled Information/Influence Warfare and Manipulation." https://fsi-live.s3.us-west-1.amazonaws.com/s3fs-public/ cyber-enabled_influence_warfare-ssrn-v1.pdf.

Lindsay, Jon R., and Erik Gartzke. 2014. "Coercion Through Cyberspace: The Stability-Instability Paradox Revisited." In *Coercion: The Power to Hurt in International Politics*. 2018, edited by Kelly M. Greenhill and Peter J. Krause. Oxford: Oxford University Press.

McDougal, Myres S., and Florentino P. Feliciano. 1957. "International Coercion and World Public Order: The General Principles of the Law of War." *The Yale Law Journal*, 67(5): 771.

New York Times. 2017. *Full Transcript and Video: James Comey's Testimony on Capitol Hill. New York Times*, June 8, 2017. https://www.nytimes.com/2017/06/08/us/politics/senate-hearing-transcript.html.

Ohlin, Jens D. 2016. "Did Russian Cyber Interference in the 2016 Election Violate International Law." *Texas Law Review,* 95: 1579.

Ohlin, Jens D. 2018. "Election Interference: The Real Harm and the Only Solution." *Cornell Law School Research Paper,* No. 18–50: 1–26.

P. R. C., Permanent Mission to the U.N. 2013. *Statement By Ms. Liu Ying of the Chinese Delegation at the Thematic Debate on Information and Cyber Security at the First Committee of the 68th Session of the UNGA*, October 30, 2013. www.china-un.org/eng/hyyfy/t1094491.htm.

Rosenau, James N. 1969. "Intervention as a Scientific Concept." *Journal of Conflict Resolution*, 13(2): 149–171.

Schmitt, Michael N. (ed). 2017. *Tallinn Manual 2.0 on the International Law Applicable to Cyber Operations*, 2nd edn. Cambridge: Cambridge University Press.

Sweden, Government Offices of Sweden, Ministry of Justice. 2018. "National Strategy for Society Information and Cyber Security." June 2018. https://www.government.se/4ac8ff/contentassets/d87287e088834d9e8c08f28d0b9dda5b/a-national-cyber-security-strategy-skr.-201617213.

Thornberry, Patrick. 1992. "The Democratic or Internal Aspect of Self-Determination with Some Remarks on Federalism." In *Modern Law of Self-Determination*, edited by Christian Tomuschat. Dordrecht, Boston and London: Martinus Nijhoff.

Tsagourias, Nicholas. 2012. "Cyber attacks, Self-Defence and the Problem of Attribution." *Journal of Conflict and Security Law*, 17(2): 229–244.

Tsagourias, Nicholas. 2012. "The Tallinn Manual on the International Law Applicable to Cyber Warfare: A Commentary on Chapter II—The Use of Force." *Yearbook of International Humanitarian Law*, 15: 19–43.

U.K. Attorney General's Office. 2018. *Cyber and International Law in the 21st Century*, May 23, 2018. https://www.gov.uk/government/speeches/cyber-and-international-law-in-the-21st-century.

U.K. Cabinet Office. 2018. National Security Capability Review. March 28, 2018. https://assets.publishing.service.gov.uk/government/uploads/system/uploads/attachment_data/file/705347/6.4391_CO_National-Security-Review_web.pdf.

U.N. General Assembly Res. 1948. *Universal Declaration of Human Rights*, December 10, 1948, 183rd Plenary Meeting, U.N. Doc. 217A (III).

U.N. General Assembly Res. 1965. *Declaration on the Inadmissibility of Intervention in the Domestic Affairs of States and the Protection of Their Independence and Sovereignty*, December 21, 1965, U.N. Doc. A/RES/20/2131 (XX), Annex.

U.N. General Assembly Res. 1970. *Declaration on Principles of International Law Concerning Friendly Relations and Co-Operation among States in Accordance with the United Nations*, October 24, 1970, U. N. Doc. A/RES/2625 (XXV), Annex.

U.N. General Assembly. 1964. *Consideration of Principles of International Law Concerning Friendly Relations and Co-Operation Among States in Accordance with the Charter of the United Nations, Report of the Special Committee on Principles of International Law Concerning Friendly Relations and Co-Operation Among States*, November 16, 1964, 19th sess., U.N. Doc. A/5746.

U.N. General Assembly. 1966. International Covenant on Civil and Political Rights "ICCPR" (Concluded December 16, 1966, entered into force March 23, 1976) 999 UNTS 171.

U.N. General Assembly. 2013. *Group of Governmental Experts on Developments in the Field of Information and Telecommunications in the Context of International Security*, June 24, 2013, 68th sess., U.N. Doc. A/68/98.

U.N. General Assembly. 2015. *Group of Governmental Experts on Developments in the Field of Information and Telecommunications in the Context of International Security*, July 22, 2015, 17th sess., U.N. Doc. A/70/174.

U.S. Department of Homeland Security and Office of the Director of National Intelligence. 2016. "Joint Statement from the Department of Homeland Security and Office of the Director of National Intelligence on Election Security". DHS Press Office. https://www.dhs.gov/news/2016/10/07/joint-statement-department-homeland-security-and-office-director-national.

U.S. Department of Homeland Security. "Election Security". https://www.dhs.gov/topic/election-security.

U.S. District Court, District of Columbia, United States v. Internet Research Agency LLC et al, (Indictment, February 16, 2018), Criminal Action No. 00032 (DLF) *and* United States v. Victor Borisovich Netyksho et al (Indictment, July 13, 2018), Criminal Action No 00215 (ABJ). https://d3i6fh83elv35t.cloudfront.net/static/2018/07/Muellerindictment.pdf.

U.S. Office of the Director of National Intelligence. 2017. "Background to 'Assessing Russian Activities and Intentions in Recent US Elections': The Analytic Process and Cyber Incident Attribution" in *Assessing Russian Activities and Intentions in Recent US Elections*. ICA 2017–01, January 6, 2017. https://www.dni.gov/files/documents/ICA_2017_01.pdf.

U.S., The White House. 2017. *National Security Strategy of the United States of America*. December 2017. Washington, DC. https://www.whitehouse.gov/wp-content/uploads/2017/12/NSS-Final-12-18-2017-0905.pdf.

Vilmer, J.B. Jeangène, Alexandre Escorcia, Marine Guillaume, and Janaina Herrera. 2018. "Information Manipulation: A Challenge for Our Democracies, Report by the Policy Planning Staff (CAPS) of the Ministry for Europe and Foreign Affairs and the Institute for Strategic Research (IRSEM) of the Ministry for the Armed Forces." August 2018. Paris.

Vincent, John. 1974. *Non Intervention and International Order*. Princeton, NJ: Princeton University Press.

Watts, Sean. 2015. "Low-Intensity Cyber Operations and the Principle of Non-Intervention." In *Cyber War: Law and Ethics for Virtual Conflicts*, edited by Jens David Ohlin, Kevin Govern and Claire Finkelstein. Oxford: Oxford University Press.

Watts, Sean. 2016. "International Law and Proposed US Responses to the DNC Hack." *Just Security*, October 14, 2016. https://www.justsecurity.org/33558/international-law-proposed-u-s-responses-d-n-c-hack/.

Zetter, Kim. 2014. "Sony Got Hacked Hard: What We Know and Don't Know So Far." *Wired*, March 12, 2014. https://www.wired.com/2014/12/sony-hack-what-we-know/.

Chapter 4

Violations of Territorial Sovereignty in Cyberspace—an Intrusion-based Approach

Przemysław Roguski

Ever since the Treaty of Westphalia established the modern legal order, the sovereignty of states is one of the foundational principles of public international law. The principles of state sovereignty and sovereign equality have been reaffirmed in Art. 2(1) of the United Nations Charter and form the bedrock of the post–World War II international legal order. This legal order, conceived in a time when global computer networks carrying information across continents in seconds and making it available without regard for location and geographical distance were but a distant dream, must evolve to account for new technological developments such as the rise of information and communication technologies (ICTs), which link states and people closer together through cyberspace. Faced with a new medium with unique characteristics of ubiquity and aterritoriality of information, states as the principal actors of the international legal order had to decide whether this new medium—cyberspace—is a unique "space," requiring a different set of rules governing state rights and state behavior, or whether existing rules of international still apply.

Gradually, a consensus has begun to form around the proposition that rules and principles of international law, as enshrined in the UN Charter, apply in cyberspace. As the former legal adviser to the US Department of State, Harold Koh, put it: "cyberspace is not a 'law-free' zone where anyone can conduct hostile activities without rules or restraint. (. . .) States conducting activities in cyberspace must take into account the sovereignty of other states" (Koh 2012, 3, 6). This consensus has been cemented through the work of the United Nations Group of Governmental Experts on Developments in the Field of Information and Telecommunications in the Context of International Security (GGE), which in 2013 and 2015 issued two reports detailing the rules and principles of international law applicable to state behavior in cyberspace (United Nations General Assembly 2013, 2015). While the Group of Governmental Experts managed to clarify many fundamental aspects relating to state sovereignty in cyberspace, including the jurisdiction of states over cyber infrastructure located on their territory (United Nations General Assembly 2013, para. 20), the prohibition on the use of force and non-intervention in the internal affairs of other states (United Nations General Assembly 2015, para. 26), the interpretation of the principle of state sovereignty and its application to state conduct in cyberspace have not been addressed in great detail.

One of the questions left open by the GGE reports is whether cyber operations which do not constitute a use of force or intervention into internal affairs of another state are nevertheless prohibited by virtue of a duty to respect the sovereignty of states, or whether the absence of a specific prohibitive rule leaves states free to conduct cyber operations within and against cyber infrastructure located on the territory of other states (provided they do not rise to the level of force or intervene into internal affairs). It is, therefore, no surprise that the question whether international law recognizes a general rule of territorial sovereignty, operating below the threshold of use of force and intervention is currently one of the most contentious issues in international law, in light of the fact that such a rule may be violated through state-conducted or state-sponsored cyber operations. Moreover, it remains unclear if this rule is recognized, then how to precisely define its scope. Maybe the most prominent academic effort to comprehensively map and describe the rules applicable to state conduct in cyberspace is the *Tallinn Manual*. Now in its second edition, the *Manual* states in Rule 4 that "[a] State must not conduct cyber operations that violate the sovereignty of another State" (Schmitt and Vihul 2017c, 17). In ascertaining when such a violation of sovereignty may occur, the *Tallinn Manual 2.0* employs an effects-based test which focuses on two bases: the degree of infringement upon the state's territorial integrity and the interference with, or usurpation of, inherently governmental functions (Schmitt and Vihul 2017c, 20). Under this test, cyber operations which violate the integrity of ICT systems in another state by installing malware containing malicious payloads are not prohibited *per se*, unless they lead to the loss of functionality of the target system. In effect, a majority of the *Manual*'s authors does not regard the act of installing and sustaining malicious code in foreign ICT systems as a violation of international law.

This chapter critically examines the *Tallinn Manual*'s Rule 4 and argues that a purely effects-based approach to violations of territorial sovereignty is at odds with the traditional understanding of sovereignty as espoused by the Permanent Court of International Justice (PCIJ) and the International Court of Justice (ICJ). If we understand sovereignty as the exclusive right of states to regulate entry into their territory and the right to forbid any assertion of jurisdiction or the performance of acts *de iure imperii* within their territory by another state without their consent, then any unauthorized presence and any act of foreign state power violates sovereignty, regardless of whether these actions cause physical harm or not. Therefore, the chapter argues for a different, intrusion-based approach to violations of territorial sovereignty in cyberspace. Under the proposed intrusion-based test, the violation of a state's territorial sovereignty is linked to the breach of the information security—especially the integrity—of the targeted ICT system. This allows for a more technical and precise determination of the boundary between permissible and impermissible acts in cyberspace and would help to reduce the legal uncertainties which currently exist in relation to low-intensity cyber operations.

This chapter proceeds in three steps. First, it discusses the traditional concept of sovereignty and addresses the question whether sovereignty is a principle of international law from which more concrete rules of state behavior—such as the prohibition on the use of force and the prohibition of intervention into internal affairs of other states—derive; or whether it is itself a rule of international law, prohibiting conduct which violates the territorial sovereignty of states. While this question has already been addressed in many publications (see, e.g., Eichensehr 2015; Heintschel von Heinegg 2012, 2013; Pirker 2013; Schmitt and Vihul 2017a, 2017b, 2017c), a recent speech by the United Kingdom attorney general, Jeremy Wright QC MP, in which he firmly spoke against the existence of such a rule of territorial sovereignty (Wright 2018), warrants a further look at this issue. Second, it addresses the *Tallinn Manual 2.0* Rule 4 and its interpretation of the rule of territorial sovereignty, with special regard to the tests proposed by the authors of the *Tallinn Manual* to ascertain when a violation of territorial sovereignty takes place. Last, it proposes a different, intrusion-based test of the violation of territorial sovereignty.

THE CONCEPT OF TERRITORIAL
SOVEREIGNTY IN CYBERSPACE

Rule 4 of the *Tallinn Manual 2.0* states that "[a] State must not conduct cyber operations that violate the sovereignty of another State" (Schmitt and Vihul 2017c, 17). It is based on the assumption that the international legal order contains, apart from the prohibition on the use of force and the prohibition of intervention into the internal affairs of other states, a separate norm requiring respect for the (territorial) sovereignty of other states, which may be violated through the performance of certain cyber activities within other states' territories without their consent. However, the existence of such a rule has recently been put into question—at least with respect to activities in cyberspace. In his

Chatham House speech of May 23, 2018, the attorney general of the United Kingdom, Jeremy Wright QC MP, has stated that he is "not persuaded that we can currently extrapolate from [the] general principle [of sovereignty] a specific rule or additional prohibition for cyber activity beyond that of a prohibited intervention. The UK Government's position is therefore that there is no such rule as a matter of current international law" (Wright 2018). The United Kingdom has been the first state to officially articulate its doubts as to the existence of a rule of territorial sovereignty in such clear terms, but this position seems to reflect earlier arguments brought forth by (at least) some branches of the US government. The then legal adviser to the US Department of State, Brian Egan, noted that "cyber operations involving computers located on another State's territory do not constitute a violation of international law. (. . .) This is perhaps most clear where such activities in another State's territory have no effects or de minimis effects" (Egan 2016). Furthermore, as has been reported by some authors (Watts and Richard 2018, 859; Schmitt and Vihul 2017a, 1641), on January 19, 2017, the outgoing general counsel of the US Department of Defence has issued a memorandum on the "International Law Framework for Employing Cyber Capabilities in Military Operations." The memo—which is not publicly available and whose content the present author can therefore only assess through secondary sources— reportedly stated that sovereignty is not a rule but a "baseline principle" which undergirds other binding rules of international law such as the prohibition on the use of force and the prohibition of intervention (Schmitt and Vihul 2017a, 1642). The 2017 DoD memo's position seems to be shared by some American authors, including authors which at the time of writing are working for US Cyber Command (Corn and Taylor 2017; Corn and Jensen 2018).

Two Arguments Against Territorial Sovereignty in Cyberspace

The case against the existence of a rule of territorial sovereignty can be summarized as resting on two arguments. First, in what may be called the argument from lack of state practice, it is stated that there is not sufficient state practice and *opinio iuris* to conclude the existence of such a rule in customary international law (Wright 2018; Corn and Jensen 2018). Second, in what may be termed the argument from cyberspace design and practicality, it is held that while sovereignty has always been tightly tied to territory, the logical and social layers of cyberspace have "at most a tenuous connection to geography" (Corn and Jensen 2018) and thus territorial concepts are not readily transposable to an aterritorial medium by way of simple analogy. Moreover, the global reach and availability of cyber infrastructure makes it possible for malicious cyber operations to be mounted from a multitude of globally dispersed locations (Corn and Jensen 2018). States wishing to protect their cyber infrastructure from such threats, therefore, need to be able to counter cyberattacks regardless of their starting location. The sovereignty-as-a-rule approach would create "unworkable hurdles to States conducting such limited but potentially important operations" (Corn 2017).

According to the lack-of-state-practice argument, sovereignty is a baseline principle of international law, from which other, more concrete prohibitive rules of international law flow. These rules, such as the prohibition on the use of force and the prohibition of intervention, exist as customary international law, because they are evidenced by a sufficiently uniform and universal practice and *opinio iuris* of states, and/or have been codified in the United Nations Charter. Below the threshold of these two rules, "international law docs not obligate other states to refrain from all activities that might infringe upon or operate to the prejudice of the territorial state's internal sovereignty" (Corn and Taylor 2017, 209). Evidence of this is to be seen in the fact that states conduct espionage operations within the territory of other states, yet international law does not prohibit espionage as such (Corn and Taylor 2017, 209). Moreover, one cannot find evidence of one single universal rule of territorial sovereignty, as the content of rights in relation to a particular territory varies depending on which domain (land, sea, air, space) is affected. While access to airspace is severely restricted, and entry without consent is a serious violation of international law which may lead to grave consequences (as has most recently been evidenced by the shoot down of a Russian fighter jet by the Turkish army for violating Turkish airspace), international law allows the innocent passage of warships through the territorial sea of states and in the case of space, orbiting objects do not violate the airspace or territory states they overfly (Corn and Taylor 2017, 210). In consequence, given that no separate regime of restricted access to a state's cyberspace domain (below the thresholds of use of force and intervention) has yet developed, states are free to act as they wish by virtue of their sovereignty, as has been found by the PCIJ in the *Lotus* case (*S.S. Lotus* [*Fr. v. Turk.*], 1927 P.C.I.J. Rep. [ser. A] No. 10, at 18).

In the author's view, both arguments are to be rejected. They disregard long-standing jurisprudence of the PCIJ and ICJ, do not take account of more recent state practice, and are based on a false understanding of the so-called *Lotus* doctrine whereby states have unlimited freedom of action barring a prohibitive rule of international law.

International Jurisprudence Supports the Existence of a Rule of Territorial Sovereignty

The essence of state sovereignty is perhaps best captured in a passage from Judge Max Huber's arbitral decision in the *Island of Palmas* case. The arbitrator stated that "Sovereignty in the relations between States signifies independence. Independence in regard to a portion of the globe is the right to exercise therein, to the exclusion of any other State, the functions of a State" (*Island of Palmas* [*Neth. v. U.S.*], P.C.A. 1928, 2 R.I.A.A 829, 838). Traditionally, this independence is understood to contain an internal as well as an external aspect (Besson 2011; Tsagourias 2015, 17). While internal sovereignty means the supreme authority within the state to regulate political, social, and legal affairs and enforce rules, external sovereignty pertains to the rights and duties of states toward each other and denotes the competence of states to engage in activities outside of their territory, subject only to binding rules of international law (Crawford 2015, 118). From this internal sovereignty arises the authority to determine *inter alia* who may enter the territory. This is exclusive in the sense that "governmental authority carried out on the territory of another state is only lawful if performed with the latter's consent" (Crawford 2015, 121). The supreme authority of a state vis-à-vis other states within its territory thus gives rise to a fundamental "restriction imposed by international law upon a State (. . .) that—failing the existence of a permissive rule to the contrary—it may not exercise its power in any form in the territory of another State. In this sense jurisdiction is certainly territorial; it cannot be exercised by a State outside its territory except by virtue of a permissive rule derived from international custom or from a convention" (*S.S. Lotus* [*Fr. v. Turk.*], Judgement, 1927 P.C.I.J. Ser. A No. 10, p. 4, 18–19). This dictum of the PCIJ has been upheld after the entry into force of the UN Charter by the ICJ. In the *Corfu Channel* case, the Court had to decide whether a demining operation conducted by the United Kingdom in Albanian territorial waters violated Albanian sovereignty even if it was a necessary self-help measure. The court held that "[b]etween independent States, respect for territorial sovereignty is an essential foundation of international relations. The Court recognizes that the Albanian Government's complete failure to carry out its duties after the explosions (. . .) are extenuating circumstances for the action of the United Kingdom Government. But to ensure respect for international law, of which it is the organ, the Court must declare that the action of the British Navy constituted a violation of Albanian sovereignty" (*Corfu Channel* [*U.K. v. Alb.*], Judgment, 1949 I.C.J. Rep. 4, 35). Furthermore, in *Nicaragua*, the court clarified the relation between the requirement of respect for territorial sovereignty and the *lex specialis* prohibition on the use of force. It held that "[t]he effects of the principle of respect for territorial sovereignty inevitably overlap with those of the principles of the prohibition of the use of force and of non-intervention. Thus the assistance to the contras (. . .) not only amount to an unlawful use of force, but also constitute infringements of the territorial sovereignty of Nicaragua, and incursions into its territorial and internal waters" (*Military and Paramilitary Activities in and Against Nicaragua*

[*Nicar. v. U.S.*], Judgment, 1986 I.C.J. Rep. 14, para. 251). What becomes clear from this brief overview is, therefore, that sovereignty is not only a principle, from which other more specific rules are derived, but that sovereignty demands respect for the supreme authority of a state within its territory and as such forms itself a prohibitive rule of international law. Territorial sovereignty is, therefore, a "baseline rule" derived from general international law (Watts and Richard 2018, 859), which reflects the structural framework of international law for the exercise of state sovereignty in order "to ensure the co-existence of independent communities and facilitate the achievement of common aims" (Hertogen 2015, 912). As Judge Shahabuddeen has noted in his dissent in the *Nuclear Weapons* advisory opinion: "It is difficult (. . .) to uphold a proposition that, absent a prohibition, a State has a right in law to act in ways which could deprive the sovereignty of all other States of meaning" (*Legality of the Threat or Use of Nuclear Weapons*, Advisory Opinion, Dissenting Opinion of Judge Shahabuddeen, 1996 I.C.J. Rep. 226, 393–394).

State Practice Is Not Uniform

With regard to state practice, it is certainly true that so far only a small number of states have publicly presented their understanding of the application of sovereignty to cyberspace. Declarations such as the speech given by the UK attorney general help to identify and clarify the content of international norms applicable to cyberspace and may, in time, be of sufficient number and uniformity to restrict the application of a rule of territorial sovereignty to cyberspace along the lines advocated by Attorney General Wright and some American authors (Schmitt 2018, 18). However, in the author's view, the current state practice on this topic is not uniform and may even point to a majority position contrary to the attorney general's. For instance, in a speech held at Chatham House London on May 18, 2015, the then commissioner for International Cyber Policy of the German Foreign Office, Ambassador Norbert Riedel, stated that "There is consensus that State sovereignty and international norms and principles that flow from sovereignty apply to State conduct of activities related to information and communication technology, and to their jurisdiction over the required infrastructure within their territory." While cyberattacks which amount to a use of force or even an armed attack are prohibited by the UN Charter and customary international law, "[e]ven in cases where one cannot speak of a use of force, the use of cyber capabilities might constitute a violation of sovereignty, if the attack can be attributed to a state" (Riedel 2015). The argument that territorial sovereignty applies in cyberspace is even more forcefully put forward by France. The French "Strategic Review of Cyberdefence" (*Revue stratégique de cyberéfense*) of February 12, 2018 offers the view that cyber incidents of a significant, but not extreme, impact fall below the threshold of armed attack, but may nevertheless constitute other internationally wrongful acts such as intervention, violation of sovereignty or use of force (*"les actions correspondant à ces niveaux pourraient néanmoins constituer d'autres faits internationaux illicites [intervention, violation de la souveraineté, usage de la force, etc.]*)" (Secrétariat général de la défense et de la sécurité nationale 2018, 80). This view is elaborated upon in the declaration on "International Law Applicable to Operations in Cyberspace" (*Droit international appliqué aux opérations dans le cyberespace"*), published by the Ministry of Defence on 9 September 2019. The document argues that since France has sovereignty over ICT systems located within its territory, any cyberattack—defined as an operation which breaches the confidentiality, integrity, or availability of the targeted system—constitutes at minimum a violation of sovereignty, if attributable to another state. Such a violation occurs not only when effects are produced on French territory, but already when there is a penetration of French computer systems (Ministère des Armées 2019, 6–7).

Similarly, the GGE consensus reports clearly conclude that states have jurisdiction over ICT infrastructure located within their territory (United Nations General Assembly 2015, akap. 28[a]). States regularly assert jurisdiction, both civil and criminal, over activities within their cyber infrastructure. For example, on July 13, 2018, the US Special Counsel filed an indictment of twelve Russian intelligence officers alleged to have hacked the servers of the Democratic National Committee and thus to have committed computer-related offenses within the United States (*United States vs. Netyksho et al.*, US District Court for the District of Columbia, Case No. 1:18-cr-00215-ABJ, filed July 13, 2018). It is thus clear that states treat activities within their cyber infrastructure as falling into the territorial confines of their sovereignty (some states even speak of "national cyberspace," e.g., the Polish cybersecurity strategy *"Polityka Ochrony Cyberprzestrzeni Rzeczpospolitej Polskiej"* [Ministerstwo Administracji i Cyfryzacji 2013]), even though some states may deny the existence of a rule of territorial sovereignty. In the author's view, it follows from sovereignty over ICT devices that sovereign activities conducted within the cyber infrastructure located on the territory of other states violate their territorial sovereignty if they constitute an exercise of power without the consent of the affected state.

In summary, it may very well be that the rule of territorial sovereignty in cyberspace will have to adapt for the (perceived) aterritoriality of the logical and social layers of cyberspace, the loss of distance typical for geographical territory and the ease of access this structural characteristic of cyberspace presents to malicious cyber actors. The practical necessity of defending against threats originating from multiple locations and using cyber infrastructure located in various states, coupled with the currently slow process of international legal assistance and the disinterest or inability of many states to actively counter malicious activity emanating from their cyber infrastructure, may require an adjustment of the international legal regime to allow for a greater degree of self-help (although, as the *Tallinn Manual* points out, legal remedies in the form of countermeasures and the doctrine of necessity are available [Schmitt and Vihul 2017c, 111–141]). But, as the law currently stands, the baseline rule of territorial sovereignty, as recognized by the ICJ in *Corfu Channel* and *Nicaragua*, still applies. States arguing for its nonexistence would have to demonstrate on the basis of universal state practice and *opinio iuris* the emergence of an exception to territorial sovereignty in cyberspace, not the other way around.

VIOLATIONS OF TERRITORIAL SOVEREIGNTY UNDER THE *TALLINN MANUAL 2.0* RULE 4

Assuming that territorial sovereignty exists as a rule of international law and further assuming that this rule is applicable to state conduct in cyberspace, the next question is to ascertain the precise content of this rule. So far, the most elaborate attempt to formulate a test for the violation of territorial sovereignty in cyberspace has been offered by the authors of the *Tallinn Manual 2.0* in Rule 4 (Schmitt and Vihul 2017c, 17). The *Tallinn Manual 2.0* stipulates that the lawfulness of remote cyber operations that manifest on a state's territory depend on the "degree of infringement upon the target State's territorial integrity" and/or on the "interference with or usurpation of inherently governmental functions" (Schmitt and Vihul 2017c, 20). With regard to the infringement upon territorial integrity, the *Manual's* authors stipulate that cyber operations, which result in physical damage, show a sufficient degree of infringement to constitute a violation of territorial sovereignty. Furthermore, the experts argue that a loss of functionality of the targeted system may constitute a violation of sovereignty, if it reaches a certain threshold. The precise threshold could not be established, but the experts agreed that cyber operations resulting in the requirement to replace and repair computer systems or their components are sufficiently akin to physical damage to constitute a violation of sovereignty (Schmitt and Vihul 2017c, 21). There was no consensus among the experts as to whether cyber operations falling below the threshold of loss of functionality violate territorial sovereignty; therefore, the *Tallinn Manual 2.0* does not take a position on this issue.

The *Tallinn Manual's* approach to territorial sovereignty is thus largely effects-based. The *Tallinn Manual* itself does not explain how the authors arrived at the abovementioned set of factors to determine the existence of a violation of sovereignty. It appears that these factors are derived from a particular interpretation of the object and purpose of sovereignty: since the physical damage of targeted computer systems and the loss of functionality requiring repair and replacement lead to similar effects as unconsented physical presence, they, therefore, infringe sovereignty, which "clearly protects territorial integrity against physical violation" (Schmitt and Vihul 2017c, 20). Furthermore, the *Manual* takes into account the traditional aspect of sovereignty of regulating access to territory (*c.f. Vilvarajah and others v UK*, ECtHR, Ser. A, 215, October 30, 1991) and concludes that territorial sovereignty is violated if a state conducts cyber operations when its agents are physically present in the target state (Schmitt and Vihul 2017c, 19). Virtual presence through remote-access cyber operations, on the other hand, seems not to be sufficient to violate territorial sovereignty.

In the author's view, this approach overemphasizes physical effects on territory, while omitting a crucial aspect of sovereignty, namely the exercise of state power. Moreover, the emphasis on the physical effects of a cyber operation does not sufficiently take into account the technical side of most cyber operations, thus leading to difficulties in the precise determination when a violation of territorial sovereignty occurs or is ongoing.

Regarding the first point, the *Tallinn Manual 2.0* seems to consider the main object and purpose of sovereignty to be "the protection of territorial integrity against physical violation" (Schmitt and Vihul 2017c, 20). However, as discussed above, the regulation of access to territory is but one of the aspects of internal sovereignty. Furthermore, the main aim of this exclusive right of the state is not to protect its territory from physical effects—after all, unconsented overflights or transboundary abductions, which are regarded as violations of territorial sovereignty (Wilske 2012), do not usually cause damage or lasting physical effects on the territory of the affected state. Rather, the object and purpose of the rule of territorial sovereignty is to be seen in the protection of the exclusivity of state authority within its territory. As held by the PCIJ in the *S.S.Lotus*: "failing the existence of a permissive rule to the contrary [a State] may not exercise its power in any form in the territory of another State" (*S.S. Lotus* [*Fr. v. Turk.*], Judgement, 1927 P.C.I.J. Ser. A No. 10, pp. 4, 18–19). While in a globalized world, and especially in cyberspace, actions undertaken by one state may very well have a substantial effect on the (cyber) territory of other states, this effect has to be tolerated by virtue of the principle of sovereign equality only insofar as it is a consequence of the exercise of the acting state's internal sovereignty. Conversely, the exercise of state power within the territory of another state violates the target state's exclusive authority and thus its territorial sovereignty. Admittedly, one has to be careful with territorial analogies with regard to cyberspace, as the medium has different characteristics. Nevertheless, every action taken through cyberspace manifests itself on cyber infrastructure located within a specific territory. As the UN GGE noted in its two reports, states have jurisdiction over the ICT infrastructure located within their territory (United Nations General Assembly 2015, akap. 28[a]) and they do assert their jurisdiction over actions performed by individuals as well as agents of other states. If the agents of a state perform cyber operations within the cyber infrastructure of another state in ways other than the intended use of said cyber infrastructure, that is, by violating the information security of computer systems, they exercise state power vis-à-vis cyber infrastructure under the jurisdiction of another state. Thereby they actively change the functioning of computer systems within the sphere of authority of another state and thus exercise a power which, by virtue of the principle of sovereignty, should remain exclusively with that state.

Secondly, if the violation of territorial integrity depended on the manifestation of physical effects, states would not have a legal remedy against cyber operations which are in their preparatory stages or ongoing. Looking at the technical side of cyber operations, one sees that conducting offensive cyber operations requires several preparatory steps: identifying a target, choosing the appropriate attack vector, bypassing the security of the attacked computer system and finally conducting the intended activity. There are many analytical models describing the various steps of a cyberoperation and its effects (Smeets 2017, 30; CCHS 2016, 5; Ducheine 2015, 230), but one of the most common models—the so-called Cyber Kill Chain, developed by employees of the Lockheed Martin Corporation—divides cyber operations into seven phases: Reconnnaisance, Weaponization, Delivery, Exploitation, Installation, Command and Control and Action on objective (Hutchins, Cloppert and Amin 2011, 5). During the reconnaissance phase, the attacker identifies and selects potential targets. Information about the target can be collected from many sources: from open-source intelligence through secret intelligence sources, to the scanning of computer systems (for a detailed description see Maybaum 2013, 217–219). After identifying the proper target and its vulnerabilities, the attackers can gain access to the targeted system (delivery and exploitation phases). This can happen remotely (in so-called remote-access cyber operations, e.g., by sending an infected message to the victim's mailbox) or directly (in so-called close-access cyber operations, e.g., by installing malicious software directly on the target system by the agent, vendor) (Owens and ors. 2009, 87). Most often, malicious code installed after gaining access does not yet contain the proper harmful payload but is used for self-replication and "raising the drawbridge" through which the system will be accessed and further payloads will be installed. In many cases, the installed code is a so-called Remote Access Tool (RAT), which makes contact with the command and control server and waits for further commands from the attackers (Maybaum 2013, 122).

The activities described above are preparatory phases of a cyber operation. The further course depends on the intentions and decisions of the attacker. If the purpose of the operation is to obtain confidential information, the payload will contain code for searching information, tracking the user's computer communication, activating the camera and microphone, and so on. If the purpose is to destroy data or impact on machines and processes controlled by a given computer system, the payload will contain appropriate mechanisms. To this end, many RATs allow the installation of additional modules, depending on the operator's current needs. It should be noted that the nature of a cyber operation is not obvious at the time the information security of the infected system is first compromised. It is only the content of the payload that determines whether it is intended for espionage or for specific damage. In the case of most cyber operations, the determination of their character is possible only after technical analysis of the payload, which requires technical expertise, adequate resources and time (the technical analysis of *Stuxnet* took several months after its initial discovery [Falliere, Murchu, and Chien 2011]). Nevertheless, the initial illegal access to the targeted computer system, irrespective of the subsequent actions, already constitutes a criminal offense against the confidentiality, integrity, and availability of computer data and systems under the domestic law of many states, as required by Art. 2 of the 2001 Cybercrime Convention (Convention on Cybercrime, Budapest, 23.11.2001, E.T.S. No. 185).

The outline of a typical cyber operation above is obviously very simplified. However, three conclusions can be drawn: first, actors conducting cyber operations use previously identified vulnerabilities to gain access to computer systems without authorization, thus breaching the information security of the targeted systems. Second, the unauthorized intrusion into computer systems constitutes a breach of their information security and thereby a criminal offense. Third, the intended effect of a cyber operation is ascertainable either after the prior detection and technical analysis of the payload, or after the activation of the payload and the materialization of its effects. If the violation of territorial sovereignty were to depend exclusively on the physical effects of a cyber operation (either through physical damage or a significant loss of functionality), the intrusion into a computer system and the compromising of its information security would not yet constitute a violation of sovereignty (although in most cases it would already constitute a criminal offense under the domestic law of the targeted state). Under the so-called *Lotus* doctrine, which presumes a state's freedom of action unless a prohibitive norm has been created through state consent (Kwiecień 2012, 48), this freedom to act would in effect create a freedom to install malware on foreign computer systems. Although the targeted state would still be free to sanction violations of information security under its domestic law, it would be powerless to prevent this under international law, as countermeasures and the obligation of cessation depend on the existence of an internationally wrongful act (United Nations International Law Commission 2001). In consequence, the international legal order would be put in a situation where, based on its external sovereignty, a state would be free to exercise its power through cyber operations, affecting the information security of computer infrastructure in other states, and to allow its agents to commit criminal offenses, while the targeted states would have no legal redress to enforce the exclusivity of their authority within their territory. To quote Judge Shahabuddeen again: "It is difficult (. . .) to uphold a proposition that, absent a prohibition, a State has a right in law to act in ways which could deprive the sovereignty of all other States of meaning" (*Legality of the Threat or Use of Nuclear Weapons*, Advisory Opinion, Dissenting Opinion of Judge Shahabuddeen, 1996 I.C.J. Rep. 226, 393–394).

AN INTRUSION-BASED APPROACH TO
VIOLATIONS OF TERRITORIAL SOVEREIGNTY

Given this unsatisfactory state of events, what could an alternative approach to violations of territorial sovereignty look like? The author proposes to start from what the rule of territorial sovereignty seeks to prohibit: the unauthorized exercise of state power in the territory of another state, as exemplified in the *Lotus* judgment (*S.S. Lotus* [*Fr. v. Turk.*], Judgement, 1927 P.C.I.J. Ser. A No. 10, pp. 4, 18–19). It is clear from this and other judgments such as *Corfu Channel*, as well as state practice, that the exercise of state power is not measured by the effects of one state's actions on the territory of another state, but rather by the nature of the action itself. Any activity of a sovereign (i.e., noncommercial) nature taken within or against another state's territory without that state's consent or a legal basis in international law constitutes an unauthorized exercise of state power and thus a violation of territorial sovereignty. This is why United Kingdom's demining operation in Albanian territorial waters (see *Corfu Channel* [*U.K. v. Alb.*], Judgment, 1949 I.C.J. Rep. 4, 35), the US training and financing of Contra rebels in Nicaragua (*Military and Paramilitary Activities in and Against Nicaragua* [*Nicar. v. U.S.*], Judgment, 1986 I.C.J. Rep. 14, para. 251) or the abduction of a person from the territory of a state by the agents of another state (Ghafur Hamid 2004, 79) constitute such violations.

It is furthermore clear that while cyberspace undoubtedly has other properties than physical space, it is by no means aterritorial, as has been claimed in the 1990s (Johnson and Post 1996). It is true that data mobility and interconnectedness pose a challenge to strictly territorial notions of jurisdiction requiring a reconceptualization or a new approach (Daskal 2015; Roguski 2019), but this challenge does not invalidate the strict link between geography and sovereignty in cyberspace (but compare Corn and Jensen 2018). This is because actions taken against specific computers or networks, even if undertaken remotely, ultimately manifest themselves in the territory of the state where the physical infrastructure is located. For this reason, states continue to assert jurisdiction over the physical components of cyberspace (United Nations General Assembly 2015) and apply their national (criminal) law to actions taken against these components, irrespective of the location of the perpetrators (U.S. District Court, ND California, *U.S. v. Dmitry Dokuchaev, et al.*, Case 3:17-cr-00103-VC).

Established notions of international law and current state practice, therefore, suggest that states can (and do) assert exclusive authority over computers and networks physically located within their territory and, in consequence, any exercise of power by other states in those networks, irrespective of its physical effects, would violate the territorial integrity of that state. What, then, should be the test for establishing the exercise of state power through cyberspace within the territory of another state? Rather than to focus on the physical effects of cyber operations, the present author proposes to focus instead on the technical aspects of a cyber operation. As has been shown above, the essence of every cyber operation is the act of "hacking," or—to use a definition well established in the technical (and legal) community, the breach of the information security of a computer system through an action compromising either the confidentiality, integrity, or availability of the information stored in the computer system (Kosseff 2018). This so-called CIA Triad, although not a legal definition, is well established in the realm of cybersecurity and is used by some states—Germany and Austria, for example—to define a cyberattack in their national cyber strategies (Bundeskanzleramt Österreich 2013, Bundesministerium des Inneren 2016). Moreover, under the Cybercrime Convention (Convention on Cybercrime, 23.11.2001, E.T.S. No. 185) states parties are obliged to penalize offenses against the confidentiality, integrity, and availability of computer data and systems (Convention on Cybercrime Articles 2–8). In particular, the Cybercrime Convention obliges states parties to criminalize illegal access to computer systems, data and system interference, computer-related fraud and so on. Most states parties have implemented these provisions into their national law or have similar provisions. The United States, for instance, have penalized computer crime, including computer intrusions, denial-of-service attacks, and viruses (Doyle 2014; US Department of Justice—Computer Crime and Intellectual Property Section 2010) through the Computer Fraud and Abuse Act (codified in 18 U.S. Code 1030).

Since computer crimes and state cyberattacks share the same techni-cal characteristics and the forensic analysis of both types of attacks is the same—the difference lying only in the attribution of the action constituting a computer crime to a state actor, thus subjecting it to international rather than (only) national law—the present author proposes to use the criterion of computer intrusion or interference to assess the moment state power is exercised in the territory (cyber infrastructure) of another state. This means that whenever a foreign state damages, deletes, deteriorates, alters, or sup-presses data stored on a computer system within the territory of another state (compare Art. 4 Cybercrime Convention), this action would be regarded as an exercise of state power and thus a violation of the territorial sovereignty of the targeted state.

The criterion of "intrusion," closely related to the integrity of data stored on a computer system, does not encompass every action of a state in foreign networks. For instance, intrusion does not mean the regular use of cyberspace infrastructure for their intended purposes, as no damage to or alteration of data is being done in this process. This is true even for actions undertaken with malicious intent, such as port scanning for the purposes of reconnais-sance and preparation of a cyberattack in the future. Since the scanning of ports is possible without interference with data stored in a network due to the technical design and functioning of global networks such as the Internet and states allow the use of their ICT infrastructure for the purposes of informa-tion transfer, regular usage, even including the routing of cyber operations through foreign infrastructure, would therefore not violate territorial sover-eignty. Similarly, even gaining access to a computer network without proper authorization (i.e., breaching the confidentiality of a computer system or net-work, for instance through phishing) would not constitute an intrusion under the proposed test as the integrity of data stored within the system would not be compromised. The present author submits that the focus on the integrity (rather than its confidentiality or availability) of a computer system or data stored therein is justified, as it is the interference with the functioning of a computer system in the territory of another state—for example, the deletion or alteration of data, the implantation of malware, remote access tools, the use of the computer system to cause effects on systems or processes controlled by that computer.—which bears the closest resemblance to the exercise of state power in the traditional sense.

The proposed intrusion-based approach would have several advantages over the no-sovereignty approach advocated by the UK attorney general (Wright 2018) or the effects-based approach proposed by the *Tallinn Man-ual 2.0* (Schmitt and Vihul 2017c). First, with respect to the sovereignty-as-a-principle view, it respects established international jurisprudence and international law, which is, in the view of the present author, unequivocal in this point. Secondly, with respect to the *Tallinn Manual 2.0* approach, focusing on a technical, rather than an effects-based criterion, has the advantage of forensic clarity and predictability, thus enhancing legal certainty. Whereas a successful hacking operation may not produce any physical effects at all or these effects may not manifest for some time, under the intrusion-based approach it is the hacking itself which constitutes the violation of sovereignty. The affected state would thus not have to wait for physical effects to emerge—or to be severe enough—to be legally entitled to enact countermeasures. Thirdly, the close resemblance of the intrusion criterion to the legal framework regulating computer crimes would allow states to rely on technical expertise and procedures established by law enforcement. In other words—the terrain would be more familiar. And lastly, treating computer intrusions as violations of sovereignty would truly establish territorial sovereignty as the "baseline" norm (Watts and Richard 2018) in cyberspace, thus creating a predictable framework of primary norms and norms-imposing consequences for their breach (such as counter-measures) and could therefore enhance the stability of cyberspace through clear legal principles.

The approach proposed in this chapter has recently gained prominent support in the form of the French declaration on "International Law Applicable to Operations in Cyberspace," which has been published after the submission date of this article and thus can only be briefly referred to. In this document, France argues that a violation of sovereignty may already exist when there is a penetration of computer systems under the sovereignty of France (Ministère des Armées 2019, 6–7). Given that a penetration occurs when there is a breach of the information security, that is, the confidentiality, integrity, or availability, of the targeted system, it is similar to the criterion of intrusion proposed in this article.

CONCLUSION

This chapter argued that territorial sovereignty, which as a primary norm of international law is also applicable to state conduct in cyberspace, requires a clear and operable criterion in order to provide a clear and predictable framework for states to operate in. Rather than concentrating on the physical effects of cyber operations, it is proposed that an intrusion-based approach, which concentrates on the technical side of cyber operations, would provide a familiar, less ambiguous and more viable tool for assessing violations of sovereignty in cyberspace. The criterion of intrusion conforms to the essence of territorial sovereignty, which is the regulation of access to territory and the preservation of exclusivity of state power within its territory. It is independent of the intent of the attacking state and the consequences of its actions and relies on a verifiable technical criterion to ascertain whether a violation of territorial sovereignty has taken place. Furthermore, if the internationally wrongful act of violating the territorial sovereignty of a state in cyberspace were to depend on the intrusion into the targeted computer system, rather than on the effects of that intrusion, the targeted state would have legal redress in the form of a right to demand cessation and to institute countermeasures before the harmful effects of the cyber operation materialize, rather than after. In conclusion, an intrusion-based approach to territorial sovereignty would more clearly reflect the object and purpose of sovereignty, allow states to counter malicious activities before their effects are manifested and would more clearly correspond to the technical side of cyber operations. Although the interpretation of international law in cyberspace has solidified with respect to many norms, for example, the use of force, only a fraction of states has thus far set out their views on the application of territorial sovereignty in cyberspace. New ideas can—and should—be explored and discussed. The new Group of Governmental Experts as well as the Open-Ended Working Group, which have been established in 2019 to further explore the interpretation and application of international law in cyberspace, would be good fora for such discussions.

BIBLIOGRAPHY

Besson, Samantha. 2011. "Sovereignty." In *Max Planck Encyclopaedia of Public International Law*, edited by Rüdiger Wolfrum. Oxford, NY: Oxford University Press.

Bundeskanzleramt Österreich. 2013. "Österreichische Strategie für Cyber-Sicherheit." http://archiv.bundeskanzleramt.at/DocView.axd?CobId=50748.

Bundesministerium des Inneren. 2016. "Cyber-Sicherheitsstrategie für Deutschland." https://www.bmi.bund.de/cybersicherheitsstrategie/BMI_CyberSicherheitsStrat egie.pdf.

CCHS. 2016. "Into the Gray Zone: The Private Sector and Active Defense Against Cyber Threats." *Center for Cyber & Homeland Security*, 86. https://cchs.gwu.edu/sites/cchs.gwu.edu/files/downloads/CCHS-ActiveDefenseReportFINAL.pdf.

Corn, Gary P. 2017. "Tallinn Manual 2.0—Advancing the Conversation." *Just Security*. https://www.justsecurity.org/37812/tallinn-manual-2-0-advancing-conver sation/.

Corn, Gary P., and Eric Jensen. 2018. "The Technicolor Zone of Cyberspace—Part II." *Just Security*. https://www.justsecurity.org/57545/technicolor-zone-cyberspa ce-part-2/.

Corn, Gary P., and Robert Taylor. 2017. "Sovereignty in the Age of Cyber." *AJIL Unbound* 111: 207–212. https://doi.org/10.1017/aju.2017.57.

Crawford, James. 2015. "Sovereignty as a Legal Value." In *The Cambridge Companion to International Law*, edited by James Crawford i Martti Koskenniemi, 117–133. Cambridge: Cambridge University Press. https://doi.org/10.1017/C CO9781139035651.009.

Daskal, Jennifer. 2015. "The Un-Territoriality of Data." *Yale Law Journal* 125 (2): 326–398.

Doyle, Charles. 2014. *Cybercrime: An Overview of the Federal Computer Fraud and Abuse Statute and Related Federal Criminal Laws*. Washington, DC: Congressional Research Service.

Ducheine, Paul. 2015. "The Notion of Cyber Operations." In *Research Handbook on International Law and Cyberspace*, edited by Nicholas Tsagourias and Russell Buchan, 211–232. Cheltenham: Edward Elgar Publishing.

Egan, Brian. 2016. "Remarks on International Law and Stability in Cyberspace." https://2009-2017.state.gov/s/l/releases/remarks/264303.htm.

Eichensehr, Kristen E. 2015. "The Cyber-Law of Nations." *Georgetown Law Journal* 103 (2): 317–380. https://doi.org/10.1525/sp.2007.54.1.23.

Falliere, Nicolas, Liam O Murchu, and Eric Chien. 2011. "W32.Stuxnet Dossier." *Symantec-Security Response*. https://doi.org/20 September 2015.

Ghafur Hamid, Abdul. 2004. "Jurisdiction Over a Person Abducted from a Foreign Country: Alvarez Machain Case Revisited." *Journal of Malaysian and Comparative Law* 31: 69–86.

Heintschel von Heinegg, Wolff. 2012. "Legal Implications of Territorial Sovereignty in Cyberspace." In *4th International Conference on Cyber Conflict*, edited by Christian Czosseck, Katharina Ziolkowski, and Rain Ottis, 7–19. Tallinn: NATO CCD COE Publications.

Heintschel von Heinegg, Wolff. 2013. "Territorial Sovereignty and Neutrality in Cyberspace." *U.S. Naval War College International Law Studies* 89: 123–156.

Hertogen, An. 2015. "Letting Lotus Bloom." *European Journal of International Law* 26 (4): 901–926.

Hutchins, Eric M., Michael J. Cloppert, and Rohan M. Amin. 2011. "Intelligence-Driven Computer Network Defense Informed by Analysis of Adversary Campaigns and Intrusion Kill Chains." In *6th Annual International Conference on Information Warfare and Security*, 1–14. http://papers.rohanamin.com/wp-content/uploads/ papers.rohanamin.com/2011/08/iciw2011.pdf%5Cnhttp://www.lockheedmartin.co m/content/dam/lockheed/data/corporate/documents/LM-White-Paper-Intel-Driven -Defense.pdf.

Johnson, David R., and David Post. 1996. "Law and Borders—The Rise of Law in Cyberspace." *Stanford Law Review* 48 (5): 1367–1402.

Koh, Harold Hongju. 2012. "International Law in Cyberspace." *Harvard International Law Journal* 54: 1–9.

Kosseff, Jeff. 2018. "Defining Cybersecurity Law." *Iowa Law Review* 103: 985–1031.

Kwiecień, Roman. 2012. "Does the State Still Matter? Sovereignty, Legitimacy and International Law." *Polish Yearbook of International Law* XXXII: 45–74.

Maybaum, Markus. 2013. "Technical Methods, Techniques, Tools and Effects of Cyber Operations." In *Peacetime Regime for State Activities in Cyberspace*, edited by Katharina Ziolkowski, 103–134. Tallinn: NATO CCD COE Publications.

Ministère des Armées. 2019. "Droit International appliqué aux opérations dans le cyberespace." https://www.defense.gouv.fr/content/download/565895/9750877/file/Droit+internat+appliqué+aux+opérations+Cyberespace.pdf.

Owens, William A., Kenneth W. Dam, Herbert S. Lin, and National Research Council. 2009. *Technology, Policy, Law and Ethics Regarding U.S. Acquisition and Use of Cyberattack Capabilities*. The National Academies Press.

Pirker, Benedikt. 2013. "Territorial Sovereignty and Integrity and the Challenges of Cyberspace." In *Peacetime Regime for State Activities in Cyberspace*, edited by Katharina Ziolkowski, 189–216. Tallinn: NATO CCD COE Publications.

Riedel, Norbert. 2015. "'Cyber Security as a Dimension of Security Policy.' Speech by Ambassador Norbert Riedel, Commissioner for International Cyber Policy, Federal Foreign Office, Berlin, at Chatham House, London." London. https://www.auswaertiges-amt.de/en/newsroom/news/150518-ca-b-chatham-house/271832.

Roguski, Przemysław. 2019. "Layered Sovereignty: Adjusting Traditional Notions of Sovereignty to a Digital Environment." In *11th International Conference on Cyber Conflict: Silent Battle*, edited by Tomáš Minárik, Siim Alatalu, Stefano Biondi, Massimiliano Signoretti, Ihsan Tolga, and Gábor Visky, 1–13. Tallinn: NATO CCD COE Publications. https://doi.org/10.23919/cycon.2019.8756900.

Schmitt, Michael N. 2018. "International Cyber Norms: Reflections on the Path Ahead." *Militair Rechtelijk Tijdschrift* 111 (3 Cyber Special): 12–20.

Schmitt, Michael N., and Liis Vihul (eds.). 2017c. *Tallinn Manual 2.0 on the International Law Applicable to Cyber Operations*. Cambridge: Cambridge University Press.

Schmitt, Michael N., and Liis Vihul. 2017a. "Respect for Sovereignty in Cyberspace." *Texas Law Review* 95: 1639–1670.

Schmitt, Michael N., and Liis Vihul. 2017b. "Sovereignty in Cyberspace: Lex Lata Vel Non?" *AJIL Unbound* 111: 213–218.

Secrétariat général de la défense et de la sécurité nationale. 2018. "Revue stratégique de cyberdéfense." http://www.sgdsn.gouv.fr/uploads/2018/02/20180206-np-revue-cyber-public-v3.3-publication.pdf.

Smeets, Max. 2017. "Organisational Integration of Offensive Cyber Capabilities: A Primer on the Benefits and Risks." In *9th International Conference on Cyber Conflict: Defending the Core*, edited by Henry Roigas, R. Jakschis, L. Lindström, i T. Minárik, 25–42. Tallinn.

Tsagourias, Nicholas. 2015. "The Legal Status of Cyberspace." In *Research Handbook on International Law and Cyberspace*, edited by Nicholas Tsagourias i Russell Buchan, 13–29. Cheltenham: Edward Elgar Publishing.

U.S. Department of Justice—Computer Crime and Intellectual Property Section. 2010. "Prosecuting Computer Crimes Manual." Washington, DC. https://www.justice.gov/criminal/cybercrime/docs/ccmanual.pdf.

United Nations General Assembly. 2013. *Report of the Group of Governmental Experts on Developments in the Field of Information and Telecommunications in the Context of International Security*. UN Doc. A/68/98.

United Nations General Assembly. 2015. *Report of the Group of Governmental Experts on Developments in the Field of Information and Telecommunications in the Context of International Security*. UN Doc. A/70/174.

Watts, Sean, and Theodore Richard. 2018. "Baseline Territorial Sovereignty and Cyberspace." *Lewis & Clark Law Review* 22 (3): 803–872.

Wilske, Stephan. 2012. "Abduction, Transboundary." In *Max Planck Encyclopaedia of Public International Law*, edited by Rüdiger Wolfrum. Oxford, NY: Oxford University Press.

Wright, Jeremy. 2018. "Cyber and International Law in the 21st Century." London. https://www.gov.uk/government/speeches/cyber-and-international-law-in-the-21st-century.

Chapter 5

What Does Russia Want in Cyber Diplomacy?

A Primer[1]

Xymena Kurowska

The standard analytical narratives regarding Russia's behavior in global diplomacy, today, revolve around great power aspirations, revisionist power games, and a threat to liberal democracy as we know it. The Russian discourse can also, however, be parsed with reference to resentment, resulting from the sense of "being betrayed" by the West (Kurowska 2014), or to anger over apparent disrespect received from other international actors (Larson and Shevchenko 2014). Demand for status recognition is a key factor in Russia's international conduct (Krickovic and Weber 2018; Schmitt forthcoming; Neumann 2016, 1996), which finds its expression in Russia's regular insistence on acknowledging its indispensability to the international order (Lo 2015, 47). Despite declarations of pragmatism in foreign policy (Omelicheva 2016; Casier 2006), this status-related rationale often overshadows what would appear more rational courses of action. Demands for recognition may also result in embarrassment. One vivid example of the latter involved the emotional outburst by the acting Russian representative to the UN, Vladimir Safronkov, toward the UK representative during a Security Council session in April 2017: famously, "Look at me!" and "Don't you dare insult Russia again!" (RFE 2017). Many looked away mortified, but Safronkov's superiors in the Ministry for Foreign Affairs commended his behavior, as part of resistance toward Western attempts at hegemonic imposition (Schreck 2017).

The current tit-for-tat clashes over models of global Internet governance, which effectively reinstate Russia to the highest echelons of international interactions, are redolent of the Cold War diplomatic ritual that Russia enjoys. It matters, once again, what Russia says. There is a timely narrative in this strategic communication, backed by effective diplomatic outreach, which is by no means "cheap talk." The contestation over global Internet governance both manifests and indicates the emerging contours of a new international order. Examining Russia's priorities in this struggle is not easy, however, due to radical political polarization but also a certain "confusion-of-tongues." In cyber diplomacy, or in international information security (as is the preferred term in the Russian discourse), actors use identical or similar terminology, but such terminology derives from different imaginaries about the international order, and, arguably, different imaginaries about the good life.[2] The place of the individual in international society remains the bone of contention across these ideational frameworks. It will inform, implicitly and explicitly, the normative stakes in global governance of the Internet for years to come, including with regard to technology-related questions.

This chapter brings these issues to sharp relief, contributing to a better-informed debate. In its substantive introduction, it lays out the basics of the current framing of Russia's cyber narrative. It then explains the priorities of Russian cyber diplomacy with reference to Russia's self-perceived standing and responsibility in maintaining peace and security. Crucial to grasping this position is understanding the conception of international law that Russia applies in cyberspace, how this ties back to its doctrine of multipolarity, and the peculiar interpretation of multilateralism that comes along with this. Further, the chapter unpacks a core trope in Russia's strategic diplomatic communication more broadly: that is, the notion of "democratizing" international relations. This is a self-serving rhetorical trope, readily dismissed by the West as nonsense. But it is not without the potential to subvert the Western normative dominance in global Internet governance. This rhetoric appeals to genuine grievances over the existing inequalities in international society and capitalizes on the West's own subversion and betrayal of the liberal ethos. Russia's strategy to advance its "democratization" agenda resembles "trickstery" (Kurowska and Reshetnikov 2018b): It is a mixture of a spoiler's tactic of sowing confusion, along with a sombre discourse of responsibility for international security.

The last two parts of this chapter look more closely at, first, the doctrine of information security, which is fundamental for grasping Russia's cyber conduct at the juncture of its domestic and foreign policy, and, second, the regional effort to codify this doctrine, which is incrementally being uploaded globally. The chapter concludes with the suggestion that Russia's posturing in cyber diplomacy is not a security threat as such but a "normative threat" (Creppell 2011) to the liberal way of life. As such, it is a manifestation of an ideological struggle that liberal cyber-norms entrepreneurs cannot afford to simply disparage or ignore. An analysis of exactly what is being contested can help to reform their effort. The rather urgent political question, in this context, involves how to smartly counteract being cast as a villain by Russia's narrative about the post-liberal world. In other words, the question concerns how to offer an appealing and inclusive alternative.

"2018—RECLAIMING THE DEBATE"

The adoption of two competing resolutions regarding global governance of the Internet in 2018, the U.S.-sponsored reaffirmation of UN Group of Governmental Experts (UN GGE) (General Assembly 2018a) and the Russia-sponsored launching of the Open-Ended Working Group (OEWG) (General Assembly 2018c), marks the final breakdown of international consensus on the issue.[3] In Russia's cyber narrative, it is, however, taken as a positive breakthrough, fortuitously overlapping with the twenty-year anniversary of 1998 when Moscow tabled its first draft resolution on Information and Communication Technology in the General Assembly's First Committee on Disarmament and International Security (Kommersant 2018, 6). In 2018, Russia in fact successfully sponsored two resolutions, the abovementioned one launching OEWG and another, adopted in the Third Committee of the General Assembly on cybercrime (General Assembly 2018b), both framed as a significant way forward instigated by Russia's cyber diplomacy (Chernukhin 2019). They are portrayed as a return to the original purpose of the UN track on International Information Security, as initiated by Russia in 1998, which is to create accountability in the fundamentally "ungovernable" cyberspace. The OEWG resolution sets thirteen rules, norms, and principles (in comparison with the eleven laid out in the U.S.-sponsored resolution) of responsible state behavior that are the first "rules of the road" in history with regard to this issue —despite them formally being "recommendations for considerations by States" (Ibid.). Specifically, the resolution includes a re-assertion of cultural diversity, enshrined in the UN Charter, in global Internet governance. The launch of OEWG is presented as ushering in a genuine democratization of global Internet governance and a potential space where negotiations over an international cyber treaty can be launched.

The aim of the resolution on cybercrime was, in turn, to launch a separate track on the matter in the UN, as an alternative to the Budapest Convention on Cybercrime. Drawn up by the Council of Europe in 2001 to foster international cooperation in cybercrime matters and promoted by the group of the "like-minded," the Budapest convention is opposed by Russia and others due to its paragraph 32b, which allows for transborder access to data during cybercrime investigations by the intelligence services. Russia's advocacy for a cybercrime treaty within the UN, recently bolstered by a new resolution adopted in the Third Committee, is portrayed as part of the attempt to extend the control of the state over the Internet and curtail the political rights of the individual (Nakashima 2019). This is, in broad terms, the crux of "the like-minded" position. Russia, similar to some other non-Western actors, charges the West with maintaining digital inequality and infringement of sovereignty in the pursuit of upholding the liberal world order. The remainder of the chapter unpacks the Russian perspective on the current state of "unpeace" (Kello 2017, 78) that thus unfolds in cyberspace and the tasks that the Russian diplomacy sets for itself in this regard.

PRIORITIES OF RUSSIA'S CYBER DIPLOMACY

The short answer to what Russia wants in and through cyber diplomacy is twofold. *First*, cyberspace promises Russia respect (уважение/uvazheniye), not only at the well-cultivated regional level, but, potentially, globally. It affords status recognition that Russia lost and craved to regain since the unsuccessful attempt to integrate into the liberal world order in the early 1990s. Status thirst is, however, difficult to engage with in politics. It is a moving target and the approaches of Western countries are likely to "fall below Moscow's expectations to be treated as it feels it deserves" (Schmitt forthcoming, 20). *Second*, the long-standing priority of Russia's cyber diplomacy is "to *create conditions* [emphasis mine] for promoting internationally the Russian initiative to develop and adopt a Convention of International Information Security by United Nations Member States" (Security Council 2013). The *lex specialis* for the cyber domain may not yet be realistic, in other words, but Russia is working to prepare the ground for it.

"The like-minded" tend to justify their objection to an international cyber treaty by reference to the consensus that existing international law applies in cyberspace, which, supported by the norms of responsible state behavior, is sufficient to defend "the rules-based international order" in cyberspace. Negotiations over a new binding instrument would, in this context, only divert efforts from implementing what is already agreed upon; they would draw the world into an unnecessary, lengthy, and divisive struggle, and, as emphasized particularly in US discourse, hinder technological development (Rõigas 2015). Russia's advocacy for the treaty relies on the claim to defend the international order in its classic version where binding legal instruments are a traditional form of regulation. An international cyber treaty is also portrayed as a means to curb the liberal international order which legitimizes intervention into the domestic makeup of states, and thus a tool against the ad hoc decisions by the strong.

The notion of "the rules-based international order"[4] is particularly contested, in this respect, as a replacement for, rather than a continuation of, an international law-based order. The idea is vehemently attacked in Russian diplomacy as an attempt to "usurp the decision-making process on key issues" by "[replacing] the universally agreed international legal instruments and mechanisms with narrow formats, where alternative, non-consensual methods for resolving various international problems are developed in circumvention of a legitimate multilateral framework" (Lavrov 2019). Such rhetoric, as the chapter lays out below in more detail, is self-serving; however, it is short-sighted of the West to disregard it. The concern with representativeness, and the instrumentalization of such a concern for both tactical and strategic gains, increasingly inform political positions in the global governance of Internet.

Finally, Russia's advocacy of an international cyber treaty has another snappy line: International law applies in cyberspace but even experts do not know how, and there is a reason for it. The very term "responsible state behavior in cyberspace" is, in the Russian interpretation, not clear. International procedural law, as a set of principles and norms governing the exercise of the rights and obligations of subjects of international law, is seen as being not adapted to the regulation of international relations in the field of Information and Communication Technology (ICT) (Strel'tsov, Sharyapov, and Yashchenko 2016, 6, para. 1.7.). The use of international customs and general principles of law is, further, unpromising in this area given the lack of a common understanding of some objects of legal regulation; for example, the use of ICT as a means of warfare (Ibid). This almost sacrosanct portrayal of international law has been part of Russia's foreign policy for two decades. After the 1999 NATO operation in Kosovo, which Russia contested passionately, the then Minister for Foreign Affairs, Igor Ivanov formulated what became a default Russian position: the objection to changing "basic principles of international law" in order to replace them with the doctrines of "limited sovereignty" (Igor Ivanov cited in, Averre 2009, 586).

This sacrosanct understanding of international law as above politics has been interrogated in the Western doctrine of international law as a political move in itself (Klabbers 2004; Koskenniemi 2011). Despite its claim to neutrality and impartiality, international law is part of the way political power is used, critiqued, and sometimes limited. The Russian initiative to create conditions conducive to negotiating an international cyber treaty needs to be seen in this light: It is part of the process of imposing a particular vision of international relations, in the process critiquing and possibly limiting the power of Western liberal states, above all the United States.

RUSSIA'S COMEBACK AS "A RESPONSIBLE CYBER POWER"

The promotion of a dedicated and legally binding instrument in cyberspace belongs to Russia's twofold strategy. On the one hand, Russia engages in intense "securitization"[5] of cyberspace: It invests in portraying everything "cyber," or digital, as a grave security threat (see below). On the other, it takes up the role of a responsible great power which can be relied upon to counter this threat. Russia thus acts simultaneously as spoiler and savior. This position yields distinct rewards: It provides discursive resources for Russia to frame itself as a concerned, influential, and capable cyber leader for the non-Western, or post-liberal world. Thus, Russia returns to the global game of international order.

The analogy with the new "Cuban missile crisis," conjured up by Andrey Krutskikh, Director of the Department of International Information Security in Russia's Ministry of Foreign Affairs (Andrey Krutskikh cited in, Kommersant 2019b) is an example of the securitizing discourse about the world at the brink of a cyber catastrophe. Russia substantively likens the hazards of nuclear weapons and digitalization because of the technological implications of the scale of threat and interlinkages between them (Sharikov 2018a). The very initiation of the cyber debate in the context of international security within the UN First Committee on Disarmament was justified in terms of the dangers of "information weapons" (the term now formally withdrawn but hardly forgotten) and modeled on the nuclear nonproliferation regime. Russia hoped to emulate the parameters of the nuclear regime for information security in cyberspace to mediate Western superiority in that domain (cf. Chernenko 2018). Cyber debates predictably proliferated across the UN landscape to include all domains of international relations. But the security tone that Russia set back in the late 1990s remains dominant.

The image of the new Cuban crisis has a wider appeal, however. It excavates the frame of the Cold War Soviet–US relationship as ruling the world, and of the international order as it was fixed in 1945 by the victorious allies, with the caveat that China has risen in the meantime. This is a reinvigorating turn for Russia's long-frustrated aspiration to regain (even symbolically) parity with the West and the image of an imminent disaster is well exploited. As the current mantra of Russian diplomats goes: "[U]nlike the US, Russia, as a *responsible* [emphasis mine] State, is not interested in new missile crises," but it has the obligation to mitigate US "destructive actions" in global politics (Vladimir Yermakov cited in, Permanent Mission 2019b, 2). An impoverished country with tangibly little to mold the world affairs, but with a reputation in need of restoring, Russia can only gain from revamping its international role by becoming "a responsible cyber power" (cf. Nocetti

2018). The role gives a shiny and topical veneer to an anachronistic understanding of the international order, reasserting Russia's special responsibility as the permanent member of the UN Security Council for shaping global cooperation and maintaining peace and security. The distinct advantage of the cyber domain is that it is highly "actionable." Nuclear weapons are, ultimately, not to be used; the international community has even managed to create a taboo over such potential use (Tannenwald 1999). By contrast, cyberspace means of disruption and interference may be, and are, in common use.

In rhetoric, Russia's chief preoccupation is then with the militarization of cyberspace, which adds urgency to global Internet regulation. In practice, cyber diplomacy provides Russia with a global platform for uploading its long-cultivated regional effort to counter the liberal world order. The frequency of cyberattacks and scandals, like that of the Snowden and Cambridge Analytica revelations, bolster Russia's claim of cyberspace as dangerous and lacking proper "rules-of-the-road." The growing populist sentiment at the global level further plays into the hands of the Kremlin, which has the ideological and operational resources to tap into this sentiment as a new structuring force in international politics. A key discourse in this respect is Russia's broad agenda of defending international law and democratizing international relations, read containing the US hegemony, revamped in the rhetoric of fighting digital inequality.

INTERNATIONAL LAW AND INTERNATIONAL NORMS IN RUSSIA'S CYBER DIPLOMACY

There is a missing link in the debate over whether international law applies in cyberspace. The explicit consensus that it does, indeed, apply is marked by different understandings of the role of international law as such.[6] The consensus is, therefore, hardly a reason to celebrate. The recent recommendation that national governments append to UN GGE reports their explanation of how international law applies in cyberspace is a move toward clarification. It will not, however, eradicate fundamental differences in interpretation.

The Kremlin interprets international law as the body of rules and conventions that govern relations between the major powers. Formally speaking, this reflects a procedural and pluralist understanding of international law as a particular kind of a legal system, with a commitment to legality in international politics as an end in itself rather than a means toward an end beyond itself (Collins 2019, 196). This traditional positivist notion contrasts with a model of international law as a way to judge, in terms of its "functional capacity to actually pre-empt political choices and realise agreed-upon objectives" (Ibid). In other words, for Moscow, international law regulates relations between states of different ideological disposition, without prejudice as to such disposition. "The like-minded" see international law more as a means toward upholding a liberal consensus, in this case an open and free Internet which belongs to the liberal vision of international order. As a result, there are different models of international law that apply in cyberspace.

The core to the Russian interpretation is the preponderance of the statist discourse of international law, with the emphasis on the classic understanding of sovereignty and a categorical rejection of the notion of the individual as a subject of international law (Dmitry 2017). At the same time, the individual becomes increasingly empowered in the Western discourse on international law which also shifts toward transnational, rather than state-based, solutions. The glorification of the state in the Russian legal doctrine (Mälksoo 2015, 100) leads to a distinct twist on the very idea of law as "speaking truth to power": In the Russian rendition, the addressee of the "truth of international law" rather is the United States, or the "West" by extension, and not the Russian government (Ibid, 81).[7] International law "à la Russe serves to restrain the exercise of American power" (Lo 2015, 95).

When the Russian foreign minister Lavrov repeats the mantra of the double standards in the application of international law (Lavrov 2016) and denounces "attacks on international law" (Sergey Lavrov cited in, Kommersant 2019a), it is this version of speaking truth to power that is being exercised. Such tirades may be interpreted as ludicrous and hypocritical by Western observers. It eludes these observers, however, that international law is often portrayed outside of the West as a hegemonic tool of the West. The Russian Investigative Committee chief Alexander Bastrykin taps into anti-hegemonic grievances in international society when he states that "international law and the justice based on it have increasingly become tools of [hybrid] war" against Moscow (Alexander Bastrykin cited in, Kommersant 2016, 20).

Such grievances are appealed to in Russia's pursuit of the "democratization" of international relations, even as the agenda serves the Russian doctrine of multipolarity, rather than the cause of a genuine democratization of decision-making in the international system. Simply put, multipolarity, or the polycentric world order, refers to a system in which power is distributed among at least three significant poles concentrating wealth and/or military capabilities and which are able to block or disrupt major political arrangements that threaten their major interests (Kurowska 2014; Makarychev and Morozov 2011). A pole is also understood as an actor capable of producing order or generating disorder, usually a regional power with a global outreach. Multipolarity, therefore, means concentrating power in the hands of a few. When Russia speaks of a polycentric world order, it also projects a value system that would support such order (Kagan 2008). This builds on civilizational diversity; that is, the notion that countries should not have the right to judge each other's domestic practices and cultures. The principle is not politically neutral; the pole exerts the normative, as well as political, influence. The principle is rather intended "to chip away at the authority of Western forms of order and empower regimes to dismiss liberal norms as intrusive and inappropriate for their culture" (Cooley 2019, 22).

Multipolarity is often conflated with multilateralism in Russian diplomacy, to the extent that it baffles external observers. Russia approaches international institutions as equalizers of liberal hegemony and as a means of guarding its own sovereignty, not as components of transnational regimes generating global governance, which contravenes sovereignty, or makes it "conditional." The insistence on the UN's central and coordinating role in world politics should be read in this light: It reasserts collective leadership by major powers through the Security Council, as fixed in 1945. It also constitutes a balancing mechanism to both prevent an imposition with regard to domestic governance and curb a unilateral action based solely on national interest (i.e., the US interest).

International law and international norms are crucial to maintaining this system, hence Russia's whole-hearted commitment to them. They do so differently from how they are envisaged in the liberal paradigm, however. As explained above, in the Russian doctrine, international law is understood procedurally. The international cyber treaty is supposed to target the current "loose" cyber regime based on the "common law" logic that reflects, enables, and reproduces the liberal consensus. A dedicated legal instrument establishes procedural rules of the game, in a supposedly politically neutral manner, to prevent acting on the liberal reflex. International norms, specifically those such as, for example, sovereignty and multilateral decision-making, have also been extremely important in the Russian foreign policy discourse because they help Russia maintain its technically great power status (Hopf 2002, 225). From this position, norms, including cyber norms, must be or should become binding, as a transitionary step toward codification. The current politically, rather than formally, binding character of cyber norms is, therefore, unsatisfactory for Russia as it reflects the suboptimal state of the regulation of the cyber domain.[8]

Norms are not, however, understood in accordance with the liberal idea of norm diffusion by enlightened norm entrepreneurs, as progressively adopted across the international community to constitute a uniform social glue and superior morality (cf. Kurowska 2019). Quite the opposite, in the Russian doctrine, norms are in place in order to regulate conduct between states of a different normative makeup, and, to be effective, they need to be formally binding. This is how Russia interprets the rules and norms of responsible state behavior in cyberspace. A global value-bound community, which does not need a binding legal instrument because it can act on a case-by-case basis on shared understandings, is an embodiment of hegemony in this interpretation. Attempts to design and implement new cyber norms are supported because they are in Russia's interests of regulating the Internet; but they need to be monitored as they potentially penetrate the state and pose the risk of "norm weaponization" in the interests of liberal interventionism.

DEMOCRATIZATION À LA RUSSE

One of the curious political implications of cyber treaty advocacy is that it furthers a fundamentally conservative process, in the spirit of the post-1945 international arrangement, by imitating the progressive politics that exposes digital inequality. A good illustration thereof is Russia's standing claim that developing states become "hostage to the cyber neocolonialism policy," as they also become the wasteland of the West's cyber refuse (Andrey Krutskikh cited in, Permanent Mission 2019a, 3). It often pushes Western countries into defensive positions, even as Russian "democratization speak" is recognized as instrumental given Russia's own practices of exclusion and domination.

The function of such rhetoric can be better understood, however, in the framework of great power management (Astrov 2011, 6). As defined by Hedley Bull, great power management consists of two practices: managing relations among themselves in the interest of international order, for example, by preserving the balance of power, and exploiting dominance in relation to the rest of international society, by acting either in concert or unilaterally (Bull 1977, 205-6; Astrov 2011). Within the framework of great power management, and in line with the doctrine of multipolarity, "democratization" of international relations denotes the decentralization of power from the United States, as the former hegemon, to a group of great powers, including Russia and now China. Despite the populist use of the term in Russia's cyber diplomacy, small states are instrumental in this configuration. They can be wooed or coerced for tactical purposes but only great powers ultimately have the responsibility to manage the international order.

This rationale is an important qualification in evaluating Russia's advocacy of the OEWG as a parallel UN track to the UN GGE. Russia's initial support for the UN GGE followed the logic of the world being governed by a few— that is, great power management, here represented by governmental experts. Formally launched in 2004, the UN GGE produced three reports in 2010, 2013, and 2015. The reports are not legally binding but they have become the main point of reference in the discourse of responsible state behavior and the question of the applicability of international law in cyberspace. The failure of the 2017 UN GGE is attributed by Andrey Krutskikh to Western experts' monopolization of the leadership of the group and the need of Russia to resist that (Andrey Krutskikh cited in, Kommersant 2019b, 6). It is the realization that Russia could not further advance its great power cyber goals within the UN GGE that led to a major diplomatic swerve in 2018 and the resolution which launched the OEWG (General Assembly 2018c). From then on, it proceeded to label the UN GGE as a U.S.-promoted mechanism driven by experts who act in their personal capacity, which makes it unrepresentative and exclusionary.

The statements about the final draft of the OEWG-launching resolution in the First Committee on November 8, 2018 demonstrate a successful application of "democratization" rhetoric for contesting the liberal order. Russia denounced the UN GGE, ironically given its role in instantiating the process, as "the practice of some club agreements [that] should be sent into the annals of history" (Disarmament and International Security Committee 2018). "The like-minded" responded with pledges to strengthen capacity building and envisaging merely a secondary and consultative role for the OEWG in implementing norms created by the UN GGE. This made them politically vulnerable to charges of maintaining the structural inequality of the global Internet governance. The Russian portrayal of the OEWG, as, first, providing equal access to all the UN membership to shape Internet governance decisions, and, second, as returning sovereign states to the driver's seat of making such decisions (Andrey Krutskikh cited in, Permanent Mission 2019c, 3), appealed to concerns over representativeness in non-Western constituencies.

The diplomatic feat of launching the OEWG unsettles the process of global Internet governance but it will not be easy to exploit. With the OEWG advocacy, Russia seeks to break its own marginalization, yet it can simultaneously harm its overall objective; that is, achieving an equal status at the table of those shaping the global governance structures of the Internet. The OEWG constitutes "a cyber agora" which, in the long run, can provide a platform for treaty negotiation. But it comes with agora-like politics which cannot be easily channelled or made conducive to intimate deals among "poles of power," something that Russia craves to be involved in.

The diplomatic downfall experienced in November 2019, after the generally positive atmosphere around the launch of the OEWG in June and September 2019, shows how "democratization agenda" is but a tool in the geopolitics of global Internet governance. The First Committee session on November 6, 2019 saw, again, two votes over competing resolutions. The U.S.-sponsored document (General Assembly 2019a) elaborates on and reasserts the primacy of the UN GGE and concedes to "also welcoming" rather than only noting the launch of the OEWG. The Russian-sponsored, and little-consulted, document (General Assembly 2019b) prioritizes the OEWG while "also welcoming" the UN GGE and underscoring the status of both as independent mechanisms under United Nations auspices that should work in parallel toward peace and stability in ICTs. This head-on rhetorical confrontation between the two main cyber orators creates confusion and divisions among "the like-minded." Caught between its commitment to working within both the OEWG and the UN GGE and its allegiance to "the like-minded" vision of cyberspace, the EU abstained rather than voting against the Russian-sponsored resolution. The explanation of the vote cited "the non-consensus based language" but reaffirmed the commitment to "work both within the UN GGE and the OEWG in a complementary and coordinated fashion, to promote and further build on the cumulative achievements of the previous UN GGEs" (EEAS 2019). Switzerland, chairing the OEWG, voted in favor. A closer look at the underpinnings of Russia's cyber narrative may help better manage the confusion it generates.

"DIGITALIZATION IS DANGEROUS"—THE DOCTRINE OF INFORMATION SECURITY

The staple of the Russian cyber narrative is that digitalization is dangerous. It is generally seen as уязвимость/uyazvimost' (vulnerability). Domestically, it constitutes a disruptive tool with regard to regime stability, a view which consolidated in the realization of the power of the social media during the Arab Spring, drove home by the extent of anti-regime protests in Russia in 2012 (Pigman 2019). Internationally, the Internet is portrayed as a dangerous instrument of foreign interference. The doctrine on information security laid out in the International Convention on Information Security stresses threats of information warfare and dangers stemming from foreign governments' exploiting information and communication technologies for undermining state sovereignty, political independence, and territorial integrity (MID 2011). Every year since 1998, Russia has put forward resolutions at the United Nations to prohibit "information aggression," which is interpreted to mean ideological attempts to undermine regime stability. Moscow seems to see itself in a particular situation vis-à-vis Western countries: a non-declared war, no peace context, but information warfare as a continuous state of flux between peace and war (Franke 2015, 42).

Russia's understanding of what constitutes information security merits scrutiny in this context. In contrast to the Western approaches focused on technology, protection of communication infrastructure, and free access to information, the doctrine of information security relates to the responsibility of the government to secure the information itself and, therefore, ultimately, national sovereignty (Sharikov 2018c). If Western countries seek security of communication, the Russian government wants control over the content of information, since content can be used as a tool of influence in the socio-humanitarian sphere (Nocetti 2018, 187). More broadly, two political principles are key to the doctrine. One is the understanding of "real" sovereignty as the stability of the political system, national unity, prevention of fundamental contradictions between the authorities, the society, and the elites (Kokoshin 2006, 26); in other words, prevention of political dissent. The other relates to the perception of the politically empowered individual, especially one who uses information technologies to advance their rights, as both a vulnerability and a security threat to the state (Sharikov 2018b, 172–4).

The Kremlin's expansion of a "digitally sovereign" Russia program is, therefore, a defence of the state against both the discontent of their own citizens and uncontrolled Western influence. The development of the Russian segment of the information and communication network, known as Runet, is part of this agenda. The Sovereign Internet Law, which came into force on November 1, 2019 and will be incrementally rolled out in the coming years, envisages technical arrangements in case of disconnection from the rest of the Internet, as, for example, due to foreign aggression. Russian telecom firms have to install, for this purpose, "technical means" to re-route all Russian Internet traffic to exchange points approved or managed by Roskomnazor, Russia's telecom watchdog. The "Runet" logic is, in essence, defensive of the regime. But it is also a local response to challenges of digitalization at the global scale, which calls for a greater technological sovereignty and economic protectionism. The championing of data localization also belongs to this agenda. Understood as storing data within the borders of the country where it was generated and justified in terms of resisting the concentration of transnational data storage in California, United States, data localization constitutes a crucial part of state digital sovereignty. If, in the United States, information regime data belongs to tech companies, and in the EU General Data Protection Regulation framework it belongs to the individual, in Russia data belongs to the state and must be strictly controlled by it (Sharikov and Stepanova 2019).

GLOBALIZING INFORMATION SECURITY THROUGH REGIONAL PLATFORMS

The regional promotion of a counter-liberal order commenced in the late 1990s by mainstreaming the counternorms of civilizational diversity and traditional values, the old-new rearticulation the norm of sovereign equality (cf. Cooley 2015). Russia could not afford, however, a global model of illiberal contestation for the utter lack of legitimacy, both in terms of its own standing and the strength of the liberal order at that time. Regional platforms have presently become regulation entrepreneurs: a laboratory for global cyber regulation and a space for coalition building for global cyber diplomacy.

Russia has uploaded to regional platforms its own solutions for countering the vulnerabilities of digitalization. Within the framework of the Shanghai Cooperation Organization (SCO), it has, for example, streamlined the norm of digital sovereignty in contrast to the U.S.-advocated "cyber-freedom" and in 2009 facilitated the SCO agreement for cooperation to ensure "international information security." Initiated in a 2011 letter to the UN General Assembly by the Russian coalition (gathering China, Uzbekistan, and Tajikistan), it includes a pledge that states subscribing to the Code "not use information and communications technologies and other information and communications networks to interfere with the internal affairs of other states or with the aim of undermining their political, economic and social stability" (General Assembly 2011). The 2011 proposal also banned the use of the Internet for military purposes, but was criticized for the very attempt at formalization, the inconsistency with the multistakeholder approach, the de facto justification of censorship in the name of national sovereignty, and the overemphasis on terrorism and extremism to the neglect of cross-border law enforcement cooperation (Rõigas 2015). The 2015 updated version retracts the term "information weapons" that generated much controversy and states the commitment that human rights apply online as they do offline, but submits this recognition to national security prerogatives (Kavanagh 2017, 25). It also, however, introduces a provision not to take advantage of a "dominant position in the sphere of IT" (section 5), which is in line with the broader agenda of "democratization," and reiterates the role of governments in Internet governance (section 8), which may be interpreted as a continuous opposition to the multi-stakeholder model propagated by "the like-minded." This acquis clashes too violently with the liberal model of Internet governance to be uploaded in its entirety. Still, the regional cyber codification is attractive to many actors who are concerned with the cyberspace being unregulated, are increasingly puzzled at the West's refusal of the international cyber treaty, and are inclined toward the state-controlled regulation of the Internet. The call for stricter regulation is gaining salience as it addresses many contemporary issues in cyberspace. The generic call for "free, safe, open, and secure" Internet will not alleviate such concerns and challenges. This is the immediate leverage that regional regulation entrepreneurs do possess.

While Russia did not fabricate the backlash against the hegemonic liberal world order and the reassertion of the conservative ideologies in these regions, it will rush to expedite such processes and turn them to its own advantage. Its traditionally strong regional expertise and the historical record of playing on regional grievances during the Cold War come in handy especially strongly vis-à-vis colonial legacies and the extractive post-colonial policies that proliferate in cyberspace. The strategy of empowering regional organizations as responsible for regional security in accordance with the UN Charter adds legitimacy to this self-serving endeavor. Many regional actors recognize the "pragmatist" logic of this rhetoric. Even if they do not necessarily fall for Russia's supposedly democratic campaign, their concern with structural inequality in the international system partially overlaps with Russia's agenda. What gets corrupted in the process of aligning such positions is the very ideal of decolonization and de-hierarchization. It is hijacked for Russia's pursuit of collective leadership by great powers which will disregard the voices of those structurally disadvantaged in the system.

CONCLUSION

Cyber diplomacy has become a way of revendicating and revalorizing Russia's global role, another rendition of the old "Gentlemen, Russia is back!" (Rossiyskayagazeta 2007). That declaration after the Munich speech (Putin 2007) which heralded a more active international politics by the Kremlin lacked, however, in the realm of legitimacy for many years to come. The realm of global Internet governance provides a new ground of legitimation because it strikes a peculiar balance between Russia being able to break and fix things. It depicts the Internet as the ultimate contemporary security threat to monger fear and justify extraordinary measures, and champions the cause of regulation in one breath. Russia often punches above its weight in this game, and its cyber narrative is simplistic. But it exposes the hypocrisy and self-subversion of the liberal order on the global stage the way populists expose the liberal hypocrisy domestically. This is where the normative threat of endangering the sustainability of the liberal way of life and the liberal international order manifests itself most clearly.

One of the distinguishing features of liberalism is, however, that it can reform and adapt itself while authoritarianism only learns how to be more effective. The Russian vision is, ultimately, anachronistic. It relies on control and subordination of the individual to the state, which ignores the extent of and the hunger for genuine democratization and freedom at the level of the cyber citizen. The liberal cyber regime should hence reinvigorate its holistic commitment to the individual as the center of gravity of international cyber society. Not only as a free entrepreneur but as a political subject with a full spectrum of political rights, and with community and national attachments as a source of self-expression rather than subservience. "Leading by example," the old liberal means of persuasion, may have lost much of its charm as an effective strategy to achieve such aim. Its righteousness also becomes anach-ronistic in international society, underpinned by normative pluralism and the contestation of hierarchies, including those created by liberal social norms. The shift from paternalism to participatory modes of engagement in building sustainable cyber societies better corresponds to the realities of the contem-porary world. It builds an alternative, human- rather than security state-based model of democratization in international relations. The major challenge in this process is to "de-securitize" the politics of the global governance of the Internet and reformulate the parameters of the debate about digital society.

NOTES

1. I thank Patryk Pawlak and Mika Kerttunen for detailed comments on this chap-ter. I would also like to acknowledge research opportunities provided by EU Cyber Direct Team and non-attributable conversations with national diplomats participat-ing in the UN processes. I further thank Bibi van den Berg and Dennis Broeders for numerous textual and terminological suggestions. Philip Conway helped with copy editing. The views expressed in this chapter are solely mine and I bear responsibility for any possible mistakes. A version of this paper was first published by EU Cyber Direct. Reprinted here with permission.

2. See Giles and Hagestad (2013) for an analysis of terminological misunderstand-ings in the domain of cyber and information security as evident in the policy docu-ments by Russia, China, United States, and United Kingdom.

3. For an alternative view, see Tikk and Kerttunen (2018).

4. "The rules-based international order" has not been neatly defined but it can be understood as "a shared commitment by all countries to conduct their activities in accordance with agreed rules that evolve over time, such as international law, regional security arrangements, trade agreements, immigration protocols, and cultural arrange-ments" (Association of Australia 2015, 3).

5. Securitization in international relations is the process of state actors transform-ing subjects into matters of "security": an extreme version of politicization that enables extraordinary means to be used in the name of security (Buzan, Wæver, and de Wilde 1998, 25). The successful securitization of ICT by the Russian Federation was noticed by Tikk and Kerttunen (2018, 56, 58).

6. Some authors speak of the Russian version as "a simulacrum or concave mirror to Western use" (Mälksoo 2015, 185). See Tikk and Kerttunen (2018), for examples, of how specific concepts of international law have been differently understood across a range of actors participating in the UN GGE.

7. This can also be interpreted as a "pragmatist relation to truth," which opens another line of interpretation of the Russian agenda of democratizing international relations. On the domestic culture of the pragmatic relation to truth as manifested in pro-Kremlin trolling, see Kurowska and Reshetnikov (2018a).

8. I thank Mika Kerttunen for highlighting this point to me.

BIBLIOGRAPHY

Association of Australia, United Nations. 2015. *The United Nations and the Rules-Based International Order.* Accessed November 23, 2019. https://www.unaa.org .au/wp-content/uploads/2015/07/UNAA_RulesBasedOrder_ARTweb3.pdf.

Astrov, Alexander. 2011. "Great Power Management without Great Powers? The Russian–Georgian War of 2008 and Global Police/Political Order." In *The Great Power (mis)Management: The Russian–Georgian War and Its Implications for Global Political Order*, edited by Alexander Astrov, 1–24. Farnham: Ashgate.

Averre, Derek. 2009. "From Pristina to Tskhinvali: The Legacy of Operation Allied Force in Russia's Relations with the West." *International Affairs* 85 (3): 575–591.

Bull, Hedley. 1977. *The Anarchical Society: A Study of Order in World Politics.* London: Macmillan.

Buzan, Barry, Ole Wæver, and Jaap de Wilde. 1998. *Security: A New Framework for Analysis.* Boulder, CO: Lynne Rienner.

Casier, Tom. 2006. "Putin's Policy Towards the West: Reflections on The Nature of Russian Foreign Policy." *International Politics* 43 (3): 384–401.

Chernenko, Elena. 2018. "Russia's Cyber Diplomacy." In *Hacks, Leaks and Disruptions. Russian Cyber Strategies*, edited by Nicu Popescu and Sergiu Secrieru, 43–49. Paris: EU Institute for Security Studies.

Chernukhin, Ernest. 2019. *Mezhdunarodnaya informatsionnaya bezopasnost': uspekhi Rossii v OON [International Information Security: Russia's Successes at the UN].* Russian International Affairs Council. Accessed November 23, 2019 https:// russiancouncil.ru/analytics-and-comments/analytics/mezhdunarodnaya-informatsi onnaya-bezopasnost-uspekhi-rossii-v-oon/.

Collins, Richard. 2019. "Two Idea(l)s of the International Rule of Law." *Global Constitutionalism* 8 (2): 191–226.

Cooley, Alexander. 2015. "Authoritarianism Goes Global: Countering Democratic Norms." *Journal of Democracy* 26 (3): 49–63.

Cooley, Alexander. 2019. "Ordering Eurasia: The Rise and Decline of Liberal Internationalism in the Post-Communist Space." *Security Studies* 28 (3): 588–613.

Creppell, Ingrid. 2011. "The Concept of Normative Threat." *International Theory* 3 (3): 450–487.

Disarmament and International Security Committee, General Assembly of United Nations . 2018. 31st meeting in the 73rd session of the General Assembly. New York.

Dmitry, Dubrovsky. 2017. "Lauri Mälksoo. Russian Approaches to International Law. Oxford: Oxford University Press, 2015." *Laboratorium: Russian Review of Social Research* 9 (1): 146–151.

EEAS. 2019. "EU Explanation of Vote—United Nations 1st Committee: Information and Telecommunications in the Context of International Security." https://eeas.eu ropa.eu/delegations/un-new-york/70041/eu-explanation-vote-%E2%80%93-un ited-nations-1st-committee-information-and-telecommunications-context_en.

Franke, Ulrik. 2015. *War By Non-Military Means. Understanding Russian Information warfare.* Swedish Defence Research Agency. http://johnhelmer.net/wp-conte nt/uploads/2015/09/Sweden-FOI-Mar-2015-War-by-non-military-means.pdf.

General Assembly, United Nations. 2011. International Code of Conduct for Information Security. New York: A/66/359.

General Assembly, United Nations. 2018a. Advancing Responsible State Behaviour in Cyberspace in the Context of International Security. Edited by 1st Committee of the General Assembly of the United Natons. New York.

General Assembly, United Nations. 2018b. Countering the Use of Information and Communications Technologies for Criminal Purposes. Edited by 3rd Committe of United Nations General Assembly. New York.

General Assembly, United Nations. 2018c. Developments in the Field of Information and Telecommunications in the Context of International Security. Edited by 1st Committe of United Nations General Assembly. New York: A/RES/73/27.

General Assembly, United Nations. 2019a. Advancing Responsible State Behaviour in Cyberspace in the Context of International Security. Edited by 1st Committee of the General Assembly of the United Nations. New York: November 6, 2019.

General Assembly, United Nations. 2019b. Developments in theFfield of Information and Telecommunications in the Context of International Security. Edited by 1st Committee of the General Assembly of the United Nations. New York: November 6, 2019.

Giles, Keir, and William Hagestad. 2013. "Divided by a Common Language: Cyber Definitions in Chinese, Russian and English." *5th International Conference on Cyber Conflict (CyCon)*: 1–17.

Kagan, Robert. 2008. *The Return of History and the End of Dreams*. New York: Knopf.

Kavanagh, Camino. 2017. *The United Nations, Cyberspace and International Peace and Security. Responding to Complexity in the 21st Century*. New York: The United Nations Institute for Disarmament Research.

Kello, Lucas. 2017. *The Virtual Weapon and International Order*. New Haven: Yale University Press.

Klabbers, Jan. 2004. "Constitutionalism Lite." *International Organizations Law Review* 1 (1): 31–58.

Kokoshin, Andrei. 2006. *Real'nyi suverenitet v sovremennoi miropoliticheskoi sisteme [Real Sovereignty in a World Political System]*. Moscow: Evropa.

Kommersant. 2016. "Pora postavit' deystvennyy zaslon informatsionnoy voyne [It's time to put an effective barrier to the information war]." Accessed November 23, 2019. https://www.kommersant.ru/doc/2961578.

Kommersant. 2018. "Rossiya i SSHA peretyagivayut vsemirnuyu pautinu [Russia and the USA are pulling the World Wide Web]." Accessed November 23, 2019. https://www.kommersant.ru/doc/3797617.

Kommersant. 2019a. "Ataki na mezhdunarodnoye pravo priobretayut opasnyye masshtaby [Attacks on international law are becoming dangerous]." Accessed November 23, 2019. https://www.kommersant.ru/doc/4109238.

Kommersant. 2019b. "Rossii nechego skryvat' i nechego boyat'sya [Russia has nothing to hide and nothing to fear]." Accessed November 23, 2019. https://www.kommersant.ru/doc/3923963.

Koskenniemi, Martti. 2011. *The Politics of International Law*. London: Hart Publishing.

Krickovic, Andrej, and Yuval Weber. 2018. "What Can Russia Teach Us About Change? Status-Seeking as a Catalyst for Transformation in International Politics." *International Studies Review* 20 (2): 292–300.

Kurowska, Xymena, and Anatoly Reshetnikov. 2018a. "Neutrollization: Industrialized Trolling as a Pro-Kremlin Strategy of Desecuritization." *Security Dialogue* 49 (5): 345–363.

Kurowska, Xymena, and Anatoly Reshetnikov. 2018b. "Russia's Trolling Complex at Home and Abroad." In *Hacks, Leaks and Disruptions: Russian Cyber Strategies*, edited by Nicu Popescu and Sergiu Secrieru, 25–32. Paris: EU Institute for Security Studies.

Kurowska, Xymena. 2014. "Multipolarity as Resistance to Liberal Norms: Russia's Position on Responsibility to Protect." *Conflict, Security & Development* 14 (4): 489–508.

Kurowska, Xymena. 2019. *The Politics of Cyber Norms: Beyond Norm Construction Towards Strategic Narrative Contestation.* Paris: EU Institute for Security Studies. https://eucyberdirect.eu/content_research/the-politics-of-cyber-norms-beyond-norm-construction-towards-strategic-narrative-contestation/.

Larson, Deborah Welch, and Alexei Shevchenko. 2014. "Russia Says No: Power, Status, and Emotions in Foreign Policy." *Communist and Post-Communist Studies* 47 (3): 269–279.

Lavrov, Sergey. 2016. "Russia's Foreign Policy in a Historical Perspective." *Russia in Global Affairs* 2. Accessed July 27, 2019. https://eng.globalaffairs.ru/number/Russias-Foreign-Policy-in-a-Historical-Perspective-18067.

Lavrov, Sergey. 2019. "World at a Crossroads and a System of International Relations for the Future." *Russia in Global Affairs.* Accessed November 11, 2019. https://eng.globalaffairs.ru/book/World-at-a-crossroads-The-future-system-of-international-relations-20199.

Lo, Bobo. 2015. *Russia and the New World Disorder.* London and Washington, DC: Chatham House and Brookings Institution Press.

Makarychev, Andrey, and Viatcheslav Morozov. 2011. "Multilateralism, Multipolarity, and Beyond: A Menu of Russia's Policy Strategies." *Global Governance* 17 (3): 353–373.

Mälksoo, Lauri. 2015. *Russian Approaches to International Law.* First Edition ed. Oxford: Oxford University Press.

MID. 2011. Convention on International Information Security. Accessed November 24, 2019. https://www.mid.ru/en/foreign_policy/official_documents/-/asset_publisher/CptICkB6BZ29/content/id/191666.

Nakashima, Ellen. 2019. "The U.S. Is Urging a No Vote on a Russian-Led U.N. Resolution Calling for a Global Cybercrime Treaty." *The Washington Post.* Accessed 23 November 2019. https://www.washingtonpost.com/national-security/the-us-is-urging-a-no-vote-on-a-russian-led-un-resolution-calling-for-a-global-cybercrime-treaty/2019/11/16/b4895e76-075e-11ea-818c-fcc65139e8c2_story.html?wpisrc=nl_cybersecurity202&wpmm=1.

Neumann, Iver. 1996. *Russia and the Idea of Europe: A Study in Identity and International Relations.* 2nd ed. London: Routledge.

Neumann, Iver. 2016. "Russia's Europe, 1991–2016: Inferiority to Superiority." *International Affairs* 92 (6): 1381–1399.

Omelicheva, Mariya Y. 2016. "Critical Geopolitics on Russian Foreign Policy: Uncovering the Imagery of Moscow's International Relations." *International Politics* 53 (6): 708–726.

Permanent Mission, of the Russian Federation to the United Nations. 2019a. Statement by Ambasador Andrey Krutskikh, Special Representative to the President of the Russian Federaton for International Cooperation in the Field of Information Security at the First Session of teh Open-Ended Working Group on Developments in the Field of Information and Telecommunication in the Context of International Security. New York: June 3–4, 2019.

Permanent Mission, of the Russian Federation to the United Nations. 2019b. Statement by Mr.Vladimir Yermakov, Head of Delegation of the Russian Federation to the First Committee of the 74th UNGA session, Director of the Department for Nonproliferation and Arms Control of the Ministry of Foreign Affairs of the Russian Federation, within the General Debate. New York: October 11, 2019.

Permanent Mission, of the Russian Federation to the United Nations. 2019c. Statement by the Special Representative of the President of the Russian Federation on International Cooperation on Information Security, Ambassador-at-Large A.V.Krutskikh. New York: September 9, 2019.

Pigman, Lincoln. 2019. "Russia's Vision of Cyberspace: A Danger to Regime Security, Public Safety, and Societal Norms and Cohesion." *Journal of Cyber Policy* 4 (1): 22–34.

Putin, Vladimir. 2007. Speech and Discussion at Munich Conference on Security Politics. Accessed July 27, 2019. http://special.kremlin.ru/events/president/transcripts/24034.

RFE. 2017. "'Look At Me!'—Russian UN Envoy Demands Attention." Accessed November 23, 2019. https://www.rferl.org/a/russia-uk-un/28427527.html.

Rõigas, Henry. 2015. "An Updated Draft of the Code of Conduct Distributed in the United Nations—What's New?" Accessed November 11, 2019 https://ccdcoe.org/incyder-articles/an-updated-draft-of-the-code-of-conduct-distributed-in-the-united-nations-whats-new/.

Rossiyskayagazeta. 2007. "Sergey Yastrzhembskiy: Gospoda, Rossiya vernulas'! [Sergey Yastrzhembsky: Gentlemen, Russia has returned!]." Accessed November 23, 2019. https://rg.ru/2007/02/22/yastrgemsky.html.

Schmitt, Oliver. forthcoming. "How to Challenge an International Order. Russian Diplomatic Practices in Multilateral Security Organisations." *European Journal of International Relations*.

Schreck, Carl. 2017. "'Look At Me!': Russian UN Envoy's Rant Stirs Buzz Back Home." Accessed July 10, 2019. https://goo.gl/xsS6Ga.

Security Council, of the Russian Federation. 2013. Osnovy gosudarstvennoy politiki Rossiyskoy Federatsii v oblasti mezhdunarodnoy informatsionnoy bezopasnosti na period do 2020 goda [Foundations of the state policy of the Russian Federation in the field of international information security for the period until 2020]. http://www.scrf.gov.ru/security/information/document114/.

Sharikov, Pavel, and Natalia Stepanova. 2019. "Podkhody SSHA, ES i Rossii k problleme informatsionnoy politiki [US, EU and Russia's approaches to information policy]." *Sovremennaya Evropa* 2: 73–83.

Sharikov, Pavel. 2018a. "Artificial Intelligence, Cyberattack, and Nuclear Weapons— A Dangerous Combination." *Bulletin of the Atomic Scientists* 74 (6): 368–373.

Sharikov, Pavel. 2018b. "Informatsionnyy suverenitet i vmeshatel'stvo vo vnutrenniye dela v rossiysko-amerikanskikh otnoshenyiakh [Information sovereignty and interference in domestic affairs in the Russian-US relations]." *Mezhdunarodnyye protsessy* 16 (3): 170–188.

Sharikov, Pavel. 2018c. "Understanding the Russian Approach to Information Security." Accessed November 23, 2019. https://www.europeanleadershipnetwork.org/commentary/understanding-the-russian-approach-to-information-security/.

Strel'tsov, A. A., R.A. Sharyapov, and V.V. Yashchenko. 2016. Kratkiy kommentariy i predlozheniya k p.13 Doklada Gruppy pravitel'stvennykh ekspertov po dostizheniyam v sfere informatizatsii i telekommunikatsiy v sfere mezhdunarodnoy bezopasnosti [Brief comment and suggestions to paragraph 13 of the Report of the Group of Governmental Experts on Developments in the field of information and telecommunications in the context of international security]. Moskva: Institut problem informatsionnoy bezopasnosti Moskovskogo gosudarstvennogo universiteta imeni M.V.Lomonosova.

Tannenwald, Nina. 1999. "The Nuclear Taboo: The United States and the Normative Basis of Nuclear Non-Use." *International Organization* 53 (3): 433–468.

Tikk, Eneken, and Mika Kerttunen. 2018. *Parabasis. Cyber-Diplomacy in Stalemate.* Norwegian Institute of International Affairs (Oslo).

Chapter 6

China's Conception of Cyber Sovereignty

Rhetoric and Realization

Rogier Creemers[1]

INTRODUCTION

Since its initial connection to the global Internet in the 1990s, China has experienced a tremendous technological leap forward. Over 850 million Chinese individuals have become network users (CNNIC 2019), using increasingly sophisticated devices to access a rapidly burgeoning digital economy. Chinese hardware and software businesses, including Alibaba, Tencent, Huawei, and ZTE, have become industry leaders with a growing global footprint. Technology questions have swiftly gained political prominence, reflected in the creation and expansion of institutions such as the Cyberspace Administration of China (CAC) and the Central Commission for Cybersecurity and Informatization, chaired by Xi Jinping personally (Creemers 2019). Yet, the nomenclature of the latter body also points at a tension fundamental to China's technology policy: while informatization—the introduction of information technologies (ITs) into social and economic life—promises considerable benefits, it equally creates considerable security concerns.

These concerns are not limited to technical questions surrounding the integrity, availability, and correct functioning of IT systems and the data stored within them. For decades, the Chinese leadership has feared ideological subversion, and has designated online content as a potential weapon for "peaceful evolution" (Wang 2011). In recent years, the growing adoption of ITs and tensions resulting from China's expanding geopolitical role have led to new worries, particularly in relation to the United States. Overall, China sees itself standing at the wrong end of a digital divide, where the distribution of resources and capabilities in cyberspace is highly asymmetric

(Shen 2016). The Snowden revelations, US technology export bans targeting ZTE and Huawei, and the discontinuation of security support for Windows XP each highlighted vulnerabilities resulting from forced reliance on currently irreplaceable US technology. Until its reform process, the Internet Corporation for Assigned Names and Numbers (ICANN) was often viewed as an extension of the US government. US-led efforts to curtail the global presence of Huawei, particularly its participation in the standardization process for fifth-generation mobile networks (5G) form one of the major elements of what some observers already call the "US-China technology cold war" (Yuan 2019). Concerns about surveillance and espionage, the survival of national economic champions and even China's basic ability to access the global Internet thus joined propaganda and ideology in Chinese technology policy.

Inasmuch as the tensions between China and the United States (or more broadly, the "like-minded" nations) result from competing national interests, they are also the product of opposed views on the role of IT in the relationship between the state, citizens, and the economy. Since the 1990s, the U.S. tech community has espoused a "free and open" view of the Internet, embodying American liberal democratic norms including free speech, access to information and free-market capitalism, as well as some of the libertarian ethics of the academic and engineering communities that created the Internet. The economic dominance of the US tech industry, and the central role played by these communities, meant these views were nearly universally disseminated without much opposition as the Internet expanded in the decades since (Demchak 2016). Over the past decade, however, China has become increasingly vocal and active in defending a different approach, one based on "cyber sovereignty" (*wangluo zhuquan*).

Cyber sovereignty has become a mainstay in documents and statements for international consumption since its first high-profile appearance in the 2010 White Paper outlining China's position on the Internet (SCIO 2010). Together with Russia, China proposed a Code of Conduct for state behavior in the United Nations General Assembly in 2011 (UN 2011) and again in 2015 (UN 2015). Sovereignty was the first of five principles for international cooperation in cyberspace that the Chinese delegation proposed at the 2012 Budapest Conference on Cyberspace (MFA 2012), and the second item in the Wuzhen Declaration that China proposed at the first World Internet Conference in 2014 (WIC 2014). It has been a repeated element in speeches by top leaders including General Secretary Xi Jinping (Xi 2015) and ex-Internet "czar" Lu Wei (Lu 2014), as well as a key objective in China's national cybersecurity strategy (CAC 2016a), its Cybersecurity Law (NPC 2016C), its development program for the ICT sector (Central Committee and State Council 2016), and its international cyber strategy (MFA 2017).

These policy documents usually define cyber sovereignty in vague and broad terms. In the words of Xi Jinping, a state has the right "to choose its online development path, its network management model and its public Internet policies, and to equal participation in international cyberspace governance." In turn, states should refrain from "engaging in cyber hegemony, interfering in other countries' internal affairs, and engaging in, tolerating or supporting online activities harming the national security of other countries" (Xi 2015). Yet, what this implies in specific national and international legal, regulatory and policy questions is often unclear, and subject to considerable debate in China itself (Zeng, Stevens and Chen 2017). Existing literature has primarily focused on the discussion of sovereignty in diplomatic processes and foreign policy, such as global Internet governance regimes including ICANN, WSIS, and the Internet Governance Forum (Shen Hong 2016; Mueller 2012; Arsène 2012), military and strategic cybersecurity (Swaine 2013; Harold, Libicky and Stuth Cevallos 2016; Kolton 2017; Lindsay 2014), and the reshaping of the global cyber order (Demchak 2016). However, in this literature, cyber sovereignty is largely taken as given, and the substance of the concept, as well as its role as an organizing principle for cyberspace, receives little attention. This chapter thus intends to bookend this body of literature by supplementing two elements: first, how the cyber sovereignty concept emerges as part of China's broader approach to foreign policy, and second, how Chinese authorities have structured the domestic legal, regulatory, and policy landscape in order to realize the goals sovereignty entails.

This chapter contains two sections. The first section explores the development of China's conception of sovereignty, both general and cyber-related, against a historical background. It will pay particular attention to how China's reading of sovereignty embodies its broader views of the global order, as well as to the multidimensional nature of the sovereignty concept. It will identify two major components of the sovereignty concept: a normative component defining how states should conduct themselves in cyberspace, and a capability component that identifies the governance and material resources and mechanisms a state requires to realize the normative component in a potentially antagonistic environment. The second section will review how China has sought to construct these governance and material resources through law, regulation, and policy. It finds the Chinese state has mainly sought to institute and consolidate effective control over online actors, activities, and content through a process of territorialization, indigenization, and investment, while maintaining technical interoperability with the global Internet. Even so, there is a considerable degree of complexity: although it is one thing to declare cyber sovereignty, it is quite another thing to unpick the tightly woven fabric of the digital society without undue harm, particularly as the interests of various Chinese stakeholders are often at odds. The conclusion will discuss practical and theoretical implications of these processes for the global Internet.

THE CONCEPT OF SOVEREIGNTY IN CYBERSPACE

Parallel Histories

While the classical attribution of sovereignty to the 1648 Peace of Westphalia has been disputed, it is generally accepted that the notion of sovereignty— supreme and exclusive political authority within a bounded territory—was consolidated across Europe in the seventeenth century. This international order was based on the principles of non-intervention and sovereign equal- ity: no foreign entity outranked the ruler of a territory, or was permitted to interfere in its internal affairs (Krasner 1999). This was particularly impor- tant with regard to religion. Religious wars had wrought havoc across the continent for over a century. In this sense, with the principle of *cuius region, eius religio*, sovereignty expressed an agreement to disagree: disputes over alleged universal moral truths would no longer form a justification for con- flict. In the centuries since, the sovereign state has become the primary form of territorial organization worldwide.

To be sure, the sovereignty principle has often been honored in the breach as much as the observance. The attempted invasion by monarchical powers into revolutionary France, for instance, was largely justified by arguments for regime change. Racist ideas concerning "civilization" withheld sovereignty from much of the non-European world until after World War II. Yet, as decolonizing states increasingly achieved sovereignty and self-determination, another trend toward constraining sovereignty started gaining traction: one to limit state cruelty and injustice. In the wake of the Holocaust, the Universal Declaration on Human Rights became the first component of a growing body of human rights law. The Helsinki Process of the 1970s created commitments on civil rights that greatly encouraged dissident and democratic movements in the USSR and its satellite states (Thomas 2001). Following the end of the Cold War, doctrines such as the Responsibility to Protect further eroded the authority of the non-intervention norm (Glanville 2013). Lastly, *de facto* if not *de jure*, economic globalization has grown to considerably curtail the space for movement of states, and consolidated the dominance of a (neo-) liberal capitalist model around the world (Stein 2016).

China's approach to sovereignty, in contrast, was predominantly concerned with a drive to counteract the presence of imperialist powers that had estab- lished extraterritorial rule in their concessions and had taken over a number of Chinese government authorities, and start China on a path back toward wealth and strength (Schell and Delury 2014). Their efforts rarely met with success. At the end of World War I, China hoped to cash its material support for the allies with the return of German-held concessions in Shandong. Delegation member (and later International Court of Justice judge) Wellington Koo eloquently argued that the Wilsonian principles of independence and self-determination implied Japan's competing claims should be rejected. The territories were subsequently handed over to Japan as part of a compromise to mitigate tensions in the Pacific and stave off Japanese calls for the explicit recognition of racial equality in the League of Nations (MacMillan 2011, chapters 23–24). In China, this disappointment triggered dejection, protests, a transformational nationalist cultural movement (Forster 2018), the establishment of the Chinese Communist Party, and a lingering sense that, in the final analysis, foreign powers were not serious in their stated commitment to international law, but would use it as an instrument of power (Kent 2008). China's task, therefore, would be to acquire power, not play the law game.

Distrust continued to color the foreign relations of the Chinese Republic and People's Republic, even with its nominal allies. During World War II, even though Chiang Kai-shek managed to secure agreements ending extraterritoriality and renouncing territorial concessions from Britain and the United States, the alliance was strained due to Chiang's—not unjustified—sense that both countries were only doing the bare minimum to keep China in the war and Japanese soldiers tied up (Mitter 2013). Ideological differences, disagreements on relationships with the West, and competition for leadership in the global Communist movement led Mao to curtail relationships with the Soviet Union in the early 1960s. China's near-total isolation from global diplomacy would last until the 1970s, when gradual overtures toward the United States led to Beijing's takeover of the Chinese membership of the UN, hitherto held by Taipei, and the recognition of the People's Republic by most nations worldwide. The Dengist reforms further spurred openness to the outside world, as China started participating in numerous global diplomatic and legal regimes. Yet, even as China developed a more pragmatic form of global engagement, the rhetorical basis of China's foreign policy remained the Five Principles of Peaceful Coexistence, developed in the mid-1950s, of which sovereignty was the most important one (Kent 2008).

The Tiananmen events of 1989 underscored the distance the regime would go to, to safeguard its existence, and in a certain sense, their aftermath has continued to shape China's relationship with the outside world. Coinciding with the end of Communist regimes in Eastern Europe and the dissolution of the Soviet Union, the West came to believe that Tiananmen indicated it would only be a matter of time until the Chinese regime would follow them into the annals of history (Pei 2006; Chang 2010). Human rights became an important part of American and European diplomatic efforts toward China, and democratization became one of the key themes of China scholarship. The Chinese leadership, however, considered its response to the Tiananmen protests as a regrettable but necessary defensive measure. Since then, stability maintenance (*weiwen*) has been one of the cornerstones of Chinese domestic politics, affecting areas ranging from media and education to policing and surveillance (Wang and Minzner 2015). The explicit Western support for the Tiananmen protests, as well as liberal activism in the decades since, has fostered further distrust among the leadership about Western intentions vis-à-vis China. Senior leaders and party media often refer to the efforts by "foreign hostile powers" (Hu 2011) that attempt to Westernize and divide China, or subvert CCP leadership. China's conception of sovereignty embodies the core of these tensions: China's definition of sovereignty primarily concerns the integrity of its political structure, while Western states consider this a defence of exactly those abuses that the more conditional, post–Cold War reading of sovereignty sought to curtail.

Sovereignty and Cyberspace

The controversy concerning cyber sovereignty is one specific manifestation of these broader tensions. Here as well, China's views of the role of the state evolved separate from those in the West, where the trend has been one of progressive withdrawal of the state. For the first few decades of their development, information technologies were primarily driven by national security interests, and more specifically, intelligence, surveillance, and encryption (Corera 2015), as well as prestige projects such as Apollo. However, the growing adoption of computers by businesses and individuals meant that states gradually lost their exclusive control over networking and encryption technologies. In the United States, a budding community of academics and engineers started building what became the Internet, on the basis of libertarian ethical principles of openness, transparency, and skepticism of government. Governments attempted to resist their efforts for a while, during the crypto wars of the 1980s. But the relaxed political environment following the end of the Cold War encouraged the broad adoption of this mind-set, including by governments. No longer a secretive part of the state's security arsenal, information technology came to symbolize the post–Cold War belief that liberal democracy and free-market capitalism were the inevitable end of history (Demchak 2016).

In this techno-optimist view, cyberspace had become a phenomenon all of its own, in which traditional government no longer played a significant role. John Perry Barlow's Declaration of the Independence of Cyberspace explicitly claimed that governments, "weary giants of flesh and steel," no longer had sovereignty in the digital domain (Morrison 2019). Technology businesses enthusiastically embraced this narrative of openness, with its rejection of strong government regulation, as it allowed them to rapidly grow on a global scale. Political and economic elites came to see digital technology as a solution for a wide variety of economic and social ills, but also as a battering ram against the remaining bastions of authoritarianism. The reduced role of the state also became clear in many aspects of Internet governance, for instance, in ICANN and the Internet Engineering Task Force (IETF), where the multi-stakeholder model became the norm (Dutton and Peltu 2008). In this model, technical and business communities, as well as civil society, became at least as important as government in creating governance rules for the Internet.

China's relative latecomer status to information technologies meant it had little influence or participation in the emergence of these processes. Nonetheless, it espoused its own version of techno-optimism, which led it to espouse information technologies enthusiastically with its agenda of "informatization" (*xinxihua*) (Qu 2010). This optimistic view shared the basic principle that digital technology could address socioeconomic questions, but fundamentally disagreed with its liberal democratic precepts. Rather, technologies were marshalled as part of the broader CCP project that sought to combine economic development with strict political control, under the exclusive authority of the party (Central Committee and State Council 2016). Related tactics the party employed elsewhere were extended into the sphere of technologies, including media control and limitations to foreign and private participation in strategic economic sectors. By design, these tactics limited both commercial opportunities for foreign players, and the political liberalization foreign observers hoped for, leading to growing criticism. It is in response to this criticism, as well as the growing prominence of cyber-related questions in the diplomatic realm, that the concept of cyber sovereignty entered the political jargon.

In 2010, the Chinese government published its first comprehensive justification of its approach to cyberspace governance. This White Paper stated that, as the Internet fell under the jurisdiction of Chinese sovereignty, everyone within Chinese territory was obliged to obey Chinese laws and regulations (SCIO 2010). In 2012, at the Budapest Conference on Cyber Issues, China proposed five principles for international cooperation on cyberspace, echoing the Five Principles of Peaceful Coexistence. Sovereignty was the first of these, defined as the entitlement of every state to "formulate its policies and laws in light of its history, traditions, culture, language and customs (MFA 2012)." At that point in time, the chief matter of concern was online content. Subsequent policy documents have slightly expanded on these principles, or were updated to reflect new concerns. The Wuzhen Declaration, circulated at the first World Internet Conference in 2014, stated that "We should respect each country's rights to the development, use and governance of the Internet, refrain from abusing resources and technological strengths to violate other countries' Internet sovereignty" (WIC 2014). Xi Jinping reiterated this stance in his Wuzhen speech the following year (XI 2015). The 2016 National Cyberspace Security Strategy explicitly defended states' rights to "prevent, curb and punish the online dissemination of harmful information endangering national security and interests, and to safeguard order in cyberspace" (CAC 2016a). The most elaborate discussion of sovereignty in a policy document can be found in the 2017 International Strategy of Cooperation on Cyberspace, and deserves to be quoted in full.

> As a basic norm in contemporary international relations, the principle of sovereignty enshrined in the UN Charter covers all aspects of state-to-state relations, which also includes cyberspace. Countries should respect each other's right to choose their own path of cyber development, model of cyber regulation and Internet public policies, and participate in international cyberspace governance on an equal footing. No country should pursue cyber hegemony, interfere in other countries' internal affairs, or engage in, condone or support cyber activities that undermine other countries' national security.
>
> Upholding sovereignty in cyberspace not only reflects governments' responsibility and right to administer cyberspace in accordance with law, but also enables countries to build platforms for sound interactions among governments, businesses and social groups. This will foster a healthy environment for the advancement of information technology and international exchange and cooperation.
>
> National governments are entitled to administer cyberspace in accordance with law. They exercise jurisdiction over ICT infrastructure, resources and activities within their territories, and are entitled to protect their ICT systems and resources from threat, disruption, attack and destruction so as to safeguard citizens' legitimate rights and interests in cyberspace. National governments are entitled to enact public policies, laws and regulations with no foreign interference. Countries should exercise their rights based on the principle of sovereign equality and also perform their due duties. No country should use ICT to interfere in other countries' internal affairs or leverage its advantage to undermine the security of other countries' ICT product and service supply chain. (MFA 2017)

China's Concept of Cyber Sovereignty: The Normative Dimension

The above descriptions, however vague, do allow the abstraction of three implicit general principles underpinning the cyber sovereignty concept. The first principle is that national governments enjoy sovereign rights against other national governments. This principle primarily is a response against the universalist claims of the proponents of online openness. By reserving the right to control all online activities under their jurisdiction to national governments, this principle rejects the applicability of universal rights, including free expression and access to information, as well as potential moves by adversaries to realize those rights, for instance, through circumvention software. It is also up to individual states to decide how to use technology for purposes such as domestic surveillance and law enforcement. At a secondary level, it defends the right of states to organize and develop their digital industries as they see fit. This can entail development strategies including state subsidies and other forms of support, but also market access and security review regimes for foreign software and hardware, as discussed below.

The second principle is that national governments enjoy sovereignty over all non-state actors, be they domestic or foreign. This principle opposes the multistakeholder model of Internet governance that had been developed through institutions such as ICANN and the IETF, and endorsed by WSIS and the IGF. Instead, even if the technical and commercial communities have an important role to play, final authority should be exercised by nation-states through intergovernmental institutions. China's call for transforming ICANN into a specialized UN body under the ITU is perhaps the most prominent manifestation of this principle. Nonetheless, China has also come to propose a "multi-party" model, in which the consultative role of non-state entities is explicitly recognized. The importance of this model should not be overstated. China's Internet ecology consists of numerous industry associations and professional bodies that fall under the formal authority of state ministries, or whose senior officials are appointed by the CCP. Business leaders, too, are often party members. While that does not mean monolithic acceptance of central state policy—often quite the opposite—this model combines a semblance of institutional pluralism while maintaining a considerable degree of political control.

The third principle is sovereign equality of states in Internet governance. Under this principle, no state should have more power than others, or seek hegemony. This principle clearly targets what China sees as the hegemonic position of the United States, but it also has important tactical considerations in the multilateral context. As evidenced by the high level of support for the reforms Russia and China proposed in the ITU meeting of 2012 (Klimberg 2013), as well as for the Open-Ended Working Group on norms for state behavior in cyberspace at the 2018 UN General Assembly, a significant number of countries worldwide at least partially share China's position. In other words, the sovereignty narrative is also attractive to small and midsize player with whom China might seek common cause.

China's Concept of Cyber Sovereignty: The Capability Dimension

The three abovementioned normative principles undergird China's diplomatic efforts, but have also inspired an ongoing expansion of domestic measures to ensuring sovereignty can be realized for China itself, even in the absence of international adoption. These measures have converged around three core strategies: territorialization, indigenization, and investment.

Territorial boundaries are a key component of the concept of sovereignty, but have been largely anathema in discussions on cyberspace. From a technical perspective, geography plays no meaningful role in the functioning of the Internet, even if the underlying infrastructure is territorial, and the absence of online borders was key to the techno-optimist view of cyberspace as a completely *sui generis* creature. Unsurprisingly, the Chinese government has taken a rather different approach. In 2013, CAC director Lu Wei stated that cyberspace is an extension of real space, and that it is, therefore, not a "land outside the law" (*fa wai zhi di*, Lu 2013). Yet, claiming jurisdiction over cyberspace implies having to define its limits and instituting border controls. Partly, the Chinese government has been able to do so through physical infrastructure: the Great Firewall's hardware is mainly located at China's international gateways (Lee 2018). But territorialization can also take place through regulatory means: by mandating that particular actors, activities, and data are located within China, jurisdictional questions are avoided altogether.

The indigenization strategy intends to increase the proportion of technology used in Chinese cyberspace that is produced by Chinese suppliers. For most of the 2000s, the vast majority of information technology products used in China originated from foreign businesses, from Cisco routers in the network infrastructure to Microsoft operating systems, from Apple smartphones and laptops to domain names purchased from foreign registrars. In 2014, a party journal claimed that 82 percent of servers, 73.9 percent of storage equipment, 95.6 percent of operating systems and 91.7 percent of databases in the country were foreign-sourced (Zhao and Xu 2014). A number of events highlighted China's vulnerability to both foreign corporate decisions and governmental acts. When Microsoft announced in early 2014 that it would no longer support Windows XP, for instance, this operating system was still in use in the majority of Chinese computers. In response, China banned Windows 8 from government systems (Kai 2014), and Microsoft reversed its position. The Snowden revelations generated widespread concern about the possible implantation of backdoors or other forms of malicious code into foreign ICT equipment (Xi 2013, *People's Daily* 2014). For both economic and political reasons, the Chinese government has increasingly sought to substitute foreign suppliers by domestic counterparts across a range of sectors. As a result, foreign content providers and online platforms have either not gained a significant foothold on the Chinese market, or in the case of Google, ended their Chinese activities as they were unwilling to comply with government demands. The four brands Huawei, Oppo, Vivo, and Xiaomi combined now hold over 80 percent of China's market share. China has also attempted to develop indigenous technological standards and stimulated its domestic businesses to participate in the formulation of global standards, most notably 5G. The success of this indigenization strategy nevertheless remains uneven. In many areas, including operating systems and semiconductors, Chinese products lag far behind foreign counterparts in quality, security, and market success (Triolo 2019). Equally, the international adoption of Chinese standards, as well as Chinese participation in global standards, remains extremely limited.

To remedy these weaknesses, the Chinese government has deployed several industrial policy schemes across the technological spectrum. One major destination of funding has been research and education, both for general purposes and specific technical capabilities. Universities have been encouraged to expand computer science and cybersecurity curricula, expanding China's talent pool, with an increasing focus on emerging technologies such as big data and artificial intelligence (State Council 2016). Support is also offered through favorable government procurement policies or direct subsidies under industrial plans such as Made in China 2015 and the Internet Plus plan (Wübbeke et al. 2016). The Digital Silk Road component of the Belt-Road Initiative supports Chinese technology businesses in their international development (Shen 2018). Some of these strategies have, however, backfired. For instance, governmental guidance funds meant to provide venture capital for the technology sector have been less successful than intended (Feng 2018). Moreover, governmental support for China's technology businesses is a major factor driving the worsening of relations with major trading partners.

REALIZING SOVEREIGNTY AT HOME

The Chinese government has used various combinations of these three strategies in order to realize its cyber sovereignty objectives, going back to the early 2000s in some cases. This process has intensified since 2013, for a number of contributory reasons. Some of these concern the rapidly expanding adoption and complexity of ITs in general. From the point of view of sovereignty, they can also be seen as a response to two trends at the international level. First, China's sovereignty stance has found little traction in existing cyber governance circles thus far. Partly, this is due to symbolic reasons. "Like-minded" governments have come to see sovereignty as a shibboleth to justify of authoritarianism. Consequently, even if many of them have come to favor a somewhat greater degree of governmental control, they have been hesitant to endorse the inclusion of national sovereignty. On the Chinese side, this has stimulated accusations of hypocrisy. Chinese commentators have argued that initiatives such as the US buildup of military cyber capabilities, and the introduction of the EU General Data Protection Regulation, are expressions of sovereign power in cyber affairs. Second, the likelihood of any agreement has become more remote as the Sino-American relationship has sharply deteriorated, most prominently through tensions concerning digital technology. During the second term of the Obama administration, the United States stepped up pressure against China on issues concerning cyber espionage, leading to an agreement in 2015 that neither state would conduct or condone such activities (Sevasto-pulo and Dyer 2015). The advent of the nationalist Trump administration, which campaigned on a strong anti-China platform, and growing disillu-sion about the treatment of American businesses severely weakened the stabilizing role of the trade component in the overall relationship. As part of a broader trade war, the US government launched an investigation con-cerning Chinese technology transfer requirements and intellectual property infringement, finding these constituted unreasonable burdens to US busi-nesses (Congressional Research Service 2018). It also imposed sanctions against ZTE and Huawei for the violation of sanctions against Iran (SCMP 2018). Reversing decades of economic integration, "decoupling" became a buzzword both in Washington and Beijing, particularly in the tech sec-tor (Panda 2019). These evolutions fostered a greater sense of urgency in Beijing to enhance resilience, autonomy, and self-reliance (*zili gengsheng*, Thomas 2019), while still maintaining the advantages of global connectiv-ity and interoperability. This section will review how this balance has been pursued in the areas of content control, the Domain Name System (DNS), data protection, and the engagement with foreign digital corporations.

Content Control

Perhaps the best-known boundary in cyberspace is the Great Firewall of China, the filtering infrastructure at the international gateways of China's telecommunications networks that filters out undesirable content. Established in the late 1990s, it has been upgraded of the years to effectively remove from Chinese audiences content produced outside of Beijing's ability to control. This includes explicitly political content, such as websites defending Falun Gong, the Tibetan or Uyghur cause, online media outlets reporting critically in China, social media networks that had been implicated in political events such as the Arab Spring and color revolutions in ex-Soviet states, as well as morally undesirable content such as pornography (Griffiths 2019). Allegedly, it was used to leverage the "Great Cannon" attack, which targeted developer platform GitHub in 2015 (Marczak et al. 2015). The Great Firewall has also been periodically updated to target circumvention software. For instance, par-ticular commercial VPN services work less effectively around major national celebrations, and The Onion Router (TOR), which enables anonymous and encrypted web access, does not function reliably from China.

Yet, the Great Firewall is not the only barrier to foreign content. Starting in 2000, authorities started expanding the previous regulatory regime for media from the traditional realm to the Internet. The first provisional regulations already contained a ban on foreign audiovisual content on Chinese websites (SARFT 2000, Art. 16[g]), and imposed licensing requirements for online operators. The permitted share of foreign participants in online information services' joint ventures was limited (State Council 2000, Art. 17), while the Chinese WTO accession schedule limited foreign market access for many media-related activities (MOFCOM 2001). Subsequent regulations barred foreign participation from activities such as news (SCIO and MII 2005, Art. 9), online publishing (CAC 2016b, Art. 10), and provision of audiovisual content (SARFT 2004, Art. 7). Unsurprisingly, these regulatory barriers, in combination with a protectionist stance in favor of Chinese businesses, meant no large foreign online operator has been able to maintain a sustained presence on Chinese territory. Google had set up operations in Beijing in 2005 but closed down its Chinese search engine in 2010 after it discovered state-backed hacking operations into its user data (Waddell 2016). More recently, Facebook attempted to open a start-up incubator subsidiary in Hangzhou, but after a miscommunication between local and central authorities meant it did not obtain the required permits (Liao 2018). Instead, the market has come to be dominated by the domestic massive online platform companies Alibaba, Tencent, and Baidu. Among a list of top 100 mobile apps on the Chinese market as measured in market penetration in 2017, only a handful are produced by a foreign entity (Jiguang n.d.).

In governing online content, Beijing thus has employed a combination of the territorialization (Great Firewall) and indigenization (barring foreign businesses) approaches, with considerable success. This not only has substantial economic benefits, it also provides the leadership with a more effectively governed landscape. Regular tussles notwithstanding, over the years, a modus vivendi has emerged between China's online businesses and the central government. Government recognizes private business has generated considerable economic and technological achievement, and thus maintains a mostly positive attitude, while businesses do not upset the governmental applecart, and are far more trusted on politically sensitive matters than their foreign equivalents (Creemers 2018).

The Domain Name System (DNS)

In the early days of the Internet, China's participation in ICANN was limited, partially due to a comparative lack of Chinese expertise, but also because of political objections against the structure and politics of ICANN. Some of these objections were quite specific. ICANN, as a private corporation, did not subscribe to usual diplomatic protocols concerning Taiwan. Rather, the Taiwanese government participated equally in ICANN institutions, including the Governmental Advisory Council (GAC). China also found ICANN lagging on technical questions affecting its claims and preferences, particularly in terms of adapting the DNS to adapt Chinese and other non-Roman alphabets. China boycotted ICANN conferences between 2001 and 2009.[2] On these matters, China and ICANN reached an agreement. China would send a MIIT representative to the GAC, while ICANN would refer to Taiwan as "Chinese Taipei." It would also create a fast track for the inauguration of top-level domains (TLDs) in non-Western scripts. Moreover, management powers for the Chinese character TLDs were handed over to CNNIC, providing a further economic incentive for the continued support of the ICANN system (Mueller 2012).

Broader problems in China's perception of ICANN were, perhaps ironically, its multistakeholder functioning on the one hand, and its close relationship with the US government on the other. From 1998 onwards, ICANN had managed the DNS through a contract with the Department of Commerce National Telecommunications and Information Administration, yet governments played a minimal role in its internal processes. On the one hand, China was concerned this meant decisions with potential strategic relevance could be taken outside of governmental control. On the other, there were fears concerning American preponderance in Internet infrastructure and traffic control. A 2012 *People's Daily* piece, for instance, laments (incorrectly) that all thirteen root servers are set up within the United States, and that 80 percent of global Internet traffic passed through the United States (*People's Daily* 2012). These objections pushed China to propose a different arrangement to govern the DNS: ICANN, or its functions, should be brought under the control of the United Nations, or more specifically, under the aegis of the International Telecommunications Union. First presented at the first World Summit on the Information Society (Segal 2017), this position quickly became a core element of its international cyber strategy. Moreover, China was not the only country dissatisfied with the ICANN status quo: India equally proposed transferring responsibilities for Internet governance to the ITU (Shen 2016, 89).

Even so, relationships between Beijing and ICANN have improved considerably over the years. For its part, ICANN has worked hard to establish good relationships with Chinese authorities during this process. It opened its first Engagement Centre in Beijing at the ICANN46 meeting (ICANN 2013). This center liaises closely with authorities in order to build mutual trust and deepen collaboration. Then-ICANN CEO Fadi Chehadé joined the high-level advisory committee for the Wuzhen World Internet Conference as cochairman (Xinhua 2015). China, equally, has made efforts to build closer relations. The ICANN50 meeting in London, most notably, was the venue for CAC director Lu Wei to make his first high-profile international appearance (Lu 2014). Furthermore, the ICANN transition away from a direct contractual relationship with the US government and toward nongovernmental, multi-stakeholder stewardship assuaged some of Beijing's concerns vis-à-vis the organization. Even so, some ambivalence remains in China's stance. While ICANN reform seems less of a priority for Beijing, the International Strategy for Cooperation in Cyberspace, as well as the Chinese submission to the UN Open-Ended Working Group on Information and Telecommunications still contain references to the need to create a multilateral Internet governance system, and to ensure that institutions governing strategic Internet resources, such as root servers, remain "truly independent of any state's control" (MFA 2019). Partly, this reflects continuing concerns that, as a U.S.-registered corporation, ICANN could be compelled to limit its services to China, for instance, through a process akin to the Department of Commerce Entity List, which limits, among others, technology exports to specific businesses or institutions. Another element is that numerous other strategic resources, such as the root servers on which the DNS depends, remain owned or operated by US entities, further increasing perceived risk.

In the meantime, China has sought to mitigate some of the risks it saw emanating from the ICANN structure through domestic regulation. Almost from the start, the administration of domain names became a government affair, eschewing the multistakeholder approach adopted elsewhere. In 1997, the newly established CNNIC, under the Chinese Academy of Sciences, became responsible for managing Chinese aspects of the DNS, including administration of the .cn domain (Xue 2004). CNNIC also required notification from server operators using other top-level domains (Ermert and Hughes 2003, 202). Successive regulations promulgated in 2002 and 2004 started to extend Chinese jurisdiction over the domain name system, referring consistently to "our country's domain name system." Not only did they encourage the adoption of Chinese-language domain names, they also applied preexisting provisions on content censorship to domain names, and required providers to cease resolving DNS addresses upon request by public security departments (MII 2002; MII 2004). But perhaps, most importantly, it unilaterally took the initiative to create an alternative system to handle Chinese-language domain names, which still remained globally compatible. While this system was operated relatively secretly at first, by 2006, the *People's Daily* proudly boasted that "[Chinese] Internet users don't have to surf the web via the servers under the management of the Internet Corporation for Assigned Names and Numbers of the United States (Cited in Mueller 2012)." Also, the continuing tensions over ICANN's role led the Chinese government to subsidize research on something that came to be known as IPv9: a separate technical protocol that allows systems to be "independent of the US Internet but [. . .] Internet compatible" (Wang and Shebzukhov 2019). Nevertheless, IPv9 seems not to play a role of any significance thus far.

New DNS regulations from 2017 illustrate the growing trend toward localization. These regulations require entities running DNS root servers registered in China to locate their servers inside Chinese territory. Domain name registries must be based domestically, and the top-level domains these registries manage thus explicitly fall under Chinese jurisdiction. Domain name registrars equally must be Chinese entities running their systems within Chinese territory. Both registries and registrars must establish domestically based emergency response systems, and create localized backups of their databases (MIIT 2017). At the same time, there has been a certain degree of restraint. A draft version of these regulations contained a provision that "domain names with network access services within the borders" must register their domain name with a Chinese provider (MIIT 2016, Art. 37). These requirements have been dropped in the final version, after they were widely seen as rendering all foreign websites in China unlawful (Global Times 2016). Even so, suspicions against foreign intelligence services' surveillance capabilities led to the inclusion of an article in draft regulations on data protection published in May 2019, which require that domestic Chinese Internet traffic must be exclusively routed through Chinese territory (CAC 2019c). The topography of China's Internet, with only a limited number of international gateways, may facilitate the implementation of this requirement.

Data Protection

Like many governments, the Chinese leadership has identified data as a crucial resource for development, but also a potential source of vulnerability. Many of those risks, such as data leaks leading to fraud and abuse, are domestic, but authorities have also voiced concern over the potential harm stemming from data on Chinese citizens and important businesses flowing abroad. Over the past few years, the leadership has thus sought to centralize its previously fragmented regulatory approach to data protection, and data localization is an important element in new regulations. Localization requirements were already issued for financial and healthcare data in 2011 and 2014 respectively (PBoC 2011; NHFPC 2014). A 2013 technical standard required consent of data subjects for data export (Chander and Le 2014). The cybersecurity law would set a general standard across all sectors. Yet, the exact categorization of data to be protected, as well as the specific limitations on their export, have been subject to a to-and-fro between different regulators and stakeholders, as the need for protection is counteracted by both the economic harm from excessive limitations as well as the actual ability of government to implement and enforce data export rules.

This tension has been on display in the drafting process of the cybersecurity law. The first draft, from July 2015, determined that "critical information infrastructure operators" must store both citizens' personal information and "other important data" gathered during their operations within Chinese territory. Critical information infrastructure was broadly defined, as "basic information networks providing services such as public correspondence and radio and television broadcasting; important information systems for important industries such as energy, transportation, water conservation, and finance, and public service areas such as electricity, water and gas utilities, medical and sanitation service and social security; military networks and government affairs networks for state organs at the sub districted city level and above; and networks and systems owned or managed by network service providers with massive numbers of users" (NPC 2015). The term "important data" remained undefined. In the second draft, published a year later, it was changed into "important business data" (NPC 2016), following suggestions from domestic stakeholders (NPC 2016A). Even so, this new term equally remained undefined. In response, forty foreign business groups submitted a statement asking for change, yet without success (Bloomberg 2016). The third draft, from November 2016, omitted the word "citizen," suggesting all personal data collected in China, also from non-Chinese nationals, should be stored locally (NPC 2016B, Art. 37). The final, enacted version of the law maintained this provision, and reverted to the original formulation of "important data," still without definition. It also refined the definition of critical information infrastructure, to "public communication and information services, power, traffic, water resources, finance, public service, e-government, and other critical information infrastructure which—if destroyed, suffering a loss of function, or experiencing leakage of data—might seriously endanger national security, national welfare, the people's livelihood, or the public interest" (NPC 2016C).

In April 2017, the first set of draft regulations addressed the export of both personal information and important data, setting out conditions under which this export was to be prohibited and outlining security review requirements for permitted cases (CAC 2017b). These draft regulations also widened the scope of regulated subjects: every "network operator," defined as "the owner of a network, a manager, and a network service provider," would be required to store personal and important data locally. Important data was defined for the first time, albeit vaguely, as "data that is closely related to national security, economic development, and social and public interests, with specific reference to national relevant standards and important data identification guidelines." A separate technical standard on data export refined the definition, providing a detailed list of specific data and their identifying features in twenty-eight industry sectors (TC260 n.d.). Nonetheless, this list is non-exhaustive, and government departments still retain wide discretion to designate other data as important. In the end, the 2017 draft regulations were not adopted, both due to continuing internal debate and opposition in the WTO under the leadership of the United States and Japan (Lu et al. 2018). Similarly, the technical standard still awaits adoption.

Regulatory efforts regained momentum in the spring of 2019, as two draft regulations emerged: one on general data protection matters, and one on cross-border personal data flows. The former again contained a vaguely worded provision on the export of important data, referring the matter to either the relevant controlling authority or cybersecurity departments. Combining elements from the previous draft regulations and draft standard, it defined important data as "data that, if divulged, may directly affect national security, economic security, social stability, or public health and safety, such as undisclosed government information or large-scale data on the population, genetic health, geography, mineral resources, etc. Important data generally does not include enterprises' production, operations, and internal management information, personal information, etc. (CAC 2019c)." For the export of personal data, it referred to the second, separate draft document. These personal data export regulations, strongly influenced by Europe's GDPR, required all network operators to conduct security assessments before exporting personal data, and to file such operations with provincial cybersecurity authorities. Moreover, they sharply curtailed data gathering activities by foreign entities, stipulating that "overseas organizations, in conducting business activities and when collecting the personal information of domestic users through the Internet and other means, shall fulfill the responsibilities and obligations of network operators in these measures through domestic legal representatives or organizations" (CAC 2019b, Art. 20). At the time of writing, these draft measures have not been approved or taken effect.

The tortuous trajectory of data localization over the past years illustrates the difficult balance regulators seek to strike. There are, on the one hand, clear political and economic incentives to localize Chinese data: it is deemed to provide a defence against overseas intelligence gathering, as well as spur the development of the Chinese cloud industry. On the other hand, particularly when it comes to important data, there are considerable costs to maintaining an overly broad definition as well: enforcement resources might become spread so thin that meaningful protection is not achieved, or business is throttled through excessive red tape. With the predicted adoption of 5G and IoT technologies, these considerations will only grow in complexity.

Tilting the Playing Field

As indicated above, the Chinese government has sought to raise the domestic capabilities of its digital sector through various means, including industrial policy and investment. It has, over the years, published highly detailed plans for the country's informatization (State Council 2016), developed special funding vehicles and structures for information technology, and provided the physical infrastructure it believes necessary. These efforts combine the imperative of economic development with a political goal: domestic players are seen as more secure and amenable to government control than foreign businesses. With this support, and by deftly leveraging the enormous size of the domestic market, Chinese technology businesses have become increasingly competitive with foreign counterparts in numerous sectors. This, in combination with the growing priority of cybersecurity, has raised expectations and intentions that indigenous technology might progressively replace foreign hardware and software.

In some cases, regulations have mandated domestic content for quite some time. For instance, in the area of encryption, China has banned foreign technology since 1999 (Segal 2016, State Council 1999). In 2007, the Ministry of Public Security introduced the first iteration of the multilevel protection system (MLPS) for cybersecurity. This categorizes information networks in five tiers, depending on the potential harm to public and private interests, as well as national security, in case of disruption. Level three and higher networks were required to use domestic cybersecurity technology, and retain domestic cybersecurity monitoring contractors (MPS 2007, Arts. 21, 11). Banking regulators issued standards on "secure and controllable" technology that, in many cases, required technology to be acquired from vendors with at least a presence in China, have domestic intellectual property rights or use domestic encryption tools (Freshfields 2016). However, these regulations were withdrawn following public protests by US officials, as well as quiet lobbying by Chinese banks harboring concerns about being pushed to adopt inferior or less secure technology.

A similar to-and-fro was seen in China's push to indigenize technical standards. In 2003, the Chinese government mandated that all wireless devices sold in China must run WAPI, a domestically developed encryption standard. International standardization bodies such as IEEE and ISO all rejected the standard, Intel announced it would stop shipments of Centrino chip technology, while the US government threatened a WTO suit. It did not take long for China to shelve WAPI at an international level. Even so, foreign device manufacturers ended up providing support for WAPI domestically, indicating the extent to which businesses might comply with Chinese policy, or form local partnerships, even if not legally mandated to do so (Ahmed and Weber

2018). Efforts to popularize a homegrown 3G standard, TD-SCDMA, floundered as the technology was inferior and was only adopted by a few handset makers. This saddled China Mobile, which had been pressured to use the standard against its business judgment, with a severe market disadvantage (Knowledge@Wharton 2011). Another domestic encryption standard, ZUC, fared slightly better: it was approved by the European Telecommunications Standards Institute, and adopted as a voluntary standard by the 3G Partnership Project. In late 2011, the adoption of domestic encryption algorithms became obligatory in 4G networks, which *de facto* mandated ZUC use (MacGregor 2012, 40). However, in 2013, China agreed in negotiations with the United States that ZUC compliance would not be a precondition for market access (USTR 2014).

The MLPS was incorporated in the cybersecurity law, which also created an overlapping mandate to the CAC for critical information infrastructure protection. When new draft regulations for the MLPS were published in June 2018, nearly all references to domestic technology and operators had been removed, with the exception of encryption technology. Instead, the document only explicitly required that operation and maintenance of high-level networks is carried out within Chinese territory (MPS 2018, Art. 29), a requirement that was also present in concurrent draft regulations on critical infrastructure protection (CAC 2017a). The MLPS regulations also banned the unauthorized participation of personnel occupying "critical positions" in highly ranked networks, or those providing cybersecurity services to them, in foreign "cyber attack and defence events," or in other words, hacking competitions (MPS 2018, Art. 54). At the same time, the MLPS draft expanded the scope of level three networks to not only include networks whose disruption affects social stability and national security, but also "particularly gravely" affects the lawful rights and interests of private actors (MPS 2018, Art. 15). The changes in the MLPS do not necessarily constitute a relaxation of constraints on foreign technology. First, the second iteration of the MLPS shifts from a greater focus on self-reporting toward more government audits and scrutiny. Second, a number of supplementary technical standards also affect MLPS, and impose more onerous requirements on operators, including source code delivery and access control (Sacks and Li 2018, 9–10).

Technical standards for cybersecurity are likely to erect market access barriers more broadly. Over the past years, Technical Committee 260 (TC260), which is in charge of developing cybersecurity standards, has published over 300 standards, many of which have since taken effect. While these standards are technically not legally binding, Chinese courts and authorities nevertheless see them as best industry practices, giving them *de facto* a similar effect. In other cases, technical standards are incorporated into regulations by reference, vicariously making them legally binding. The various requirements of this thicket of standards create a range of possible compliance considerations for foreign entities. Where they mandate source code disclosure, businesses rightly worry about disclosure, leaks, and intellectual property loss. Where they mandate data sharing with Chinese government authorities, they may break laws elsewhere or contribute to reputational damage. They may require developing China-only versions of software and hardware, increasing business costs. Ironically, however, this latter element may also limit the export potential of Chinese enterprises. Moreover, the vagueness of these standards (and, more broadly, the cybersecurity law and its attendant regulations) opens the door for uneven enforcement, either for direct political reasons such as the trade war, or as fallout of interdepartmental bickering. These points are, by the very nature of the system's opacity, necessarily opaque. What is certain is that the extent to which foreign businesses can influence standard-setting in China is limited: a limited number of companies, including Microsoft, Cisco and Intel, were invited to join TC260 as late as 2016. They are only allowed in five of the eight Working Groups, and barred from those addressing encryption, classified information system security, and the information security standard system. In at least one case, a standard initiative was moved from an "open" Working Group to a "closed" one after opposition by the former's foreign members (Sacks and Li 2018).

Chinese measures increasingly clearly show the imprint of Sino-American strife, and the US actions against Huawei and ZTE. One example of this is the debate that took place in the framework of the security review process for critical network products and specialized cybersecurity products, also introduced in the cybersecurity law. Draft measures from 2019, which create a mandatory security review process for technology used in critical infrastructure, identify both the possibility of factors such as "politics, diplomacy and trade" to disrupt the controllability, security, and supply chain integrity of products or services, as well as "situations in which product or service providers are funded, controlled, etc., by foreign governments" as priority elements in cybersecurity reviews (CAC 2019a). Moreover, the Chinese government announced it might create an "unreliable entity list," sanctioning foreign businesses boycotting or cutting off supplies to Chinese companies for noncommercial purposes. The Ministry of Foreign Affairs explicitly connected the actual introduction of this list with the extent to which Sino-American trade ties improved (Reuters 2019).

Yet, even if there is broad agreement among Chinese policy makers how foreign technology should be managed, the specific way to do so remains disputed. The controversy surrounding the adoption of a specific version of Windows for government systems provides an instructive example. In the summer of 2017, Ni Guangnan, member of the Chinese Academy of Engineering and a prominent advocate for the development of indigenous operating systems (Ni 2017B) claimed this version should remain outside the government procurement catalogue (Ni 2017), and more broadly, that government operating systems should be "indigenous and controllable (Ni 2017A)." In response, Wang Jun, general engineer at one of the approved third party security evaluators, the China Information Technology Security Evaluation Centres (CNITSEC), stated that the cybersecurity review regime does not discriminate on the basis of nationality. Moreover, Wang indicated that replacing Windows with an indigenous alternative would "not necessarily [be] the best choice" (Transpacifica 2017), citing switchover costs, software incompatibilities, and software quality as reasons. In contrast, Wang hailed the fact that the government edition was developed by a Sino-US joint venture, in which Microsoft cooperated with the China Electronics Technology Group (CETC), with the aim of providing software better responding to user needs and security requirements. Lastly, Wang argued domestic operating systems might not necessarily provide a more secure alternative, merely that the risk profile might be somewhat different. This debate encapsulates many of the key points surrounding the technology substitution question in China, many of which are nonideological or political. Some businesses, such as CETC, care well through technological openness, others would do better if foreign competitors were absent from the market. In many cases, foreign technology is better than Chinese alternatives, and even a Huawei executive has indicated the virtuous effects of competition on innovation and security provide a strong reason to maintain openness (Shih 2015). The existing installed base of foreign technology and integration with other systems means "rip-and-replace" might be very costly.

It is often claimed that the Chinese government uses its close ties to businesses to advance the cause of national champions. This is especially salient in the area of 5G, which lies at the heart of tensions between China and its major trading partners. State-owned telecommunications operator China Mobile granted over half the contracts for its 5G equipment to Huawei (Li 2019), and specific policy plans often indicate local content targets in various sectors and network systems. Furthermore, state-run media outlets regularly target foreign businesses in order to pressure them toward greater compliance, or send political signals. The technology sector is no exception. In July 2019, for instance, Apple was targeted on national radio for allegedly allowing fake reviews to appear on its App Store (CNR 2019). This compounded an already negative picture for Apple in China: Apple's smartphone share plummeted from a high of 27 percent in 2015 to 5 percent in late 2019 (Kirton 2019). Huawei not only took 42 percent of the Chinese domestic market at that time, it also had surpassed Apple as the second largest smartphone manufacturer worldwide. Partly, this may be due to political influence and nationalism among Chinese buyers, but the rapidly growing quality and feature set of Huawei's more competitively priced handsets is likely to be at least as important (Rapoza 2019). Moreover, the handset market may provide one example of how American trade sanctions might backfire: Huawei has prepared by developing or sourcing alternatives for technologies it might not be able to access reliably in the future. The Google Android operating system is one of these. As a plan B, Huawei developed HarmonyOS, a multi-platform system that might replace Android not only in smartphones, but in all kinds of connected devices (Hall 2019). Given Huawei's global market share, this would be a severe blow to the existing duopoly of Google and Apple technology. Even so, it must be remembered that it is not a complete one-way street, and openness continues in other areas: British Telecom became the first foreign mobile operator to gain a nationwide Chinese operating licence in early 2019 (*China Daily* 2019). Moreover, the difficulties still facing Chinese businesses in gaining parity with their foreign counterparts should not be underestimated. China still lags behind in software and hardware components ranging from PC operating systems to semiconductors, chip manufacturing equipment to business software (Triolo 2019). The most important question remains how the decoupling that both the Chinese and American stances are likely to cause will impact the highly integrated global digital economy. With some observers already warning about an "innovation winter" (Houser, forthcoming), sovereignty might come at a high cost.

CONCLUSION AND IMPLICATIONS

China's conception of cyber sovereignty is primarily defensive and reactive, as it aims to ensure CCP control over processes that, in its view, may endanger its leading position. It reflects a legal position, entrenching the party-state's exclusive ability to regulate and police the online world, and rejecting any form of foreign interference. But it is not merely a talking point in international diplomatic processes or a propaganda slogan for domestic consumption. It also refers to the capabilities the leadership deems necessary to realize that legal position in actual reality. To this end, it disposes of a set of policy, legal and regulatory tools that fall under the categories of territorialization, indigenization, and investment.

Within the Chinese policy and academic landscape, cyber sovereignty is nearly universally accepted as a foundation for engagement with global cyber affairs at a matter of principle, and it thus constitutes an organizing principle in domestic cyber governance. Domestic technology use requirements, data localization, increasing scrutiny of foreign content and VPNs, security standards that privilege domestic players and government procurement and subsidy programs are all marshalled in pursuit of sovereignty. Overall, China has sought to maintain interoperability with the global Internet, at the same time as striving to ensure dominance of indigenous online businesses, as well as technological autonomy to the greatest possible extent. Moreover, the increasing tensions with the United States have fostered a greater sense of urgency and unity in Beijing. Nevertheless, there are considerable arguments and differing views among different constituencies on important questions of how this principle is best realized in practice. How, and in which fields, to collaborate with foreign players, the extent to which specific foreign technologies should be banned from certain fields or merely regulated, and how to determine the sort of data that should be nationalized are still open questions.

This trend has not taken place in a vacuum. China's insistence on cyber sovereignty has both been a response to and a catalyst of broader evolutions in global cyber governance. In some cases, other governments have recognized the desirability of jurisdictional powers, referring explicitly to the sovereignty principle. EU digital commissioner Günther Oettinger, for instance, mentioned "digital sovereignty" as an objective for European digital policy (Tost 2015). Sovereignty was recognized as applying to states' use of information technologies in the 2013 and 2015 reports of the United Nations Group of Governmental Experts (Schmitt and Vihul 2017), and is recognized in the *Tallinn Manual*, a comprehensive expert analysis of how international law applies to cyber operations (Schmitt 2017). China is not the only country to institute data localization policies; the EU's General Data Protection Regulation equally requires local storage of personal data under certain circumstances. As governments increasingly assert control over the digital sphere, and as national security questions grow increasingly prominent in global cyber debates, it seems China's approach to sovereignty has to be seen as part of a complex spectrum. While Beijing's stance seems clear-cut and diametrically opposed to that of the United States and its "like-minded" allies in diplomatic discourse, the complexity of the domestic policy and regulatory landscape reveals a more nuanced picture.

To a significant degree, the difference in approaches reflects the contrast in security concepts between Beijing and its Western counterparts. China primarily defines cybersecurity through the lens of "information security" (CAC 2016a), and focuses on the potential impact the uncontrolled circulation of information might have on political, economic, and social stability. It is thus no surprise that content control has historically been the most elaborate component of the cybersecurity landscape. American and European governments, conversely, have largely defined cybersecurity in technical terms, focusing on the integrity, stability, and functioning of information systems and the data stored on them. This, in turn, explains the attention these governments have directed toward the security of telecommunication networks, and in some cases, resorted to banning Chinese suppliers from their domestic markets. It is worth remembering that China, thus far, has not banned specific hardware or software makers from its markets. Equally, China puts a far greater emphasis on economic development its cyber policy, while the United States stresses military, intelligence, and other national security questions relatively more. It is likely that these views will converge somewhat over the years, as illustrated by greater Western attention to disinformation campaigns and fake news, and China's efforts to establish a cybersecurity review regime. The United States seems more amenable to greater state influence over economic affairs, while China is building up its cyber military and intelligence capabilities. Yet, even that convergence is unlikely to lead to greater cooperation or coordination. It is overshadowed by the growing U.S.–China tensions, in which technology plays a central role. It seems that, increasingly inevitably, arrangements in cyberspace will reflect unadorned great power competition, with interests overshadowing values in importance, and political expediency replaces pragmatic cooperation as a key virtue.

This has important implications on the future development of both the development of the digital economy, and of interstate relations pertaining to cyber affairs. The global digital economy as it exists today, developed since the 1990s in a context where there were few national and international regimes on matters ranging from data flows to supply chains. The current process of increasing regulatory nationalization inaugurates a new paradigm in which multinational companies must operate. One likely scenario is that the world will fragment into separate spheres of cooperation with high degrees of internal harmonization, and significant barriers between them. An example of this is the supply of telecommunications equipment. If China's push for technology indigenization is matched by other major states, or leads to reciprocal measures, the global market for telecommunications devices may equally become segregated along the lines of political alignment. What will be the impact on global connectivity, data and information flows is an important subject for future research. Yet, the tightrope that China needs to walk is a precarious one. In the diplomatic realm, China's strong insistence on sovereignty has contributed to a low level of trust between Beijing and its major international interlocutors. It also has, thus far, overshadowed the question in which areas, how and for which purposes China can cooperate with other states—even those ostensibly more closely aligned—in order to enhance cyber governance, continue to stimulate interoperability and innovation, and tackle shared issues affecting the global online ecosystem. Yet, in the economic realm, greater economic internationalization and technical interoperability is imperative for the flourishing of China's digital industry. Moreover, the global digital economy is, seemingly inextricably, linked with China as a manufacturing base and market. With the nature of cyber issues increasing in complexity, and tensions increasing in intensity, the way Beijing will seek to preserve this balance, and how its foreign counterparts will respond, will be a prime factor shaping outcomes in the decades to come.

LIST OF ABBREVIATIONS

CAC: Cyberspace Administration of China
CNNIC: China Internet Network Information Centre
CNR: China National Radio
ICANN: Internet Corporation for Assigned Names and Numbers
MFA: Ministry of Foreign Affairs
MII: Ministry of Information Industry
MIIT: Ministry of Industry and Information Technology
MOFCOM: Ministry of Commerce
MPS: Ministry of Public Security
NHFPC: National Health and Family Planning Commission
NPC: National People's Congress
PBoC: People's Bank of China
SARFT: State Administration of Radio, Film and Television
SCIO: State Council Information Office
SIIO: State Internet Information Office
TC260: Technical Committee 260
USTR: United States Trade Representative
UN: United Nations
WIC: World Internet Conference

NOTES

1. This chapter has been written with the generous support of the Dutch Ministry of Foreign Affairs and the NWO (Netherlands Organization for Scientific Research).

2. Members of the technical community and sector institutions such as the Internet Society of China did attend. Given that these organizations function under party leadership and maintain direct connections with the bodies in charge of Internet governance, this meant that Chinese governmental preferences were still represented, albeit indirectly.

BIBLIOGRAPHY

Ahmed, Shazeda and Steven Weber. 2018. "China's Long Game in Techno-Nationalism." *First Monday* 23 (5–7). http://dx.doi.org/10.5210/fm.v23i5.8085.

Arsène, Séverine. 2012. "The Impact of China on Global Internet Governance in an Era of Privatized Control." Presented at the *Chinese Internet Research Conference*, Los Angeles, May 2012. Accessed November 25, 2019. http://hal.archives-ouver tes.fr/hal-00704196/document.

Bloomberg. 2016. "China Adopts Cybersecurity Law Despite Foreign Opposition." November 7, 2016. Accessed November 29, 2019. https://www.bloomberg.com/ news/articles/2016-11-07/china-passes-cybersecurity-law-despite-strong-foreign-opposition.

CAC. 2016a. "Guojia wangluo kongjian anquan zhanlüe (National Cyberspace Security Strategy)." December 27, 2016. Translation, accessed November 22, 2019. https://chinacopyrightandmedia.wordpress.com/2016/12/27/national-cyberspace-security-strategy/

CAC. 2016b. "Wangluo chuban fuwu guanli guiding (Online Publishing Service Management Rules)." February 4, 2016. Translation, accessed November 29, 2019. https://chinacopyrightandmedia.wordpress.com/2016/02/04/online-publish ing-service-management-rules/

CAC. 2017a. "Guanjian xinxi jichu sheshi anquan baohu tiaoli (zhengqiu yijian gao) (Critical Information Infrastructure Security Protection Regulations)." July 10, 2017. Translation, accessed November 29, 2019. https://chinacopyrightandmedia .wordpress.com/2017/07/10/critical-information-infrastructure-security-protectio n-regulations/

CAC. 2017b. "Geren xinxi he zhongyao shuju chujing anquan pinggu banfa (zhengqiu yijian gao) (Measures for the Assessment of Personal Information and Important Data Exit Security (Draft for Soliciting Opinions))." April 11, 2017. Translation, accessed November 29, 2019. https://chinacopyrightandmedia.wordpress.com/ 2017/04/11/circular-of-the-state-internet-information-office-on-the-public-consu ltation-on-the-measures-for-the-assessment-of-personal-information-and-impo rtant-data-exit-security-draft-for-soliciting-opinions/

CAC. 2019a. "Wangluo anquan shencha banfa (zhenqiu yijian gao) (Cybersecurity Review Measures (Draft for Comment))." May 21, 2019. Translation, accessed November 29, 2019. https://www.newamerica.org/cybersecurity-initiative/digichin a/blog/chinas-cybersecurity-reviews-critical-systems-add-focus-supply-chain-fore ign-control-translation/

CAC. 2019b. "Shuju anquan guanli banfa (zhenqiu yijian gao) (Data Security Management Measures (Draft for Comment)." May 28, 2019. Translation, accessed November 29, 2019. https://www.newamerica.org/cybersecurity-initiative/digichin a/blog/translation-chinas-new-draft-data-security-management-measures/

CAC. 2019c. "Geren xinxi chujing anquan pinggu banfa (zhengqiu yijian gao) (Personal Information Outbound Transfer Security Assessment Measures (Draft for Comment)." June 13, 2019. Translation, accessed November 29, 2019. https://ww w.newamerica.org/cybersecurity-initiative/digichina/blog/translation-new-draft-r ules-cross-border-transfer-personal-information-out-china/

Central Committee and State Council. 2016. "Guojiaxinxihua fazhan zhanlüe gang-yao (Outline of the National Informatization Development Strategy)." July 27, 2016. Translation, accessed November 22, 2019. https://chinacopyrightandmedia

.wordpress.com/2016/07/27/outline-of-the-national-informatization-developme nt-strategy/

Chander, Anupam and Uyen P. Le. 2014. "Breaking the Web: Data Localization vs. the Global Internet." *UC Davis Legal Studies Research Paper Series* 378. Accessed November 29, 2019. https://aicasia.org/wp-content/uploads/2017/06/ SSRN-id2407858-1.pdf.

Chang, Gordon G. *The Coming Collapse of China*. New York: Random House, 2010.

China Daily. 2019. "BT Becomes First Foreign Telecoms Firm to Secure Chinese License." January 29, 2019. Accessed November 29, 2019. http://www.chinadail y.com.cn/a/201901/29/WS5c4fbdfca3106c65c34e70b2.html.

CNNIC. 2019. "Di 44 ci 'Zhongguo hulian wangluo fazhan zhuankuang tongji baogao' (44th 'China Statistical Report on Internet Development')." August 30, 2019. Accessed October 19, 2019. http://www.cac.gov.cn/2019-08/30/c_11249 38750.htm.

CNR. 2019. "App Store xian 'shuahaoping' wudao yonghu kewu: ruo bu manyi ke gei chaping ('Good Review Paint" Emerges on App Store, Misleading Customers: In Case of Dissatisfaction, Bad Marks May be Awarded)." July 8, 2019. Accessed November 29, 2019. http://china.cnr.cn/yaowen/20190708/t20190708_524682741 .shtml.

Congressional Research Service. 2018. "Tricks of the Trade: Section 301 Investi- gation of Chinese Intellectual Property Practices Concludes." March 29, 2018. Accessed November 29, 2019. https://crsreports.congress.gov/product/pdf/LSB/ LSB10109.

Corera, Gordon. 2015. *Intercept: The Secret History of Computers and Spies*. Lon- don: Hachette UK.

Creemers, Rogier. 2018. "Disrupting the Chinese State: New Actors and New Fac- tors." *Asiascape: Digital Asia* 5(3): 169–197.

Creemers, Rogier. 2019. "The International and Foreign Policy Impact of China's Arti- ficial Intelligence and Big-Data Strategies." In *Artificial Intelligence, China, Russia, and the Global Order: Technological, Political, Global, and Creative Perspectives*, edited by Wright, Nicholas, 129–135. Maxwell AFB: Air University Press.

Demchak, Chris. 2016. "Uncivil and Post-Western Cyber Westphalia: Changing Interstate Power Relations of the Cybered Age." *The Cyber Defense Review* 1(1): 49–74.

Dutton, William H., and Malcolm Peltu. 2008. "The New Politics of the Internet: Multi-stakeholder Policy-making and the Internet Technocracy." In: *Routledge handbook of Internet politics*, edited by Chadwick, Andrew and Philip Howard, 400–416. Abingdon: Routledge.

Ermert, Monika and Christopher Hughes. 2003. "What's in a Name? China and the Domain Name System." In: *China and the Internet: Politics of the Digital Leap Forward*, edited by Hughes, Christopher and Gudrun Wacker, 127–138. Abingdon: Routledge.

Feng, Emily. 2018. "China's State-Owned Venture Capital Funds Battle to Make an Impact." *Financial Times*. December 23, 2018. Accessed November 29, 2019. https://www.ft.com/content/4fa2caaa-f9f0-11e8-af46-2022a0b02a6c.

Forster, Elisabeth. 2018. *1919—The Year That Changed China: A New History of the New Culture Movement.* Berlin: De Gruyter.

Freshfields. 2016. "China Introduces Comprehensive New Cyber Security Rules for Banking Procurement." Accessed November 29, 2019. http://knowledge.freshfields.com/m/Global/r/1514/china_introduces_comprehensive_new_cyber_security_rules.

Glanville, Luke. 2013. *Sovereignty and the Responsibility to Protect: A New History.* Chicago: University of Chicago Press.

Global Times. 2016. "Hulianwang xingui bing fei 'fengsha jingwai wangzhan', IT jie wangyou jiedu zhuanye shuyu (New Internet Rules Don't 'Wipe Out Foreign Websites', Netizens from IT Circles Explain Specialized Jargon)." March 29, 2016. Accessed November 29, 2019. https://world.huanqiu.com/article/9CaKrnJUT0p.

Griffiths, James. *The Great Firewall of China: How to Build and Control an Alternative Version of the Internet.* London: Zed Books.

Hall, Chris. 2019. "Huawei HarmonyOS Update: Without Google What Is Huawei's plan B?" *Pocket Lint.* September 18, 2019. Accessed November 29, 2019. https://www.pocket-lint.com/phones/news/huawei/148118-huawei-alternative-os-without-google-huawei-plan-b.

Harold, Scott Warren, Martin C. Libicki, and Astrid Stuth Cevallos. 2016. "Getting to Yes with China in Cyberspace." *Rand Corporation.* Accessed November 25, 2019. https://www.rand.org/content/dam/rand/pubs/research_reports/RR1300/RR1335/RAND_RR1335.pdf.

Houser, Kimberley. Forthcoming. "The Innovation Winter Is Coming: How the U.S.-China Trade War Endangers the World." *San Diego Law Review* 57(3). Accessed November 29, 2019. https://papers.ssrn.com/sol3/papers.cfm?abstract_id=3473902. https://opinion.huanqiu.com/article/9CaKrnK3qF3.

Hu, Jintao. 2011. "Jianding buyi zou Zhongguo tese shehuizhuyi wenhua fazhan daolu: nuli jianshe shehuizhuyi wenhua qiangguo (Resolutely Walk the Path of Socialist Culture Development with Chinese Characteristics: Striving to Construct a Strong Socialist Culture Country)." *Qiushi.* Translation, accessed November 28, 2019. https://chinacopyrightandmedia.wordpress.com/2012/01/04/hu-jintaos-article-in-qiushi-magazine-translated/

ICANN. 2013. "ICANN Engagement Center to Open In Beijing." April 8, 2013. Accessed November 29, 2019. https://www.icann.org/en/system/files/press-materials/release-08apr13-en.pdf.

Jiguang. S.d. "Jiguang dashuju: 2017 nian yidong hulianwang hangye pandian app bangdan (Jiguang data: a 2017 list of apps in the mobile Internet sector)." Accessed November 29, 2019. https://www.jiguang.cn/reports/195.

Kai, Jin. 2014. "Why China Banned Windows 8." *The Diplomat.* May 28, 2014. Accessed November 29, 2019. https://thediplomat.com/2014/05/why-china-banned-windows-8/.

Kent, Ann. 2008. "China's Changing Attitude to the Norms of International Law and Its Global Impact." In *China's "New" Diplomacy,* edited by Kerr, Pauline, Stuart Harris and Yaqing Qin, 55–76. New York: Palgrave Macmillan.

Kirton, David. 2019. "Huawei Tightens China Market Hold with 42% Share at Expense of iPhones: Canalys." *Reuters.* October 30, 2019. https://www.reuters.

com/article/us-china-smartphone/huawei-tightens-china-market-hold-with-42-s
hare-at-expense-of-iphones-canalys-idUSKBN1X907R.

Klimburg, Alexander. 2013. "The Internet Yalta." *Center for a New American Security*. Accessed November 29, 2019. http://dragon-report.com/Dragon_Report/h
ome/home_files/The%20Internet%20Yalta.pdf.

Knowledge@Wharton. 2011. "China's 3G Technology Gamble: Who Has the Last
Laugh?" Accessed November 29, 2019. https://knowledge.wharton.upenn.edu/arti
cle/chinas-3g-technology-gamble-who-has-the-last-laugh/

Kolton, Michael. 2017. "Interpreting China's Pursuit of Cyber Sovereignty and Its
Views on Cyber Deterrence." *The Cyber Defense Review* 2(1), 119–154.

Krasner, Stephen D. 1999. *Sovereignty: Organized Hypocrisy*. Princeton: Princeton
University Press.

Lee, Jyh-An. 2018. "Great Firewall." *The Chinese University of Hong Kong Faculty
of Law Research Papers* 2018–10.

Li, Tao. 2019. "Huawei Wins Half of China Mobile's 5G Network Contracts While
Ericsson Picks Up a Third." *South China Morning Post*. June 17, 2019. https://
www.scmp.com/tech/big-tech/article/3014766/china-mobile-awards-half-its-5g-ne
twork-contracts-huawei-while.

Liao, Shannon. 2018. After a Single Day, Facebook Is Pushed Out of China Again."
The Verge. July 25, 2018. Accessed November 29, 2019. https://www.theverge
.com/2018/7/25/17612162/facebook-technology-subsidiary-blocked-china-censor.

Lindsay, Jon. 2014. "The Impact of China on Cybersecurity: Fiction and Friction."
International Security 39(3): 7–47.

Lu, Wei. 2013. "Wang ju zhengnengliang, gong zhu Zhongguo meng: zai di shisan
jie Zhongguo wangluo meiti luntan shang de zhuzhi yanjiang (Concentrate Positive Online Energy, Jointly Build the Chinese Dream: Speech at the 13th China
Online Media Forum)." October 30, 2013. Translation, accessed November 29,
2019. https://chinacopyrightandmedia.wordpress.com/2013/10/30/siio-director-
outlines-eight-objectives-for-online-media/.

Lu, Wei. 2014. "Gongxiang de wangluo, gongzhi de kongjian: zai ICANN Lundun
huiyi kaimushi de zhuzhi yanjiang (A Network Shared Together, A Space Governed Together: Keynote Speech at the Opening Ceremony of the London ICANN
Meeting)." June 23, 2014. Translation, accessed November 22, 2019. https://ch
inacopyrightandmedia.wordpress.com/2014/06/23/a-network-shared-together-a-s
pace-governed-together/

Lu, Xiaomeng, Paul Triolo, Samm Sacks, Rogier Creemers, and Graham Webster.
2018. "Progress, Pauses, and Power Shifts in China's Cybersecurity Law Regime."
Digichina. Accessed November 29, 2019. https://www.newamerica.org/cybersec
urity-initiative/digichina/blog/progress-pauses-power-shifts-chinas-cybersecurit
y-law-regime/

Macmillan, Margaret. 2011. *Peacemakers: Six Months That Changed the World*.
London: Hachette, UK.

Marczak, Bill, Nicholas Weaver, Jakub Dalek, Roya Ensafi, David Fifield, Sarah
McKune, Arn Rey, John Scott-Railton, Ron Deibert, and Vern Paxson. 2015.
"China's Great Cannon." *CitizenLab*. Accessed November 29, 2019. https://citizen
lab.ca/wp-content/uploads/2009/10/ChinasGreatCannon.pdf.

McGregor, James. 2012. *No Ancient Wisdom, No Followers: The Challenges of Chinese Authoritarian Capitalism*. London: Easton Studio Press.

MFA. 2012. "Statement at Budapest Conference on Cyber Issues." October 4, 2012. Accessed November 22, 2019. http://www.chinesemission-vienna.at/eng/zgbd/t977627.htm.

MFA. 2017. "Wangluo kongjian guoji hezuo zhanlüe (International Strategy of Cooperation on Cyberspace)." January 3, 2017. Translation, accessed November 22, 2019. https://chinacopyrightandmedia.wordpress.com/2017/03/01/international-strategy-of-cooperation-on-cyberspace/

MFA. 2019. "China's Submissions to the Open-ended Working Group on Developments in the Field of Information and Telecommunications in the Context of International Security." Accessed November 29, 2019. https://s3.amazonaws.com/unoda-web/wp-content/uploads/2019/09/china-submissions-oewg-en.pdf.

MII. 2002. "Zhongguo hulianwangluo yuming guanli banfa (Management Rules for Domain Names on the Chinese Internet)." August 1, 2002. Accessed November 29, 2019. http://www.people.com.cn/GB/14677/21980/22078/1898076.html.

MII. 2004. "Zhongguo hulianwangluo yuming guanli banfa (Management Rules for Domain Names on the Chinese Internet)." November 5, 2004. Accessed November 29, 2019. http://www.miit.gov.cn/n1146295/n1146592/n1146754/n1234736/n1234739/n1234740/c3099778/content.html.

MIIT. 2016. "Hulianwang yuming guanli banfa (xiuding zhengqiu yijian gao) (Internet Domain Name Management Rules (Opinion-seeking Revision Draft))." March 25, 2016. Translation, accessed November 29, 2019. https://chinacopyrightandmedia.wordpress.com/2016/03/25/internet-domain-name-management-rules-opinion-seeking-revision-draft/

MIIT. 2017. "Hulianwang yuming guanli banfa (Internet Domain Name Management Regulations)." August 16, 2017. Accessed November 29, 2019. https://baike.baidu.com/item/互联网域名管理办法/23443734?fromtitle=中国互联网络域名管理办法&fromid=1778530.

Mitter, Rana. 2013. *China's War with Japan, 1937–1945: The Struggle for Survival*. London: Penguin.

MOFCOM. 2001. "China's Schedule of Specific Commitments." Accessed November 29, 2019. http://fta.mofcom.gov.cn/pakistan/xieyi/fwmyxieding-zfcrb_en.pdf.

Morrison, Aimée Hope. "An Impossible Future: John Perry Barlow's' Declaration of the Independence of Cyberspace'." *New Media & Society* 11(1-2): 53-71.

MPS. 2007. "Xinxi anquan dengji baohu guanli banfa (Information Security Multi-level Protection Management Rules)." June 22, 2007. Accessed November 29, 2019. http://www.gov.cn/gzdt/2007-07/24/content_694380.htm.

MPS. 2018. "Wangluo anquan dengji baohu tiaoli (zhenqiu yijian gao) (Cybersecurity Multi-level Protection Management Rules (Opinion-seeking Draft))." June 27, 2018. Accessed November 29, 2019. http://www.mps.gov.cn/n2254536/n4904355/c6159136/content.html.

Mueller, Milton. 2012. "China and Global Internet Governance: A Tiger By the Tail." In *Access Contested: Security, Identity and Resistance in Asian Cyberspace*, edited by Deibert, Ronald, 177–194. Cambridge: MIT Press.

NHFPC. 2014. "Renkou jiankang xinxi guanli banfa (shixing) (Population Health Information Management Rules (Trial))." May 5, 2014. Accessed November 29, 2019. http://www.cac.gov.cn/2014-08/20/c_1112064075.htm.

Ni, Guangnan, 2017A. "Zhengfu caozuo xitong ying quebao zizhu kekong (Government Operating Systems Should Be Guaranteed Indigenous and Controllable)." *Global Times.* June 13, 2007. Accessed November 29, 2019.

Ni, Guangnan. 2017. "Jianyi zhengfu tingzhi caigou he shiyong 'Win10 zhengfuban' (I Suggest the Government Ceases to Buy and Use the 'Win10 Government Edition')." *QQ Tech.* June 8, 2017. Accessed November 9, 2019.

Ni, Guangnan. 2017B. "Jiandingbuyi de fazhan guochan caozuo xitong (Unwaveringly Develop Domestically Produced Operating Systems)." *Global Times.* June 29, 2017. Accessed November 29, 2019. https://opinion.huanqiu.com/article/9CaK rnK3MJr.

NPC. 2015. "Zhonghua renmin gongheguo wangluo anquan fa (cao'an) (Cybersecurity Law of the People's Republic of China (Draft))." July 6, 2015. Translation, accessed November 29, 2019. https://chinacopyrightandmedia.wordpress.com/ 2015/07/06/cybersecurity-law-of-the-peoples-republic-of-china-draft/

NPC. 2016. "Zhonghua renmin gongheguo wangluo anquan fa (cao'an—erci shenyi gao) (Cybersecurity Law of the People's Republic of China (Second Reading Draft)." July 6, 2016. Translation, accessed November 29, 2019. https://chinaco pyrightandmedia.wordpress.com/2016/07/06/peoples-republic-of-china-cybersec urity-law-second-reading-draft/

NPC. 2016. "Zhonghua renmin gongheguo wangluo anquan fa (cao'an—sanci shenyi gao) (Cybersecurity Law of the People's Republic of China (Third Reading Draft)." November 2, 2016. Translation, accessed November 29, 2019. https://ch inacopyrightandmedia.wordpress.com/2016/11/02/cybersecurity-law-of-the-peop les-republic-of-china-third-reading-draft/

NPC. 2016A. "Wangluo anquan fa (cao'an) de xiugai qingkuang (The Situation of the Revision of the Cybersecurity Law (Draft))." July 8, 2016. Translation, accessed November 29, 2019. https://chinacopyrightandmedia.wordpress.com/2016/07/08/ the-situation-of-the-revision-of-the-cybersecurity-law-draft/

NPC. 2016C. "Zhonghua renmin gongheguo wangluo anquan fa (Cybersecurity Law of the People's Republic of China." November 7, 2016. Translation, accessed November 22, 2019. https://chinacopyrightandmedia.wordpress.com/2016/11/07/ cybersecurity-law-of-the-peoples-republic-of-china/

Panda, Ankit. 2019. "Huawei's Legal Woes and Tech 'Decoupling' Between China and the West." *The Diplomat.* February 4, 2019. Accessed November 29, 2019. https://thediplomat.com/2019/02/huaweis-legal-woes-and-tech-decoupling-betw een-china-and-the-west/

PBoC. 2011. "Guanyi yinhangye jinrong jigou zuohao geren jinrong xinxi baohu gongzuo de tongzhi (Notice concerning Protecting Personal Financial Information in Financial Bodies in the Banking Sector)." January 21, 2011. Accessed November 29, 2019. http://www.gov.cn/gongbao/content/2011/content_1918924.htm.

Pei, Minxin. 2006. *China's Trapped Transition.* Cambridge: Harvard University Press.

People's Daily. 2012. "Wangzhan xiaoyenmiman, women ruhe yingdui (Smoke over the Network Warfare Battlefield, How Do We Respond)." June 6, 2012. Accessed November 29, 2019. http://media.people.com.cn/GB/18088684.html.

People's Daily. 2014. "Guojia Hulianwang Bangongshi fuzhuren Wang Xiujin: wangluo anquan shi zhongda zhanlüe wenti (SIIO Vice-Director Wang Xiujin: Cybersecurity Is a Major Strategic Question)." May 18, 2014. Translation, accessed November 29, 2019. https://chinacopyrightandmedia.wordpress.com/2014/05/30/siio-vice-director-wang-xiujun-cybersecurity-is-a-major-strategic-question/

Qu, Weizhi. 2010. *China's Path to Informatization*. Singapore: Cengage Learning Asia.

Rapoza, Kenneth. 2019. "Huawei Has Taken Over Apple's Market Share in China; It Will Get Worse." *Forbes*. May 2, 2019. Accessed November 29, 2019. https://www.forbes.com/sites/kenrapoza/2019/05/02/huawei-has-taken-over-apples-market-share-in-china-it-will-get-worse/#3530820385f1.

Reuters. 2019. China Publication of 'Unreliable Entities List' Depends on Sino-U.S. Trade Talks: Sources." October 11, 2019. Accessed November 29, 2019. https://www.reuters.com/article/us-usa-trade-china-entities/china-publication-of-unreliable-entities-list-depends-on-sino-u-s-trade-talks-sources-idUSKBN1WQ28L.

Sacks, Samm and Manyi Kathy Li. 2018. "How Chinese Cybersecurity Standards Impact Doing Business in China." *CSIS Briefs*. Accessed November 29, 2019. https://csis-prod.s3.amazonaws.com/s3fs-public/publication/180802_Chinese_Cybersecurity.pdf?EqyEvuhZiedaLDFDQ.7pG4W1IGb8bUGF.

SARFT. 2000. "Xinxi wangluo chuanbo guangbo dianying dianshi lei jiemu jiandu guanli zanxing banfa (Provisional Information Network Dissemination of Radio, Film and Television-Type Programme Supervision and Management Rules)." April 7, 2000. Translation, accessed November 29, 2019. https://chinacopyrightandmedia.wordpress.com/2000/04/07/provisional-information-network-dissemination-of-radio-film-and-television-type-programme-supervision-management-rules/

SARFT. 2004. "Hulianwang deng xinxi wanluo chuanbo shiting jiemu guanli banfa (Internet and Other Information Networks Audiovisual Programme Dissemination Management Rules)." July 6, 2004. Translation, accessed November 29, 2019. https://chinacopyrightandmedia.wordpress.com/2004/07/06/internet-and-other-information-networks-audiovisual-programme-dissemination-management-rules/

Schell, Orville, and John Delury. 2014. *Wealth and Power: China's Long March to the Twenty-First Century*. New York: Random House, 2014.

Schmitt, Michael N., and Liis Vihul. 2017. "Sovereignty in Cyberspace: Lex Lata Vel Non?" *AJIL Unbound* 111: 213–218.

Schmitt, Michael N., ed. 2017. *Tallinn Manual 2.0 on the International Law Applicable to Cyber Operations*. Cambridge: Cambridge University Press.

SCIO and MII. 2005. "Hulianwang xinwen xinxi fuwu guanli guiding (Internet News Information Service Management Regulations)." September 25, 2005. Translation, accessed November 29, 2019. https://chinacopyrightandmedia.wordpress.com/2005/09/25/internet-news-information-service-management-regulations/

SCIO. 2010. "The Internet in China (White Paper)." June 8, 2010. Accessed October 22, 2019. http://www.chinadaily.com.cn/china/2010-06/08/content_9950198.htm.

SCMP. 2018. "Timeline: Chinese Telecoms Giants Huawei, ZTE Incur Wrath of Washington Over Iran Sanction Violations." December 6, 2018. Accessed November 29, 2019. https://www.scmp.com/tech/big-tech/article/2176664/timeline-chine se-telecoms-giants-huawei-zte-incur-wrath-washington.

Segal, Adam. 2016. "China, Encryption Policy, and International Influence." *Hoover Institution.* Accessed November 29, 2019. https://www.hoover.org/sites/default/fil es/research/docs/segal_webreadypdf_updatedfinal.pdf.

Segal, Adam. 2017. "Chinese Cyber Diplomacy in a New Era of Uncertainty." *Hoover Institution, Aegis Paper Series* 1703. Accessed November 29, 2019. https://ww w.hoover.org/sites/default/files/research/docs/segal_chinese_cyber_diplomacy.pdf.

Sevastopulo, Demetri and Geoff Dyer. 2015. "Obama and Xi in Deal on Cyber Espio- nage." *Financial Times.* September 15, 2015. Accessed November 29, 2019. https ://www.ft.com/content/0dbcab36-63be-11e5-a28b-50226830d644.

Shen, Hong. 2016. "China and Global Internet Governance: Toward an Alternative Analytical Framework." *Chinese Journal of Communication* 9(3): 304–324.

Shen, Hong. 2018. "Building a Digital Silk Road? Situating the Internet in China's Belt and Road Initiative." *International Journal of Communication* 12: 2683–2701.

Shen, Yi. 2016. "Cyber Sovereignty and the Governance of Global Cyberspace." *Chinese Political Science Review* 1(1): 81–93.

Shih, Gerry. 2015. "Huawei CEO Says Chinese Cybersecurity Rules Could Back- fire." *Reuters.* April 21, 2015. Accessed November 29, 2019. http://www.reuters.c om/article/2015/04/21/us-huawei-cybersecurity-idUSKBN0NC1G920150421.

State Council. 1999. "Shangyong mima guanli guiding (Commercial Encryption Management Regulations)." October 7, 1999. Accessed November 29, 2019. https ://zh.wikisource.org/zh-hans/中华人民共和国国务院令第273号

State Council. 2000. "Hulianwang xinxi fuwu guanli banfa (Internet Information Service Management Rules)." September 25, 2000. Translation, accessed Novem- ber 29, 2019. https://chinacopyrightandmedia.wordpress.com/2000/09/25/internet- information-service-management-rules/

State Council. 2016. "'Shisan wu' guojia xinxihua guihua ('13th Five-Year Plan' for National Informatization)." December 15, 2016. Accessed November 29, 2019. http://www.gov.cn/zhengce/content/2016-12/27/content_5153411.htm.

Stein, Arthur A. 2016. "The Great Trilemma: are Globalization, Democracy, and Sovereignty Compatible?" *International Theory* 8(2): 297-340.

TC260. n.d. "Xinxi anquan jishu—shuju chujing anquan pinggu zhinan (Information Security Technology- Guidelines for Data Cross-Border Transfer Security Assess- ment)." Accessed November 29, 2019. https://www.tc260.org.cn/ueditor/jsp/upl oad/20170527/87491495878030102.pdf.

Thomas, Daniel C. 2001. *The Helsinki Effect: International Norms, Human Rights, and the Demise of Communism.* Princeton: Princeton University Press.

Thomas, Neil. 2019. "Mao Redux: The Enduring Relevance of Self-Reliance in China." *MacroPolo.* April 25, 2019. Accessed November 29, 2019. https://ma cropolo.org/analysis/china-self-reliance-xi-jin-ping-mao/

Tost. 2015. "Oettinger Calls for 'Europeanisation' of Digital Policy." *EurActiv.* March 17, 2015. Accessed November 29, 2019. https://www.euractiv.com/section/ digital/news/oettinger-calls-for-europeanisation-of-digital-policy/

TransPacifica. 2017. "Chinese IT Security Examiner Describes Review Process, Clarifies Status of Chinese Government Windows Edition." Accessed November 29, 2019. http://transpacifica.net/2017/06/1963/

Triolo, Paul. 2019. "China Is Not A Technology Superpower. Stop Treating It Like One." *SupChina.* October 1, 2019. https://supchina.com/2019/10/01/china-is-not-a-technology-superpower-stop-treating-it-like-one/

UN. 2011. "International Code of Conduct for Information Security." A/66/339. September 12, 2011. Accessed October 22, 2019. https://www.un.org/ga/search/v iew_doc.asp?symbol=A%2F66%2F359&Submit=Search&Lang=E.

UN. 2015. "International Code of Conduct for Information Security." A/69/723. January 9, 2015. Accessed October 22, 2019. https://digitallibrary.un.org/recor d/786846/files/A_69_723-EN.pdf.

USTR. 2014. "Fact Sheet: Successes in Reducing Technical Barriers to Trade to Open Markets for American Exports." Accessed November 29, 2019. https://ustr.gov/ about-us/policy-offices/press-office/fact-sheets/2014/March/Successes-Reducing -Technical-Barriers-to-Trade-to-Open-Markets-for-US-Exports.

Waddell, Kaveh. 2016. "Why Google Quit China—and Why It's Heading Back." *The Atlantic.* Accessed November 29, 2019. https://www.theatlantic.com/technology/a rchive/2016/01/why-google-quit-china-and-why-its-heading-back/424482/

Wang Yonggui. 2011. "Zhongguo gongchandang 90 nian lai tuijin yishixingtai gongzuo de lishi jingyan (The Historical Experience of the Chinese Communist Party's 90 Years of Moving Ideological Work Forward)." Translation, accessed October 19, 2019. https://chinacopyrightandmedia.wordpress.com/2011/09/09/ the-historical-experience-of-the-chinese-communist-partys-90-years-of-moving-id eological-work-forward/

Wang, Yubian, and Yuri Shebzukhov. 2019. "From Network Security to Network Autonomous." *International Journal of Advanced Network, Monitoring and Controls* 4(1): 61–65.

Wang, Yuhua, and Carl Minzner. 2015. "The Eise of the Chinese Security State." *The China Quarterly* 222: 339–359.

WIC. 2014. "Wuzhen Declaration." November 21, 2014. On file with author.

Wübbeke, Jost, Mirjam Meissner, Max J. Zenglein, Jaqueline Ives and Björn Conrad. 2016. "Made in China 2025." *MERICS Papers on China* 2016(2). Accessed 29 November 2019. https://www.merics.org/sites/default/files/2017-09/MPOC_No.2 _MadeinChina2025.pdf.

Xi, Jinping. 2013. "Zai quanguo xuanchuan sixiang gongzuo huiyi de jianghua (Speech at the Nationwide Propaganda and Ideology Work Conference)." August 19, 2013. Trranslation, accessed November 29, 2019. https://chinacopyrightand media.wordpress.com/2013/11/12/xi-jinpings-19-august-speech-revealed-transl ation/

Xi, Jinping. 2015. "Zai di'er jie shijie hulianwang dahui kaimushi de jianghua (Speech at the 2nd World Internet Conference Opening Ceremony)." December 16, 2015. Translation, accessed November 22, 2019. https://chinacopyrightandmedia .wordpress.com/2015/12/16/speech-at-the-2nd-world-internet-conference-openi ng-ceremony/

Xinhua. 2015. "High-level Advisory Committee Established for World Internet Conference." December 21, 2015. Accessed November 29, 2019. http://www.wuzh enwic.org/2015-12/21/c_48303.htm.

Xue, Hong. 2004. "Voice of China: A Story of Chinese-Character Domain Names." *Cardozo Journal of International and Comparative Law* 12: 559–592.

Yuan, Li. 2019. "As Huawei Loses Google, the U.S.-China Tech Cold War Gets Its Iron Curtain." *New York Times*, May 20, 2019. https://www.nytimes.com/2019/0 5/20/business/huawei-trump-china-trade.html.

Zeng, Jinghan, Tim Stevens and Yaru Chen. 2017. "China's Solution to Global Cyber Governance: Unpacking the Domestic Discourse of 'Internet Sovereignty'." *Politics & Policy* 45(3): 432–464.

Zhao, Zhoujian and Zhilian Xu. 2014. "Xinxi jiashu fazhan qushi yu yishixingtai anquan (Information Technology Development Trends and Ideological Security)." *Red Flag Manuscripts*. Translation, accessed November 29, 2019. https://ch inacopyrightandmedia.wordpress.com/2015/01/01/information-technology-develo pment-trends-and-ideological-security/.

Part II

POWER AND GOVERNANCE

INTERNATIONAL ORGANIZATIONS, STATES, AND SUBSTATE ACTORS

Chapter 7

A Balance of Power in Cyberspace

Alexander Klimburg and Louk Faesen

Cyberspace[1] is managed by stakeholders from civil society, the private sector, and, to a lesser degree, by governments. The latter, however, is increasingly asserting its role in cyberspace, leading to a redistribution of power in which states are not only competing with other stakeholders, but also among each other. All cyberspace users thus face a power struggle between states that stands to affect the private sector and civil society, the multistakeholder approach to managing Internet resources, and therefore cyberspace writ large.

This chapter appropriates a realist model in international relations—the balance of power theory (BOP)—and adjusts it with neoliberal concepts of power to help better understand the challenge of stability between states in and on cyberspace. It specifically enables the "cybered" international relations of governments to be analyzed against the backdrop of the complex ecosystem of stakeholders. This does not presuppose that states are or should be the most important or influential actors in cyberspace. Instead, this chapter focuses on state interests. It identifies two conditions of the BOP theory and applies them to cyberspace in three different scenarios previously suggested by states, and offers one suggestion on the way forward.

THE BALANCE OF POWER

"The greatest need of the contemporary international system is an agreed concept of order. In its absence, the awesome available power is unrestrained by any consensus as to legitimacy . . . without it stability will prove elusive."[2]

The balance of power theory is one of the most enduring and protean concepts in international relations.[3] It has also sometimes proven to be the

145

battle line between both neorealist and neoliberal interpretations in international relations scholarship. This largely has been because of different interpretations of the term "anarchy" in international relations, and different assessments of the propensity of states to actually collaborate, besides a fundamentally different assessment of what constitutes "power." This has sometimes amounted to wasted opportunity, since it is possible to apply more neoliberal views to BOP, both by stressing the importance of institutions as well as including a wider concept of power per se. This is even possible when taking many neorealist positions as a starting point.

For instance, a common point of departure for BOP is the basic assumption that states act rationally to maximize their security or power in anarchic systems without a higher authority to regulate disputes.[4] Robert Jervis lists four realist assumptions that constitute the foundation of this premise: (i) all states must want to survive, (ii) they are able to form alliances with each other based on short-term interests, (iii) war is a legitimate instrument of statecraft, and (iv) several of the actors have relatively equal military capabilities.[5] The system ensures that any one state's power will be checked by a countervailing (coalition of) power that is alarmed by the potential hegemonic threat it poses to the system. From here on, the perspectives on the BOP theory diverge: one of them views the active goal of states as pursuing strategies designed to maintain the balance, while another maintains that it is an automatic consequence of state behavior, a side effect.[6] As its name implies, the distribution of power, usually defined in terms of military capabilities, is central to the BOP theory.[7] In particular, rough parity among several competing actors is frequently posed as a necessary feature of such a system. Even though the invisible hand of the balance of power regulates the system, states must be moved by explicit concerns over a potential hegemon and be ready to counter it with checks and balances as they struggle to curb the rise of a potential hegemon. As we shall see later, this becomes complicated if one departs from the realist definition of power as being purely military and adopts a wider understanding of what power may entail.

Fundamentally, the balance of power is based on a compromise—it cannot satisfy every actor in the international system completely. As Kissinger described, "Paradoxically, the generality of dissatisfaction is a condition of stability, because were any one power totally satisfied, all others would have to be totally dissatisfied. The foundation of a stable order is the relative security—and the relative insecurity—of its members."[8] The balance of power works best when it keeps one state from predominating and prescribing laws to the rest, and prevent the aggrieved parties from seeking to overthrow the international order. It does not purport to avoid crises or even wars. Its goal is not aimed at reaching peace, but rather moderation and stability.

Defining Cyber Power

Traditional understanding of the balance of power where states seek to survive as independent entities in an anarchic global system can seem particularly challenged when confronted with the concepts of *cyber power*. In a contemporary world with powerful norms against conquest, states no longer fear the same degree of physical extinction. The empirical evidence of limited military intervention for balancing purposes attests to the need to expand the traditionally military-security notion to include a wider range of means—including not only economic but also "soft power" factors.[9] Indeed, the challenge is that in cyberspace many (but not all) of the traditional realist measures of state power do not seem to hold up, and it is, therefore, necessary to reconceive of what power means in cyberspace.

Power, however elusive and difficult to measure, goes beyond the physical or military supremacy over another. Joseph S. Nye offers guidance by describing *cyber power* as a unique hybrid regime of physical properties (the infrastructures, resources, rules of sovereignty, and jurisdiction) and virtual properties that make government control over the former difficult. Low-cost attacks from the virtual or informational realm can impose high impacts and costs on the physical layer. The opposite is also true; control over the physical layer can have territorial and extraterritorial effects on the virtual layer.[10] Daniel Kuehl defines *cyber power* as "the ability to use cyberspace to create advantages and influence events in other operational environments and across the instruments of power."[11] In line with his distinction between hard and soft power, Nye conceptualizes three faces of power: (i) the *coercive* ability to make an actor do something contrary to their preferences or strategies, (ii) *agenda setting* or framing to preclude the choices of another by exclusion of their strategies, and (iii) *shaping* another's initial preferences so that some strategies are not even considered.[12] This chapter focuses on the first face, gives a cursory glance at the second, and only touches upon the third. This is not a reflection of relative importance of the respective faces of power (indeed some scholarship might consider the opposite to be the case), but rather a focus on the measurability (or at least observability) of the faces of power. It must be noted that none of the faces of power are easily quantifiable. There is no question that the measurement becomes abstract. The more indirect the power relation is, the more difficult measurement becomes—that is, the third face of power is more difficult to measure using traditional international relations methods.

The *hard power* manifestation of the first face of power in cyberspace, which comes close to the realist interpretation of power, is the ability to infringe on the availability and integrity of data. This can be accomplished either through denial of services (e.g., DDoS) or by various methods designed to influence data integrity (e.g., destructive malware insertion by various means). To accomplish these activities, some capability is often equally required in the non-kinetic field of "espionage"—that is, the ability to violate the confidentiality of data. This precursor, formally known as Computer Network Exploitation (CNE),[13] has since been refined to include capabilities known as ISR (intelligence, surveillance and reconnaissance) and OPE (operational preparation of the environment, a.k.a. "preparing the battlefield").[14] Thus, it is logical that the capability of states to inflict kinetic-effect harm in cyberspace requires (to various extents) the ability to conduct intelligence gathering.[15] However, the exact nature of these "kinetic-equivalent" effects, formally simply known as "Computer Network Attack" and now known as "Offensive Cyber Effect Operations" (OCEO),[16] is in doubt. While some cyber capabilities are reserved for the battlefield (e.g., to take out a radar to enable an air strike) and are at least somewhat defined and even considered as "cyber fires,"[17] other capabilities are less clear. For instance, OCEO targeted at a power grid could of course mean "switching off the grid." But it could also mean "destroying the grid" to many different degrees, including to the extent that it was not easily reconstitutable. And finally, it could also mean something completely different—where, for instance, the power grid is simply repositioned to be used as an espionage tool,[18] or even as a weapon itself. This lack of clarity on what exact capabilities in cyberspace are means that it is very difficult to describe comprehensively what the "means" (delivery systems or weapons) are. In some cases, this might seem relatively easy—Stuxnet, Flame, Duqu Shamoon, Ouroboros, and Dark Energy, come to mind as examples of somewhat classifiable "cyber weapons," but in other cases, this would be much more difficult. For the purposes of arms control or similar, the lack of transparency in presumed force deployment and even the method of operation or intended effects make the task extremely difficult, at least if an "arms control treaty" is the goal. At best, a "cyber weapon" remains a weapon system of "omni-use" technologies that is extremely difficult for another state to verify due to a lack of transparency. Otherwise, however, states are only left with the ability to presume—basically to guess—the overall capability of another state (albeit at widely variating degrees of detail) without, in most cases, being able to detail the exact order of battle, table of equipment, tactics, techniques, and procedures or other basic information—unless the intelligence assessment is very complete.

Leaving the definitional hurdles aside, the equilibrium of forces or the military balance of power in cyberspace is further complicated by characteristics unique to these tools:

- The success of an attack is more a reflection of the overall quality of defence rather than the quality of offense. An attacker will, therefore, always use the "cheapest" tools available, and not necessarily the most advanced.[19]

- The vast majority of offensive cyber effects can only be deployed using civilian intermediaries (networks, products) that also can be part of a neutral or even friendly third nation.
- The difference between imminent preparation for attack (e.g., OPE) and simple espionage can be hard to distinguish for the defender, making inadvertent escalation much more likely due to a failure to correctly interpret intent.
- Offensive capabilities are much cheaper and much easier to develop and deploy than the total sum of necessary defensive measures.[20]
- Unlike conventional weapons, "cyber weapons" can be reused but are also perishable—an entire arsenal can be rendered useless without ever being used once the vulnerability is patched.[21]
- These tools are specific—the outcomes are dependent on the victim's network—and can be immediate or time-delayed. They upend conventional ways of response.
- They can also be reverse engineered, weaponized and reused by the victim or another party that gets their hands on the technology.[22]
- They not only undermine the target's security but also compromise the security of other actors using systems with the same vulnerabilities.[23]

These are just a small range of examples describing how the fundamental differences between cyber and conventional weapons greatly complicate the process of parsing state offensive cyber capabilities.

But even in the physical world, Kissinger states that "an exact balance is impossible, and not only because of the difficulty of predicting the aggressor. It is chimerical, above all, because while powers may appear to outsiders as factors in a security arrangement, they appear domestically as expressions of a historical existence. No power will submit to a settlement, however well-balanced and however secure, which seems totally to deny its vision of itself."[24] Power is thus conceived and assessed not merely as a mathematical exercise (the number of weapons or military capabilities) but takes into account the perception of a nation's leaders, the quality of its strategies, military doctrines, and its will to use power effectively. Therefore, the common perception of a state's cyber capabilities, even if founded on incomplete knowledge, can function as a basis for calculating the respective balance of power.

Legitimacy

A balance of power makes the overthrow of international order physically difficult, deterring a challenge before it occurs. A broadly based principle of legitimacy produces reluctance to assault the international order. A stable peace testifies to a combination of physical and moral restraints.[25]

According to Kissinger's theory, a balance of power is not in itself an adequate basis for order. It is regarded as a minimal condition, but if it becomes an end in and of itself, it becomes self-destructive: "a system based purely upon power will turn every decision into a contest of strength, whereas the essence of stability is the recognition of limits by major actors."[26]

If nations desire peace, they cannot seek it directly. Instead, they must focus on creating stable relations among nations, which, according to Kissinger, is based on two major conditions: the existence of a balance of power and the acceptance of an international system of mediation and legitimacy by the major powers—an acceptance he terms "the legitimizing principle" or "the principle of legitimacy." These two terms should be conceptualized as conditions that form the basic hypotheses about the ideal conditions for the effective functioning of the system.[27]

This brings us to the second condition of stability—which commonly results not from a quest for peace but from a generally accepted legitimacy. It means no more than an international agreement about the nature of workable arrangements and about the permissible aims and methods of foreign policy. It implies the acceptance of the framework of the international order by all major powers, at least to the extent that no state is so dissatisfied that it expresses its discontent in terms of a revolutionary foreign policy. The legitimizing principle reflects the prevailing values of the historical epoch, especially how the international order should be organized in a specific context, and captures a general acknowledgment or consensus among the major actors in a system on what is considered to be the principal form of organization and order.[28] This principle identifies the *what*—the central actors—and the *how*—the types of interactions—in the international system. The peace of Westphalia, for example, marked a change in the legitimizing principle from feudalism to the system of sovereign nation-states. The legitimizing principle is often summarized as a "recognition of limits" by the state. It is important to understand that these limitations are not necessarily only legal or institutional but also include the understanding of what the actual and normative reality means.

In the context of cyberspace, the system for governing global cyber activities is primarily construed within its technical reality. The various interlocking but separate governance processes that together define cyberspace have been described by Joseph S. Nye as forming a "regime complex."[29]

This regime complex is only partially influenced by state actors, and by bilateral, regional, or multilateral processes. The private sector and civil society both generate products, common practices, and norms of behavior largely separate from government involvement, although these developments can have significant impacts on state-led processes and discussions on international peace and security. Despite states' traditional dominance over all questions related to international peace and security, governments make up only one out of three actor groups in the overall cyber regime complex, and its role within it is no greater than that of the private sector or civil society. The state-oriented regimes do not necessarily have the ability to speak on behalf of other equally crucial regimes. This creates a situation unique in international peace and security, where governments cannot decide on all aspects of the international cybersecurity domain itself, as responsibility and ownership for this domain is shared with non-state actors.

This could arguably be described as the multistakeholder reality of the domain. The multistakeholder model does not go uncriticized. First, there are those who say it's too vacuous a term to describe a chaotic arrangement of actors and agreements that works at odds. Second, the exact legitimacy in determining the relevant stakeholders, especially from civil society and the private sector, is often mentioned as a possible stumbling block. While the term does not have a single overriding definition, it does have an implicit definition. Its core idea is that some issues are too complex and have too many independent operational stakeholders to be decided on by one inevitably self-interested group and, therefore, require the participation of all stakeholders: civil society (including academia and technical community), the private

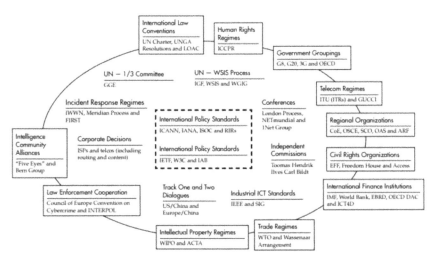

Figure 7.1 **"The Regime Complex for Managing Global Cyber Activities."** *Source*: Joseph S. Nye Jr. "The Regime Complex for Managing Global Cyber Activities," Global Commission on the Internet Governance, May 2014. Available at: www.cigionline.org/s ites/default/files/gcig_paper_no1.pdf.

sector, and governments. For the Internet, this is seemingly grounded in reality. It is the members of civil society (which includes state-funded university researchers, as well as corporate engineers working on their own time) who write the code of the Internet. It is the private sector that builds and owns most aspects of the Internet, ranging from the cables to the services, to products and software which runs on and in it. Government's role is relatively limited in that respect. Its power is manifested through its sovereign rights and jurisdiction. While there are fine-tuned differences between the exact definition of the multistakeholder approach, for instance, between Western nations and China (Russia, by and large, still rejects the term entirely), there are more questions of applicability and responsibility. Both definitions, however, implicitly agree that the cyberspace domain overall is a multistakeholder one—even if they disagree on exactly what the respective authorities of the actors among each other are, or at what "level" of governance and what kind of authority is applicable.

The ability of governments to successfully manage the threat of major conflict in cyberspace is, therefore, not only hampered by the rapid development of digital technologies but also the dominant role of non-state actors in all shapes and forms (attacker, victim, media or carrier of attacks), as well as their unclear relationships with the government. Traditionally, all questions related to international peace and security occur within the governmental remit of states and the UN First Committee, while in reality governments only constitute one of three stakeholder groups in the wider cyberspace ecosystem. Failure to reach meaningful progress at the multilateral level has led other civil society and industry to become more involved in developing rules of the road.[30] This is not the first time that this has occurred—nongovernmental groups have previously helped reshape global discussions on responsible behavior.[31] Governments and international organizations are beginning to recognize the need for industry and civil society involvement at the traditionally state-led multilateral level. Initiatives such as the "Paris Call for Trust and Security in Cyberspace,"[32] the "UN Secretary General's High-Level Panel on Digital Cooperation,"[33] and the civil society and industry consultations of the "UN Open-Ended Working Group on Developments in the Field of Information and Communications Technologies in the Context of International Security"[34] are testament to this development.

Finally, there is the question of the ideological connotation of the multistakeholder model itself, opening the door for further neo-corporatist influence over the governance structure. While many of these points are worthy of further examination and debate, there is often the assessment on par with liberal democratic systems that it might be one of the worst systems out there, but still better than the alternatives. Support for the multistakeholder approach should not just be based on the notion of simply being "inclusive." Instead, they allow for decision- and policy making to be informed and shaped by the relevant and authoritative sources. Within the complex context of cyberspace, it's not an ideology, but a necessity—the removal of the private sector and civil society from the Internet governance architecture is simply not physically possible.

Given this complex landscape, it is unlikely there can be a singularly encompassing entity successfully acting unilaterally across the entire regime complex. If, for instance, governments, as an overall actor group, were to agree to make definitive changes to the current non-state-dominated Internet governance structures, then there would almost certainly be a strong reaction—not only from the private sector but also from the engineers and hobbyists who have coded most of the backbone of the Internet. Installing an intergovernmental organization instead of, for instance, the Internet Engineering Task Force, would not simply make these volunteers stop working on Internet technology. Therefore, the most basic reality of the wider cyber regime complex is that it is in its own, precarious, multistakeholder balance. While states can and may expand their own arrangements among each other, certain basic realities of how the domain is managed cannot be changed. Nothing that completely goes against the diffused power structure of cyberspace can, therefore, be considered viable or "legitimate"—the multistakeholder approach is, therefore, in effect, the Westphalian System of the Internet.

BALANCING POWER IN CYBERSPACE

Thus far, it has become apparent that an equilibrium of state forces in cyberspace remains elusive because of the lack of a basic understanding of each other's capabilities and doctrines and, therefore, also a minimum amount of agreed definitions. Moving beyond power, the legitimizing principle reflects the recognition of the limits of states in the prevailing reality of the historical epoch. In cyberspace, this arguably can be expressed as the multistakeholder approach because of the technical reality of cyberspace that prevents one party from deciding universally and unilaterally.

From a state perspective, there are different ways to achieve a balance of power. In the next section, the guiding principles will be applied to three scenarios proposed by states that roughly correspond to the first three committees of the UN General Assembly to see how likely they can actually lead to a balance of power that upholds to the legitimizing principle. This does not mean that the UN is or should be the sole means through which to establish international peace and stability in cyberspace. Instead, it offers a starting point to identify initiatives that have been previously proposed by governments, and one suggestion on the way forward.

First Basket, First Committee Issues

The First Committee of the United Nations General Assembly deals with issues of disarmament and international security. As previously mentioned, states make up only one of the three actor groups within the overall cyber regime complex despite their traditional dominance over all questions related to international peace and security in cyberspace, meaning they cannot decide on all aspects by itself—ownership is shared with the private sector and civil society. Yet, the involvement of non-state stakeholders in the international state-led processes remains limited at best. The last UN GGE Consensus Report (described below) seems to acknowledge the need to involve other stakeholders in its conclusions: "while States have a primary responsibility to maintain a secure and peaceful ICT environment, effective international cooperation would benefit from identifying mechanisms for the participation, as appropriate, of the private sector, academia and civil society organisations."[35]

Using Nye's cyber regime complex as a point of departure, one of the authors expands Joseph Nye's regime complex to offer an impression of the stakeholders and respective processes affecting the political-military dimension of cybersecurity, a.k.a. "international cybersecurity" or "international peace and security in cyberspace" that could be considered UN First Committee issues.

In the UN context, the First Committee is most concerned with guiding responsible state behavior in terms of international peace and security in cyberspace. To this end, there have been three major state efforts in the UN.[36]

1. **The United Nations Group of Governmental Experts (GGE) and the Open-Ended Working Group (OEWG) on Developments in the Field of Information and Telecommunications in the Context of International Security.** Since its inception in 2010, the GGE has convened five times and issued three consensus reports. Each group had a mandate of only one year—which, until now, has been renewed on an annual basis. The first consensus report recommended that states consider norms, confidence-building measures (CBMs), and capacity-building initiatives to "reduce the risk of misperception" in cyberspace.[37] In the second consensus report, major powers explicitly recognized for the first time that the application of international law, in particular the Charter of the United Nations, is essential to maintaining peace and stability in cyberspace.[38] It also encouraged the development of regional confidence-building

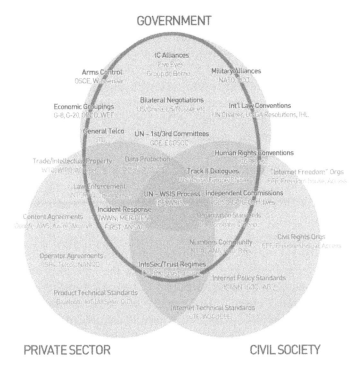

Figure 7.2   The Cyber Regime Complex by Stakeholder Group: The "International Cybersecurity" Cluster. *Source*: Alexander Klimburg, "To the GGE and beyond," UNIDIR Cyber Stability Conference Series, 17 July 2016, Geneva. Available at: www.unidir.ch/f iles/conferences/pdfs/looking-ahead-the-gge-and-beyond-en-1-1173.pdf.

measures. The third consensus report outlines voluntary peacetime norms states are encouraged to follow. The 2016–2017 iteration failed to reach a consensus report. The stumbling block: the application of international law to cyber operations.[39] In more recent developments, the 73rd Session of the UN General Assembly saw proposals from the United States[40] and Russia[41] to create two parallel working groups, a reiteration of the GGE and a proposal for a new Open-Ended Working Group (OEWG), within the disarmament machinery to develop rules for responsible state behavior in cyberspace, which are widely seen as two competing processes. Both processes establish modalities for multilateral engagement, yet the OEWG presents a wider scope for consultation with non-state stakeholders in the private sector and civil society communities. Meaningful participation and input is by no means a given, as it is still unclear as to what kinds of results these modalities will lead to in practice.

2. Members of the **SCO have circulated a draft international code of conduct for information security at the UN General Assembly.**[42]

The code proposes that states voluntarily forego the "use of [ICTs] . . . to carry out activities which run counter to the task of maintaining international peace and security." It predominantly focuses on interstate cooperation against the use of ICTs to incite the "three evil –isms"—terrorism, separatism or extremism—as well as reinforces a multilateral model for Internet governance and the notion of noninterference in the internal affairs of states through ICTs. The code has been floated at the UN since 2011, but has attracted criticism for its perceived incompatibility with human rights law.[43]

3. Finally, the **UN General Assembly adopted a resolution in 2003**, calling on states to build a culture of cybersecurity by encouraging domestic stakeholders to be aware of cybersecurity risks and to take steps to mitigate them.[44]

Other multilateral initiatives to enhance international security and stability have been agreed outside of the auspices of the UN, most notably, the work of the Organization for Security and Cooperation in Europe (OSCE), the ASEAN Regional Forum (ARF), and other regional organizations on CBMs. In addition, previous efforts have been made toward potential control of "intrusion software" by the Wassenaar Arrangement that aimed at "creating a consensus approach to regulate conventional arms and dual-use goods and services."[45] It has forty-one signatories that regulate the export of both conventional weapons and dual-use goods, which includes certain categories of information systems.[46] In 2013, the member states agreed to include certain categories of intrusion software to this list.[47] Although this may bolster states against network intrusions, it also significantly impedes the ability of information security researchers to exchange findings without risking criminal proceedings.

Despite these efforts, the year 2017 marked the shortcomings of meaningful interstate efforts to advance norms and legal interpretations to bring international security and stability. This is just one way to do so. Some experts foresee a more fruitful future for operational cooperation—for example, in CBMs,[48] while others are exploring countering efforts to the proliferation of offensive cyber capabilities.[49]

The most likely application of a balance of power framework could be through the field of arms control, which is traditionally the only venue where states openly consider trade-offs in their individual security in the name of broader peace. It would also be the most difficult to achieve—the last twenty years have shown that the arms control discussion in cyberspace has been beset with challenges, from applying overtly traditional models of negotiation (only including governments) to the inability to even agree on basic terms. As noted before, the notion of what constitutes a "cyberweapon" is as open and contentious as the concept behind "cyber power" per se, and there is no definition of a cyberweapon or even cyber capabilities that would lend itself to negotiations. Russia and China still view cyber threats in fundamentally different ways as the United States (e.g., information weapons versus cyber tools), making it difficult to establish and enforce such a framework. There are some workarounds that have been suggested, such as the focus on simply regulating certain "effects" rather than trying to define the weapons. However, they also stumble over some basic differences in understanding of international law. Currently, the open questions in international law, particularly the status of data as an object,[50] are almost as difficult as technical understanding of what could comprise a "weapon" in cyberspace, mainly due to the dual-use or omni-use nature of many of the potential subcomponents in a "cyberweapon," and the need for the technical community, researchers, or the private sector to be able to provide security tools for testing.

The introduction of two competing processes within the First Committee neither represent encouraging developments in this regard, signifying that divergent views between UN member states, in particular between liberal democracies and autocracies, persist even despite progress that may have previously been made through the GGE. However, if these hurdles can be overcome, the ability to at least agree on a counter-proliferation agreement (similar to the Missile Technology Control Regime or the Treaty on the Non-Proliferation of Nuclear Weapons) is theoretically possible.[51] Such an agreement would clarify both concepts and capabilities of signatory states, as well as limit the transfer of those capabilities to other actors (including non-state actors). If such a treaty neither violated the need of the technical community to have simple and easy access to security testing tools, nor set a dangerous precedent by trying to "outlaw" individual pieces of code globally, then it could arguably provide for a much-needed dose of predictability among states.

Second Basket, Second Committee Issues

The Second Committee of the United Nations General Assembly focuses primarily on economic and financial issues, and has a strong connection to the United Nations Development Programme and the United Nations Economic and Social Council (ECOSOC). The council is covered by the schedule officers from both the Second and Third Committees. The primary issue on the committee's agenda is the "digital economy"—an issue predominantly discussed outside of the auspices of the United Nations, by institutions such as the EU, OECD, G20, G7, WEF, to name but a few. The digital economy includes specific issues such as digital trade, e-commerce, infrastructure development, and industry 4.0.

In this context, however, a closer look will be taken at law enforcement cooperation as a potential approach to establish a balance of power. Admittedly, law enforcement cooperation can also be categorized under the First or Third Committee issues. The Budapest Convention on Cybercrime established by the Council of Europe and open to third party members is one of the most authoritative in this context, but has been criticized because it seemingly enforces a Western narrative.[52] In response, Russia has reportedly proposed a draft convention on countering cybercrime and promoting law enforcement cooperation under the auspices of the United Nations, as it apparently believes previous conventions threaten the sovereignty of independent states.[53]

The area of law enforcement cooperation offers some possibilities for pursuing a balance of power approach between states. First, in this context, the power of states is at least partially framed by the second and the third face of power considerations—co-option and conviction of soft power, besides the overall perceived coercive "hard power" strength of its suspected military and intelligence cyber capabilities. Second, a state can relatively easily ramp

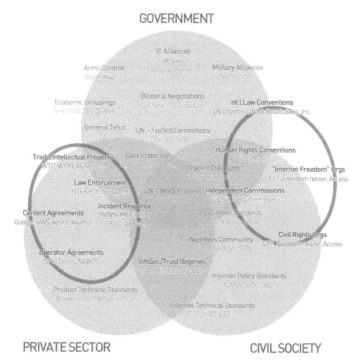

Figure 7.3   The Cyber Regime Complex by Stakeholder Group: "Law Enforcement" and "Civil Rights" Clusters. *Source*: Alexander Klimburg, "To the GGE and beyond," UNIDIR Cyber Stability Conference Series, 17 July 2016, Geneva. Available at: www.unidir.ch/f iles/conferences/pdfs/looking-ahead-the-gge-and-beyond-en-1-1173.pdf.

up its engagement in negotiations in this space, but it will be a credible actor only if it has a strong reputation in general and in the "rule of law" in particular—not necessarily the easiest of all criteria to fulfill. Third, it allows states to address the issue of malicious non-state actors that impact their national security concerns, including, for instance, countering the terrorist use of ICTs. Finally, a law enforcement approach that concentrates on mutual legal assistance treaties (MLATs), rather than specifying specific crimes, does not contradict the legitimizing principle.

The limitations of the benefits of the law enforcement treaty approach to achieve a balance of power are based upon a simple understanding of what power in cyberspace is. Such a treaty would theoretically have little bearing on a state's ability to conduct offensive cyber operations and, therefore, would not impact its "hard power" capabilities, unless the government in question clandestinely leverages cybercrime actors to buttress its own governmental capabilities. In the latter case, such a treaty would represent a clear loss for the cybercrime-supporting side, and a number of governments probably do fall into this category, limiting decisively their actual power gains as well.

A law enforcement approach is theoretically possible and more likely to succeed than the arms control approach described above and the Internet governance approach that will follow below, but it falls short in what it delivers for the balancing of states. Although it does not necessarily address the hard powers of states, it deals with the contentious issue of non-state actors that governments have struggled to manage, and, more importantly, builds confidence among states. A final disclaimer would be that the proposed solutions to "double-bad" issues (illegal in both jurisdictions) can be a slippery slope for increasingly intrusive surveillance measures that the Western like-minded states would not condone.

Third and Fourth Basket, Third Committee Issues

The Third Committee of the United Nations General Assembly focuses the social, humanitarian and cultural issues. Most notably, human rights are discussed within this committee, and also in other UN institutions, such as the Human Rights Council and UNESCO, as well as outside the UN context: the Council of Europe, EU, OSCE, Freedom Online Coalition (FOC), IGF, WSIS, APC, Human Rights Watch, and many more. The application of international law (including human rights law) has already been established by the United Nations, and a human rights-based approach has been reiterated in many other contexts such as the NETmundial Declaration in 2014. It is, however, unlikely to create a balance of power among states by and of itself as many of the *multilateralist* countries that promote a state-governed Internet through notions such as "cyber sovereignty" remain critical of human rights. Moreover, human rights law governs mainly the relations between governments and their citizens. Instead, it needs to be incorporated into other approaches.

Finally, there have been several attempts by states to assert power in cyberspace by pushing for a state-led Internet governance approach through the International Telecommunications Union (ITU) of the United Nations. Internet governance is largely treated as a Second Committee issue (primarily through ECOSOC and the Internet Governance Forum) but there are options to connect it to the Third Committee as well. The IGF has no formal decision-making power or government policy-making impact, but instead helps to coordinate and facilitate among the different Internet governance constituencies. If the Third Committee link to Internet governance can be strengthened, this might also reinforce the notion of a rights-based Internet.

The Internet governance regime complex best represents the complexity of dealing with the larger issues of managing resources and behaviors in cyberspace. It encompasses a wide range of different institutions, from established international organizations like the International Telecommunications Union (ITU)[54] to the critical Internet Engineering Task Force (IETF)[55] that is characterized by its informal structure, and the nonprofit public-benefit corporation known as the Internet Corporation for Assigned Names and Numbers (ICANN).[56] Most importantly, the Internet governance ecosystem is resolutely representative of the multistakeholder approach, with civil society, the private sector and government stakeholders each working more or less equally according to their strengths. As such, it is a "proof" of the legitimizing principle of cyberspace: nothing that is determined about resources and behaviors in cyberspace can be legitimate if it fully violates the basic reality of how the Internet is actually managed.

As such, a major question of the state's influence on Internet governance was solved by a momentous decision by the Obama administration. The day of October 1, 2016 marked a historic moment, when the US government officially cut the final strings to its influence over ICANN by handing over the IANA function—the management of the root zone file of the Internet—to ICANN in its entirety.[57] The process of slowly moving the Internet away from government influence was arguably part of the basic US approach to the Internet since as far back as the 1980s. A number of steps under various administrations conformed to this principle—slowly moving the Internet "back into the Internet community" that gave birth to it, even if that community was heavily financed by the US government in its early years. The commitment of the US government to fully disinvest itself from the last vestiges of direct control over the Internet was given new urgency after the June 2013 Snowden revelations and the significant impact this had on US "soft power," particularly in and through cyberspace. Although it marks an awkward bent in realist thinking

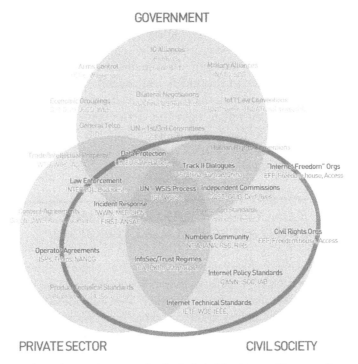

**Figure 7.4   The Cyber Regime Complex by Stakeholder Group: "Internet Governance"
Cluster.** *Source*: Alexander Klimburg, "To the GGE and beyond," UNIDIR Cyber Stability
Conference Series, 17 July 2016, Geneva. Available at: www.unidir.ch/files/conferences/
pdfs/looking-ahead-the-gge-and-beyond-en-1-1173.pdf.

that a state would voluntary give up power, the Obama administration made
the assessment that sticking to previous political commitments and "releas-
ing" the last shreds of government control over the Internet confirmed to
three objectives, namely it reinforced the US soft power when it gave up its
first "potentially coercive" face of power, to (i) gain a stronger position in the
second face, that is, in agenda setting or framing, (ii) it confirmed a self-image
of the United States as a leader of a "Free Internet," and (iii) it finally reinforced the basic legitimizing principle of the Internet altogether: it is run by the
multistakeholder approach, and no one government can exercise a hegemonic
position on it. Instead, all states enjoy the same relative power. Therefore, the
US IANA disinvestment played a significant role in bringing a "balance of
power" to the Internet governance domain itself.

The internal balance of power within Internet governance means that it is,
in effect, a poor choice for states to advance their power through this approach
as it would disrupt the current system and the legitimizing principle. If a state
tried to do so at the expense of the multistakeholder model, it would conflict

with the basic reality of the domain, in which the key technical standard setting bodies, such as the IETF, are resolutely outside of governmental control and due to their voluntary nature cannot be co-opted by it. If a state tried to expand its power while at the same time maintaining the multistakeholder model, it would be limited to very small, incremental increases, thus limiting its attractiveness. Restructuring the Internet governance ecosystem to that of an intergovernmental structure is, therefore, a poor choice for states to seek a different balance of power among states as they already enjoy the same relative power under the current ICANN structure that respects the legitimizing principle of the multistakeholder model.

CONCLUSION: TOWARD A BASKET-BASED APPROACH FOR CYBERSPACE

This chapter sets out to assess the application of the balance of power theory to cyberspace to establish international stability and order. It did so by pursuing a more neoliberal interpretation of power. Two conditions of the balance of power theory were applied to three approaches or scenarios that roughly correspond to the first three committees of the United Nations General Assembly, to see how they could contribute to such a stable environment, leading to the following preliminary observations.

Overall, merit can be found in the realist approach to stability and international order in cyberspace by describing it in terms of compromise and of relative security and relative insecurity. By adopting a neoliberal interpretation of the notion of cyber power, the balance of power theory can be applied to certain aspects of cyberspace. Establishing stability in this environment hinges upon the acceptance of the framework of the international order by all major powers, at least to the extent that no state is so dissatisfied that it expresses it in a revolutionary foreign policy. At least for now, the Internet governance domain enjoys a balance of power among states in accordance with the legitimizing principle. This principle, described as a "recognition of limits" by the state, is construed by the technical reality of the domain inhibiting one party from deciding universally and unilaterally, arguably defined as the multistakeholder reality in the context of cyberspace.

However, the condition of an equilibrium of forces that lies at the core of the balance of power theory is currently impossible to establish as it requires states to have a basic understanding of each other's capabilities and, therefore, a minimum amount of agreed definitions as to what constitutes a "cyberweapon." In this context, compared to the other options, an arms control treaty has most to offer for the balance of power for states in cyberspace. If nearly all difficulties could be overcome, it would clarify those concepts of capabilities that are in much need of more transparency. This transparency can be delivered in the short term through CBMs, agreements of self-restraint or norms, but those fall short in terms of visibility, verification, and rigor in the long run compared to the former approach.

Each of the other baskets has its own specific merit, but falls short in establishing a balance of power for states in adherence to the legitimizing principle. Instead, a holistic basket-based approach could serve as an alternative. In a thought piece for the Global Commission on the Stability of Cyberspace, Wolfgang Kleinwächter describes the need, dilemmas, and possibilities of such an approach.[58] Using the context of the "Helsinki Process" of the 1970s as a source of inspiration, Kleinwächter identifies four baskets: (1) cybersecurity, (2) digital economy, (3) human rights, and (4) technology. These correspond to the previously discussed baskets with the addition of "technology." Each basket includes a different constellation of actors and constituencies involved and, therefore, enjoys different levels of multistakeholder and multilateral engagement, as appropriate. Kleinwächter in particular highlights the attraction of the Helsinki Process: namely, that the basket-based approach is the only way to align the vastly different interests of the two per-dominant power blocks and that of the G77, as well as fitting the essential multistakeholder reality that underpins all aspects of cyberspace.

The baskets are not "joined" or organized in a hierarchical fashion. Instead, they are brought together under a decentralized Conference on Security and Cooperation in Cyberspace (CSCC) and connected through a system of liaisons and mechanisms of reciprocal reporting to increase information exchange, cross-fertilization, and eventually, more coherence across these topics. Like its historical precedent, each basket is negotiated individually, but remains interconnected with the others, allowing asymmetric compromises in the negotiation processes—as the British foreign minister argued in 1972, "if we don't lay eggs in the third basket, there will be none in the other ones either." Ideally, over time, the actions of states would balance out across all baskets, enabling not only information exchange but also a more concerted level of negotiation between states. The conference would aim at drafting a "Final Act on Security and Cooperation in Cyberspace" (FASCC), legally nonbinding commitments from governments, the private sector, civil society and the technical community.[59]

Fundamentally, the inspiration drawn from the Helsinki Process revolves around the same essential complex "bottom-up" nature of negotiations, its emphasis on "soft law" (none of the Helsinki agreements have treaty status), the strengthening of human rights, and the weak institutional basis (the OSCE was set up only in 1995). Furthermore, through the Helsinki Watch groups and earlier inclusion of nongovernmental organizations, formal involvement and consultation of non-state actors are facilitated. Just like in the 1970s, when the idea to have a discussion about conventional forces in Europe side-by-side with a human rights discussion, the same "basket-based" approach could be applied to the wide variety of issues in cyberspace: International peace and security issues, cybercrime (terrorist use of the Internet) and economic and development issues, human rights and Internet governance issues. These also nicely align with the UN First to Third Committees.

Most importantly, it needs to be pointed out that the Helsinki Final Act did not create new norms but reinforced existing norms within the UN charter. It provided for an "enhanced explanation" of the Charter, something that could be very welcome in the context of cyberspace. It would also help define the exact role of the multistakeholder model and its application across the baskets. Just like the original Helsinki Process, it does require the full-fledged support of all major powers to get underway—the United States was notably hesitant on the Helsinki Process from the very start, and a new Helsinki Process might be equally popular, for similar reasons. However, the legally nonbinding status here is key—it provides assurances to the doubters that the process can be reversed if necessary, while at the same time does not undermine existing international law.

A basket-based model inspired by the Helsinki Process could create an environment in which all major players can expand their foreign policy interests in the respective baskets, while leaving room for others to do the same, leading to a more stable situation whereby all states are equally (dis)satisfied and at the same time respect the legitimizing principle of a multistakeholder reality in cyberspace. No matter how likely its success, it needs to be seen as a collaborative effort where progress toward stability can be made on several fronts.

The basket-based approach is obviously just one approach that need not frame a "final answer" to the overarching problem of balancing states' interests in cyberspace. But it may form a beginning.

NOTES

1. U.S. National Security Presidential Directive 54/Homeland Security Presidential Directive 23 (NSPD-54/HSPD-23) defines cyberspace as "the interdependent network of information technology infrastructures, and includes the Internet, telecommunications networks, computer systems, and embedded processors and controllers in critical industries. Common usage of the term also refers to the virtual environment of information and interactions between people."

2. Kissinger, Henry. 1969. *Central Issues of American Foreign Policy*. Available at: https://history.state.gov/historicaldocuments/frus1969-76v01/d4

3. For an overview of the evolution of the balance of power theory, see Schweller, Rendall L. May 2016. *The Balance of Power in World Politics*. Oxford: Oxford

University Press, USA. For examples of the competing theoretical and empirical claims see Vasquez, J. A. and C. Elman. eds. 2003. *Realism and the Balancing of Power: A New Debate*. Saddle River, NJ: Prentice Hall.

4. See, for example, Mearsheimer: "The international system creates powerful incentives for States to look for opportunities to gain power at the expense of rivals, and to take advantage of those situations when the benefits outweigh the costs" (Mearsheimer, John. 2001. *The Tragedy of Great Power Politics*. New York: Norton); and Morgenthau: "the aspiration for power on the part of several nations, each trying to maintain or overthrow the status quo, leads of necessity, to a configuration that is called the balance of power and to policies that aim at preserving it" (Morgenthau, Hans. 1948. *Politics Among Nations: The Struggle for Power and Peace* [4th ed.], New York: Alfred Knopf).

5. Jervis, Robert. 1978. *Cooperation under the Security Dilemma*, pp. 186–189.

6. Waltz, for example, maintains that "these balances tend to form whether some or all States consciously aim to establish and maintain balance, or whether some or all States aim for universal domination" in Waltz, K. N. 1979. *Theory of International Politics*. Reading, MA: Addison-Wesley. p. 119; and Morgenthau who considers a balance of power as a result from a State's policies in Morgenthau, Hans. *Politics Among Nations: The Struggle for Power and Peace* (4th ed.). New York: Alfred Knopf. Statecraft based on balancing polices has been lauded by figures such as Metternich, Castlereagh, Churchill, and Kissinger.

7. Schweller, R. L. 2006. *Unanswered Threats: Political Constraints on the Balance of Power*. Princeton, NJ: Princeton University Press: "Balancing means the creation or aggregation of military power through either internal mobilization or the forging of alliances to prevent or deter the occupation and domination of the State by a foreign power or coalition. The State balances to prevent the loss of *territory*, either one's homeland or vital interests abroad (e.g., sea lanes, colonies, or other territory considered of vital strategic interest). Balancing only exists when States target their military hardware at each other in preparation for a possible war."

8. Kissinger, Henry. 1957. *A World Restored: Metternich, Castlereagh, and the Problems of Peace 1812–1822*. Echo Point Books & Media.

9. See Nye, Joseph S., Jr. 2011. "The Future of Power." *Public Affairs*.

10. Nye, Joseph S., Jr. 2010. *Cyber Power*. Harvard University Belfer Center for Science and International Affairs, pp. 7–8. Available at: www.belfercenter.org/sites/default/files/legacy/files/cyber-power.pdf.

11. Kuehl, Daniel T. "From Cyberspace to Cyberpower: Defining the Problem." In: Kramer, Franklin D., Stuart Starr, and Larry K. Wentz, eds. 2009. *Cyberpower and National Security*. Washington, DC: National Defense University Press. Available at: http://ctnsp.dodlive.mil/files/2014/03/Cyberpower-I-Chap-02.pdf.

12. Ibid., p.10.

13. CNE was initially defined in JP1-02 as "Enabling operations and intelligence collection capabilities conducted through the use of computer networks to gather data from target or adversary information systems or networks." In JP 3-13 (2012), its removal from JP-02 was approved.

14. Cyberspace Operational Preparation of the Environment (OPE) is defined in JP3-12 (2013) as "consist[ing] of the non-intelligence enabling activities conducted to

plan and prepare for potential follow-on military operations. OPE requires cyberspace forces trained to a standard that prevents compromise of related IC operations. OPE in cyberspace is conducted pursuant to military authorities and must be coordinated and deconflicted with other USG departments and agencies."

15. Network attacks are usually preceded by network exploitation. As former NSA and CIA director Michael Hayden states in his book, *Playing to the Edge* (2017): "Reconnaissance should come first in the cyber-domain. . . . How else would you know what to hit, how, when—without collateral damage?"

16. Offensive Cyber Effects Operations (OCEO) is defined in PPD-20 as "Operations and related programs or activities—other than network defense, cyber collection, or DCEO—conducted by or on behalf of the United States Government, in or through cyberspace, that are intended to enable or produce cyber effects outside United States Government networks."

17. See FM3-38 (2014) for examples. Electronic Attacks, for example, is "considered a form of fires" (see 4–3).

18. Exploiting, for instance, the ability to conduct differential power analysis on individual computers.

19. Klimburg, Alexander. 2017. *The Darkening Web: The War for Cyberspace.* New York: Penguin Press.

20. Slayton, Rebecca. 2016. "What Is the Cyber Offense-Defense Balance? Conceptions, Causes, and Assessment." *International Security* 41, no. 3. Slayton argues that this perception leads to unnecessary escalation and militarization of cyberspace. According to Klimburg (2017), using DDoS costs as a point of departure, defense can be conceived as being up to 1,000 times more costly than offense.

21. In *Zero Days, Thousands of Nights* by Lillian Ablon and Timothy Bogart of RAND, the average lifespan of zero-days is set at 6.9 years, and for a given stockpile of zero days, about 5.7 percent will be publicly disclosed after one year. The report is available at: www.rand.org/pubs/research_reports/RR1751.html.

22. The EternalBlue exploit is a good example of a weapon or exploit developed by the NSA that was leaked by the Shadow Brokers, and was used in several malware epidemics afterward, including NotPetya and WannaCry. See, for example, Fox-Brewster, Thomas. May 12, 2017. "An NSA Cyber Weapon Might Be Behind A Massive Global Ransomware Outbreak." *Forbes.* www.forbes.com/sites/thomasbre wster/2017/05/12/nsa-exploit-used-by-wannacry-ransomware-in-global-explosio n/#2ff505c2e599; and Perlroth, Nicole, Mark Scott, Sheera Frenkel. June 27, 2017. "Cyberattack Hits Ukraine Then Spreads Internationally." *The New York Times,* www.nytimes.com/2017/06/27/technology/ransomware-hackers.html?_r=0.

23. Several examples include NotPetya, Turla and Black Energy. These are all malware attacks generally thought to be sponsored by the Russian Federation. Nevertheless, it went rogue and the malware hit Russian organizations and companies as well. More information available at: www.cfr.org/interactive/cyber-operations

24. Kissinger. *A World Restored.*

25. Kissinger, Henry. 1989. *War Roared Into Vacuum Formed by a Sidestepping of Statesmanship.* Available at: http://articles.latimes.com/1989-08-27/opinion/op-1559_1_eastern-europe.

26. Ibid., p. 145.

27. Schweller, Randall. 2016. *The Balance of Power in World Politics.* 10.1093/acrefore/9780190228637.013.119.

28. The *legitimizing principle* is not a traditional element of the Balance of Power theory. Although the concept appears in other contexts and modes of thought, Henry Kissinger introduced it as an addition to Balance of Power in order to establish stability—see: Kissinger. *A World Restored.* Similar definitions of the notion are included below:

"*The legitimizing principle represents the prevailing values of the historical epoch. It is in the name of the legitimizing principle that nations accept the international order.*" In Cleva. Gregory D. *Henry Kissinger and the American Approach to Foreign Policy*, p. 66.

"*By "order" is meant the legitimizing principle by which authority receives its sanction in the eyes of the association. [. . .] It goes to the problem of discovering the operative ideals, the expectations, the rules of concerted action to which the group members believe it necessary to conform in order to give their leaders the necessary authority to realize their own desires and objectives.*"

In Leiserson, Avery. 1949. "Problems of Representation in the Government of Private Groups." *The Journal of Politics* 11, no. 3: 569.

"*The urge for formally declared and generally acknowledged legitimacy approaches the status of a constant feature of political life. This urge requires that power be converted into authority [...]. Politics is not merely a struggle for power but also a contest over legitimacy, a competition in which the conferment or denial, the confirmation or revocation, of legitimacy is an important stake. [. . .] [t]here is, of course, a correlation between the nature of the legitimizing principle and the identity of its applicator. For instance, the principle of divine right tends to call for an ecclesiastical spokesman, and the consent theory implies reliance on a democratic electoral process.*" In Claude, Inis L. Jr. 1966. "Collective Legitimization as a Political Function of the United Nations." *International Organization* 20, no. 3: 367.

"*Legitimizing principles are called into question during major systemic crises, such as world wars or widespread political upheavals [...]. This dynamic occurs because it is impossible to completely satisfy the statist and nationalist principles simultaneously. Therefore, the new system tends to generate its own crisis, leading to a reevaluation of the normative principle.*" In Barkin, S.J. and B. Cronin. 1994. "The State and the Nation: Changing Norms and the Rules of Sovereignty in International Relations." *International Organization* 48, no. 1: 108.

29. Nye, Joseph S., Jr. May. 2014. "The Regime Complex for Managing Global Cyber Activities." *Global Commission on the Internet Governance.* Available at: www.cigionline.org/sites/default/files/gcig_paper_no1.pdf.

30. See, for example, initiatives from Microsoft on the Digital Geneva Convention, the Cybersecurity Tech Accord, the Charter of Trust, the Paris Call for Trust and Security in Cyberspace and the Global Commission on the Stability of Cyberspace (GCSC). These efforts were initiated by major tech corporations or civil society actors in cooperation with each other and/or states. They have stepped into the norm-setting arena largely because of a sense of societal responsibility, with a view to fill the void created by the influential states.

31. For instance, the Brundtland Commission created norms for Sustainable Development. A Carnegie Commission on Preventing Deadly Conflict led to the International Commission on Intervention and state Sovereignty and a commitment by all UN member states on the duty to prevent and protect against war crimes, genocide, ethnic cleansing and other crimes against humanity. The Ilves Commission helped set the framework for the NETmundial Initiative. The Brandt and Palme Commissions represented important steps both in development and disarmament, respectively.

32. The Paris Call for Trust and Security in Cyberspace (2018) is a high-level multistakeholder declaration with norms and principles to enhance cybersecurity that is signed by 552 official supporters from all stakeholder groups and launched by French President Emmanuel Macron. For more information see: Ministry for Europe and Foreign Affairs of France. 2018. *The Paris Call for Trust and Security in Cyberspace* https://www.diplomatie.gouv.fr/IMG/pdf/paris_call_text_-_en_cle06f918.pdf.

33. The UN Secretary-General's High-Level Panel on Digital Cooperation, a multistakeholder initiative dealing with a variety of digital challenges, argue in favor of a distributed co-governance architecture that bridges multilateralism and multistakeholderism. UN Secretary-General's High-level Panel on Digital Cooperation. 2019. *The Age of Digital* Interdependence. 33, https://digitalcooperation.org/wp-content/upl oads/2019/06/DigitalCooperation-report-web-FINAL-1.pdf.

34. United Nations General Assembly Resolution A/RES/73/27. 2018. https://undocs.org/A/RES/73/27

35. UNGGE 2015 Report, paragraph 31 on p. 13, a vailable at: www.un.org/ga/s earch/view_doc.asp?symbol=A/70/174.

36. For a comprehensive overview of cyber diplomatic initiatives see: Grigsby, Alex. 2017. *Overview of Cyber Diplomatic Initiatives*, and Housen-Couriel, Deborah. 2017. *An Analytical Review and Comparison of Operative Measures Included in Cyber Diplomatic Initiatives*, both published as Briefings from the Research Advisory Group for the Global Commission on the Stability of Cyberspace, available at: https ://cyberstability.org/wp-content/uploads/2017/12/GCSC-Briefings-from-the-Researc h-Advisory-Group_New-Delhi-2017.pdf.

37. The UN General Assembly, Group of Governmental Experts on Developments in the Field of Information and Telecommunications in the Context of International Security, A/65/201. July 30, 2010, available at: www.unidir.org/files/medias/pdfs/fi nal-report-eng-0-189.pdf.

38. The UN General Assembly, Group of Governmental Experts on Developments in the Field of Information and Telecommunications in the Context of International Security, A/68/98. June 24, 2013, www.un.org/ga/search/view_doc.asp?symbol =A/68/98.

39. The United States argues it failed over states' unwillingness to explain how specific bodies of international law, such as the law of armed conflict (LOAC) or state responsibility, apply to cyberspace. Cuba, echoing the views of Russia and China, argues that acknowledging LOAC would legitimize cyberspace as a domain for military conflict, giving state-sponsored cyber operations a green light.

Sources: Markoff, Michele G. *Explanation of Position at the Conclusion of the 2016–2017 UN Group of Governmental Experts (GGE) on Developments in the*

Field of Information and Telecommunications in the Context of International Security, available at: www.state.gov/s/cyberissues/releasesandremarks/272175.htm. "71 UNGA: Cuba at the final session of Group of Governmental Experts on developments in the field of information and telecommunications in the context of international security," Cuba's Representative Office Abroad, available at: http://misiones.minr ex.gob.cu/en/un/statements/71-unga-cuba-final-session-group-governmental-experts -developments-field-information.

For a non-State expert commentary of the failure of the 2016–2017 GGE, see, for example: Lewis, James A. August 6, 2017. *The Devil Was in the Details: The Failure of UN Efforts in Cyberspace*, available at: www.thecipherbrief.com/devil-w as-details-failure-un-efforts-cyberspace-1092.

40. The UN General Assembly, Resolution Adopted by the General Assembly on 22 December 2018 Advancing responsible State behavior in cyberspace in the context of international security, (A/RES/73/266) January 2, 2019, available at: https://undocs.org/en/A/RES/73/266.

41. The UN General Assembly, Resolution Adopted by the General Assembly on 5 December 2018 Developments in the field of information and telecommunications in the context of international security, (A/RES/73/27) December 11, 2018, available at: https://undocs.org/en/A/RES/73/27.

42. The UN General Assembly, Letter dated January 9, 2015, from the Permanent Representatives of China, Kazakhstan, Kyrgyzstan, the Russian Federation, Tajikistan and Uzbekistan to the United Nations addressed to the Secretary-General, (A/69/723) January 13, 2015, available at: https://ccdcoe.org/sites/default/files/d ocuments/UN-150113-CodeOfConduct.pdf.

43. The UN General Assembly, Letter dated September 12, 2011, from the Permanent Representatives of China, the Russian Federation, Tajikistan and Uzbekistan to the United Nations Addressed to the Secretary General, A/66/359 (September 14, 2011), available at: www.un.org/ga/search/view_doc.asp?symbol=A%2F66%2F 359&Submit=Search&Lang=E; Grigsby, Alex. January 28, 2015. "Will China and Russia's Updated Code of Conduct Get More Traction in a Post-Snowden Era?" *Net Politics* (blog), the Council on Foreign Relations, available at: www.cfr.org/blo g/will-china-and-russias-updated-code-conduct-get-more-traction-post-snowden-era ; McKune, Sarah. September 28, 2015. "An Analysis of the International Code for Conduct for Information Security," *The Citizen Lab*, available at: https://citizenlab.c a/2015/09/international-code-of-conduct/.

44. The UN General Assembly, Resolution 57/239. January 31, 2013. Creation of a global culture of cybersecurity, A/RES/47/239, available at: www.oecd.org/sti/iec onomy/UN-security-resolution.pdf.

45. The Wassenaar Arrangement was criticized as lacking in technical expertise— partially because governments had no prior history of engaging with issues related to cybersecurity. For similar point see: Goodwin and Fletcher. *Export Controls and Cybersecurity Tools.*

46. More information available at: www.wassenaar.org/about-us/.

47. More information available at: www.wassenaar.org/wp-content/uploads/201 5/06/WA-Plenary-Public-Statement-2013.pdf.

48. Grigsby, Alex. 2017. "The End of Cyber Norms", *Survival*, 59(6).

49. Morgus, Robert, Max Smeets, Trey Herr. 2017. *Countering the Proliferation of Offensive Cyber Capabilities*. Published by the Global Commission on the Stability of Cyberspace, and available at: https://cyberstability.org/wp-content/uploads/2017/12/GCSC-Briefings-from-the-Research-Advisory-Group_New-Delhi-2017.pdf.

50. The second edition of the *Tallinn Manual* states that, in the opinion of its experts, data is not an object in legal terms (*Tallinn Manual* at p. 127). This view is, however, disputed by other scholars. See for example: Adams, Michael J. January 04, 2017. "A Warning About Tallinn 2.0 ... Whatever It Says." *Lawfare*, available at: www.lawfareblog.com/warning-about-tallinn-20-%E2%80%A6-whatever-it-says.

51. For more information on the feasibility of the application of the counter-proliferation model to cyberspace see: Morgus, Robert, Max Smeets, Trey Herr. 2017. *Countering the Proliferation of Offensive Cyber Capabilities*. Published by the Global Commission on the Stability of Cyberspace, and available at: https://cyberstability.org/wp-content/uploads/2017/12/GCSC-Briefings-from-the-Research-Advisory-Group_New-Delhi-2017.pdf. For more information on the application of the feasibility of a Cyber Weapons Convention based off the Chemical Weapons Convention, see Geers, Kenneth. September 2010. "Cyber Weapons Convention." *Computer Law & Security Review,* Volume 26, Issue 5, pp. 547–551.

52. Council of Europe. 2001. *Convention on Cybercrime*. European Treaty Series—No. 185, available at: www.coe.int/en/web/conventions/full-list/-/conventions/rms/0900001680081561.

53. "Russia Presents Draft UN Convention on Fighting Cyber Crimes in Vienna." *Sputnik*, May 25, 2017, https://sputniknews.com/science/201705251053959333-russia-un-convention-cybercrimes/.

54. The ITU is a United Nations agency established in 1865, whose mission includes developing technical standards, allocating the radio spectrum, and providing technical assistance and capacity building to developing countries.

55. The IETF is one of the most important organizations working on Internet protocols and effectively decides much what constitutes the Internet's nervous system; most protocols, such as DNS and BGP. Its mission is to "make the Internet work better" from an engineering point of view. They try to avoid policy and business questions as much as possible, which are mostly managed by the Internet Society.

56. ICANN is a nonprofit public-benefit corporation with the purpose to coordinate at the overall level, the global Internet system of unique identifiers and manage the Internet names and addresses (IANA function) www.icann.org/resources/pages/what-2012-02-25-en,

57. On 1 October 2016, the contract between ICANN and the United States Department of Commerce National Telecommunications and Information Administration (NTIA) to perform the IANA functions officially expired, handing over the stewardship of IANA functions to the global Internet community. You can read the announcement here: www.icann.org/news/announcement-2016-10-01-en.

58. Kleinwächter, Wolfgang. 2018. *Towards a Holistic approach for Internet Related Public Policy Making: Can the Helsinki Process of the 1970s Be a Source of Inspiration to Enhance Stability in Cyberspace?* Published by the Global Commission

on the Stability of Cyberspace, available at: https://cyberstability.org/wp-content/up loads/2018/02/GCSC_Kleinwachter-Thought-Piece-2018-1.pdf.

59. A priori, it is interesting to note that the Conference on Security and Coopera- tion in Europe (CSCE) was very much a European product, in particular a German one, that the United States only grudgingly supported. Therefore, the context for the Helsinki Process is arguably more complex than a bipolar negotiation between the United States and the Soviet Union. The Soviet Union was primarily interested in gaining recognition and legitimacy of their sphere of influence. Western interests, while not fully homogenous, can be summarized in pushing forward the military security and humanitarian issues, such as the free flow of individuals, information and ideas between East and West. At least as important, the was the work of the Helsinki Watch groups—the formally protected NGOs that in particular monitored human rights abuses in Eastern Europe. The Helsinki Final Act fundamentally led to NGOs being institutionalized in the East.

Chapter 8

International Law in Cyberspace

Leveraging NATO's Multilateralism, Adaptation, and Commitment to Cooperative Security

Steven Hill and Nadia Marsan[1]

Cybersecurity has become a key component of national security calling for effective international cooperation. As the NATO Secretary-General highlighted, "today, a cyber-attack can be as destructive as a conventional attack, and practically every conflict has a cyber dimension. So being able to defend ourselves in cyber space, is just as important as defending ourselves on land, at sea and in the air."[2] A credible international legal framework is a necessary enabler to a peaceful, secure, and stable cyberspace. The application of international law to cyberspace is now broadly accepted.[3] However, the lack of clarity as to how international law applies has fueled debates on the application of important areas of international law to cyberspace, such as the law of state responsibility, the law of self-defense, and international humanitarian law. Toward maintaining peace and security in cyberspace in line with Article 1 of the Charter of the United Nations[4] and Article 3 of the North Atlantic Treaty,[5] there is value in gaining greater clarity on what constitutes acceptable peacetime behavior in cyberspace and what actions could call for legally justified responses.

Within this context, normative constraints can contribute to preventing conflict in cyberspace by promoting stability and the rule of law and by facilitating transparency and confidence building between states. States set the parameters which form the basis of norms for responsible state behavior according to their consistent practice and expressed intentions. States have at times been reluctant to establish potentially binding rules when the underlying technology and the corresponding threats to cybersecurity are evolving in such a dynamic way. Nevertheless, there has generally been broad consensus

173

and support for the development of voluntary cyber norms themselves in order to set some parameters and build trust between states in cyberspace in the context of the United Nations.[6] These efforts continue to be underway at this time of publication. Despite such support for the establishment of voluntary norms in cyberspace, reaching agreement on the substance of those norms has proven to be difficult at times.[7] Without prejudice to ongoing discussions at the United Nations and other fora, NATO, bringing together twenty-nine sovereign nations for collective defense within the legal framework of the North Atlantic Treaty,[8] can potentially add value to this debate. The organization provides a forum for daily multilateral discussions and exchanges of views on collective security issues, including cyber defense. Multilateralism as practiced at NATO is a process of continuous consultation based on shared values in the spirit of cooperation.[9] NATO also provides a venue where member states can express support or alignment with a position or with principles expressed by individual allies. The regular meetings of heads of state and government provide an opportunity for member states to make clear public statements on common security priorities. Since 2008, cyber defense has featured prominently in all summit declarations. For example, at the Warsaw Summit in 2016, allies affirmed that cyberattacks present a clear challenge to the security of the alliance and could be as harmful to modern societies as a conventional attack.[10] At the Wales Summit in 2014, NATO heads of state and government underlined that NATO's cyber policy must reaffirm, "the principles of the indivisibility of Allied security and of prevention, detection, resilience, recovery, and defense."[11]

NATO is not a state but an international organization. As such, NATO does not create international law or voluntary norms that regulate state behavior. There would be little appetite among allies and in the broader international community for NATO to lead the global debate on the development of voluntary norms for responsible state behavior in cyberspace. That said, as a multinational intergovernmental organization, NATO provides a good vantage point from which to observe and note emerging state practice. The organization has followed with interest the debates in various international fora on how to make cyberspace safer and more secure since such efforts actually set important parameters and frame policy discussions on collective defence. At the Brussels Summit in July 2018, allies affirmed NATO support for "work to maintain international peace and security in cyberspace and to promote stability and reduce the risk of conflict, recognizing that we all stand to benefit from a norms-based, predictable, and secure cyberspace."[12]

Written from the perspective of two practitioners, this chapter will begin by expanding on the role of norms in the promotion of international peace and security, and will then propose four areas within NATO's mandate where allies could potentially contribute to the socialization of broad voluntary norms. The chapter concludes that although states are responsible for norms, given the proliferation of cyber threats to transatlantic security, NATO cannot but both contribute to and draw guidance from the ongoing debates on the development of norms of responsible state behavior and stability in cyberspace. Furthermore, recent experience in NATO and in other international fora has underlined the importance of reinforcing effective enforcement mechanisms and potential response options.

NORMATIVE CONSTRAINTS AND CYBERSECURITY

NATO heads of state and government affirmed at the Wales Summit in 2014 that international law, including international humanitarian law and the UN Charter, applies in cyberspace.[13] Although there is now general consensus on the fundamental role that international law can play in promoting peace and stability in cyberspace, questions remain as to how international law applies in a cyber context. For example, questions relating to attribution and state responsibility, which have always been difficult topics in international law, have become even more so given the intrinsically anonymous and asymmetrical nature of cyberspace. There are also questions as to whether a particular cyber activity is of such a nature to warrant a response, preventative or defensive. The "below-the-threshold" nature of most malign cyber incidents challenges our understanding of what counts as an internationally wrongful act which could form the basis of a legally justified response such as countermeasures. The lack of clarity in these crucial and contentious areas makes it difficult to predict state action in the cyber realm and the existence of divergent views among states risks leading to misperceptions and potential escalations.[14]

Several important international initiatives have provided some guidance on these and other questions. The development of the two *Tallinn Manuals* under the auspices of the NATO-accredited Cooperative Cyber Defense Centre of Excellence (CCDCOE) in Estonia has helped identify the key legal issues and provides an academic assessment of the application of international law to cyberspace. As the development of the manuals was not a process formally endorsed by states, experts were free to thoroughly explore the implications of legal issues and states had an opportunity to offer comments during the so-called Hague Process. The manuals have become indispensable desk books for lawyers and cyber policy experts. However, although the *Manuals* help us interpret the law, they are not official NATO doctrine and do not constitute the law itself.

There has been progress in advancing the norms debate in international fora, many of which have largely been aspirational in nature.[15] The United Nations

Group of Government Experts, a United Nations working group of experts from member states, was created to study "potential threats in the sphere of information security." The 2016/2017 Group was to consider measures to address these threats, including "norms, rules, and principles of responsible behavior of states, confidence building measures, and capacity building."[16] The Group's failure to arrive at a consensus report and robust substantive rules highlighted, for some, the reluctance of states to seriously engage on the question of the application of international law in cyberspace. These efforts continue at the time of publication under the auspices of two bodies: a Group of Governmental Experts and an Open-Ended Working Group.

National initiatives such as the London and the Hague Processes as well as recent statements made by NATO allies have contributed to further clarifying some elements of contention on the application of international law to cyberspace. A former legal adviser at the US Department of State, Harold Koh, set out early in the process that international law applies to cyberspace and that the development of common understandings about how these rules apply will promote greater stability in cyberspace.[17] In 2017, another former legal adviser at the US Department of State, Brian Egan, confirmed that from the US perspective, the international law of state responsibility supplies the needed standards for attributing acts, including cyber acts to states.[18] More recently, the former UK attorney general Jeremy Wright elucidated the UK interpretation of several key components of international law as they apply in cyberspace, including on the application of the UN Charter, the unlawful intervention on state sovereignty and the corresponding use of countermeasures.[19] Commemorating one year of the *Tallinn Manual 2.0*, the Minister of Foreign Affairs of the Netherlands, HE Mr. Stef Blok, affirmed the Dutch position that there is no need to develop a new system of international law for cyberspace, arguing that the clear application of existing laws in cyberspace is the best guarantee of an open, free, and stable Internet in the future.[20]

These important statements and international efforts have all contributed to setting some important parameters for the debate. Indeed, clear national statements about the applicable legal framework enhance cyber stability by increasing predictability. States, especially those with advanced cyber capabilities, should be "open and clear in setting out the rules" they feel bound by since, in doing so, they "demonstrate not just [their] commitment to the rules based international order, but also [their] leadership in its development."[21] States themselves set out the normative constraints that bind them in their international relations; domestic sources of "law are found in statutes and in court judgments—but there are few of either in international law, instead there are treaties, and customary international law formed from the general and consistent practice of states acting out of a sense of obligation."[22]

Cyber defense is part of NATO's core task of collective defense, within NATO's broader deterrence and defense posture which was strengthened at the NATO Summit in Wales in 2014. Mechanisms used in deterrence, including denial by defense and the development of voluntary norms, are intended to dissuade or diminish the likelihood of unacceptable behavior by making the costs of the bad actions exceed the benefits to be gained therefrom.[23] A "norm" is broadly understood as "a collective expectation of proper behavior of actors with a given identity."[24] Although norms are not legally binding in themselves, "laws can serve as a basis for formulating norms, just as norms can be codified by law."[25] In distinguishing between formal international law and voluntary nonbinding norms, Brian Egan notes that norms "set out standards of expected state behavior that may, in certain circumstances, overlap with standards of behavior that are required as a matter of international law. Such norms are intended to supplement existing international law. They are designed to address certain cyber activities by States that occur outside the context of armed conflict that are potentially destabilizing."[26]

Within NATO's legal framework of the North Atlantic Treaty, the utility of norms is not so much geared toward inducing a negative impact on detractors' reputation or soft power, but rather toward elucidating how allies apply and interpret their commitments under the North Atlantic Treaty in cyberspace, thereby increasing predictability and clarifying where collective NATO action may be legally justified.

As described above, NATO can provide an important forum for member nations to discuss cyber defense. The foundational elements of NATO's approach to cyber defense include a respect for and inviolability of the sovereign nature of allies' cyber defense capabilities, strong political oversight by allies, and the requirement for consistency with NATO obligations and international law. These commitments provide a reassuring environment where allies show mutual respect of each other's sovereignty and need for political oversight, while encouraging constant dialogue, cooperation, and assurance that threats to cybersecurity will be addressed in line with international law.

In their chapter "International Norm Dynamics and Political Change," Martha Finnemore and Kathryn Sikkink develop the idea of a three-stage "norm life cycle" from norm emergence to norm acceptance to internalization. Between the first and second stages, they identify a "tipping point" whereby a critical mass of relevant state actors adopt the norm.[27] The second stage also called "norm cascades" is animated by states and international organizations toward increasing legitimacy through institutionalization.[28] NATO could act as a socialization venue precisely at the tipping point between norm emergence and norm acceptance. Indeed, the multilateralism of the alliance can function as an agent of socialization by encouraging states within the alliance, by virtue of their identity as members of a group tied by shared values, to adopt common policies and to subscribe to the set standards of expected state behavior in cyberspace.[29] If we look at the timeline of UNGGE decisions[30] and NATO heads of state and government decisions on cyber since 2012, we see that NATO provided an opportunity for a group of nations united by shared values to socialize and affirm principles that emerged in other international fora, the UN GGE in this case. This should not be underestimated as what may begin as a general, shared and nonbinding principle can, by virtue of state practice and a sense of legal obligation, "crystallize into binding customary international law" over time.[31]

NORMS, DETERRENCE, AND NATO

Within NATO, allies have coalesced on a few fundamental areas that can serve as building blocks for the development and particularly the socialization of norms: the rule of law, restraint, resilience, and mutual cooperation and assistance. These areas are well anchored in the North Atlantic Treaty and in the most recent Summit Communiques, which supplement the work of international expert groups regarding how well-established areas of international law apply to cyberspace.

Rule of Law

Allies express their commitment to the rule of law in the preamble to the North Atlantic Treaty which states that "the Parties to this Treaty . . . are determined to safeguard the freedom, common heritage and civilization of their peoples, founded on the principles of democracy, individual liberty and the rule of law." At the NATO Summit in Wales in 2014, allies recognized that "international law, including international humanitarian law and the UN Charter, applies in cyberspace."[32] More recently, at the Brussels Summit in July 2018, allies reaffirmed their "commitment to act in accordance with international law, including the UN Charter, international humanitarian law, and human rights law, as applicable."[33]

The broad affirmation of the application of the body of international law to cyberspace cannot be underestimated. It is the essential starting point toward ensuring predictability and stability as it places a duty on states to exercise diligence in the application of international law in cyberspace. At the NATO Summit in Warsaw in 2016, NATO heads of state and government recognized cyberspace as an operational domain "in which NATO must defend itself as effectively as it does in the air, on land, and at sea."[34] Together with the commitment to respect the UN Charter and international humanitarian law, the designation of cyberspace as an operational domain indirectly reinforces the tenet that the general corpus of international law applying in the air, land, and sea domains also applies in cyberspace. Although every situation is unique and states must be able to respond to cyber incidents using a wide variety of means, states have the obligation to act in accordance with international law before (*jus ad bellum*) and during an armed conflict (*jus in bello*) as well as during peacetime.

With the application of international law in cyberspace, it can be inferred that there is no immediate requirement to create new legal instruments to govern state behavior in cyberspace. Such proposals, including the idea of a Digital Geneva Convention[35] or of an International Code of Conduct for Information Security,[36] have raised a number of concerns on the part of some states related to enforcement, verification, volatile technological change, and fear that tailored instruments may discredit rather than reinforce the international legal order.[37] With respect to the proposal for an International Code of Conduct for Information Security, the primary concern was that such a code could potentially enshrine state sovereignty and information control in cyberspace.[38]

Restraint

Flowing from the previous point on the rule of law, NATO discussions and statements also support an evolving consensus on the application of the principle of restraint in cyberspace. Article 1 of the North Atlantic Treaty embodies the principle of restraint which echoes the principles set out in Article 1 of the UN Charter: "the Parties undertake, as set forth in the Charter of the United Nations, to settle any international dispute in which they may be involved by peaceful means in such a manner that international peace and security and justice are not endangered, and to refrain in their international relations from the threat or use of force in any manner inconsistent with the purposes of the United Nations."[39]

At the Warsaw Summit in 2016, allies agreed that they "will continue to follow the principle of restraint and support maintaining international peace, security and stability in cyber space."[40] States have shown that they generally respond to cyber incidents at a lesser threshold than would be permitted under international law, thereby demonstrating a commitment to restraint and de-escalation. Some good examples of such responses include network shutdown to stop the spread of a particular attack, public attribution, diplomatic demarches, economic sanctions, and increased exchanges of information with like-minded states. Self-restraint in cyberspace is especially important as actions in that realm may have unintended and serious follow-on consequences for other state and non-state actors: "the very newness of cyberwar and the fear of unforeseen consequences in unpredictable systems may contribute to prudence and self-restraint that could develop into a norm of non-use or limited use or limited targets."[41] The importance of self-restraint in cyberspace is further highlighted within the context of "broad deterrence," which includes the notion of entanglement. Entanglement is "the existence of various interdependences that make a successful attack simultaneously impose serious costs on the attacker as well as the victim."[42]

Resilience

At the Warsaw Summit in 2016, allies adopted the Cyber Defense Pledge toward strengthening and enhancing the cyber defenses of national networks and infrastructures, thereby bolstering the alliance's resilience to cyber threats and enhancing the resilience of the alliance itself. This emphasis on cyber resilience was reaffirmed at the NATO Summit in Brussels in July 2018, where allies declared that they "are determined to deliver strong national cyber defenses through full implementation of the Cyber Defense Pledge, which is central to enhancing cyber resilience and raising the costs of a cyber-attack."[43]

The commitment to resilience is anchored in the North Atlantic Treaty at Article 3: "in order more effectively to achieve the objectives of this Treaty, the Parties . . . will maintain and develop their individual and collective capacity to resist armed attack."[44] Although Article 3 refers to the capacity to resist *armed attack*, NATO's approach to cyber defense through the pledge has prioritized resilience in peacetime, precisely to prevent armed attacks from occurring in the first place. Effective cyber defense and deterrence relies on resilience of networks and their capacity to recover.[45] Resilience of networks deters malicious cyber actors by increasing the effort, raising the risk, and reducing the rewards.[46]

The priority for NATO itself is the protection of the communication and information systems owned and operated by the alliance. In light of our increasing dependence on information technologies and the escalatory potential of state action in cyberspace, the resilience of our cyber networks is necessary to limit the damages of any malicious cyber incidents including cyberattacks and, correspondingly, reinforce collective defense mechanisms themselves. The emphasis on cyber resilience highlights a fundamental element of collective defense; that allies' "interconnectedness means that we are only as strong as our weakest link."[47]

Mutual Assistance and Cooperation

An important enabler to resilience is mutual assistance and cooperation, which is a fundamental principle animating the collective defense engagement of the North Atlantic Treaty.[48] Just as for resilience, Article 3 of the treaty is the anchor for collective assistance: "in order more effectively to achieve the objectives of this Treaty, the Parties, separately and jointly, *by means of continuous and effective self-help and mutual aid*, will maintain and develop their individual and collective capacity to resist armed attack."

As part of efforts to enhance information sharing, allies committed to a model memorandum of understanding which sets out arrangements for the exchange of cyber defense-related information and assistance to improve allies' cyber incident prevention, resilience, and response capabilities. In his chapter "The Cyberhouse Rules: Resilience, Deterrence and Defence in Cyberspace," the current assistant secretary-general for Emerging Security Challenges at NATO Headquarters underlined that "cyber defence is a quintessential team sport, and the Alliance recognises that it cannot go it alone in cyberspace: partnerships are instrumental for strengthening resilience and deterrence."[49] This pledge for mutual assistance is a key element toward ensuring the resilience of networks and was reaffirmed at the NATO Summit in Brussels in July 2018.[50]

Although NATO has a regional focus, its commitment to collective security calls for close cooperation with other international organizations, including cooperative relationships with more than forty countries around the world and international organizations. For example, in 2016, a Technical Arrangement on cyber defense was concluded between the NATO Computer Incident Response Capability (NCIRC) and the Computer Emergency Response Team of the European Union (CERT-EU), thereby providing a framework for exchanging information and sharing best practices between emergency response teams. NATO has also recognized the importance of cooperation with the private sector in confronting threats and challenges to cybersecurity, especially as industry develops and operates the vast majority of networks worldwide. Toward increased cooperation with industry, NATO established the NATO-Industry Cyber Partnership at the Summit in Wales in 2014. This was further reaffirmed at the NATO Summit in Brussels in 2018 where allies committed to "further develop our partnership with industry and academia from all Allies to keep pace with technological advances through innovation."[51]

CONCLUSION

There is no need to create specific and tailored law to govern state behavior in cyberspace. It is more a question of applying and adapting existing law to a new and evolving context. Existing multilateral institutions such as NATO, working within the clear international legal framework of the North Atlantic Treaty, could add value in the process of socialization of voluntary norms regulating responsible state behavior in cyberspace, without prejudice to ongoing efforts by states either bilaterally or multilaterally.

To complement these efforts, a multilateral organization such as NATO could be a vehicle for a driver toward identifying common approaches between states. Indeed, multilateral discussions in NATO generally complement and are coordinated with bilateral efforts. As an alliance of sovereign states, NATO has shown that multilateralism and bilateralism can overlap in an effective way. National commitments and positions can be much more effective from a defense and deterrence perspective when supported more broadly by other states. Despite the challenges that broad consultations present, multilateralism will continue to be attractive as a force multiplier and as a foundation for mutual assistance.

It is argued in this chapter that the alliance's role in channeling state positions regarding voluntary norms for responsible state behavior in cyberspace should not be underestimated. NATO's multilateralism can function as a socialization vector by encouraging member states, by virtue of their identity as members of an alliance united by shared values, to adopt policies and national legislation that are animated by their common interests and commitment to a set of fundamental principles including the rule of law, restraint, resilience, and mutual cooperation and assistance. This, in turn, forms a strong basis for the acceptance and eventual internalization of certain voluntary norms for responsible state behavior in cyberspace.[52]

The multilateral nature of discussions at NATO enables another fundamental characteristic of the organization, which is its ability to learn, change, and adapt to emerging security challenges. The former UK attorney general Jeremy Wright recently underlined that "one of the biggest challenges for international law is ensuring it keeps pace as the world changes. International law must remain relevant to the challenges of modern conflicts if it is to be respected, and as a result, play its critical role in ensuring certainty, peace and stability in the international order."[53] NATO's ability to adapt has been one of its greatest strengths over the years. The ever-shifting power dynamics in cybersecurity are what make setting clear rules, consequences, and expectations so difficult. NATO allies, united by shared values and animated by a spirit of continuous adaptation, are well placed to contribute to novel applications of international law within the parameters set out by the North Atlantic Treaty.

Through its broad network of cooperative partnerships, NATO brings together many different actors including nations, international organizations, and industry. As an alliance focused on collective defense, there is a prerogative for greater cooperation in cyber defence, including in information sharing and the building of expert networks, toward establishing a common language, standardized procedures and expertise to ensure the resilience of national and NATO systems. It is by encouraging regular high-level interaction between national cyber policy experts, lawyers, academics, and industry, that we will gain more clarity on the application of international law.

The application of international law depends heavily on important political factors and will rarely be clarified in a factual vacuum. NATO's regular multilateral cyber defense exercises engage the highest level of government decision makers and are crucial to the development of effective capabilities. These exercises also provide an opportunity to "test" the application of international law and clarify national positions in some particularly contentious areas, albeit in a virtual and usually classified context. Exercises are also a good vehicle for assessing the implementation of practical measures, thereby clarifying the range of actions that can form the basis of acceptable responses to malicious cyber activity.

With cyber defence now being a fundamental facet of North Atlantic security, NATO must continue to be a forum where allies address the collective security implications of cybersecurity. NATO supports the establishment of a norms-based, stable and secure global cyberspace. NATO does not set norms, states do. But with greater cooperation and multilateral dialogue, states could begin to take common national positions regarding the limits of appropriate behavior in well-defined areas. As such, NATO will continue to provide an important forum for multilateral cooperation and engagement in the context of cyber defense, which will in turn support and facilitate debates on how international law should apply especially in collective defense contexts.

NOTES

1. The views expressed here are ours alone and do not necessarily represent the views of NATO or its allies.

2. Stoltenberg, Jens. 2018. "Why Cyber Space Matters as Much to NATO as Land, Sea and Air Defence," *Financial Times*, July 12, 2018. https://www.ft.com/content/9c3ae876-6d90-11e8-8863-a9bb262c5f53.

3. NATO Wales Summit 2014 Communiqué, paragraph 72.

4. United Nations, *Charter of the United Nations*, October 24, 1945, 1 UNTS XVI, hereafter *UN Charter.*

5. *The North Atlantic Treaty 1949.*

6. See the NATO Warsaw Summit 2016 Communiqué, paragraph 70: *We welcome the work on voluntary international norms of responsible state behavior and confidence-building measures regarding cyberspace.*

7. See Nye, Joseph S. 2018. "Normative Restraints on Cyber Conflicts," *Cyber Security: A Peer-Reviewed Journal* 1, no. 4 (August): 331–342. https://www.belfercenter.org/sites/default/files/files/publication/ Nye%20Normative%20Restraints%20Final.pdf.

8. *The North Atlantic Treaty*, Preamble.

9. As reflected in *The North Atlantic Treaty*, Article 9.

10. NATO Warsaw Summit 2016 Communiqué, paragraph 70.

11. NATO Wales Summit 2014 Communiqué, paragraph 72.

12. NATO Brussels Summit 2018 Communiqué, paragraph 20.

13. NATO Wales Summit 2014 Communiqué, paragraph 72.

14. Egan, Brian J. 2017. "International Law and Stability in Cyberspace," *Berkeley Journal of International Law* 35, no. 1, (2017): 169–180, 172. http://scholarship.l aw.berkeley.edu/bjil/vol35/iss1/5.

15. Including the production of the Cyber Norms Index by the Carnegie Endowment for International Peace, the work of the Global Commission on the Stability of Cyberspace, the London Process and the G20, to name only a few international initiatives.

16. United Nations General Assembly resolution 68/243, *Developments in the field of information and telecommunications in the context of international security*, A/RES/68/243 (December 27, 2013), available from undocs.org/A/RES/68/243.

17. Koh, Harold Hongju. 2012. "International Law in Cyberspace," *Yale Law School Faculty Scholarship Series* 4854 (2012): 1–12. http://digitalcommons.law .yale.edu/lfss_papers/4854.

18. See Egan 2017.

19. Speech delivered by the UK attorney general Jeremy Wright QC MP, *Cyber and International Law in the 21st Century,* May 23, 2018, https://www.gov.uk/govern ment/speeches/cyber-and-international-law-in-the-21st-century. Hereafter *Wright*.

20. Blok, Stef. 2018. "Keynote by HE Mr. Stef Blok MA, Minister of Foreign Affairs," *Militair Rechtelijk Tejdschrift* 111, 3 Cyber Special (2018): 8–10. https://pu c.overheid.nl/mrt/doc/PUC_248137_11/1/.

21. See Wright.

22. *Ibid.*

23. Nye Jr., Joseph S. 2017. "Deterrence and Dissuasion in Cyberspace," *International Security* 41, no. 3 (Winter): 44–71, 53. doi:10.1162/ISEC_a_00266.

24. Nye 2018, 11 citing Finnemore, Martha and Duncan B. Hollis. 2016. "Constructing Norms for Global Cybersecurity," *The American Journal of International Law* 110, no. 3 (July): 425–479, 442. http://www.jstor.org/stable/10.5305/amerjinte law.110.3.0425.

25. *Ibid.*

26. Egan 2017, 180.

27. Finnemore, Martha, and Kathryn Sikkink. 1998. "International Norm Dynamics and Political Change." *International Organization* 52, no. 4 (Autumn): 887–917, 895.

28. *Ibid.*, 898.

29. *Ibid.*, 902.

30. For example, the UNGGE 2013 affirmed the application of existing international law to states' cyber activities, while NATO did so at its summit in Wales in 2014; the UNGGE 2015 affirmed a state's inherent right to act in self-defense in response to a cyber operation meeting the threshold of an armed attack, while NATO

did so at its Summit in Wales in 2014; UNGGE 2015 confirmed the application of IHL principles to cyberspace, NATO did so at its summit in Wales in 2014.

31. Egan 2017, 180.

32. NATO Wales Summit 2014 Communiqué, paragraph 72.

33. NATO Brussels Summit 2018 Communiqué, paragraph 20.

34. NATO Warsaw Summit 2016 Communiqué, paragraph 70.

35. Proposal initially made by the president of Microsoft Incorporated, Brad Smith, at the RSA Conference in February 2017.

36. Originally presented to the United Nations General Assembly in 2011 by China, Russia, Tajikistan, and Uzbekistan. Subsequently, a revised version was submitted to the United Nations General Assembly in January 2015 by the founding members of the Shanghai Cooperation Organization (SCO).

37. Maurer, Tim, and Kathryn Taylor. 2018. "Outlook on International Cyber Norms: Three Avenues for Future Progress," *Just Security*, March 2, 2018. www.justsecurity.org/53329.

38. *Ibid.*

39. *The North Atlantic Treaty*, Article 1.

40. NATO Warsaw Summit 2016 Communiqué, paragraph 70.

41. Nye 2018, 15.

42. See Keohane, Robert O. and Joseph S. Nye Jr. 1977. *Power and Interdependence: World Politics in Transition.* Boston: Little, Brown.

43. NATO Brussels Summit 2018 Communiqué, paragraph 20.

44. *The North Atlantic Treaty*, Article 3.

45. Nye 2017, 56.

46. *Ibid.*, citing Bruce Schneider, page 56.

47. The NATO Cyber Defense Pledge, issued on July 8, 2016, paragraph 2. https://www.nato.int/cps/en/natohq/official_ texts_133177.htm

48. *The North Atlantic Treaty*, Preamble: *They are resolved to unite their efforts for collective defense and for the preservation of peace and security.*

49. Missiroli, Antonio. 2018. "The Cyberhouse Rules: Resilience, Deterrence and Defence in Cyberspace," *Italian Institute for International Political Studies*, May 2, 2018. https://www.ispionline.it/sites/default/files/ pubblicazioni/commentary_missiroli_02.05.2018.pdf

50. NATO Brussels Summit 2018 Communiqué, paragraph 20.

51. *Ibid.*

52. See, for example, the NATO Cyber Defence Pledge. https://www.nato.int/cps/en/natohq/official_texts_133177.htm

53. See Wright.

Chapter 9

Cybersecurity Norm-Building and Signaling with China

Geoffrey Hoffman

In the endeavor to establish global cybersecurity norms, China's Internet censorship presents an obstacle for democracies. China, with over 800 million Internet users (CINIC 2018), is the largest and least free entity on the Internet (Freedom House 2017), but democracies often couple cybersecurity norms with Internet freedom. Nevertheless, China and democracies share an objective to improve global cybersecurity cooperation in order to make the Internet a safer place—both from each other and from the other myriad hostile actors—and establishing norms is a primary means of attaining this end (Finnemore and Hollis 2016, 436). Using the Operation Aurora cyber espionage campaign as a case study, the hypothesis emerges that cybersecurity norm-building between democracies and China is more likely to succeed when democracies decouple cybersecurity from Internet freedom, and that signaling can address some of the difficulties inherent in this decoupling.

It can be challenging to define cybersecurity norms: many norms already exist, many of those norms dovetail, and multiple lower-level norms may, together, construct a single, higher-level norm. Martha Finnemore and Duncan B. Hollis (2016, 426–427) point out that, while "calls for 'cybernorms' to secure and govern cyberspace are now ubiquitous," cybersecurity is actually "a diverse array of problems." Yet, they further contend that much of the power of norms "lies in the processes by which they form and evolve" (Finnemore and Hollis 2016, 427). Aurora provides a novel context in which to examine this process. Further, the concept of decoupling here refers to democracies working with China to establish mutually beneficial cybersecurity norms that are wholly independent from Internet freedom—the 2015 Obama-Xi cybersecurity pact is one example (Sanger 2016).

Early idealists had hoped that the Internet, by virtue of the unfettered access it provided to information, would act as a force of liberal reform in authoritarian states—and, indeed, it might have, had the Internet remained free and open (Hwang 2018). Instead, China, via the Great Firewall, retooled its domestic Internet into the world's largest censorship apparatus and, despite the efforts of the United States and other democracies, further tightens its Internet controls every year (*Bloomberg News* 2017). China's refusal to adopt domestic or international liberal norms for the Internet presages that the cybersecurity norms among democracies will be different from those between democracies and China—and from those between China and other authoritarian states. Indeed, China has already demonstrated this difference in norms by signing a cybersecurity pact with Russia based on sharing Great Firewall technology (*The Guardian* 2016), and by selling censorship technology to Iran (Stecklow 2012). In other words, while democracies are building cybersecurity norms coupled with Internet freedom, authoritarian states are building cybersecurity norms coupled with Internet censorship. The common bridge between the two sets is cybersecurity, alone.

Margaret Roberts (2018, 37) defines censorship as "the restriction of the public expression of or public access to information by authority when the information is thought to have the capacity to undermine the authority by making it unaccountable to the public." Democracies engage in censorship to different degrees; the flooding of misinformation during the last US election, for instance, has spurred debate on the culpability of Internet companies and whether they should censor their users (Reynolds 2018). However, democracies generally have laws defending free speech (Roberts 2018, 15–16), whereas China argues for its sovereign right to censor. China's government tells private companies, directly, what to censor (Zhuang 2018). Lu Wei, the former head of the Cyberspace Administration of China, said, "I, indeed, may choose who comes into my house. They can come if they are friends," and, "Freedom is our goal. Order is our means" (Martina 2015). Thus, censorship is a nuanced concept, and contrasting democracies as having Internet freedom with China as having Internet censorship is a porous abstraction. Nevertheless, for a broad look at cybersecurity norm-building, this abstraction is useful—with the caveat that, as a complex issue, its purpose is to underscore the fundamental difference that democracies seek the best approach to information freedom, whereas China seeks greater information control.

There are three barriers to decoupling cybersecurity from Internet freedom. The first barrier is that democracies view Internet freedom as a human right while China does not, which compels democracies to pressure China on Internet censorship. Article 19 of the Universal Declaration of Human Rights (1948) recognizes freedom of opinion and expression as a human right, and Internet freedom is that right on the Internet. One cybersecurity expert illustrates the resistance to decoupling cybersecurity from Internet freedom by criticizing the 2015 Obama-Xi cybersecurity pact: "There is nothing in this agreement that addresses Chinese censorship or abuse of human rights. While some might argue that those are not issues related to hacking, a government that shuts off access to portions of the Internet that allow free communication is essentially no different than a party that executes denial-of-service attacks. And human rights cannot be left off the table" (Steinberg 2015).

The second barrier is that cybersecurity and Internet freedom are operationally entangled. To varying degrees, democracies engage in open or collaborative cybersecurity, while China uses censorship as a cybersecurity tool. From the US Department of Defense's bug bounty programs (Newman 2017) to NATO's (2018) collective cyber defense in which "allies are committed to enhancing information-sharing and mutual assistance in preventing, mitigating and recovering from cyber attacks," Internet freedom is an important part of the liberal approach to cybersecurity. On the other hand, China uses the Great Firewall's censorship capabilities for cybersecurity; for instance, China used the Great Firewall to crack down on anonymity tools like Virtual Private Networks (VPNs) (Lin and Kubota 2018)—which hackers can use to hide their location. Conversely, China also uses cybersecurity for censorship purposes; for example, one analyst argues that a cybersecurity regulation that permits both local and central authorities to search the offices of Internet service providers is "designed to more effectively implement China's censorship directives" (Gan 2018).

The final barrier is the moral question of whether this decoupling should occur. Do the benefits of greater Internet peace and security outweigh the risks of further censorship normalization that might arise from cooperative cybersecurity efforts with China? That is, even if democracies can overcome the first two barriers to cybersecurity norm-building with China, it is not clear that they should. However, both governments and technology companies have signaled that this decoupling is already occurring: from the tenuous bilateral cybersecurity pacts China has signed with the United States and a number of other democracies that make no mention of censorship (Burgess 2017) to Apple removing censorship-evading apps from its App Store in China and Google's leaked plans to reintroduce a censored version of its search engine in China (Doubek 2018).

Robert Jervis (1989, 18) defines signals as "statements or actions . . . issued mainly to influence the receiver's image of the sender." In order for signals to be credible, they must be costly—this cost establishes the sender's commitment to the signal. During Aurora, most of the costly signaling that occurred was the *ex post*, tying-hands type—commitments that would result in audience costs if abandoned (Fearon 1997). Simply put, if an actor adopts a stance but does not follow through, they suffer reputation loss. James D. Morrow (1999, 86) writes, "In international politics, signaling is a way to consider the problem of unknown motivation." Signaling, then, is an important tool in the

U.S.-China diplomatic toolbox because it helps to frame the norm formation and evolution process.

China has been signaling that it was open to cybersecurity norm-building at least since the release of its white paper *The Internet in China* in 2010, which called for multilateral cooperation to combat "the increasingly serious problem of transnational network crimes" (IOSCPRC 2010). This white paper was a by-product of an early clash of incompatible cybersecurity norms: Google and the US conflict with China over the Aurora cyber espionage campaign. Using this clash as a case study, it appears that signaling offers an answer to the first two barriers to decoupling. Specifically, signaling can allow cybersecurity norms to cultivate in a separate channel from Internet freedom pressures, and it can help identify and extricate the elements of cybersecurity bound to Internet freedom or censorship.

THE OPERATION AURORA ATTACKS: BACKGROUND

Google has had a difficult relationship with China beyond the inherent market challenges (Madden 2010). It entered China in January 2006 with google.cn, a censored version of its search engine (*CNN* 2006). A Google statement explained its calculus: "While removing search results is inconsistent with Google's mission, providing no information (or a heavily degraded user experience that amounts to no information) is more inconsistent with our mission" (Crampton 2006). Although Google said it would report to users when information was removed from search results (*CNN* 2006), there was, nevertheless, a widespread belief that google.cn violated the company's "don't be evil" policy (*BBN News* 2006). For instance, the following month, a congressional subcommittee on human rights summoned Google—along with other Internet companies—to defend their "sickening collaboration," as the subcommittee chairman put it, with the Chinese government (Zeller 2006).

Google's founders struggled with the choice. Sergey Brin, who claimed that his childhood in the authoritarian Soviet Union influenced his views on censorship (Lohr 2010), spent a year with Larry Page weighing the decision to censor on their "evil scale" (Walker 2010). Reflecting on it a year later, he said, "On a business level, that decision to censor . . . was a net negative" (Martinson 2007). He also remarked that the company had suffered because of the damage to its reputation in the United States and Europe (Martinson 2007). However, he eventually defended the moral reasoning behind google.cn, believing that it was the best decision for the Chinese people (McManus 2010).

In 2010, Google and the US government clashed with the Chinese government over cybersecurity norms. There were two central issues: China's Aurora cyber espionage campaign and China's Internet censorship (Lau

2010). Although not the first—nor most recent—Chinese cyber espionage campaign against the United States (Denning 2017), Aurora's high degree of politicization was unique. As a result, government signaling played a new and interesting role in the cybersecurity norm-building process.

The clash began in January 2010, when Google announced the discovery of a cyberattack, originating in China, that stole its intellectual property and also targeted at least twenty other businesses (Drummond 2010a). Google also noted that "a primary goal of the attackers was accessing the Gmail accounts of Chinese human rights activists" and that, as a consequence, Google would no longer censor google.cn for China (Drummond 2010a). Later that day, in an official statement, US secretary of state Hillary Clinton (2010b) expressed concern over Google's allegations and sought an explanation from China. She also announced that she would be giving a speech on Internet freedom.

Clinton delivered her speech, "Remarks on Internet Freedom," nine days later. It was a *tour de force* on the virtues of Internet freedom and cooperation. She argued that the Internet—as "a new nervous system for our planet"—when free and open, was an unprecedented force for good for individuals, societies, governments, and businesses, but that it could also be repurposed for oppression—and authoritarian regimes were using it this way through censorship. This censorship, she contended, contravened the United Nations Universal Declaration of Human Rights (Clinton 2010a).

At its core, Clinton's speech called for the establishment of global Internet freedom and cybersecurity norms, which she coupled together. She stated, "New technologies do not take sides in the struggle for freedom and progress, but the United States does. We stand for a single Internet where all of humanity has equal access to knowledge and ideas. And we recognize that the world's information infrastructure will become what we and others make of it." Tying this theme to cybersecurity, she remarked that online commerce and intellectual property "are all at stake if we cannot rely on the security of our information networks," that "disruptions in these systems demand a coordinated response by all governments, the private sector, and the international community," and, further, that "we have taken steps as a government, and as a Department, to find diplomatic solutions to strengthen global cyber security." She also announced that the US Department of State would support the development of new circumvention technologies to help evade Internet censorship (Clinton 2010a).

The broader issue, Clinton explained, is "whether we live on a planet with one internet, one global community, and a common body of knowledge that benefits and unites us all, or a fragmented planet in which access to information and opportunity is dependent on where you live and the whims of censors. Information freedom supports the peace and security that provides a foundation for global progress." She made a point of speaking directly to the private sector, arguing that "censorship should not be in any way accepted by any company from anywhere. And in America, American companies need to make a principled stand. This needs to be part of our national brand. I'm confident that consumers worldwide will reward companies that follow those principles" (Clinton 2010a).

Unsurprisingly, she also addressed the Chinese government, asking it to conduct a thorough and transparent investigation into Google's allegations. She noted that, while the United States and China had different views on Internet censorship, they should "address those differences candidly and consistently in the context of our positive, cooperative, and comprehensive relationship." She further warned of censorship's implications for international peace and security: "Historically, asymmetrical access to information is one of the leading causes of interstate conflict. When we face serious disputes or dangerous incidents, it's critical that people on both sides of the problem have access to the same set of facts and opinions" (Clinton 2010a).

In short, Google and the United States were arguing that China's Internet censorship was a human rights violation. China, however, countered that Google needed to obey its laws if it wished to operate there (Fletcher 2010a). In agreement with China was J. Stapleton Roy, a former US ambassador to China, who said, "I don't understand their calculation. I do not see how Google could have concluded that they could have faced down the Chinese on a domestic censorship issue" (Wong 2010). Also siding with China were Microsoft Corporation's Steve Ballmer (2010), who said "we are all subject to local laws," and Bill Gates, who said, "You've got to decide: do you want to obey the laws of the countries you're in or not? If not, you may not end up doing business there" (Johnson and Branigan 2010).

Furthermore, it is important to note that it is unclear whether human rights or, in fact, economics was the deeper motivation for the coordinated Google and US response to Aurora. Not doing well in China despite censoring its search engine, Google's best business decision may have been to improve its international reputation by sacrificing its China operations for a noble cause (Lacy 2010). Similarly, the United States was eager to push back against China's recurring cyber espionage efforts (Metzl 2011). From this perspective, the issue of human rights served as convenient pressure point to achieve other goals.

THE OPERATION AURORA ATTACKS: TIMELINE

Following Jervis's (1989) definition of signals, the methodology for recognizing signals is to identify, from the narrative of this clash, statements, or actions that were intended to alter another actor's perception. Thus, a timeline of the Aurora conflict follows.

January

On January 12, 2010, Google revealed the Aurora cyber espionage campaign to the public, beginning the escalation with the Chinese government (Drummond 2010a). Google announced that they, along with a wide range of other businesses, had been hacked (Drummond 2010a). Google claimed that the target was both its intellectual property and the e-mail accounts of human rights activists, and that the attacks originated in China (Drummond 2010a). Later that day, Clinton (2010b) made her statement seeking an explanation from the Chinese government. Google and Clinton implied that the Chinese government was responsible but had not explicitly assigned blame.

Two days later, a Chinese Foreign Ministry spokeswoman said that Chinese law prohibits any form of hacking attacks and she emphasized that foreign companies needed to respect Chinese law (Fletcher 2010a). She declined, however, to answer a question about whether the illegality of hacking extended to government hacking (Fletcher 2010a). That same day, security researchers at Verisign declared that the Chinese government was behind the attack, claiming that "the government of China has been engaged for months in a massive campaign of industrial espionage against U.S. companies" (Paul 2010). Security researchers at McAfee also investigated the attack, naming it "Operation 'Aurora' " (Goodin 2010a).

On January 18, Google began an investigation into its Chinese employees (Branigan 2010), and, the next day, it postponed the launch of two Android mobile phones in China (Lee and Buckley 2010). On January 21, Clinton (2010a) gave her speech on Internet freedom. The following day, China rebuffed Clinton, warning that her words were dangerous to U.S.–China relations (Fletcher 2010b). At the World Economic Forum at Davos, Google CEO Eric Schmidt remarked, "We like what China is doing in terms of growth . . . we just don't like censorship. We hope that will change and we can apply some pressure to make things better for the Chinese people" (Blumenstein and Fidler 2010).

February

Google began coordinating with the US National Security Agency to analyze the attacks, with the objective to better defend against future attacks (Nakashima 2010). On February 10, evidence emerged that the attacks were still ongoing and had targeted many more companies than Google originally estimated (Higgins 2010). On February 12, Brin said that, given the size of the Chinese government, it was not important whether it was behind the attacks (Zetter 2010). He also remarked that Google was hopeful that it could remain in China and was willing to permit some types of censorship, such as for adult content and gambling, but not political censorship (Zetter 2010). On February 17, the cybersecurity company iSEC published a report detailing the difficulty of defending against Aurora and claimed that it had actually targeted over one hundred companies. The next day, investigators linked Aurora to two Chinese universities (Goodin 2010b). On February 23, for the first time, the Chinese government officially rejected Google's allegations (Graham-Harrison 2010).

March

The United States then considered taking the issue of China's forcing censorship on Google to the WTO as an unfair trade barrier (Drajem 2010). On March 12, China's chief Internet regulator insisted Google must obey its laws or "pay the consequences" (Pomfret 2010). The state-run news agency Xinhua attacked Google's "intricate ties with the U.S. government" on March 21 (*BBC News* 2010). The following day, Google ended its google.cn censorship and tested a new strategy of automatically redirecting visitors from google. cn to google.com.hk, whose servers were located in Hong Kong and so not subject to the mainland's censorship laws (Drummond 2010b). In response, an official in China's State Council Information Office said that Google's move was "totally wrong" and "violated its written promise" (Metz 2010). As a result, on March 23, the Chinese government attempted to restrict the mainland's access to Google's Hong Kong-based servers (Metz 2010).

April–November

On April 20, referencing Article 19 of the Universal Declaration on Human Rights, Google launched a new worldwide tool that displayed the number of government requests for user data or content removal (Drummond 2010d). The Chinese government, on June 8, released the white paper *The Internet in China* defending its Internet policies (Bristow 2010). On June 28, Google announced that the Chinese government would not accept its redirect solution and would deny the renewal of its business license (Drummond 2010c). Consequently, Google attempted a new strategy, turning google.cn into a static webpage that only contained a link to their uncensored Hong Kong-based site, rather than forcing an automatic redirect (Drummond 2010c). Google stated, "This new approach is consistent with our commitment not to self censor and, we believe, with local law (Drummond 2010c)." The new strategy worked: on July 9, Google's China business license was renewed (Drummond 2010c).

From that point on, both sides remained relatively peaceable, even after a WikiLeaks cable, released on November 28, implicated the Chinese Politburo in the Aurora attacks (Shane and Lehren 2010).

THE OPERATION AURORA ATTACKS: SIGNALS

During Aurora, there were roughly four groups of tying-hands signals that used reputation as an audience cost. The first signal of significance occurs at the beginning of the conflict: Google revealing Aurora to the public and tying its hands by announcing the plan to end its censorship. To the international community and to its users, Google signaled a recommitment to its "don't be evil" policy. To the Chinese government, it signaled that there were both physical and virtual consequences to China's hostile actions in cyberspace. These potential consequences included Google no longer abiding China's censorship laws—possibly even leaving China—and China suffering international reputation loss.

The second signal was the response of the US government. Google and the US Department of State may have coordinated the initial public response to occur on the same day for greater impact. From this viewpoint, it was a two-pronged act of Thomas Schelling's (1966, 69) concept of compellence, with the threat being that the United States would escalate the issue in Clinton's upcoming speech if China did not justify itself before then. China did not, and, with Clinton's speech and the later threat to take the matter to the WTO, the United States signaled that it would respond in both the physical and virtual spheres to actions that harm its interests in cyberspace. Broadly, the United States was tying its hands to a willingness to escalate matters.

The third set of signals was the cumulative reaction of the Chinese government. There were four important individual responses: first, the response two days after the first statements by Google and Clinton; second, the response the day after Clinton's address on Internet freedom; third, the response after more evidence had accumulated linking the Chinese government to the attacks, and finally, the publication of *The Internet in China*, the Chinese government's white paper defending its Internet practices. Each response added something: the first, that foreign companies must follow China's domestic laws; the second, that what was best for the Chinese people was China's concern, and so Clinton's comments were damaging to U.S.–China relations; and the third, that Google's allegations in its January 12 statement were "groundless," stating that "China administers its Internet according to law, and this position will not change. China prohibits hacking and will crack down on hacking according to law" (Graham-Harrison 2010). This was the first time China had directly refuted the allegations, over five weeks after Aurora came to light.

China's fourth response, the white paper *The Internet in China*, both reiterated and expanded on the messages of the first three responses. Like Clinton's speech, it expressed the importance of international cooperation on cybersecurity. The white paper was both China's version of and ultimate response to the speech, and it was an argument for China's Internet sovereignty within its borders. Interestingly, apparently in response to Clinton's call for Internet freedom, it claimed that the Chinese government "guarantees the citizens' freedom of speech on the Internet as well as the public's right to know, to participate, to be heard and to oversee in accordance with the law" (IOSCPRC 2010). China was tying its hands to the argument that both the United States and China permit Internet freedom in accordance with law, but that those laws were different.

The final signals occurred during rapprochement. Because Google and the United States confronted China publicly, China had to respond in a way that would mitigate its international reputation loss. By emphasizing the illegality of hacking and making the issue of censorship a matter of legal compliance, China was able to defend its requirements for renewing Google's business license. By permitting Google to adhere to the letter of the law but not the spirit, China signaled that, even in sensitive areas like censorship, legal compliance had some flexibility.

The silence that followed the renewal of Google's business license— silence that even the new WikiLeaks evidence did not interrupt—signaled that both sides were eager to move forward from the clash. China and Google continued their tenuous relationship, although China never fully relented: it slowed down and intermittently disrupted Google's services—a form of censorship (Roberts 2018, 42)—finally blocking google.com.hk altogether in 2014 (Levin 2014). Nevertheless, at the time, Google was able to offer a link to an uncensored search engine for users who sought it, and China was satisfied that Google capitulated to its regulations. In the end, however, all three actors suffered some reputation loss: evidence had implicated the government of China in the attack, the international community remembered that Google had "spent four years, and earned vast sums of money, operating under China's censorship laws" (Carr 2010), and Clinton's appeal for global Internet freedom had achieved little.

DECOUPLING CYBERSECURITY AND INTERNET FREEDOM

Despite working in conjunction, it is clear that Google's efforts in the Aurora conflict were relatively successful, while the United States' efforts were not. To wit, although Google was struggling in a hostile market environment and the victim of cyber espionage, Google's public retaliation eventually resulted in the renewal of its business license without continuing to censor its search engine. On the other hand, as powerful as Clinton's speech and the following WTO threat were, the United States did not succeed in compelling China to lessen its information controls, in preventing businesses from becoming increasingly interdependent with China, or in yielding from China a transparent investigation into Aurora or an admission of wrongdoing. Nor did it substantially lessen China's cyber espionage efforts against the United States (Denning 2017). Thus, Google's actions serve as the better model: Google received and responded to China's signals and made more progress. It is important to consider two points, however: first, that without the accompanying pressure from the United States, China might not have been as willing to accept Google's solution; and second, Google's business interests are minor in scope in comparison to the US foreign policy interests.

From the beginning, China signaled that Google could stay by obeying China's laws. Google found it could obey these laws by rerouting traffic to its uncensored Hong Kong site, first testing China's limits with an automatic redirect before retreating to a link that required manual effort. Simultaneously, Google increased its pressure on China to reduce censorship by adding a reporting tool for government censorship requests—but it added this tool separately from its effort to renew its business license. Thus, Google overcame the first barrier—that Internet freedom is a human right—to decoupling cybersecurity from Internet freedom. Google funneled pressure against censorship through a different channel—an unrelated reporting tool, in this case—while cultivating a cybersecurity norm of following China's laws and expecting, in return, a more secure operating environment. Google achieved this favorable outcome despite its "don't be evil" policy and Brin's personal enmity toward censorship.

Through its white paper, China signaled that it desired to cooperate on cybersecurity relating to "transnational network crimes," but also that its cyber sovereignty commitment was uncompromising (IOSCPRC 2010). Clinton signaled a similar intransigence on cybersecurity cooperation, stipulating Internet freedom as an elemental component. The United States made its appeal to the international community for Internet freedom, its ambitions to create anti-censorship tools, and its threat to take the matter to the WTO in conjunction with the appeal for global cybersecurity norm-building. If the United States had separated these efforts, as it did during the later Obama-Xi summit, it might have made more progress in overcoming the first barrier.

Google's success, however, illustrates how signaling can help democracies pressure China on censorship separately from cybersecurity norm-building; it suggests that democracies can decouple the two without giving up on Internet freedom. Google's experience also demonstrated the second barrier—that cybersecurity and Internet freedom are operationally entangled—by working with the US government and international security researchers on analyzing Aurora. China had, in its white paper, stated that different states have different needs for Internet cooperation: "Though connected, the Internet of various countries belongs to different sovereignties, which makes it necessary to strengthen international exchanges and cooperation in this field" (IOSCPRC 2010). In other words, it signaled that cybersecurity norm-building requires calibrating the norms to those differences. In Google's case, the expectation of not being the target of government-sponsored cyber espionage was not contingent on having Internet freedom in China. That is, while Google could not expect full operational freedom in China, it could still seek to build a norm of operational cybersecurity.

China, by proclaiming that hacking was illegal—despite that it, itself, was doing the hacking—signaled that this concept served as a foundation to build on, and Google accepted the signal by seeking ways to continue its China operations. The secure business environment that China signaled was a norm-building effort operationally disentangled from Internet freedom or censorship. Perhaps to validate the honesty of this signal, Aurora eventually did stop. In contrast, Clinton's speech operationally coupled Internet freedom with cybersecurity, implying that improving global cybersecurity would only be possible alongside Internet freedom, and so it did not overcome the second barrier. Google's relative progress here suggests that signaling can offer insights into operational disentanglement.

The final barrier to decoupling cybersecurity from Internet freedom is the moral component. Even if democracies can decouple the two for norm-building with China, should they? Although this question will endure, a couple points worthy of consideration stand out. The fact that cybersecurity norm-building is separable from Internet freedom goals, without preventing efforts to achieve those goals, is an argument in favor. On the other hand, these efforts might be weaker, overall, and so further entrench China's censorship practices. The condemnation from human rights groups over the recent capitulations of US companies to China's censorship demands illustrates this concern (Doubek 2018).

In the Aurora conflict, China offered valuable information through signaling. Although signals can be dishonest (Jervis 1989, 18), China's renewal of Google's business license, after Google responded to China's signals, demonstrated honesty. Google used these signals to decouple Internet freedom—without abandoning it—from cybersecurity norm-building with China, as well as to discern the operational requirements of such norms. Conversely, the United States showed that not decoupling the two is a dead end. Thus, the hypothesis emerges that cybersecurity norm-building between democracies and China is more likely to succeed if cybersecurity is not coupled with

Internet freedom, and that signaling can help overcome two of the barriers to this decoupling.

Interestingly, the literature on signaling has argued that authoritarian regimes are less effective than democracies at sending tying-hands signals with *ex post* costs because the domestic audience costs are lower or obfuscated (Weiss 2013, 1–2). Jessica Chen Weiss (2013, 2) shows that authoritarian states can employ nationalist, anti-foreign protests as a substitute for the way democracies use official statements as tying-hands signals. Yet, during Aurora, China's official statements appeared to be honest signals. The first possibility is that the signals were costless but happened to be honest anyway. The second possibility, which seems more likely, is that the costs were not domestic but rather from the international audience. The world was watching, and if China had backed down from its stance of being in the legal right, the international political and business community's perception of China would adjust accordingly.

Although China's authoritarianism might intrinsically restrict the bandwidth of potential cybersecurity cooperation, something changed in democracies' willingness to seek it in the time between Clinton's speech on Internet freedom in 2010 and 2015 Obama-Xi cybersecurity summit. The summit occurred while the US Department of State was funding the development of censorship evasion tools, and the resulting pact, which temporarily succeeded in reducing the frequency of Chinese cyberattacks on the United States (Sanger 2016), made no mention of censorship (Brown and Yung 2017). The pact, along with China's other cybersecurity pacts in recent years, overcame the three barriers to decoupling and may suggest that democracies are becoming more receptive to the idea. As cybersecurity becomes more important to international security, democracies may increasingly view cybersecurity norms as independent from others.

BIBLIOGRAPHY

Ballmer, Steve. 2010. "Microsoft & Internet Freedom." Official Microsoft Blog, Microsoft. January 27, 2010. https://blogs.microsoft.com/blog/2010/01/27/micros oft-internet-freedom/.

Blumenstein, Rebecca and Stephen Fidler. 2010. "Google Takes Aim at Beijing Censorship." *Wall Street Journal*, January 30, 2010. https://www.wsj.com/articles/ SB10001424052748703389004575033100778834196.

Branigan, Tania. 2010. "Google Investigates China Staff Over Cyber Attack." *Guardian*, January 18, 2010. https://www.theguardian.com/technology/2010/jan/18/chin a-google-cyber-attack.

Bristow, Michael. 2010. "China Defends Internet Censorship." *BBC News*, June 8, 2010. http://news.bbc.co.uk/2/hi/americas/8727647.stm.

Brown, Gary and Christopher D. Yung. 2017. "Evaluating the US-China Cybersecurity Agreement, Part 1: The US Approach to Cyberspace." *Diplomat*, January 19, 2017. https://thediplomat.com/2017/01/evaluating-the-us-china-cybersecurity-agreement-part-1-the-us-approach-to-cyberspace/.

Burgess, Christopher. 2017. "Dissecting China's Global Bilateral Cybersecurity Strategy." *Security Boulevard*, October 9, 2017. https://securityboulevard.com/2017/10/dissecting-chinas-global-bilateral-cybersecurity-strategy/.

Carr, Paul. 2010. "Soul Searching: Google's Position on China Might Be Many Things, But Moral It Is Not." *TechCrunch*, January 13, 2010. https://techcrunch.com/2010/01/13/not-safe-for-wok/.

"China Denounces Google 'US ties.'" *BBC News*, March 21, 2010. http://news.bbc.co.uk/2/hi/asia-pacific/8578968.stm.

China Internet Network Information Center. 2018. "第42次《中国互联网络发展状况统计报告》发布." August 20, 2018. https://cnnic.net.cn/gywm/xwzx/rdxw/20172017_7047/201808/t20180820_70486.htm.

Clinton, Hillary. 2010a. "Remarks on Internet Freedom." U.S. Department of State. January 21, 2010. https://2009-2017.state.gov/secretary/20092013clinton/rm/2010/01/135519.htm.

Clinton, Hillary. 2010b. "Statement on Google Operations in China." U.S. Department of State. January 12, 2010. https://2009-2017.state.gov/secretary/20092013clinton/rm/2010/01/135105.htm.

Crampton, Thomas. 2006. "Google Puts Muzzle on Itself in China." *New York Times*, January 24, 2006. https://www.nytimes.com/2006/01/24/technology/google-puts-muzzle-on-itself-in-china.html.

Denning, Dorothy. 2017. "How the Chinese Cyberthreat Has Evolved." *Conversation*, October 4, 2017. https://theconversation.com/how-the-chinese-cyberthreat-has-evolved-82469.

Doubek, James. 2018. "Google Testing a Censored Search Engine Just for China." *NPR*, August 2, 2018. https://www.npr.org/2018/08/02/634827587/google-testing-a-censored-search-engine-just-for-china.

Drajem, Mark. 2010. "Google Wants U.S. to Weigh Challenging China in WTO." *Bloomberg*, March 3, 2010. https://www.bloomberg.com/news/articles/2010-03-03/google-wants-u-s-to-weigh-challenging-china-in-wto.

Drummond, David. 2010a. "A New Approach to China." *Official Blog*, Google. January 12, 2010. https://googleblog.blogspot.com/2010/01/new-approach-to-china.html.

Drummond, David. 2010b. "A New Approach to China: An Update." *Official Blog, Google*. March 22, 2010. https://googleblog.blogspot.com/2010/03/new-approach-to-china-update.html.

Drummond, David. 2010c. "An Update on China." *Official Blog, Google*. July 9, 2010. https://googleblog.blogspot.com/2010/06/update-on-china.html.

Drummond, David. 2010d. "Greater Transparency Around Government Requests." *Official Blog, Google*. April 20, 2010. https://googleblog.blogspot.com/2010/04/greater-transparency-around-government.html.

Fearon, James D. 1997. "Signaling Foreign Policy Interests: Tying Hands versus Sinking Costs." *The Journal of Conflict Resolution*. 41, no. 1 (February): 68–90. http://www.jstor.org/stable/174487.

Finnemore, Martha and Duncan B. Hollis. 2016. "Constructing Norms for Global Cybersecurity." *American Journal of International Law*. 110, no. 3 (July): 425–479. https://doi.org/10.1017/S0002930000016894.

Fletcher, Owen. 2010a. "China Emphasizes Laws as Google Defies Censorship." *PCWorld*, January 14, 2010. https://www.pcworld.com/article/186881/article.html.

Fletcher, Owen. 2010b. "China slams Clinton's Call for Internet Freedom." *Computerworld*, January 22, 2010. https://www.computerworld.com/article/2523071/enterprise-applications/china-slams-clinton-s-call-for-internet-freedom.html.

"Freedom on the Net 2017." Freedom House, November 2017. https://freedomhouse.org/report/freedom-net/freedom-net-2017.

Gan, Nectar. 2018. "Chinese Police Get Power to Inspect Internet Service Providers." *South China Morning Post*. October 6, 2018. https://www.scmp.com/news/china/politics/article/2167240/chinese-police-get-power-inspect-internet-service-providers.

Goodin, Dan. 2010a. "IE Zero-Day Used in Chinese Cyber Assault on 34 Firms." *Register*, January 14, 2010. https://www.theregister.co.uk/2010/01/14/cyber_assault_followup/.

Goodin, Dan. 2010b. "Most Resistance to 'Aurora' Hack Attacks Futile, Says Report." *Register*, March 1, 2010. https://www.theregister.co.uk/2010/03/01/aurora_resistence_futile/.

"Google move 'black day' for China." *BBC News*, January 25, 2006. http://news.bbc.co.uk/2/hi/technology/4647398.stm.

"Google to Censor Itself in China." *CNN*, January 26, 2006. http://www.cnn.com/2006/BUSINESS/01/25/google.china/.

Graham-Harrison, Emma. 2010. "China Says Google Hacking Claims 'groundless.'" *Reuters*, February 23, 2010. https://www.reuters.com/article/us-china-google/china-says-google-hacking-claims-groundless-idUSTRE61M2FM20100223.

Higgins, Kelly Jackson. 2010. "'Aurora' Attacks Still Under Way, Investigators Closing In On Malware Creators." *Darkreading*, February 10, 2010. https://www.darkreading.com/attacks-breaches/aurora-attacks-still-under-way-investigators-closing-in-on-malware-creators/d/d-id/1132922.

Hwang, Tim. 2018. "The Four Ways That Ex-Internet Idealists Explain Where It All Went Wrong." *MIT Technology Review*, August 22, 2018. https://www.technologyreview.com/s/611805/the-four-ways-that-ex-internet-idealists-explain-where-it-all-went-wrong.

IOSCPRC (Information Office of the State Council of the People's Republic of China). 2010. *The Internet in China*. June 8, 2010. http://www.china.org.cn/government/whitepaper/node_7093508.htm.

Jervis, Robert. 1989. *The Logic of Images in International Relations*. New York: Columbia University Press.

Johnson, Bobbie and Tania Branigan. 2010. "Web Censorship in China? Not a Problem, Says Bill Gates." *Guardian*, January 25, 2010. https://www.theguardian.com/technology/2010/jan/25/bill-gates-web-censorship-china.

Lacy, Sarah. 2010. "Google's China Stance: More About Business Than Thwarting Evil." *TechCrunch*, January 12, 2010. https://techcrunch.com/2010/01/12/google's-china-stance-more-about-business-than-thwarting-evil/.

Lau, Justine. 2010. "A History of Google in China." *Financial Times*, July 9, 2010. http://ig-legacy.ft.com/content/faf86fbc-0009-11df-8626-00144feabdc0#axzz5P hJFzwqh.

Lee, Melanie and Chris Buckley. 2010. "Google Postpones Cellphone Launch in China." *Reuters*, January 19, 2010. https://www.reuters.com/article/idINIndia-455 11720100119.

Levin, Dan. 2014. "China Escalating Attack on Google." *New York Times*, June 2, 2014. https://www.nytimes.com/2014/06/03/business/chinas-battle-against-goog le-heats-up.html.

Lin, Liza and Yoko Kubota. 2018. "China's VPN Crackdown May Aid Government Surveillance." *Wall Street Journal*. January 17, 2018. https://www.wsj.com/artic les/chinas-vpn-crackdown-may-aid-government-surveillance-1516189155.

Lohr, Steve. 2010. "Interview: Sergey Brin on Google's China Move." *New York Times*, March 22, 2010. https://bits.blogs.nytimes.com/2010/03/22/interview-ser gey-brin-on-googles-china-gambit/.

Madden, Normandy. 2010. "Google Isn't the Only Silicon Valley Company Strug- gling in China." *Business Insider*, January 19, 2010. https://www.businessinsid er.com/google-isnt-the-only-silicon-valley-company-struggling-in-china-2010-1.

Markoff, John and David Barboza. 2010. "2 China Schools Said to Be Tied to Online Attacks." *New York Times*, February 18, 2010. https://www.nytimes.com/2010/0 2/19/technology/19china.html.

Martina, Michael. 2015. "China's Cyber Chief Defends Censorship Ahead of Internet Conference." *Reuters*, December 9, 2015. https://www.reuters.com/article/us- china-internet/chinas-cyber-chief-defends-censorship-ahead-of-internet-conferenc e-idUSKBN0TS0X720151209.

Martinson, Jane. 2007. "China Censorship Damaged Us, Google Founders Admit." *Guardian*, January 27, 2007. https://www.theguardian.com/technology/2007/j an/27/news.newmedia.

McManus, Emily. 2010. "Sergey Brin on Google's China Decision." TEDBlog, TED. February 24, 2010. https://blog.ted.com/our_focus_has_b/.

Metz, Cade. 2010. "China Hits Back at Google's Uncensored Hong Kong Servers." *Register*, March 23, 2010. https://www.theregister.co.uk/2010/03/23/china_mov es_to_restrict_google_hong_kong_services/.

Metzl, Jamie. 2011. "China and Cyber-Espionage." *HuffPost*, October 22, 2011. https ://www.huffingtonpost.com/jamie-metzl/china-and-cyberespionage_b_931918.html.

Morrow, James D. 1999. "The Strategic Setting of Choices: Signaling, Commitment, and Negotiation in International Politics." In *Strategic Choice and International Relations*, edited by David A. Lake and Robert Powell, 77–114. Princeton: Princ- eton University Press.

Nakashima, Ellen. 2010. "Google to Enlist NSA to Help It Ward Off Cyberattacks." *Washington Post*, February 4, 2010. http://www.washingtonpost.com/wp-dyn/con tent/article/2010/02/03/AR2010020304057.html.

Newman, Lily Hay. 2017. "The Pentagon Opened Up to Hackers—And Fixed Thou- sands of Bugs." *Wired*, November 10, 2017. https://www.wired.com/story/hack-th e-pentagon-bug-bounty-results/.

NATO (North Atlantic Treaty Organization). 2018. "Cyber Defense." July 16, 2018. https://www.nato.int/cps/en/natohq/topics_78170.htm.

Paul, Ryan. 2010. "Researchers Identify Command Servers Behind Google Attack." *Ars Technica*, January 14, 2010. https://arstechnica.com/information-technolog y/2010/01/researchers-identify-command-servers-behind-google-attack/.

Pomfret, John. 2010. "China Holds Firm Against Google, Says Firm Must Obey Its Laws." *Washington Post*, March 13, 2010. http://www.washingtonpost.com/wp-dy n/content/article/2010/03/12/AR2010031203564.html.

"Putin Brings China's Great Firewall to Russia in Cybersecurity Pact." *The Guardian*, November 29, 2016. https://www.theguardian.com/world/2016/nov/29/puti n-china-internet-great-firewall-russia-cybersecurity-pact.

"Quicktake: The Great Firewall of China." *Bloomberg News*, November 30, 2017. https://www.bloomberg.com/quicktake/great-firewall-of-china.

Reynolds, Glenn Harlan. 2018. "When Digital Platforms Become Censors." *Wall Street Journal*, August 18, 2018. https://www.wsj.com/articles/when-digital-pla tforms-become-censors-1534514122.

Roberts, Margaret E. 2018. *Censored: Distraction and Diversion Inside China's Great Firewall*. Princeton: Princeton University Press.

Sanger, David E. 2016. "Chinese Curb Cyberattacks on U.S. Interests, Report Finds." *New York Times*, June 20, 2016. https://www.nytimes.com/2016/06/21/us/politics/ china-us-cyber-spying.html.

Schelling, Thomas. 1966. *Arms and Influence*. Fredericksburg: BookCrafters.

Shane, Scott and Andrew W. Lehren. 2010. "Leaked Cables Offer Raw Look at U.S. Diplomacy." *New York Times*, November 28, 2010. https://www.nytimes.com/2 010/11/29/world/29cables.html.

Stecklow, Steve. 2012. "Special Report: Chinese Firm Helps Iran Spy on Citizens." *Reuters*, March 22, 2012. https://www.reuters.com/article/us-iran-telecoms/specia l-report-chinese-firm-helps-iran-spy-on-citizens-idUSBRE82L0B820120322.

Steinberg, Joseph. 2015. "10 Issues With the China-US Cybersecurity Agreement." *Inc.*, September 27, 2015. https://www.inc.com/joseph-steinberg/why-the-china -us-cybersecurity-agreement-will-fail.html.

UN General Assembly. 1948. *Universal Declaration of Human Rights*. December 10, 1948, 217 A (III). http://www.un.org/en/universal-declaration-human-rights/.

Walker, Tim. 2010. "Sergey Brin: Engine Driver." *Independent*, January 16, 2010. https://www.independent.co.uk/news/people/profiles/sergey-brin-engine-drive r-1869546.html.

Weiss, Jessica Chen. 2013. "Authoritarian Signaling, Mass Audiences, and National-ist Protest in China." *International Organization*. 67, no. 1 (January): 1-35. http:// journals.cambridge.org/abstract_S0020818312000380.

Wong, Edward. 2010. "Google Faces Fallout as China Reacts to Site Shift." *New York Times*, March 23, 2010. https://www.nytimes.com/2010/03/24/technology /24google.html.

Zeller, Tom, Jr. 2006. "Web Firms Are Grilled on Dealings in China." *New York Times*, February 16, 2006. https://www.nytimes.com/2006/02/16/technology/web-firms-are-grilled-on-dealings-in-china.html.

Zetter, Kim. 2010. "TED 2010: Google Optimistic It Can Remain in China." *Wired*, February 12, 2010. https://www.wired.com/epicenter/2010/02/ted-2010-google-optimistic-it-can-remain-in-china/.

Zhuang, Pinghui. 2018. "Weibo Falls Foul of China's Internet Watchdog for Failing to Censor Content." *South China Morning Post*, January 29, 2018. https://www.scmp.com/news/china/policies-politics/article/2130931/weibo-falls-foul-chinas-internet-watchdog-failing.

Chapter 10

Ambiguity and Appropriation

Cybersecurity and Cybercrime in Egypt and the Gulf

James Shires

On October 4, 2018, the United Kingdom strongly denounced "reckless" and "irresponsible" cyberattacks conducted by the Russian military intelligence service against a wide range of targets, including the Organization for the Prevention of Chemical Weapons, the United Kingdom's Foreign and Commonwealth Office, and its Defence and Science Technology Laboratory. The UK statement emphasized that these attacks were "without regard for international law or established norms," contrasting Russian actions with the "united" approach of the United Kingdom, its allies, and the international community (UK Government 2018). The UK defence secretary even drew on language previously used to describe North Korean cyberattacks (Greenberg 2017), labeling Russia a "pariah state" (Lambert, Deutsch, and Faulconbridge 2018).

This extreme rhetoric, portraying cyberspace as a black-and-white competition between the good guys and the bad, obscures a more complicated global context. To understand the true nature of this supposed bipolar division in cyber norms, it may be instructive to turn away from the headline-grabbing (and undoubtedly illegitimate) activities of Russian intelligence agencies and to look at more complex edge cases. States in the Middle East exhibit this complexity in abundance, given the variety of conflicts and tensions in the region involving both internal struggles and international interventions. More specifically, where do Egypt and the six states of the Gulf Cooperation Council (GCC)—Bahrain, Kuwait, Oman, Qatar, Saudi Arabia, and the United Arab Emirates (UAE)—fit into this picture? Despite their many differences, these states share a curious position: on the one hand, their regulations, laws, and participation in international institutions place them with Russia, China, and other proponents of cyber sovereignty; on the other, their private sector cybersecurity collaborations, intelligence relationships, and offensive cyber operations are closely aligned with the United States and Europe.

This chapter argues that this contradictory position has led to two innovations in state responses to global cyber norms. First, these states have developed deliberately *ambiguous* national cybersecurity strategies that disguise differences between domestic cybersecurity priorities and those of their international partners. Second, these states have *appropriated* international norms on cybercrime—specifically the Council of Europe's Budapest Convention of 2001—in order to counter political opposition and restrict their online public spheres through new cybercrime legislation. This chapter has three sections. The first section details the contradictory position of Egypt and the Gulf states in relation to international cyber norms. The second section examines their national cybersecurity strategies, and the third section examines their cybercrime laws. Finally, it concludes that these two innovations are closely linked: the cybersecurity practices of these states, especially their appropriation of cybercrime laws, illustrates the calculated nature of the ambiguity present in their strategy documents. Finally, one caveat is necessary: the research for this chapter was conducted up to August 2018, and so developments following this date, including a recent increase in publicly available documents, are not factored into the analysis.

A COMPLEX MIDDLE GROUND

Many scholars and policy makers lament the current state of "cyber norms," especially after the failure of the U.N. Group of Governmental Experts to agree on the application of international law in cyberspace in 2017 (Grigsby 2017). The difficulty of reaching global agreement on cyber norms is generally attributed to a bipolar division in cybersecurity governance, reflecting two opposing sets of values. On one hand, there is a group of what experts have called "like-minded" states (Kaljurand 2017). This group generally includes the United States and European countries, and it believes in an open and free Internet driven largely by global market competition with some government regulation and civil society observation, known as multistakeholderism (Savage and McConnell 2015). The second group includes Iran, Russia, and China, and prioritizes state control over national "borders" in cyberspace with strict governmental limits on content, known as cyber sovereignty (Segal 2018). These differences have been described as the cyberspace element of a resurgent Cold War, in which neoliberal and democratic structures confront information control, authoritarianism, and rule-breaking (Ignatius 2016).

In fact, this picture is much more complex, with a variety of approaches to Internet governance in both camps.[1] For example, Carr highlights how multistakeholder governance masks the exercise of state power, especially regarding the diminished role of civil society groups in decision-making rather than deliberative fora; what she terms "power plays" (Carr 2015). On the other side of the coin, Cornish has shown how the Chinese approach to digital sovereignty is in fact much more nuanced than simple blanket control (Cornish 2015). Taking this argument further, Raymond and Denardis have argued that multistakeholderism is heterogeneous and inchoate, as administrative and regulatory bodies are routinely captured by specific coalitions of both public and private sector actors (Raymond and DeNardis 2015). Instead, they identify five overlapping "sets of procedural rules" for Internet governance: the liberal ("OECD") view, the authoritarian ("Shanghai Cooperation Organisation") view, a G77 postcolonial view, and technical and corporate views. This section argues that Egypt and the Gulf states occupy a hybrid position in the simpler bipolar model; however, a similar argument could be made regarding Raymond and DeNardis's fivefold model.

The GCC states and Egypt are not liberal democracies. They have all—to varying degrees—adopted a position of quiet cooperation and hostile confrontation with the regional cyber powers of Israel and Iran, respectively. There are also many wider differences in their economies, societies, and access to Internet technologies. There are deep political disputes between Egypt and the GCC states, illustrated starkly by the split between Qatar and the "quartet" states—Bahrain, Egypt, Saudi Arabia, and the UAE—in June 2017, with Oman and Kuwait taking a neutral position.

Despite their differences, all these states' approaches to cyber issues exhibit some similarities with the authoritarian, cyber sovereignty-focused approach of Russia, China, and Iran. Cyber sovereignty emphasizes the strong assertion of territorial boundaries and state control over internal infrastructure, transnational connections, and content produced within or by citizens of that state. For example, Article 31 of Egypt's 2014 constitution, drafted after the 2013 coup and subsequent election of President Abdel Fattah Al-Sisi, states: "the security of information space is an integral part of the system of national economy and security. The state commits to taking the necessary measures to preserve it" (The Arab Republic of Egypt 2014). Given the wide powers allocated to military and security agencies under this constitution, and the censorship practiced under Al-Sisi, it is safe to assume that "the security of information space" (*'amn al-fida' al-mu'alumati*) is defined broadly along Russian or Chinese lines.

The GCC states have similar outlooks on the control of national information, also demonstrated through broad practices of censorship (Dalek et al. 2018; Haselton 2013). Also, all these states have supported an increased role for the United Nations in cybersecurity regulation and standards (Dourado 2012). The United Nations is generally the preferred venue for proponents of cyber sovereignty because its state-only structures increase the relative power of non-Western states. In contrast, multistakeholderism also includes (mainly Western) private companies and civil society representatives. Despite occasional reports of bilateral cooperation with Russia and China—for example, Egypt's 2014 intent to work with China on combatting "cybercrimes" (*The Economic Times* 2014)—the United Nations appears to be the main forum where these states work together on cybersecurity.

But despite their embrace of cyber sovereignty over multistakeholderism, Egypt and the Gulf states work more closely with the "like-minded" states than their rivals. This is based on broader security and intelligence partnerships: for example, the United Kingdom relies on Oman for signals intelligence collection highly valued by its Five Eyes partners (Campbell 2014a), while Saudi Arabia and the UAE are approved "Third Parties," able to access some U.S. signals intelligence (Campbell 2014b). These links extend into cybersecurity, which is a key commercial and diplomatic pillar of the U.K.'s Gulf Initiative (UK Trade & Investment 2013). The UAE has allegedly discussed joint "cyber tools . . . to contain and defeat Iranian aggression" with a Washington think tank, another sign of potential cooperation in the cyber realm (Jilani and Grim 2017). More broadly, there are U.K.–Saudi Arabia agreements to develop "strategic cooperation in cybersecurity" (Foreign & Commonwealth Office 2018), and U.S.–Egypt joint military exercises including cybersecurity scenarios against a background of increased U.S. military aid (Belnap 2018; Malsin 2018). Due to these extensive associations, these states cannot simply be labeled as spoiler forces against multistakeholder proponents—a label more appropriately applied to Russia, China, and Iran.

Cybersecurity links to Western liberal democracies extend beyond state-to-state relationships, as the profile of commercial cybersecurity has risen following several significant cyberattacks (Bronk and Tikk-Ringas 2013; Krebs 2013). Private companies based in the United States and Europe sell a wide range of defensive cybersecurity solutions and cybersecurity consultancy services to most major companies and government organizations in Egypt and the Gulf, which they see as a lucrative market, while arms companies with a long-standing presence in the region offer national surveillance and offensive cyber capabilities (Shires 2018). In these ways, Egypt and the Gulf states present a challenge to bipolar models of Internet governance that presume the two sides simply form Cold War-style blocs.

These states' approach—extensive cooperation despite substantive disagreement—echoes wider contradictions between the normative and strategic components of the relationships between Egypt and the Gulf states and their international allies. In the Cold War, the oil wealth of the Gulf states and Egypt's central position in pan-Arabism and the Israel–Palestine conflict motivated the United States and Europe to work with these countries, over-looking inconsistencies with the rhetoric of worldwide democracy promotion (Chase and Hamzawy 2008). After the Cold War, joint concerns over Islamist terrorism and growing arms sales encouraged an equally muted public response to human rights violations from allied governments. Both sides have attempted to square this circle. International allies argued that influence in private was more effective than public condemnation, and that working with these regimes was more likely to bring change than breaking away from them (van Rij and Wilkinson 2018). The regimes themselves paid lip service to democracy and human rights, and activists and social movements made some genuine progress (Hosseinioun 2017).

In cybersecurity, the same puzzle presents itself. There has been no indication of opposition by the US and UK governments to the raft of new cybercrime laws. More seriously, their offensive cyber activities do not fall within the limits set both rhetorically and in practice by the United States, the United Kingdom, and other "like-minded" states, which condemn the destabilizing use of cyber tools and permit cyber espionage only for narrow national security purposes. The GCC split itself was reportedly triggered by a cyber operation carried out by contractors working for the UAE, who implanted fake text praising Iran on the website of the Qatari national news agency (DeYoung and Nakashima 2017). The leaking of private e-mails of the UAE ambassador to the United States may have been a Qatari response (Ahmed 2017). Finally, as part of the ongoing dispute between Canada and Saudi Arabia, Israel-manufactured spyware was identified on the devices of Saudi dissidents in Canada, and assessed to be controlled by the Saudi government (Hubbard and Porter 2018; Marczak et al. 2018). Egypt has conducted similar cyberattacks on journalists and civil society (Scott-Railton et al. 2017). Overall, the contradictions between cyber norms and long-standing security alliances have been left unresolved, undermining the force of the norms the United Kingdom stresses in regard to states like Russia.

This complex picture, which reflects the broader tensions in these states' historical relationships with Western democracies dating back to the Cold War, suggests that a binary understanding of global cyber norms is incomplete. Amid deep conflict over basic norms, Egypt and the GCC states have maneuvered between two poles while enjoying the tacit, if not explicit, support of both sides. This suggests that global cyber norms are much more complex—and much more entangled with traditional governance practices, diplomatic relationships, and strategic concerns—than Western officials may like to admit. More broadly, to understand the complexity of cyber norms we must look outside the framework of great power competition.

AMBIGUOUS CYBERSECURITY STRATEGIES

National strategy documents are a key element of the global cybersecurity landscape: they are a requirement of many cybersecurity maturity models, and international bodies collect and compare cybersecurity strategies from around the world. The language of these strategies can be hyperbolic, vague, and full of jargon: for example, the Qatari strategy claims that "this is an integrated and holistic approach that will enhance synergies, avoid duplication, and maximize resource utilisation in managing the dynamic environment and emerging threats in cyberspace" (ictQatar, May 2014, vii). Such language is easy to dismiss as mere marketing, with no significant role more broadly. Instead, I argue that national cybersecurity strategies in Egypt and the Gulf states are *ambiguous*, reflecting the contradictory position of these states in cybersecurity governance.

Ambiguity is a common attribute of international politics outside the cybersecurity arena. There are many varieties of vagueness and indeterminacy in the discourse of international politics, some of which are not deliberately cultivated; ambiguity can simply stem from lack of knowledge, time pressures, or rapidly changing circumstances (especially in cybersecurity). However, other ambiguities are entirely purposeful. In Hansen's extensive analysis of ambiguity in European arms control regulations, she notes that what Henry Kissinger described as "constructive ambiguity"—ambiguity enabling differences between parties to be bridged through the presence of several alternative meanings—generally results from heterogeneity and resistance within the negotiating parties (Hansen 2016). Cornish has even used Kissinger's phrase to describe potential avenues for dialogue between multistakeholder and cyber sovereignty proponents (Cornish 2015). In this section, I focus on a more specific version of deliberate ambiguity present in cybersecurity strategy documents: ambiguity used by *one (state) author* to disguise deviations from global norms, rather than Hansen's heterogeneous ambiguity used by many negotiating parties to reach an agreement.

To put cybersecurity strategies in context, "national strategies" are themselves a peculiar text in this region. National cybersecurity strategies for the Gulf states follow broader state policy. All GCC states have long-term national plans—the most well-known being Saudi Arabia's bold "Vision 2030," championed by the Crown Prince Muhammad bin Salman—and these display three broad similarities. First, they claim to refocus the economy from extractive industries toward technology and innovation, whether through smart cities, e-government, or other skilled sectors such as health and finance. Second, they aim to reduce the role of the public sector in all areas of life. Third, they aim to reduce high expatriate numbers through extensive training and preferential treatment for citizens. Egypt has also had many strategic plans both internally and delivered by development consultants. National cybersecurity strategies echo these wider characteristics, presenting an image of carefully planned cybersecurity governance to their audiences.

The sources are not quite as simple as the phrase "national strategies" might suggest, given the lack of availability of many government documents in this region. At the time of writing in August 2018, there was only one national cybersecurity strategy named as such that has been published in a final form in Egypt and the Gulf states, in English or Arabic, that of Qatar. Although other cybersecurity strategy documents are now available, especially through the UN Cyber Policy Portal, they were not included in the following analysis. Instead, I used publicly available documents that are as close to national cybersecurity strategies as possible. The sources for this analysis are listed in table 10.1.

The object of cybersecurity in these strategies is described variously as cyber, digital, information, or electronic security (in Arabic: *al-ʾamn al-sibrani, al-ʾamn al-raqmi, ʾamn al-muʿalumat*, or *al-ʾamn al- al-ʾiliktruni* respectively). In other contexts, scholars have argued that this linguistic difference captures important differences in national approach; for example, the societal concerns included in Russian or Chinese concepts of "information security" rather than "cybersecurity" (Giles and Hagestad II 2013). However, this is too simplistic a conclusion for situations where there are many terms in play. The focus of this chapter is on shifts in the scope of cybersecurity, not whether such shifts can be captured in a binary distinction between the term "cyber" on one hand and "electronic" or "information" on the other.

Table 10.1 Documents Used to Analyze National Cybersecurity Strategies

State	Document	Available	Secondary sources
Egypt	National ICT strategy 2012–2017 (2012)	Yes	New Egyptian constitution (2014)
UAE	National Cybersecurity Strategy (NCS) (2014)	No	Presentation at RSA conference on the strategy (2015), Dubai NCS (2017)
Saudi Arabia	National Information Security Strategy (NISS) (2013)	No	Draft NISS (2011), National Cybersecurity Centre profile (2017)
Qatar	National Cybersecurity Strategy (2014)	Yes	N/A
Oman	High-Level Cybersecurity Strategy and Master Plan (2013)	No	E.Oman strategy (2010), ITA cybersecurity mission and goals (2018)
Kuwait	National Cybersecurity Strategy (2017)	No	Announcement and summary of NCS (2017)
Bahrain	National Cybersecurity Strategy (2017)	No	NCS summary on TRA website (2017), e.Gov strategy (2016)

First, national cybersecurity strategies generally include only an abstract summary of the issue at stake. For example, the Bahrain strategy claims to "establish a secure cyber-space (*fida' al-'iliktruni 'amin*) to safeguard national interests and protect the Kingdom of Bahrain against cyber-threats (*tahdidat al-'amn al-'iliktruni*) to reduce risks" (Government of Bahrain 2017). In Dubai, this is phrased even more broadly: "The goal is to build a more secure information society that is perfectly aware of cyber security risks (*makhatir al-'amn al-'iliktruni*). One of the key objectives of this strategy is to address any risks, threats or attacks" (Government of Dubai 2017). In Saudi Arabia, the strategy aims to build "an effective and secure national information security environment (*bia'at 'amn al-mu'alumat*)" (MCIT [Saudi Arabia] 2011), while the National Cybersecurity Centre claims to "build a resilient and secure cyberspace that protects national and citizens' interests" (National Cyber Security Center 2017). The generalized tone of these summaries gives no indication of the cybersecurity priorities of these states.

Given this abstract tone, the term "malicious actor" is the most prominent characterization of cybersecurity threats in these strategies. For example, the Dubai strategy states that "An open and free cyber space provides value . . . It is important to protect this value against the risks of malicious activities and disruptions . . . Dubai is a major target for malicious actors" (Government of Dubai 2017, 9). Qatar also claims that it is "an attractive target for malicious actors who seek to cause disruption and destruction" (ictQatar, 3). It is worth noting that the adjective "malicious" has several translations. In the sentence from the Dubai strategy above, the phrase "malicious actors" is replaced by electronic attacks (*al-hujumat al-'iliktruniyya*), while the Qatar strategy uses "biased sides" (*jihat mughrida*) in the sentence above and elsewhere "malicious/evil intentions" (*nawaya khabitha*) for insider threats (ictQatar, 4). The latter echoes a similar description for malicious software (*barmajiyyat khabitha*). The term "malicious" thus performs a similar role in incorporating a range of cyber threats into a single term in both English and Arabic.

Interestingly, these strategies endorse human rights values, especially individual freedom and privacy, in an equally abstract style. For example, the objectives of Saudi Arabia's strategy aims to "enable information to be used and shared freely and securely," while the National Cyber Security Centre seeks "to realize a safe, open and stable information society" (MCIT [Saudi Arabia] 2011, iv, National Cyber Security Center 2017, 12). The Dubai strategy desires "a free and secure cyber world," claiming that "cyber space needs to remain open to innovation and free flow of ideas, information, and expression," although "due consideration should be made to maintain the proper balance between open technology and the individual rights of privacy"

(Government of Dubai 2017, 7, 13). The Qatar strategy claims that their "values in cybersecurity" are to "show tolerance and respect," and embrace "the free flow of ideas and information" (ictQatar, 17). In Bahrain, the aim is to "maintain the rights and values of individuals" (Government of Bahrain 2017). This language echoes wider contests over human rights values in the region, where alternative institutions are set up to mimic the language of genuine human rights bodies.

However, even in the rarefied world of cybersecurity strategies, this endorsement of human rights values is qualified by vague references to safety and care. The Saudi strategy emphasizes the cultural and economic threats of information to the state, although, crucially, these qualifications are *not* made by senior Saudi figures writing in U.S. journals about the Saudi cybersecurity strategy, suggesting that such figures present a calculated portrayal of abstracted Internet rights and freedoms to their international audience (Al-Saud 2012). Other Gulf states offer similar qualifications. In Kuwait, "the strategy is primarily intended to promote the culture of cyber-security which supports the safe and right use of the electronic space" (*Arab Times* 2017), while Qatar aims to "foster a culture of cyber security that promotes safe and appropriate use of cyberspace" (ictQatar, 17). In both cases, the ambiguity of "safe and right/appropriate" disguises significant content restrictions, discussed in the next section. Finally, the Dubai strategy states that "cyber space attacks lead to a variety of threats, such as: fraud, espionage, terrorism, violation of privacy, and defamation" (Government of Dubai 2017, 12). These last two threats mean that "careful use of social media" is a "baseline control" that "should be established, maintained and supported by Dubai individuals in their implementation," along with system updates, firewalls, and password management (Government of Dubai 2017, 25). The phrase "careful use" is ambiguous between care in clicking on links and sharing potentially infected documents on the one hand, and self-policing of content on the other.

Egypt's ICT strategy demonstrates this ambiguity clearly, partly due to its publication date in 2012, shortly after the January 2011 revolution and before the higher security imperatives initiated by President Al-Sisi from 2013. It was then relaunched under Al-Sisi as a 2014–2017 rather than 2012–2017 strategy, but no other changes were made. On the one hand, it states that "Telecommunications Law No. 10 of 2003 . . . contains certain articles that require amendment in line with Egypt's democratic transition that will pro-mote political openness and protect freedom of expression" (MCIT [Egypt] 2014, 9). On the other hand, it also qualifies this aim, claiming to "bring about the desired balance between the considerations of freedom as a funda-mental human right and privacy considerations and national security" (MCIT [Egypt] 2014, 33). Consequently, "the availability of information [that] could harm national security of Egypt or the exposure of relations with other countries at risk under the banner of freedom is not acceptable" (MCIT [Egypt] 2014, 33). Here the national ICT strategy incorporates both an expansive definition of national security *and* an abstract endorsement of human rights values: the ambiguity of both masks the significant extent to which Egyptian cybersecurity governance differs from U.S. and European states who adopt similar language.

On top of this ambiguity, some cybersecurity strategy documents display a contradictory orientation to international cyber norms, most relevantly the Budapest Convention on Cybercrime (treated further in the next section). The Budapest Convention is only referenced in the Omani and Egyptian strategies. In Oman, the Budapest Convention is described as one source among many for its cybercrime law:

> As the Omani society nowadays witnesses an enormous revolution in information technology, it was necessary to set a law that protects networks and devices from illegal hacking attempts . . . . The issuance of the Cyber-Crimes Law was based on the Budapest Convention as well as local, regional and international legislations. (Government of Oman 2018)

This statement portrays the Budapest Convention as a genuine influence, although not to the extent that Oman acceded to the convention. However, in Egypt the situation is less clear. In the English version of the strategy, the draft cybercrime law is explicitly claimed to originate from both international and domestic sources, including:

> International Telecommunication Union (ITU) recommendations regarding cybersecurity; relevant Indian law; the Legislation Management Draft Law of the Ministry of Justice; the Decision Support Center Draft Law; the Convention on Cybercrime (Budapest Agreement) of the Council of Europe; and "Cybercrime," by information security expert Ahmed El-Sobky. (MCIT [Egypt] 2014, 35)

Again, the Budapest Convention is presented as an influence on national cybersecurity strategy in a similar manner to Oman. However, the Arabic version of the strategy strangely omits this paragraph. The most plausible interpretation of this omission is that the English strategy aims to communicate internationally that it is based on a range of sources including the Budapest Convention, whereas this is not a relevant consideration for an Arabic-speaking audience. If correct, this reading suggests that the Budapest Convention is merely utilized by governments to appease international audiences, rather than being a genuine influence on their national policy.

Finally, the Saudi Arabian strategy contains a similar contradiction between domestic and international stances on cybercrime. After claiming that Saudi Arabia is "quickly aligning itself with international standards and capabilities to detect and respond to cybercrime," the strategy states:

> The NISS makes an important distinction between internal cybercrime laws and procedures and the requirements necessary when dealing with these issues at the international level. In order to effectively operate on the international cybercrime stage, the Kingdom may need to forego a rigid interpretation of its own legal standards and procedures and adopt a more flexible legal approach to work cooperatively with international partners. (MCIT [Saudi Arabia] 2011, 65)

It explains that this is because "domestic and international, as well as legal and cultural challenges arise when dealing with cybercrime and the interpretation of legal standards, procedures and law." Specifically, Sharia law is "applied to some forms of cybercrime," which "on the international stage, will be more difficult" (MCIT [Saudi Arabia] 2011, 66). As in Egypt, the Saudi Arabian strategy suggests that international agreements such as the Budapest Convention have limited influence on domestic cybercrime law. However, it also acknowledges that there are substantial differences in the concept of cybercrime between domestic and international levels.

In sum, although cybersecurity strategy documents in Egypt and the Gulf states have mirrored the language of human rights and a free and open Internet, this has not been matched by these states' practices. The abstract tone and internationally oriented language of national cybersecurity strategies disguises the differences between them and their Western liberal democratic allies. Furthermore, although some of these strategy documents acknowledge the Budapest Convention on Cybercrime as an international cyber norm—suggesting a Western orientation—closer analysis suggests that this acknowledgment is calculated to appeal to an international audience, and other documents explicitly argue for deviations from this norm in favor of domestic interpretations of cybercrime. In the next section, I examine these cybercrime laws in more detail.

CYBERCRIME LAWS

Ra'if Badawi, the creator of the "Free Saudi Liberals" website, was arrested by the Saudi authorities on 17 June 2012. He had run the website since 2006 and had been detained and questioned about its content in 2008. A month before his arrest, he used it to declare a celebratory day for Saudi liberals. Badawi was charged under the 2007 cybercrime law—among others[2]—for posts made by him and others on this website (BBC 2015a; 2015b; Al-Barqawi 2015). He was sentenced to 10 years in prison and 1,000 lashes; the first 50 were carried out in January 2015, but after international protests the remainder were deferred on health grounds. While recognizing the severity of the human rights violations in this incident, this section focuses on a slightly different question: is Ra'if Badawi a cybercriminal?

Cybercrime laws were drafted between 2006 and 2018 throughout Egypt and the Gulf states. In this section, I argue that these laws consisted of an expansion of the scope of "cybercrime" from economic concerns such as fraud and espionage to also include political speech online. I first stress that "cybercrime" is an English term with no equivalent in Arabic. While many professional documents in Arabic use the loan word *sibrani* (cybercrimes would thus be *al-jara'im al-sibraniyya*), this neologism is not used in legal terminology. Instead, the legal Arabic equivalents are electronic crimes (*al-jara'im al-'iliktruniyya*), information crimes (*jara'im al-mu'alumat*), or information technology crimes (*jara'im tiqniyyat al-mu'alumat*). The English translation of these terms is nearly always "cybercrime."

The main international norm regarding cybercrime is the Budapest Convention on Cybercrime agreed by the Council of Europe in 2001, considered briefly in the previous section. None of the states considered here have acceded to the Budapest Convention (accession is available to nonmembers of the Council of Europe, while signature is only available to members). At the time of writing, there were sixty-four ratifications or signatures/accessions to the Convention, only two of which are in the Middle East: Tunisia and Israel (Council of Europe 2018). Consequently, this section argues that the wide definitions of cybercrime by Egypt and the Gulf states are not a "localization" of this norm, in Acharya's terms, as these states are not "norm-takers": they have not accepted it as an international norm in the first place (Acharya 2004). Instead, it is a more active *appropriation* of this norm. "Appropriation" is a term used by some norm scholars to describe changes made by states to norms more generally (Zimmerman 2017, pp. 217–222). Here, I use it to specify the expansion of the professional discourse to fit a particular cluster of values; namely, a broad definition of national security historically prevalent in the region.

First, it should be noted that domestic cybercrime laws emerged against the backdrop of a regional agreement on cybercrime: the Convention on Combating Information Technology Offences (*jara'im tiqniyyat al-mu'alumat*) by the Arab League (the Arab Convention). This convention was signed in December 2010, and it has been ratified by Egypt and all GCC states other than Saudi Arabia. The Arab Convention is different in several key ways to the earlier Budapest Convention. Hakmeh highlights the similarities between the two, claiming that "provisions [of the Arab Convention] are in fact almost the same as those of the Budapest Convention, especially in relation to procedural powers and international cooperation" (Hakmeh 2017, 11). However, the key word here is "almost," as none of the articles that include political and socially controversial content in the Arab Convention (12, 14, 15 or 21) are in the Budapest Convention. The Arab Convention is thus a mixture of direct influence from the earlier text and additions that repurpose the Budapest Convention toward political speech online (Al-Tahir 2015). This is an expansion of, rather than a shift away from, an economic concept of cybercrime, as the convention also includes articles on copyright infringement, fraud, and electronic payment.

The Arab Spring and near contemporaneous signing of the Arab Convention was the catalyst for the spread of cybercrime laws in the GCC. Between 2011 and 2018, Saudi Arabia, Oman, and the UAE all updated earlier laws while Egypt, Bahrain, Qatar, and Kuwait implemented new laws (table 10.2).

Like the Arab Convention, several scholars have recognized that these cybercrime laws expand the concept of cybercrime to cover political speech online (Hakmeh 2018). Hakmeh argues that all GCC countries other than Bahrain have "additional offences not foreseen in other legal instruments" in their cybercrime laws, and "most GCC cybercrime laws have been subject to heavy criticism by human rights organisations for limiting free speech and imposing self-censorship on citizens and activists" (Hakmeh 2018, 9). Duffy's 2014 analysis also concludes that these laws put forward wide definitions of "public morals" and "national unity," which means that many social media comments, including any political opposition, could be considered a cybercrime (Duffy 2014).

The updated laws all strengthen existing penalties. For example, the cybercrime law in Saudi Arabia was updated in 2015 with what was termed

Table 10.2 Cybercrime Laws in Egypt and the GCC

State	Electronic transactions law	Cybercrime law
Oman	2008	Penal code amended with chapter on computer crime 2001, Cyber Crime Law 2011
UAE	2002	Law No. 2 of 2006, Law No. 5 of 2012 Concerning Combating Information Technology Crimes
Saudi Arabia	2007	Anti-Cyber Crime Law 2007, updated 2015
Qatar	2010	Cybercrime Prevention Law 2014
Bahrain	2002	Law No. 60 of 2014 Concerning Information Technology Crimes
Kuwait	2014	Law No.63 of 2015 Concerning Combating Information Technology Crimes
Egypt	2004	Laws 2015 and 2016 Concerning Electronic Crimes discussed by Parliament, approved 2018

a "naming and shaming" clause for offenders, allowing a name and details of their offense to be published in local newspapers with the costs to be paid by the person convicted (Al-Sharq Al-'Awsat 2015). Similarly, the updated Omani law in 2011 has a section explicitly titled "content crimes," covering any use of ICTs to "produce or publish or distribute or purchase or possess whatever might prejudice the public order or religious values" (Government of Oman 2011). The updated UAE law in 2012 is one of the starkest examples, as Article 9 prevents almost any form of online political debate:

> Shall be punished by temporary imprisonment and a fine not in excess of one million dirhams whoever publishes information, news, statements or rumors on a website or any computer network or information technology means with intent to make sarcasm or damage the reputation, prestige or stature of the State or any of its institutions or its president, vice-president, any of the rulers of the Emirates, their crown princes, or the deputy rulers of the Emirates, the State flag, the national peace, its logo, national anthem or any of its symbols. (Government of the UAE 2012)

New laws, such as the Kuwait cybercrime law, include very similar provisions to the updated laws above. Human rights organizations argued that the Kuwait law was "an effective barrier to critical political speech over the Internet" (Human Rights Watch 2015b), and "a direct assault on the right to freedom of opinion and belief and the right to freedom of expression" (Reporters without Borders 2016). Interestingly, this law had been considered even before the Arab Spring: a leaked U.S. cable in 2010 quoted Minister of the Interior Sheikh Jabar Al-Khalid Al-Sabah as complaining that "politics was hindering progress on . . . many other important bills, including one to criminalize cyber crimes" (Wikileaks 2010). The expansion of cybercrime in these laws is thus far more than localization of an existing norm: it is the active renegotiation of both cybercrime and national security.

Importantly, these cybercrime laws do not just have content provisions in their texts but have all been *used* to target political speech online. In the UAE, the cybercrime law was used in 2013 to charge the son of one of ninety-four defendants associated with Al-Islah, a political group accused by the UAE government of affiliation with the Muslim Brotherhood, after he published details about their trial (Human Rights Watch 2013). Al-Islah was then designated a terrorist group by the UAE in 2014. A prominent political dissident, Nasser bin Ghaith, was charged under the cybercrime law in 2016 after he criticized the UAE and Egyptian government. In this case, the cybercrime law was used to criminalize his claims of mistreatment in an earlier trial as the posting of information "intended to damage the UAE" (Human Rights Watch 2016a). Ahmed Mansoor, a well-known dissident, was also tried under cybercrime laws (Al-Jazeera 2018). In 2016, an Omani was jailed for three years after criticizing the UAE's conduct in the war in Yemen in a Whatsapp audio recording (Al-ʿArabi Al-Jadid 2016). After the Qatar crisis in June 2017, the UAE attorney general stated that showing sympathy for Qatar online would be treated as a cybercrime, resulting in prison sentences between three and fifteen years (Al Subaihi 2017).

In Saudi Arabia, the cybercrime law was also used regularly to prosecute political opposition. The liberal dissident Raʾif Badawi was sentenced under the cybercrime law in 2013 (Human Rights Watch 2012). A year later, the head of a human rights organization in Saudi Arabia was also sentenced to seven years' imprisonment under the cybercrime law (Reporters without Borders 2014). In 2015, a lawyer who had represented Raʾif Badawi, and who founded the rights organization Saudi Monitor for Human Rights, was sentenced to fifteen years imprisonment for a range of offenses, including some under the new cybercrime law (Human Rights Watch 2014a). Other lawyers confirmed the use of the cybercrime law to prosecute the "spreading of rumours" over Twitter in 2017 (Al-Barqawi 2017). Most recently, in October 2018, the Saudi Public Prosecution reiterated their willingness to use the provisions against spreading rumors in the updated cybercrime law in an oblique reference to the alleged murder of Saudi journalist Jamal Khashoggi by the Saudi government in its Turkish consulate (Saudi Gazette 2018).

Kuwait's cybercrime law was used in 2016 to charge a blogger who criticized the emir (FIDH 2016). In Bahrain, the most consistent use of the cybercrime law was against Nabeel Rajab, a prominent political activist, who led demonstrations in the 2011 protests and has been given prison sentences multiple times for his opposition to the government. According to his own testimony, he was arrested and interviewed in 2015 and 2016 by the Cyber Crimes Department following anti-government tweets, and remained in prison at the time of writing (Rajab 2016). His charges included "insulting a neighbouring country" in relation to Saudi Arabia (Bahrain Center for Human Rights 2017). In Oman, the cybercrime law was used to charge an individual who interviewed striking oil workers in 2012 and made other political statements online, although he was then convicted of an older criminal offense—insulting the Sultan—rather than under the cybercrime law (Human Rights Watch 2014b). In 2015, a government critic was sentenced to three years in prison for critical blog posts under the cybercrime law (Human Rights Watch 2015a). The editor of a politically independent newspaper in Oman, Al-Zaman, was charged under the cybercrime law after an article that criticized the judiciary in 2016 (Human Rights Watch 2016b). The newspaper was shut down a year later. I identified no instances of Qatar's cybercrime law being used to suppress political opposition. However, human rights organizations highlight risks of this law through the example of a poet sentenced to fifteen years in prison in 2013 for indirectly criticizing the ruling family (Amnesty

International 2014). This poet, Muhammad Rashid Al-Ajami, was pardoned in 2016.

Finally, Egypt's cybercrime law has followed a more contentious path than its equivalents in the Gulf states. A draft cybercrime law was first mentioned in a government-wide ICT strategy in 2012. In a similar manner to those in the Gulf states, this draft law doubled the penalties for those committing "information crimes" (*jara'im al-mu'alumat*) with the intent to damage public interest or an individual public authority (MCIT [Egypt] 2014, 35). At least three further drafts have been proposed since the June 2013 coup, in April 2015, May 2016, and June 2018 (Yusif 2016; Negm 2015). One of the main sponsors of the 2015 draft, Minister for Communications and Information Technology Khalid Negm, claimed that it was in part prompted by the Arab Convention (Saad 2015). The 2016 draft then increased the severity of the first in a similar way to the updated cybercrime laws in the GCC states, increasing the punishments for vaguely defined crimes of harming national unity and public morals (Abdelaal 2016). The latest draft was approved by parliament in June 2018 (Hassan 2018) and passed into law in August 2018 (Salama 2018). It is not included in the analysis here, although its provisions appear similar. Criticism of the law has focused on its broad definition of websites subject to censorship, including any that "threaten national security or expose the nation's security or economy to risk" (Article 7) ('Ali 2018). Critics have also pointed to heavy punishments for privacy infringements of public figures, penetration testing practices by security experts, and high data management burdens on ISPs, despite insistences by officials that these are unintended or at least limited (El-Gundy 2018).

Overall, Egyptian law follows the expansive definitions of cybercrime in the other laws above (Miller 2018). Due to the recent approval of this law, Egypt has no cybercrime prosecutions at the time of writing. However, as Ben Hassine argues, Egypt already uses a variety of anti-terror and anti-protest laws to control online political activity (Ben Hassine 2016). The anti-protest laws are especially successful in this aim, as encouraging or inciting people to protest online is a more serious offense in these laws than taking part in the protest itself. This focus on protests as a conduit for political opposition reflects Egypt's experience of the January revolution in 2011 (Abdulla 2014). It also highlights the violent responses of security forces to later protests, including the massacre of at least 700 people at Rabi'a Square in 2013, and the regular disappearance and torture of activists and protesters since (Guerin 2018).

In sum, this section has demonstrated that the governments of Egypt and the Gulf states appropriated the concept of cybercrime to counter political opposition. This tactic was combined with a similarly broad definition of other key legal terms such as terrorism, and strict anti-protest and media laws. This innovation is important for the global development of cyber norms because it demonstrates how states that are not "norm-takers" (who did not sign up to the Budapest Convention) nonetheless incorporate such norms into their practices in a strategic maneuver, signaling their alignment with the norm through national strategy documents and then deviating from the norm in their domestic laws.

CONCLUSION

This chapter has argued that the emergence of cyber norms in Egypt and the Gulf states is characterized by ambiguity and appropriation. First, I argued that these states occupy a complex position in international cybersecurity governance, with both strong security ties to multistakeholder proponents in the United States and Europe and support for cyber sovereignty measures in multilateral forums. Second, these states' cybersecurity strategy documents accommodate the contradictions of this position by adopting an abstract and *ambiguous* description of cybersecurity threats and human rights values designed for international consumption. Although this ambiguous tone is partly a reflection of the many uses and causes of ambiguity more generally in international politics, in this case it also disguises the differences in conceptions of cybersecurity and cybercrime between these states and their international allies. Third, in the turbulent political situation after the Arab Spring, cybercrime laws and regional agreements across Egypt and the GCC *appropriated* the concept of cybercrime to provide an additional means to criminalize political speech online in an already restricted public sphere. These two innovations are closely linked: the cybersecurity practices of these states, especially their appropriation of cybercrime laws, illustrates the calculated nature of the ambiguity present in their strategy documents.

Both ambiguity and appropriation are innovations in state responses to the development of global cyber norms that could be analyzed in comparative perspective elsewhere. Future work could compare the production of ambiguity and appropriation in other regions with similar contradictory positions in global cybersecurity governance or test the logic of the argument presented here by exploring whether such maneuvers take place in states without such contradictory pressures. This chapter has thus provided an original contribution to the study of cyber norms, based on a rich empirical analysis of an important and largely unstudied region in cybersecurity. It highlights how states outside the cyber "great powers" have reached novel horizons in their sophisticated engagement with cyber norms, as—through their embrace of ambiguity and appropriation—these states participate in the constant undermining and redefining of responsible behavior itself.

NOTES

1. Daniel W. Drezner, "The Global Governance of the Internet: Bringing the State Back In," *Political Science Quarterly* 119, no. 3 (2004): 477–498; Milton Mueller, Andreas Schmidt, and Brenden Kuerbis, "Internet Security and Networked Governance in International Relations," *International Studies Review* 15, no. 1 (March 1, 2013): 86–104; Roger Hurwitz, "The Play of States: Norms and Security in Cyberspace," *American Foreign Policy Interests* 36, no. 5 (September 3, 2014), p. 328.

2. Other charges included apostasy and insulting his father. It is unclear from public reports in both English and Arabic what combination of charges led to the specific sentence imposed, although the apostasy charge is the most severe; it allows capital punishment and was advocated by some Saudi conservatives.

REFERENCES

Abdelaal, Mohamed. 2016. "Egypt's New Cybercrime Law: Another Legislative Failure". *Jurist*, July 9, 2016. https://perma.cc/HED5-X2G7.

Abdulla, Rasha A. 2014. "Egypt's Media in the Midst of Revolution". Carnegie Endowment for International Peace, July 2014.

Acharya, Amitav. 2004. "How Ideas Spread: Whose Norms Matter? Norm Localization and Institutional Change in Asian Regionalism". *International Organization*, 58(2): 239–275.

Al-Barqawi, ʿAbdallah. 2017. "Mutalabat Bimuʿaqaba Murawaji Shaʾiʿat ʿAl-Qurarat' ʿabr Muwaqiʿa Al-Tawassul [Demands to Punish the Promotion of 'Low' Rumours on Social Media]". *Sabq*, November 18, 2017. https://perma.cc/5K8R-SV5G.

———. 2015. "Tanfiz Hukm Al-Jild ʿala Raʾif Badawi Bisubbub ʿibarat Kufriyya Wa ʿuquq Walidihi [Sentence of Lashes Imposed against Raif Badawi for Expressions of Unbelief and Insulting His Father]". *Sabq*, January 9, 2015. https://perma.cc/Q99Y-5F39.

Al Subaihi, Thamer. 2017. "Supporting Qatar on Social Media a Cybercrime, Says UAE Attorney General". *The National*, June 7, 2017. https://perma.cc/K7Y2-8ST5.

Al-Saud, Naef bin Ahmed. 2012. "A Saudi Outlook for Cybersecurity Strategies: Extrapolated from Western Experience". *Joint Forces Quarterly*, 64: 75–81.

Al-Tahir, Muhammad. 2015. "Taʿliq ʿala Al-Itifaqiyya Al-ʿarabiyya Limukafahat Jaraʾim Tiqniyyat Almuʿalumat [Comments on the Arab Convention for Combatting Information Technology Crimes]". *Muʾassasat Huriyyat Al-Fikr Wa Al-Taʿbir [Foundation for the freedom of thought and expression]*, March 12, 2015. https://perma.cc/DUB8-6END.

ʿAli, ʾIman. 2018. "Nanshura Al-Nus Al-Kamil Liqanun Mukafihat Jaraʾim Al-ʾintarnat Baʿad Tasdiq Al-Raʾis Al-Sisi ʿalaihi [We Publish the Complete Text of the Law against Internet Crimes After the Ratification of President Al-Sisi]". *Al-Masry Al-Yaum*, August 19, 2018. https://perma.cc/89P6-KZJ7.

Amnesty International. 2014. "Qatar: New Cybercrimes Law Endangers Freedom of Expression". Amnesty International, September 18, 2014. https://perma. cc/4ZBS-732Q.

Bahrain Center for Human Rights. 2017. "Updates: Arrest and Detention of BCHR's President Nabeel Rajab". Bahrain Center for Human Rights, August 8, 2017. https://perma.cc/39UJ-KBFH.

BBC. 2015. "Saudi Arabian Blogger 'Flogged'". *BBC News*, January 9, 2015. https:// perma.cc/36JH-YJUS.

Belnap, Jeffrey Dallin. 2018. "Bright Star Command Post Exercise Pursues Strategic Partnership". *U.S. Army Central*, September 15, 2018. https://perma. cc/3GPY-C2CN.

Ben Hassine, Wafa. 2016. "The Crime of Speech: How Arab Governments Use the Law to Silence Expression Online". Electronic Frontier Foundation, April 2016.

Carr, Madeline. 2015. "Power Plays in Global Internet Governance". *Millennium* 43(2): 640–659.

Cornish, Paul. 2015. "Governing Cyberspace Through Constructive Ambiguity". *Survival* 57(3): 153–176.

Council of Europe. 2018. "Chart of Signatures and Ratifications of Treaty 185: Convention on Cybercrime". European Treaty Series—No.185, August 15, 2018. https://perma.cc/7NQM-U764.

Dalek, Jakub, Lex Gill, Bill Marczak, Sarah McKune, Naser Noor, Joshua Oliver, John Penney, Adam Senft, and Ronald J. Deibert. 2018. "Planet Netsweeper". Citizen Lab, April 25, 2018.

Dourado, Eli. 2012. "Behind Closed Doors at the UN's Attempted 'Takeover of the Internet'". *Ars Technica*, December 20, 2012. https://perma.cc/TCG3-2LST.

Drezner, Daniel W. 2004. "The Global Governance of the Internet: Bringing the State Back In". *Political Science Quarterly*, 119(3): 477–498.

Duffy, Matt. 2014. "Arab Media Regulations: Identifying Restraints on Freedom of the Press in the Laws of Six Arabian Peninsula Countries". *Berkeley Journal of Middle Eastern & Islamic Law*, 6(1): 1.

El-Gundy, Zeinab. 2018. "Q&A: Egypt's New Cybercrime Law 'Not about Putting Barriers on the Internet'". *Ahram Online*, August 20, 2018. https://perma.cc/ QA7T-EFUR.

FIDH. 2016. "Kuwaiti Cyber Crimes Law Silences Dissent: Ongoing Prosecution of Sara Al-Drees". *Worldwide Movement for Human Rights*, December 12, 2016. https://perma.cc/YR93-Q4B8.

Foreign & Commonwealth Office. 2018. "United Kingdom-Saudi Arabia Joint Communiqué". GOV.UK, March 10, 2018. https://perma.cc/R9C7-LZVC.

Giles, Keir, and William Hagestad II. 2013. "Divided by a Common Language: Cyber Definitions in Chinese, Russian and English". In: *2013 5th International Conference on Cyber Conflict*, K. Podins, J. Stinissen, and M. Maybaum (eds.). Tallinn: NATO CCDCOE, 2013.

Government of Bahrain. 2017. "Kingdom of Bahrain—EGovernment Portal Cybersecurity Strategy". eGovernment Portal, October 3, 2017. https://perma.cc/RSL4-FPJA (ENG), https://perma.cc/NNP2-CGBJ (AR).

Government of Dubai. 2017. "Dubai Cyber Security Strategy". Dubai Electronic Security Center.

Government of Oman. 2011. "Royal Decree No 12/2011 Issuing the Cyber Crime Law". Government of Oman.

———. 2018. "Information Security—Omanuna Portal". Omanuna, 26 March 2018. https://perma.cc/8VYS-5KSW.

Government of the UAE. 2012. "Federal Decree-Law No. (5) of 2012 On Combating Cybercrimes". *Official Gazette*, Issue 540 (unofficial English translation), 13 August 2012.

Greenberg, Andy. 2017. "North Korea's Sloppy, Chaotic Cyberattacks Also Make Perfect Sense". *Wired*, June 15, 2017. https://perma.cc/A5QK-PHPH.

Guerin, Orla. 2018. "The Shadow over Egypt". *BBC News*, 23 February 2018. https://perma.cc/B5UW-PZKE.

Hakmeh, Joyce. 2017. "Cybercrime and the Digital Economy in the GCC Countries". Chatham House—The Royal Institute for International Affairs, June 2017.

———. 2018. "Cybercrime Legislation in the GCC Countries—Fit for Purpose?" Chatham House—The Royal Institute for International Affairs, July 2018.

Hansen, Susanne Therese. 2016. "Taking Ambiguity Seriously: Explaining the Indeterminacy of the European Union Conventional Arms Export Control Regime". *European Journal of International Relations*, 22(1): 192–216.

Hassan, ʿAbd Al-Basir. 2018. "Majlis Al-Nuwab Al-Misri Yaqirru Qanun Mukafahat Al-Jarimat Al-ʾiliktruniyya [Egyptian Parliament Decides on Cybercrime Law]". *BBC News*, June 7, 2018. https://perma.cc/5DWF-Y64S.

Hubbard, Ben, and Catherine Porter. 2018. "Saudi Arabia Escalates Feud With Canada Over Rights Criticism". *The New York Times*, October 10, 2018. https://perma.cc/8H5W-MGGD.

Human Rights Watch. 2012. "Saudi Arabia: Free Editor Held Under Cybercrime Law". *Human Rights Watch*, July 16, 2012. https://perma.cc/3EEJ-XYXJ.

———. 2013. "UAE: Unfair Mass Trial of 94 Dissidents". *Human Rights Watch*, April 3, 2013. https://perma.cc/43WC-NSG2.

———. 2014a. "Saudi Arabia: 15-Year Sentence for Prominent Activist". *Human Rights Watch*, July 7, 2014. https://perma.cc/8QNA-8U4K.

———. 2014b. "Oman: Rights Routinely Trampled". *Human Rights Watch*, December 18, 2014. https://perma.cc/66TQ-TDS6.

———. 2015. "Kuwait: Cybercrime Law a Blow to Free Speech". *Human Rights Watch*, July 22, 2015. https://perma.cc/265U-VVAB.

———. 2016. "Oman: Journalists Arrested for Criticizing Judiciary". *Human Rights Watch*, August 5, 2016. https://perma.cc/FX3Y-6RBR.

———. 2016. "UAE: Free Two Jailed for Criticizing Egypt". *Human Rights Watch*, May 15, 2016. https://perma.cc/JJX2-RNGR.

Hurwitz, Roger. 2014. "The Play of States: Norms and Security in Cyberspace". *American Foreign Policy Interests*, 36(5): 322–331.

ictQatar. 2014. "Qatar National Cyber Security Strategy". Government of Qatar, May 2014.

Ignatius, David. 2016. "The Cold War Is Over. The Cyber War Has Begun". *Washington Post*, September 15, 2016. https://perma.cc/G2TK-NNAL.

Kaljurand, Marina. 2017. "An Interview with Marina Kaljurand, Former Minister of Foreign Affairs". *Journal of Complex Operations*, December 21, 2017. https://perma.cc/K7F8-9MNX.

Khalid Negm. 2015. "Draft Law Concerning Electronic Crimes". Leaked draft available on Scribd, April 2015. https://perma.cc/H4BS-VLGQ.

Lambert, Lisa, Anthony Deutsch, and Guy Faulconbridge. 2018. "West Accuses "pariah State" Russia of Global Hacking Campaign". *Reuters*, October 5, 2018. https://perma.cc/YF3L-LV3N.

Malsin, Jared. 2018. "U.S. Releases $195 Million in Military Aid to Egypt". *The Wall Street Journal*, July 25, 2018. https://perma.cc/Y7EY-F7UD.

Marczak, Bill, John Scott-Railton, Adam Senft, Ronald J. Deibert, and Bahr Abdul Razzak. 2018. "The Kingdom Came to Canada: How Saudi-Linked Digital Espionage Reached Canadian Soil". Citizen Lab, October 1, 2018.

MCIT (Egypt). 2012. "National ICT Strategy 2012–2017: Towards a Digital Society and Knowledge-Based Economy". MCIT, 2012.

———. 2014. "Publications—Egypt's ICT Strategy 2014–2017". Ministry of Communications and Information Technology. https://perma.cc/X6G3-WT3F.

MCIT (Saudi Arabia). 2011. "National Information Security Strategy". Ministry of Communications and Information Technology, January 2011.

Miller, Elissa. 2018. "Egypt Leads the Pack in Internet Censorship Across the Middle East". Atlantic Council, August 28, 2018. https://perma.cc/8DAC-LXYW.

Mueller, Milton, Andreas Schmidt, and Brenden Kuerbis. 2013. "Internet Security and Networked Governance in International Relations". *International Studies Review* 15(1): 86–104.

National Cyber Security Center. 2017. "Profile—Introducing the National Cyber Security Center". Governnment of Saudi Arabia.

Rajab, Nabeel. 2016. "Letter From a Bahraini Jail". *The New York Times*, September 4, 2016. https://perma.cc/HH4R-6WZP.

Raymond, Mark, and Laura DeNardis. 2015. "Multistakeholderism: Anatomy of an Inchoate Global Institution". *International Theory*, 7(3): 572–616.

Reporters without Borders. 2014. "Cyber Crime Law Used Again to Silence Dissident Voices". July 1, 2014. https://perma.cc/2M9U-S5E2.

———. 2016. "New Cyber Crimes Law Restricts Free Expression and Targets Online Activists", January 21, 2016. https://perma.cc/M9ZB-6VRH.

Rij, Armida van, and Benedict Wilkinson. 2018. "Security Cooperation with Saudi Arabia: Is It Worth It for the UK?". The Policy Institute at King's, September 2018.

Saad, Ragab. 2015. "Egypt's Draft Cybercrime Law Undermines Freedom of Expression". Atlantic Council, April 24, 2015. https://perma.cc/9ATE-HNNA.

Salama, Samr. 2018. "Barlimani Yu'akid 'an Qanun Mukafihat Jara'im Al-Mu'alumat Al-Jadid Yauqif Al-Jara'im Al-'iliktroni [Parliament Confims That the New Law against Information Crimes Stops Electronic Crimes]". *Al-Masry Al-Yaum*, August 19, 2018. https://perma.cc/D6HS-DFG4.

Savage, John E., and Bruce W. McConnell. 2015. "Exploring Multi-Stakeholder Internet Governance". EastWest Institute, January 2015.

Segal, Adam. 2018. "Year in Review: Chinese Cyber Sovereignty in Action". Council on Foreign Relations, January 8, 2018. https://perma.cc/L3UB-CDEN.

Staff Report. 2015. "Al-Shura Al-Saʿudi Yudifu ʿaqubat Al-Tashhir ʾila Nizam Mukafahat Al-Jaraʾim Al-Muʿalumatiyya [Saudi Council Adds Naming and Shaming Punishment to the Cybercrime Law]". *Al-Sharq Al-ʾAwsat*, March 18, 2015. https://perma.cc/4QXP-Y8JR.

———. 2016. "Omani Jailed for Insulting UAE on Whatsapp". *Al-ʾArabi Al-Jadid*, February 29, 2016. https://perma.cc/2ULR-LTFQ.

———. 2017. "CAIT Chief Briefs HH the Amir on National Cybersecurity Strategy—Vision to Protect Kuwait's National Interest". *Arab Times*, July 31, 2017. https://perma.cc/KTQ7-GW8G.

———. 2018a. "5-Year Jail, 3 Million Fine for Rumormongers". *Saudi Gazette*, October 13, 2018. https://perma.cc/3D68-SFJC.

———. 2018b. "UAE Rights Activist Ahmed Mansoor Put on Trial in Abu Dhabi". *Al-Jazeera*, April 18, 2018. https://perma.cc/8MWW-JCMV.

The Arab Republic of Egypt. 2014. "Egypt's Constitution of 2014". Constituteproject.org, translated by International IDEA.

The Economic Times. 2014. "China, Egypt Sign Strategic Partnership Agreement", December 24, 2014. https://perma.cc/G5M4-KPHW.

UK Government. 2018. "UK Exposes Russian Cyber Attacks", October 4, 2018. https://perma.cc/6UTX-TXYC.

UK Trade & Investment. 2013. "Cybersecurity: The UK's Approach to Exports". UK Government, April 2013.

Wikileaks. 2010. "US Embassy Kuwait City—Kuwait Interior Minister Sounds Alarm on Iran; Offers Assurances on GITMO Returnees and Security". Wikileaks Public Library of US Diplomacy, February 17, 2010. Public Library of US Diplomacy. https://perma.cc/A79J-WF2E.

Yusif, Muhammad. 2016. "Al-Watan Tanshuru Nus Qanun Al-Jarimat Alʾiliktruniyya ʾamam Al-Nuwab [Al Watan Publishes the Text of the Electronic Crimes Law before Parliament]". *Al-Watan*, May 11, 2016. https://perma.cc/KAX8-SUQH.

Zimmermann, Lisbeth. 2017. *Global Norms with a Local Face: Rule-of-Law Promotion and Norm Translation*. Cambridge, UK; New York: Cambridge University Press.

Chapter 11

The Power of Norms Meets Normative Power

On the International Cyber Norm of Bulk Collection, the Normative Power of Intelligence Agencies and How These Meet

Ilina Georgieva

The world has been witnessing unprecedented intelligence revelations ever since the whistleblower Edward Snowden took on his role in the summer of 2013. What started off as an affair concerning the National Security Agency (NSA) and the Government Communications Headquarters (GCHQ), quickly evolved in a debate that transcended the Anglo-American context of security breaches and fundamental rights intrusions, and established itself as a long-lasting point on the policy agendas of most liberal states. Governments and agencies caught in the act had to regroup to regain public trust, and to do so quickly. What followed was a wave of inquiries (UK 2015; DoD 2013) and committees (Bundestag 2014), further disclosures induced by government officials to strengthen counter-narratives (Schulze 2015, 211), eventually crowned with the adoption of legislation amendments concerning the intelligence sector. In other words, regulation was called to the rescue in an intelligence crisis that seemed omnipresent. However, as limitations proved difficult (Boeke 2017) or even impractical, the formal re-evaluation of the controversial intelligence methods led to their (renewed) codification.

At the same time, the increasing legalization of intelligence practices, a phenomenon sometimes referred to as "intelligence legalism" (Schlanger 2015), has been gaining a foothold internationally as well (Deeks 2016, 13). The taboo of talking about intelligence methods and rationales has been lifted, and with it a possibility has arrived to further evaluate them and their impact. In light of this, international actors of all shapes and sizes have been increasingly concerned with the systematic application of (binding and non-binding) norms to intelligence practices (Deeks 2016, 17). While states, for instance, used to only occasionally make use of international rules to contest other states' intelligence mischief, international law (and international human rights law in particular) (Cole 2013; Borger 2013; Gallagher 2013; Scheinin 2014) has been enjoying quite the comeback in recent scholarship (Buchan 2016; Kittichaisaree 2017). Further, the United Nations Group of Governmental Experts (UNGGE) cyber-norms process (United Nations 1999), although indirectly related to intelligence activities, paved the way for further exploration of international norms applicable to the world's second oldest profession and its particularities in cyberspace. Scholars have been thus piecing together the intelligence practices puzzle in the cyber domain, putting forward the existence of a cyber norm on counterespionage and a cyber norm prohibiting economic espionage (Libicki 2017), to name just a few.

This chapter aims to add to the cyber-norms scholarship by tracing the evolution of an international cyber norm on *foreign* bulk data collection (as opposed to data collection by means of more targeted and/or solely domestic intelligence-gathering methods). What is more, by looking into recent legislative developments in Germany, France, and the United Kingdom (UK) covering that very same intelligence methodology, the present contribution purposes to also make the case that the cyber norm on foreign bulk data collection has been already "fortified" in black letter law. This approach offers a unique opportunity to test in practice theoretical international relations (IR) concepts on international norms development and to contribute to understanding which norms become law and how exactly by exploring the connection between the proliferation of leaks and expanding legalization (Deeks 2016, 13). Last but not least, by focusing on the role of the intelligence agencies, this contribution makes the implicit claim that the debate on norms for responsible behavior in cyberspace needs to cast a wider net to consider not only top-down but also bottom-up approaches to regulation.

When speaking of the normative capacity of the intelligence agencies at hand, pinpointing the norm is only half of the story. To complete the circle, one needs to ask not only whether the agencies promote their own norms and what their impact is on (cyberspace) regulation practices, but to also look into how and what power dynamics make that possible. This chapter thus argues that the other side of the coin is the normative power (Manners 2002) of the intelligence agencies, which makes itself particularly noticeable in the "legitimacy narrative" many of the agencies adopt defending their behavior (their norms) in the post-Snowden era. What that approach accomplishes is to add to our understanding of the role of the intelligence agencies in world politics and regulation on the one hand, while contributing to the conceptions of normal in IR scholarship on the other. Thus, following Manners's conceptualization, this chapter puts forward that to see the intelligence agencies as a normative power internationally is not "a contradiction in terms" (Manners 2002, 236), but a natural complementation of the normative process.

The main reasons for choosing to look into foreign bulk collection practices are threefold. For one, the oversea focus intends to circumvent the heated domestic debates on the checks and balances that pertain (at least to a certain extent) to rather specific domestic contexts, and have already enjoyed the attention of a number of scholars and practitioners. Second, by focusing on intelligence practices that cross national borders by default, thematic priority can be given to their relevance for both the ongoing debate on international cyber norms and for the emerging normative framework relating to cyber espionage activities. Last, bulk data is the epitome of the information age; it is what the information society in many instances thrives on, but also fears. This contribution thus takes on the opportunity to look further into the normative implications of bulk data collection.

The choice to look into the legislative developments of Germany, France and the United Kingdom bears on the following points. For one, it allows to consider both common and civil law traditions. Second, their intelligence practices (and alliances) prior to the respective intelligence reforms are well documented by primary sources, which provide for a good *ex ante—ex post* normative comparison. One can thus trace the behavioral norms the intelligence agencies were abiding by prior to the leaks, whether and how those were codified, and contrast them to current practices and legal frameworks. Further, the consideration of the normative developments in Germany, France and the United Kingdom covers a number of intelligence contexts—the United Kingdom as one of the initial driving forces behind the Five Eyes and its role as a bridge between Europe and United States; Germany, which is particularly interesting for being marked by its Stasi past and thus bound by very restrictive domestic rules regarding surveillance; and last but not least France for its rather silent development of one of the most comprehensive bulk collection mechanisms able to match the Five Eyes' ambitions long before other "elite" intelligence actors were able to do so. In addition, as the revelations and other public sources give away, all three countries are affiliated with the Five Eyes in different capacities—an interaction governed by its own diplomacy, elaborate agreements and countless treaties (Aldrich 2004, 739), creating an indisputable community culture.

The present contribution continues as follows. Section II briefly makes some terminology references and gives a few prominent examples of bulk collection which were brought to light mainly by Snowden. Section III evaluates those through the lens of IR norms scholarship to pinpoint the normativity in the agencies' behavior. Section IV presents evidence of how these methods have been fortified in legal instruments. Section V takes on the task to trace the normative power of the intelligence agencies, followed by some concluding remarks on norms and actorship in the international system.

"TAKING THE DATA STRAIGHT FROM THE TUBES"— SOME NECESSARY CONTEXT AND TERMINOLOGY

Information collection in bulk has been central to the debate in the post-Snowden era. Naturally, definitions of the practice differ according to jurisdiction and operational context (see, for instance, Anderson 2016, 1, 2 as an example of the UK context). As a rule, bulk collection refers to an intelligence collection practice by which vast amounts of data (both content and metadata) are acquired for multiple purposes/databases without a "determinant" (Boeke 2017, 312), that is to say without aiming at a particular target, be it a geographical location or an individual. Leaving the domestic context aside, it is a standard feature of the foreign intelligence portfolio of almost any intelligence or national security agency and falls by default under its respective signals intelligence (SIGINT) capabilities. As such the practice is exercised on the premise "first collect, then select" (Boeke 2017, 312), hence the familiar-sounding metaphor of the haystack and the needle. For the sake of simplicity, the rest of this article uses "bulk data collection" or "bulk collection" as references to the collection of both content and metadata unless otherwise specified. Further, the terms are used to denote communications taking place entirely abroad, as well as communications originating/ending in the intercepting country. Consequently, *a foreign* factor is always implied.

As Snowden's revelations developed in time and scope, it became increasingly clear that a number of states had been making use of bulk collection methods (Inkster 2014, 57), either unilaterally or in peer cooperation. Valuable insights on the subject were delivered by leaks relating to the NSA's Special Source Operations (SSO) division, the crown jewel of the agency (Electrospaces 2014b). Documents pertaining to the SSO allow a rare peek into the collection practices of a number of the NSA's oversea partners including the GCHQ, the German Federal Intelligence Service (*Bundesnachrichtendienst* or BND) and the French General Directorate for External Security (*Direction Générale de la Sécurité Extérieure* or DGSE) (Electrospaces 2014a). While those liaison relationships necessarily vary in scope, durability, and authorization, they also hold commonalities when it comes to obtaining communications data in bulk. As will be explained, the common features of their operational practices are particularly telling for the intelligence community's culture and corresponding intelligence collection norms. The following examples illustrate the agencies' methodology.

Operation TEMPORA allowed GCQH to tap into the fiber optic cables that carry Internet data in and out of the United Kingdom and to collect it in bulk (MacAskill et al. 2013). By exploring the United Kingdom's unique geographical advantage and placing interceptors on the approximately 200 transatlantic cables where they come ashore (Shubber 2013), GCHQ has not only managed to secure a direct access to vast amounts of Internet data, but to do so on a scale that ranked it first in that regard among its partners the Five Eyes (Shubber 2013). The process has been facilitated by secret partnerships (voluntary or forced) with the companies that operate the cables (MacAskill et al. 2013; Obermaier et al. 2014). The legal framework for the collection appears to have been the rather broad provision of s8 RIPA 2000 (Shubber 2013). The latter allows the Foreign Secretary to issue certificates for broad interception of data categories relating to terrorism, organized crime, and so on. Inception pertains to entirely foreign communications, but also to communications whereby one of the communicating parties (either the receiver or sender) is on UK soil.

France and Germany's involvement in bulk data collection is evidenced for one thing by the RAMPART-A program (Gallagher 2014; Information. dk 2014). The leaked material pertaining to the program show that the NSA considers France and Germany "third party" countries—strategic partners outside of the Five Eyes ("second parties") providing access to transition cables and hosting equipment. The majority of the RAMPART-A missions are carried out by its partners "under the cover of an overt COMSAT effort," implying that the tapping takes place at Cold War eavesdropping stations in the intercepting countries (Gallagher 2014).

Besides additional leaks, France's engagement in bulk intelligence collection is further substantiated by a handful of investigative reports that trace the practice back to 2008 (Tréguer 2017, 2). The latter confirm the involvement of the telecommunications operators Orange and the Alcatel-Lucent group as facilitating the French DGSE's access to about two dozen undersea communications cables (Tréguer 2017, 2). Designated teams within the companies would manage the so-called landing stations, where the submarine cables touch French shore and would forward the data caught in transit to the DGSE's systems in Paris (Follorou 2014). Although lacking an actual legal framework, intelligence officials familiar with the practices have argued that the practices were not illegal, but operated rather in the grey zones of the law (Follorou and Johannès 2013).

The German BND in turn is known to have (jointly with the NSA) run the EIKONAL bulk interception program (Electrospaces 2014c)—the tapping into Deutsche Telecom cables (Biermann 2014). Sources confirm that the NSA has provided the equipment for the interception in 2003 (Electrospaces 2014c). The operation was ended in 2008, although the explanations put forward in that regard differ. Legal authorization for the tapping of the transit cables has been provided by the G10-commission, which is required to step in once the collection of G10-data—communications data originating/ending in Germany and thus affecting nationals— is involved. Enabling statutes for fully foreign data traffic seems to have been of a lesser concern (Electrospaces 2015). EIKONAL and the agency's foreign partnerships aside, once the BND had learned how to collect Internet traffic from fiber optic cables, G10-orders were used to extract communications from about twenty-five domestic and foreign Internet service providers that made use of the DE-CIX cables positioned in Frankfurt (Electrospaces 2015).

The following section examines the examples from a normative perspective.

ALL ABOARD! GETTING ON THE NORMATIVE BANDWAGON

Norms are built by actors that have strong ideas about appropriate behavior in their community (Finnemore and Sikkink 1998, 896). What is appropriate in turn is very much linked to the role the actors in that community are performing (Sunstein 1996, 903). Norms are thus often role-specific (Sunstein 1996, 921). Consequently, evaluating the intelligence practices discussed above through the lens of IR norms literature mandates looking into them by adopting an *inwards* perspective and finding that shared understanding of the appropriateness of bulk collection within the community. Said communal perspective is particularly valuable when thinking of regulation in terms of bottom-up influences (as presently looking into the influences of substate entities on international cyber norms) that play out on the national and ultimately on the international level as well.

As the previous paragraph hints, the conventional wisdom holds that a norm is a standard of appropriate behavior for actors with a particular identity (Katzenstein 1996, 5; Finnemore and Sikkink 1998, 891; Finnemore and Hollis 2016, 438). This section thus focuses on highlighting the behavioral standards that give away the normative nature of bulk data collection for the intelligence community.

It appears that upon developing the necessary technological tools and know-how, all three agencies not only carry out extensive bulk collection programs but also operationalize the collection (their behavior) in a very similar way—by casting a wide net for foreign communications data and tapping into the accessible fiber optic cables. This *regularized, standardized* behavior exercised on a large-scale and without real-time constraints runs like a red thread through the examples above. The fact that the practice is not contested within the intelligence community, but seen as appropriate to serve

SIGINT purposes, encouraged through data-sharing partnerships such as the ones revealed through the NSA documents, and thus rather taken for granted with the attitude "Everybody does it," indicates norm-conforming behavior on the part of the GCHQ, the BND, and the DGSE. In IR terminology, this is one of the best examples of *norm-internalization* (Finnemore and Sikkink 1998, 895).

Note that the quality of the norm itself, that is, whether outsiders perceive it as good or bad, is not decisive, as long as the community that exercises it deems it appropriate or as inevitable to accept it (Finnemore and Sikkink 1998, 892). Put simply, the post-Snowden outrage does not abolish the bulk collection norm. It rather illustrates that the intelligence norm appeared to be in direct competition with strongly held by other actors' domestic norms on privacy and transparency of governmental agencies. Norm competition, however, is not unusual. New norms come into being in highly contested normative spaces, and while creating alternative perceptions of both interests and appropriateness, they clash with other such standards (Finnemore and Sikkink 1998, 897). Cyberspace is by no means a normative vacuum (Finnemore and Hollis 2016, 444). The extensive communication among different stakeholders upon the emergence of the bulk collection norm, accompanied by a strong and versatile rhetoric that aimed at justifying the contested behavior, on the contrary made the norm traceable and evidenced its development (Finnemore and Sikkink 1998, 892). It further means that once the leaks were out there and the necessary damage control by the use of a changed intelligence narrative and extensive communications was done, there was less fear the agencies' reputations would be additionally challenged—something Sunstein calls "social sanctions" (Sunstein 1996, 915) or in this case preempting them. Society's tolerance of the practices was secured, reputational costs lowered and thus the road ahead cleared for further fine-tuning of the bulk collection norm. That standing not only reinforced the norm within the intelligence community under scrutiny, but also paved the way for an ever-increasing number of agencies to join the bulk data collection "bandwagon" (Sunstein 1996, 930). This has had a profound knock-on effect in the legislative processes discussed below.

THE FORTIFIED CYBER NORM OF
FOREIGN BULK DATA COLLECTION

A number of comprehensive intelligence reforms saw the daylight since 2013 and the ones that recently took place in France, Germany, and the United Kingdom are of particular interest here. As research into these particular legislative processes and their outcomes yielded, the contested bulk collection—once resting on wobbly legal grounds if at all—has found its way into the statutes of these countries. The following subsection briefly presents these developments in a chronological order before moving to evaluate their meaning in the normative process.

The French Intelligence Act (FIA) (France 2015b), adopted on 24 July 2015, is the result of a long-deliberated intelligence reform.[1] The law is considered the most extensive piece of legislation relating to French surveillance practices, creating entirely new sections in the Code of Internal Security and finally legalizing already operational intelligence practices (Tréguer 2016, 2017). The FIA significantly broadens the intelligence community's collection capacities with regard to communications' content and metadata. In November of the same year, the reform was rounded off with the law on "International Surveillance" (France 2015a)—now also part of the Code of Internal Security, which focuses on international communications exclusively. The latter term is broadly defined to encompass both communications going in and out of the country (Tréguer 2016). Article L.854-2-I stipulates which network infrastructures are to be targeted for large-scale, *bulk* interception and authorizes among other things tapping into international undersea cables.

The United Kingdom followed suit by introducing the Investigatory Powers Act (IPA) in 2016 (UK 2016). The piece of legislation is understood to expand electronic surveillance powers for both law enforcement and intelligence actors. The competences outlined in the bill replace communications interception and retention powers codified by the Regulation of Investigatory Powers Act (RIPA) 2000, the Telecommunications Act (TA) 1984, the Data Retention and Investigatory Powers Act (DRIPA) 2001 and sixty-five other statutes (Anderson 2016). Further, IPA introduced new computer network exploitation powers and the ability to require retention of Internet connection records (Anderson 2016, 7). Its Part 6 and the corresponding Chapter 1 and 2 deal with bulk interception and bulk acquisition. The provisions on bulk interception replace the unclear provisions of s8 (4) RIPA and focus on "overseas-related communication," meaning communications sent or received by individuals outside the United Kingdom. The bulk acquisition powers (requiring a telecommunications provider to retain communications and disclose them pursuant to a warrant) expand the practices regulated by s94 TA that prior to the introduction of IPA was a well-kept secret (Anderson 2016, 29). The latter rules, however, affect individuals within the United Kingdom as well.

By December 2016, Germany's new surveillance laws were also on the books. The reformed BND Law introduced a number of significant new provisions with regard to the collection of foreign intelligence and international intelligence cooperation (Bundestag 2016). In its current form, the BND

Law complements the BND's collection powers by updating its *strategische Fernmeldeaufklärung* (strategic surveillance) capabilities. Adding to the agency's already existing operational powers regarding communications to and from Germany, sections 6–18 of BND Law codify for the first time the interception of communications that have both their origin and destination abroad (Wetzling 2017, 4, 5; Bundestag 2016). In that context, the amended intelligence framework covers the authorization, collection, handling, transfer and oversight of content and metadata the BND acquires in bulk. It is estimated that even prior to the legislative changes, that is to say before the existence of a proper enabling statute, the bulk collection practice made up to 90 percent of the BND's overall strategic activities (Löffelmann 2015, 1). Further, the reform allows the BND to explicitly direct intelligence operations at EU member states and EU institutions for the purpose of gathering information relevant to the country's foreign policy and security (Chase 2016).

For the sake of completeness, it should be noted that all pieces of legislation introduced above have generated significant public debates (Cobain 2018). They have further been and continue to be regularly challenged in front of judicial and other platforms by civil society groups as failing to meet international human rights and surveillance standards (ECJ 2016; Heathman 2016; Bowcott 2016; NewsWire 2018; Chase 2016).

Scholars conceptualizing the final stages of normative processes argue that institutionalization portrays the broad domestic receptiveness to a norm (Finnemore and Sikkink 1998, 906)—that the latter has been evaluated as successful (Florini 1996) to tackle ongoing societal challenges, and that putting it into binding legal instruments establishes *that* particular behavior as the credible solution for future references (Finnemore and Sikkink 1998). Thus, when prevailing norms are fortified by legal requirements (Sunstein 1996, 923), the law has a rather expressive function—it stipulates the social value of the norm encouraging it to move in a particular direction (Sunstein 1996, 953).

The above legislative summary exemplifies that the emerging bulk collection norm has reached a further phase in the normative process and it has become institutionalized (Finnemore and Sikkink 1998, 900) in specific sets of rules. The intelligence agencies studied here have thus not only developed a cyber norm on bulk collection, a norm that guides their communal practice in that regard, but have also made sure to appeal through their norm-entrepreneurial efforts (although reluctantly in the immediate post-Snowden climate) to the contemporary political context and its inherent security challenges. This has made the norm dismissal more difficult (see on the matter Keck and Sikkink 1998).

A few words need to be added here on the fact that this contribution puts forward the existence of an *international* cyber norm on bulk collection, while drawing from *national* institutionalization examples to substantiate it. This approach goes to the core of the fundamental question where international norms come from and implicate the relationship between domestic and international norms as well. International norms must always work their way through domestic structures (Finnemore and Sikkink 1998, 893), but the process is known to work the other way around too—domestic norms also influence the emergence of widely recognized, international standards. Domestic norms are intrinsically bound with the international scene's contemporary dynamics that inevitably intervene in the local realm as well.

THE POWER OF NORMS MEETS NORMATIVE POWER

This chapter so far dealt with establishing an international cyber norm on bulk data collection developed and promoted by the intelligence agencies, a norm that later became officially codified by a number of governments placing a bet on the norm's legitimacy. It thus made a strong case for studying the international norms developed by substate agencies and their impact.

While that in itself is a curious phenomenon to trace and to learn from, it nevertheless leaves the normative puzzle at hand incomplete, as it does not tell us where that normative impact comes from. Thus, to specify the argument further, this section looks into the means and mechanisms the intelligence agencies studied here use to diffuse norms in the international system and to influence other actors.

Establishing norms for the international community implies the capacity to develop new behavioral standards and *to portray* them as appropriate *for others*. This is the mission of "norm entrepreneurs" (Sunstein 1996) put in a nutshell. Once such a pursuit has been successful, the newly established norm dictates what is *normal* in a particular context. Not that long ago, Manners studied that very capacity and came to the conclusion that "the ability to define what passes for 'normal' in world politics is extremely rich" (Manners 2002, 236). He termed it "normative power"—the power to shape what can be considered normal in international life (Manners 2002, 239)—and made a proposition that international relations are often shaped by forces beyond traditional IR power structures, by a power that works through ideas and opinions (Diez 2005, 615) using norms in instrumental ways. This notion, however, while seen as a valuable addition to the concept of soft power, has found little resonance in the analysis of power dynamics brought about by other (nontraditional) international actors, like the intelligence agencies at hand. This state of affairs is surprising, as unlike other concepts of power in IR, normative power focuses much more on cognitive processes and ideational impacts than on institutions (Manners 2002, 239), and is as such particularly suitable to look into actors without state-like features.

The most important factor shaping the international role of the intelligence agencies as normative actors is not what they are, but what they do and what they say. As the previous sections dealt with what they do, in the following we touch upon what they say in more detail. Of course, just because a behavior can be labeled normative does not mean that all actors exercising it are normative powers. The crucial point is the ability *to frame* the responses of *others* (Kavalski 2013, 250). The post-Snowden reality delivers an example of exactly that—of the agencies' ability to change other actors' perception of, and response to, their norm of bulk data collection. The agencies (or rather their senior officers) and other related figures used a particular rhetoric to support a claim of urgency in their actions, induce credibility, and to thus normalize the practice. Covering a number of topics from the importance of counterintelligence efforts, the success of surveillance missions to track terrorists and to thwart plots (Sullivan 2013), the financial damage suffered by national security institutions that continues to grow five years after Snowden (Riechmann 2018), to even systematically downplaying the leaks where appropriate or proposing long-term privacy regulation solutions that would appeal to the public (Schulze 2015, 211), the strategy palette is rich in colors. The exact use of strategies corresponds to the escalation of the leaks (Schulze 2015, 211). Studies looking into the media coverage of the revelations confirm that the rhetoric has been successful. They illustrate that the media has largely picked up the "normalization trend" and appeared to report on bulk collection issues with reference to concerns over national security, while minimizing the attention given to individual rights (Wahl-Jorgensen, Bennett, and Taylor 2017, 740, 741). This finding feeds into Kavalski's conceptual qualification of normative power—it shows the intelligence agencies as agents of change, and what is more, is recognized as such by others (Kavalski 2013, 247). They have gained a position of credibility (Zupančič and Hribernik 2014, 79) by understanding the importance of interaction and instrumentalizing it.

In light of the above, it does not seem too far-fetched to suggest that the agencies' normative power has to do with their role and the context in which it is carried out, the particular community culture and the professional norms that result from it, supported by the successful framing of their missions and practices in the post-Snowden debates. Normative power is thus a way to conceptualize their toolbox. The latter is complemented by IR norms scholarship that tells us what is in there by studying the agencies' behavior and promoting understanding of its meaning (Finnemore 1996, 2).

CONCLUSION

This contribution embarked on a journey to make various claims. It dove into the complex debate on international cyber norms and made the case that the basis of what is deemed appropriate internationally may also arise among actors other than states—the intelligence agencies. It did so by studying their bulk collection practices, attempting to place some of Snowden's leaks in normative context and meaning. While the intelligence community did not have an interest to make its norms public, upon inevitably finding itself in the spotlight and setting irreversible precedents, it made the best of it—gained the states' support and pushed the norm on bulk data collection further. The agency's capacity to do so reflects their normative power—something assigned so far to rather state-like structures only. The chapter thus hopes to have identified various areas for future research—the involvement of substate agencies in international regulation efforts, and the basis on which such efforts may propel.

NOTE

1. Up until that date, France was one of the few Western democracies without a legal framework pertaining to the intelligence agencies. The latter's mandates were based on executive decrees and decisions in combination with other pieces of legislation such as the 1991 Wiretapping Act.

BIBLIOGRAPHY

Aldrich, Richard J. 2004. "Transatlantic Intelligence and Security Cooperation." *International Affairs* 80 (4): 731–53.

Anderson, David. 2016. "Report of the Bulk Powers Review." www.gov.uk/government/publications.

Biermann, Kai. 2014. "Daten Abfischen Mit Lizenz Aus Dem Kanzleramt." *Zeit*, 2014. https://www.zeit.de/politik/deutschland/2014-12/bnd-kanzleramt-eikonal-nsa.

Boeke, Sergei. 2017. "Reframing 'Mass Surveillance'." In *Terrorists' Use of the Internet: Assessment and Response*, edited by Maura Conway, Lee Jarvis, Orla Lehane, Stuart Macdonald, and Lella Nouri, 307–318. IOS Press.

Borger, Julian. 2013. "Brazilian President: US Surveillance a 'Breach of International Law.'" *The Guardian*, 2013.

Bowcott, Owen. 2016. "Investigatory Powers Bill Not Fit for Purpose, Say 200 Senior Lawyers." *The Guardian*, March 14, 2016.

Buchan, Russell. 2016. "The International Regulation of Cyber Espionage." In *International Cyber Norms: Legal, Policy and Industry Perspectives*, edited by Anna-Maria Osula and Henry Rõigas, 65–86. NATO CCD COE Publications.

Bundestag. 2014. "Antrag Der Fraktionen CDU/CSU, SPD, DIE LINKE. Und BUNDNIS 90/DIE GRUNEN: Einsetzung Eines Untersuchungsausschusses."
———. 2016. *Gesetz Zur Ausland-Ausland-Fernmeldeaufklärung Des Bundesnachrichtendienstes.* Bonn: Bunderstag. http://www.bundesgerichtshof.de/SharedDocs/Downloads/DE/Bibliothek/Gesetzesmaterialien/18_wp/BND-Gesetz/bgbl.pdf?__blob=publicationFile.
Chase, Jefferson. 2016. "Germany Reforms Its Main Intelligence Service." *Dw.Com*, 2016.
Cobain, Ian. 2018. "UK Has Six Months to Rewrite Snooper's Charter, High Court Rules." *The Guardian*, 2018. https://www.theguardian.com/technology/2018/apr/27/snoopers-charter-investigatory-powers-act-rewrite-high-court-rules.
Cole, David. 2013. "We Are All Foreigners: NSA Spying and the Rights of Others." Just Security, 2013.
Deeks, Ashley. 2016. "Intelligence Services, Peer Constraints, and the Law." In *Global Intelligence Oversight—Governing Security in the Twenty-First Century*, edited by Zachary K. Goldman and Samuel J. Rascoff, 3–36. New York: Oxford University Press.
Diez, Thomas. 2005. "Constructing the Self and Changing Others: Reconsidering `Normative Power Europe'." *Millennium: Journal of International Studies* 33 (3): 613–636.
DoD. 2013. "DoD Information Review Task Force-2: Initial Assessment- Impact Resulting from the Compromise of Classified Material by a Former NSA Contractor." https://nsarchive2.gwu.edu/NSAEBB/NSAEBB534-DIA-Declassified-Sourcebook/documents/DIA-48.pdf.
ECJ. 2016. Judgment in Joined Cases C-203/15 Tele2 Sverige AB v Post-och telestyrelsen and C-698/15 Secretary of State for the Home Department v Tom Watson and Others.
Electrospaces. 2014a. "NSA's Foreign Partnerships." Electrospaces.Blogpost.Com. 2014. https://electrospaces.blogspot.com/2014/09/nsas-foreign-partnerships.html.
———. 2014b. "Slides about NSA's Upstream Collection." January 17, 2014. https://electrospaces.blogspot.com/2014/01/slides-about-nsas-upstream-collection.html.
———. 2014c. "The German Operation Eikonal as Part of NSA's RAMPART-A Program." Electrospaces.Blogpost.Com. 2014. https://electrospaces.blogspot.com/2014/10/the-german-operation-eikonal-as-part-of.html.
———. 2015. "New Details About the Joint NSA-BND Operation Eikonal." Electrospaces.Blogpost.Com. 2015. https://electrospaces.blogspot.com/2015/05/new-details-about-joint-nsa-bnd.html.
Finnemore, Martha. 1996. "Defining State Interests." In *National Interests in International Society*, 1–33. Ithaca, NY: Cornell University Press.
Finnemore, Martha, and Duncan B Hollis. 2016. "Constructing Norms for Global Cybersecurity." *American Journal of International Law* 110. https://doi.org/10.5305/amerjintelaw.110.3.0425.
Finnemore, Martha, and Kathryn Sikkink. 1998. "International Norm Dynamics and Political Change." *International Organization* 52 (4): 887–917. http://www.jstor.org/stable/2601361.

Florini, Ann. 1996. "The Evolution of International Norms." *International Studies Quarterly* 40 (3): 363–389.

Follorou, Jacques. 2014. "Espionnage: Comment Orange et Les Services Secrets Coopèrent." *Le Monde*, 2014.

Follorou, Jacques, and Franck Johannès. 2013. "Révélations Sur Le Big Brother Français." *Le Monde*, July 4, 2013. https://www.lemonde.fr/societe/article/2013/07/04/revelations-sur-le-big-brother-francais_3441973_3224.html.

France. 2015a. *LOI N° 2015–1556 Du 30 Novembre 2015 Relative Aux Mesures de Surveillance Des Communications Électroniques Internationales (1)*. France: https://www.legifrance.gouv.fr/eli/loi/2015/11/30/DEFX1521757L/jo/texte.

———. 2015b. *LOI N° 2015–912 Du 24 Juillet 2015 Relative Au Renseignement (1)*. France.

Gallagher, Ryan. 2013. "After Snowden Leaks, Countries Want Digital Privacy Enshrined in Human Rights Treaty." *Slate.Com*, September 2013. https://slate.com/technology/2013/09/article-17-surveillance-update-countries-want-digital-privacy-in-the-iccpr.html.

———. 2014. "How Secret Partnerships Expand NSA's Surveillance Dragnet." *The Intercept*, June 19, 2014. https://theintercept.com/2014/06/18/nsa-surveillance-secret-cable-partners-revealed-rampart-a/.

Heathman, Amelia. 2016. "EU Court Deals Major Blow to UK's Controversial Snooper's Charter." *WIRED*, 2016.

Information.dk. 2014. "NSA 'Third Party' Partners Tap the Internet Backbone in Global Surveillance Program," June 19, 2014. https://www.information.dk/udland/2014/06/nsa-third-party-partners-tap-the-internet-backbone-in-global-surveillance-program.

Inkster, Nigel. 2014. "The Snowden Revelations: Myths and Misapprehensions." *Survival* 56 (1): 51–60. https://doi.org/10.1080/00396338.2014.882151.

Katzenstein, Peter J. 1996. "Introduction: Alternative Perspectives on National Security." In *The Culture of National Security: Norms and Identity in World Politics*, edited by Peter J. Katzenstein, 1–32. Columbia University Press. https://books.google.nl/books?id=bPjkBhKWBOsC&dq=the culture of national security norms and identity in world politics&hl=nl&source=gbs_book_other_versions.

Kavalski, Emilian. 2013. "The Struggle for Recognition of Normative Powers: Normative Power Europe and Normative Power China in Context." *Cooperation and Conflict* 48 (2): 247–267. https://doi.org/10.1177/0010836713485386.

Keck, Margaret E., and Kathryn Sikkink. 1998. *Activists beyond Borders: Advocacy Networks in International Politics*. Cornell University Press.

Kittichaisaree, Kriangsak. 2017. "Cyber Espionage." In *Public Internatinal Law of Cyberspace*, 233–62. Springer.

Libicki, Martin. 2017. "The Coming of Cyber Espionage Norms." In *2017 9th International Conference on Cyber Conflict (CyCon)*, 1–17. Tallinn: IEEE.

Löffelmann, Markus. 2015. "Regelung Der Routineaufklärung." *Recht + Politik* 6.

MacAskill, Ewen, Julian Borger, Nick Hopkins, Nick Davies, and James Ball. 2013. "GCHQ Taps Fibre-Optic Cables for Secret Access to World's Communications." *The Guardian*, June 21, 2013. https://www.theguardian.com/uk/2013/jun/21/gchq-cables-secret-world-communications-nsa.

Manners, Ian. 2002. "Normative Power Europe: A Contradiction in Terms?" *JCMS: Journal of Common Market Studies* 40 (2): 235–258. https://doi. org/10.1111/1468-5965.00353.

NewsWire. 2018. "Germany's Highest Court Reviewing Country's Permissive New Surveillance Laws." *Homeland Security News Wire*, 2018. http://www.homelands ecuritynewswire.com/dr20180130-germany-s-highest-court-reviewing-country-s-permissive-new-surveillance-laws.

Obermaier, Frederik, Henrik Moltke, Laura Poitras, and Jan Strozyk. 2014. "Vodafone-Firma Soll Für Spähauftrag Kassiert Haben." *Süddeutsche Zeitung*, November 21, 2014. https://www.sueddeutsche.de/digital/neue-snowden-dokumente-v odafone-firma-soll-fuer-spaehauftrag-kassiert-haben-1.2229546.

Riechmann, Deb. 2018. "Costs of Snowden Leak Still Mounting 5 Years Later." *AP News*, June 4, 2018. https://www.apnews.com/797f390ee28b4bfbb0e1b13cfed f0593.

Scheinin, Martin. 2014. "Letter to the Editor from Former Member of the Human Rights Committee." Just Security. 2014.

Schlanger, Margo. 2015. "Intelligence Legalism and the National Security Agency's Civil Liberties Gap." *Harvard National Security Journal* 6: 112–205.

Schulze, Matthias. 2015. "Patterns of Surveillance Legitimization. The German Discourse on the NSA Scandal." *Surveillance & Society* 13 (2): 197–217. http://ojs.libr ary.queensu.ca/index.php/surveillance-and-society/article/view/snowden_patterns.

Shubber, Kadhim. 2013. "A Simple Guide to GCHQ's Internet Surveillance Programme Tempora." *WIRED*, June 2013. https://www.wired.co.uk/article/gchq-tem pora-101.

Sullivan, Sean. 2013. "NSA Head: Surveillance Helped Thwart More than 50 Terror Plots." *The Washington Post*, June 18, 2013. https://www.washingtonpost.com /news/post-politics/wp/2013/06/18/nsa-head-surveillance-helped-thwart-more-than-50-terror-attempts/?noredirect=on&utm_term=.a517418b486a.

Sunstein, Cass R. 1996. "Social Norms and Social Roles." *Columbia Law Review* 96 (4): 903–968.

Tréguer, Félix. 2016. "Internet Surveillance in France's Intelligence Act." halshs-01399548.

———. 2017. "Intelligence Reform and the Snowden Paradox: The Case of France." *Media and Communication* 5 (1). https://doi.org/10.17645/mac.v5i1.821.

UK. 2015. "Privacy and Security: A Modern and Transperant Legal Framework." https://www.justsecurity.org/wp-content/uploads/2015/03/UK-ISC-Post-Snowden -Report.pdf.

———. 2016. *Investigatory Powers Act 2016*. www.tsoshop.co.uk.

United Nations. 1999. *Resolution Adopted by the General Assembly, Developments in the Field of Information and Telecommunications in the Context of International Security, A/RES/53/70*. https://documents-dds-ny.un.org/doc/UNDOC/GEN/N99/ 760/03/PDF/N9976003.pdf?OpenElement.

Wahl-Jorgensen, Karin, Lucy Bennett, and Gregory Taylor. 2017. "The Normalization of Surveillance and the Invisibility of Digital Citizenship: Media Debates After the Snowden Revelations." *International Journal of Communication* 11: 740–762.

Wetzling, Thorsten. 2017. "Germany's Intelligence Reform: More Surveillance, Modest Restrains and Inefficient Controls." Berlin. https://www.stiftung-nv.de/sites/default/files/snv_thorsten_wetzling_germanys_foreign_intelligence_reform.pdf.

Zupančič, Rok, and Miha Hribernik. 2014. "'Discovering' Normative Power as a State Strategy in the Framework of Security, Foreign, and Defense Policy: The Case of Japan." *Philippine Political Science Journal* 35 (December 2014): 78–97. https://doi.org/10.1080/01154451.2014.903566.

Part III

MULTISTAKEHOLDER AND CORPORATE DIPLOMACY

Chapter 12

Non-State Actors as Shapers of Customary Standards of Responsible Behavior in Cyberspace

Jacqueline Eggenschwiler and Joanna Kulesza

Over the past two decades, the public domain has experienced far-reaching phases of reconstitution (Ruggie 2004). Forces of globalization and technological advancement have added new degrees of complexity to international affairs and have given rise to a pluralization of actors. Polymorphous non-state actors have come to inhabit central areas of international steering and policy-making, including among others, cybersecurity.

A realm of rising political, economic, and cultural relevance, cybersecurity has been subject to considerable non-state actor engagement. Non-state actors have been key contributors to the development and expansion of cyberspace. In addition to producing hard- and software and providing technological services, they have also come to contribute to the development of global cybersecurity norms. Their normative contributions have, however, received little academic attention so far (Hall and Biersteker 2002; Ruggie 1993). With a view to addressing this deficiency, this chapter seeks to uncover the parts played by non-state actors in processes of international cybersecurity norm-construction.

Drawing on secondary academic literatures in the fields of international relations and international law, as well as primary case materials, this chapter claims that non-state actors have come to exert considerable clout over endeavors of international norm-construction, particularly as active proposers of norms of responsible behavior for state and non-state actors, and contributors to the emergence of international custom. As non-state actors continue to make their voices heard in debates about appropriate conduct in cyberspace, it is important to shed light on their contributions with a view to better understanding current practices and frames of international cybersecurity governance. The discussions of the roles of non-state actors are exemplary rather than comprehensive but help identify key features and developments.

The term *non-state actors* comprises and refers to a great number of different agents, including among others, multinational enterprises, academic communities, non-governmental organizations, as well as civil society entities, all of which would warrant their own in-depth analysis. Rather than engaging in single case studies, this chapter seeks to identify common threads of normative engagement across a broad variety of non-state actors.

The remainder of this chapter is organized along three sections. The first section summarizes key literatures related to the topic under investigation, recaps important developments, and specifies central concepts such as non-state actors and norms. The second section examines and appraises the contributions of non-state actors to processes of international cybersecurity norm-construction. Finally, the third section sums up the findings and highlights avenues for further research.

LITERATURE REVIEW

The advent of non-state actors on the international plain has presented state-oriented scholarly disciplines, including international law and international relations, with formidable theoretical and practical challenges. Non-state actors have added new layers of complexity to traditional (hierarchical) schemes of international ordering and have challenged conventional sources of agency. Yet, in order to "understand how change occurs in the world polity, [it is necessary] to unpack the different categories of transnational actors and understand the quite different logic and processes in these different categories" (Keck and Sikkink 1999, 99).

Defined in the negative, the term *non-state actors* constitutes a residual category that comprises a broad range of actors other than states (Bianchi 2011). It encompasses both bene- and malevolent individuals and entities. According to Wagner, it is impossible to identify these entities "by common sociological features as they include, inter alia, international organisations, corporations, non-governmental organisations (NGOs), de facto regimes, trade associations, and transnational corporations, terrorist groups and transnational criminal organisations" (Wagner 2009). To somewhat narrow the group of possible subjects of inquiry, this chapter only considers the contributions of benevolent non-state actors to processes of international cybersecurity norm development, that is, the contributions of those that actively seek to promote appropriate conduct in cyberspace and aspire to *improve* the overall state of global cybersecurity.

Debates about the need for rules of the road regulating the conduct of state and non-state entities in cyberspace have acquired increasing prominence over the past decade. In the face of proliferating cybersecurity incidents and reluctance on the parts of governments to agree on and enact legally binding rules at the global level, less formal, norms-based discussions have emerged as alternative pathways to formal regulation.[1] In contrast to binding legal statutes, norms as understood here denote voluntary "standard[s] of appropriate behaviour for actors with a given identity" (Finnemore and Sikkink 1998, 891). They define legitimate social purposes that enable and constrain the behavior of international actors (Florini 1996). "What distinguishes norms from other social facts (e.g., customs, traditions, values, or fashions) is their prescriptive quality, the sense of oughtness attached to them. . . . They are 'prescriptive generalization'. Or, in Onuf's more extended definition, norms (or rules) 'address some class of agents, describe some class of actions as appropriate conduct for those agents, and link agents and standards with ought-statements: agents ought to behave in accordance with standards'" (Sandholtz 2017, 2).

Since the late 1990s, norms have figured prominently across a great variety of research agendas and have witnessed extensive theorization (Keck and Sikkink 1999; Sandholtz 2017; Winston 2017). Constructivist international relations scholars, in particular, have made important contributions to advancing analytically more rigorous understandings of international norms and the roles of non-state actors in changes to normative ideas. Ideational efforts conducted by non-state actors have been subsumed under the analytical umbrella of norm entrepreneurship. Norm entrepreneurship refers to activities conducted by agents with a view to persuading others to adopt new standards of appropriateness and change social understandings (Sjöström 2010; Finnemore and Sikkink 1998). Agents engaging in norm entrepreneurship, so-called norm entrepreneurs, typically promote new understandings of appropriate conduct and mobilize other entities or network of entities to support their normative ideas. These coalitions then "bring pressure to bear from above (transnationally) and below (domestically)" and help the norms advocated to cascade, and eventually become internalized into domestic and international legal codes and institutions (Sandholtz 2017, 2).

A field of growing political importance and social relevance, cybersecurity has seen a number of noteworthy initiatives relating to the creation of international norms (Nye 2018; Hinck 2018). Discussions concerning the creation of rules of the road to curb malicious behavior in cyberspace can be traced back to the mid-1990s. In 1996, the Council of the European Union endorsed a proposal put forward by the French government for a *Charter for International Cooperation on the Internet* (Mačák 2017). At the time, "the French

Minister for Information Technology expressed hope that the initiative would lead eventually to an accord comparable to the international law of the sea" (Wu 1998, 660). The French proposition was followed by a Russian bid in the remit of the UN General Assembly, which sought to ban information weapons and their use by way of enacting legally binding rules. Moscow's draft resolution emerged in consideration of a perceived Western dominance of the ICT landscape, and gave rise to more institutionalized international discussions.

In reaction to Russia's proposal of 1998, and as a result of concerns over the appropriateness of legally binding provisions, particularly on the parts of Western states, the UN GA's First Committee called to life a Group of Governmental Experts to study existing and emerging threats emanating from the digital realm and possible normative measures to address them. The first of a total of five groups met in 2004. While the UN GGEs meeting between 2009 and 2015 managed to issue non-binding consensus reports, the groups convening between 2004–2005 and 2016–2017 did not produce corresponding documents (Väljataga 2017).

Subsequent to the 2016–2017 UN GGE's inability to agree on a consensus report, and following major cybersecurity incidents of transnational magnitude, including WannaCry and Petya/NotPetya, there has been a noticeable surge in the number of non-state initiatives directed at fostering responsible behavior in the virtual domain (Hern 2017). Examples include, among others, the University of Leiden's and ICT4Peace Foundation's co-sponsorship of a *Global Commentary on Voluntary, Non-Binding Norms for Responsible State Behaviour in the Use of Information and Communications Technology*, Microsoft's proposal for a *Digital Geneva Convention*, its adoption of a *Cybersecurity Tech Accord*, its initiation of a *Digital Peace Now* campaign, and its support of *the Paris Call for Trust and Security in Cyberspace*, Siemens' conclusion of a *Charter of Trust*, as well as the Global Commission on the Stability of Cyberspace's (GCSC) calls for the *Protection of the Public Core of the Internet*, the safeguarding of electoral infrastructures, and the release of the *Singapore Norms Package* (Smith 2017b, 2018; Siemens 2018a; Global Commission on the Stability of Cyberspace 2017a; ICT4Peace Foundation 2018; Global Commission on the Stability of Cyberspace 2018a).

In what follows, the activities of these actors are highlighted in more detail. Against the background of lacking political agreement at the intergovernmental level and a halting emergence of international hard law directed at addressing the challenges pertaining to nefarious conduct in the digital realm, efforts led by non-state actors deserve particular analytical attention in terms of fostering international peace, security, and stability.

THE NORMATIVE CONTRIBUTIONS
OF NON-STATE ACTORS

Non-state actors have been central to the growth and spread of ICTs.[2] As operators of key network infrastructures, developers of products and suppliers of services, they have made important contributions to the "international [. . .] architecture for the governance of cyberspace" (Radu 2014, 4). Apart from acting as executors of public initiatives (e.g., public-private partnerships), they have also been seen to drive normative agendas.

The subsequent paragraphs summarize the norms-based activities conducted by some of the most vocal proponents for rules of the road for cyberspace. The selection of relevant initiatives was informed by substantive as well as temporal considerations. Only proposals by benevolent non-state actors, and only proposals launched post-2017 were selected for examination.

The ICT4Peace Foundation

Since its inception in the context of the United Nations World Summit on the Information Society in Geneva and Tunis in 2004, the ICT4Peace Foundation has actively stipulated the peaceful use and employment of ICTs and new media. Against the background of rapidly emerging threats and acts of cybercrime and -sabotage, in 2011, the ICT4Peace Foundation publicly called for a *Code of Conduct for Cyberconflicts* (Stauffacher, Sibilia, and Weekes 2011). The corresponding report titled *Getting Down to Business: Realistic Goals for the Promotion of Peace in Cyberspace* maintained that

> *nations . . . need to examine and assess the need for modifying existing laws to address cyber-specific issues. At both . . . national and international levels, taskforces need to be established including all the key players to exchange information, provide early warning and explore possible solutions to existing or future challenges.* (Stauffacher, Sibilia, and Weekes 2011)

With the intention of building on the outcomes of the UN GGEs, most recently, the ICT4Peace Foundation has, in a joint initiative with Leiden University's Program for Cyber Norms, co-sponsored the publication of a *Global Commentary on Voluntary, Non-Binding Norms for Responsible State Behaviour in the Use of Information and Communications Technology*, which brings together comments and guidance for understanding and operationalizing the recommendations contained in the UN GGE reports of 2010, 2013, and 2015 (Tikk et al. 2017; ICT4Peace Foundation 2017; Adamson 2017). Furthermore, ICT4Peace has commissioned a series of cyber-norms blogposts commenting on developments in the field, and has actively participated in UN GGE and UN OEWG consultation meetings with a view to contributing to the promotion of peaceful settlements of disputes in cyberspace (Tikk 2019; ICT4Peace Foundation 2019).

Microsoft

Among the first corporate stakeholders to instigate debates about responsible conduct in cyberspace was Microsoft (Betz 2015). Following preceding efforts in 2013, 2014, and 2016, in February 2017, Microsoft president and chief legal officer Brad Smith introduced the idea of a *Digital Geneva Convention to Protect Cyberspace* (Smith 2017a; Microsoft 2013; McKay et al. 2014; Charney et al. 2016). Grounded in the belief that deep-rooted collaboration among states, and between states, the private sector and civil society is needed to curb nefarious doings in the digital realm, the convention as outlined by Smith, asks governments to "come together, affirm international cybersecurity norms that have emerged in recent years, adopt new and binding rules, and get to work implementing them" (Smith 2017b). Furthermore, it pleads global technology companies to behave as neutral actors, and recommends the setting-up of an independent non-governmental organization capable of investigating and publicly attributing (nation-state) cyberattacks (Smith 2017b; Maurer and Taylor 2018).

Microsoft's call for a *Digital Geneva Convention to Protect Cyberspace* was succeeded by the unveiling of a *Cybersecurity Tech Accord* among leading industry partners in April 2018 (Smith 2018). In September 2018, Microsoft unveiled a Digital Peace Now campaign, which calls on citizens to protect cyberspace, for example, through measures of cyberhygiene, and urges governments to refrain from endangering the global digital environment. Only two months later, in November 2018, it supported the release of the *Paris Call*, a multistakeholder initiative seeking to safeguard peace and security in the virtual realm by means of nine principles, including the prevention of nefarious interference or theft of intellectual property by foreign actors, the condemnation of hack-backs, and the securing of supply chains (Ministère de l'Europe et des Affaires Étrangères 2018). So far, the *Paris Call* has been acceded to by more than 1000 supporters: 78 governments, 29 public authorities, 343 civil society organizations, and 633 private sector entities (Ministère de l'Europe et des Affaires Étrangères 2018).

Siemens

Two months before the launch of Microsoft's *Cybersecurity Tech Accord*, Siemens, together with eight partner corporations, issued a *Charter of Trust for a Secure Digital World* (Siemens 2018a). Adopted at the sidelines of the 2018 Munich Security Conference, the charter calls for binding rules, and postulates ten principles ranging from ownership of cyber and IT security, responsibility throughout the digital supply chain, security by default, user-centricity, innovation and co-creation to education, certification for critical infrastructure and solutions, transparency and response, regulatory framework, and joint initiatives (Siemens 2018b; Hinck 2018; Kaeser 2018).

Calling for binding legal rules, the charter recognizes that

> *in order to keep pace with continuous advances in the market as well as threats from the criminal world, companies and governments must join forces and take decisive action. This means making every effort to protect the data and assets of individuals and businesses; prevent damage from people, businesses, and infrastructures; and build a reliable basis for trust in a connected and digital world.* (Siemens 2018a, 1)

In contrast to the politically worded norms advanced as part of the Digital Geneva Convention or the Paris Call, the areas of activities identified by the charter signatories are skewed toward key tenets of responsible product development and engineering practices (Horenbeeck et al. 2019).

Global Commission on the Stability of Cyberspace (GCSC)

A year prior to the postulation of Siemens' *Charter of Trust for a Secure Digital World*, the Munich Security Conference (2017) saw the inauguration of the Global Commission on the Stability of Cyberspace (GCSC), a multi-stakeholder consortium composed of regionally diverse scholars, CEOs, and (former) policy makers. The commission's expressed goal is the development of "proposals for norms and policies to enhance international security and stability and guide responsible state and non-state behaviour in cyberspace" (Global Commission on the Stability of Cyberspace 2017b). Composed of twenty-eight commissioners and supported by a research team and a governmental advisory network, the GCSC draws on a rich pool of technical and political expertise. According to one of its commissioners, Dr. Wolfgang Kleinwächter, "the GCSC has the potential, to become a trusted source of inspiration for global internet policy making in the 2020s" (Kleinwächter 2017).

The GCSC has convened several times along major Internet policy meetings, including the Munich Security Conference, CyCon, Black Hat, the Global Conference on Cyber Space, GLOBSEC, ICANN, EuroDIG, UNI-DIR, and G20. During one of its early meetings in November 2017, the GCSC issued its first norm, *A Call to Protect the Public Core of the Internet*, which states: "Without prejudice to their rights and obligations, state and non-state actors should not conduct or knowingly allow activity that intentionally and substantially damages the general availability or integrity of the public core of the Internet, and therefore the stability of cyberspace" (Global Commission on the Stability of Cyberspace 2017a, 1). The proclamation of the norm drew considerable attention from the international community and the norm has since made its way into a number of political fora, including the Paris Peace Forum, and the European Union (Global Commission on the Stability of Cyberspace 2019; Ministère de l'Europe et des Affaires Étrangères 2018). According to some observers, including the Electronic Frontier Foundation's global policy analyst, Jeremy Malcolm, "the idea of a duty on stakeholders not to attack the internet's core technical infrastructure has the potential to become an influential and important guiding principle for policymakers and business leaders" (Malcolm 2017).

The concept of the public core as advanced by the GCSC was first articulated by associate professor of Security and Technology, Dennis Broeders, in a study published by Netherlands Scientific Council for Government Policy (Broeders 2016). The study argued for the establishment of an international norm directed at protecting "the internet's public core—its main protocols and infrastructure, which are a global public good . . . against unwarranted intervention by states" (Broeders 2017, 367).[3]

Since the publication of its first norm, the commission has issued seven further norms addressing issues such as product tampering, the commandeering of botnets, and the creation of a vulnerability equities process (Global Commission on the Stability of Cyberspace 2018b).

NON-STATE ACTORS AS SHAPERS OF CUSTOMARY STANDARDS OF RESPONSIBLE BEHAVIOR IN CYBERSPACE

The cases introduced above demonstrate that non-state actors have come to insert their voices in debates about responsible behavior in cyberspace. They have taken seats at political tables and have started to behave as diplomatic protagonists. Their proposals are deliberately targeted at the international level and consciously employ policy-oriented language. Naming norms-based endeavors *Charter, Accord, or Convention* underscores the underlying political ambitions of these efforts.

In terms of agency, the norm-building activities conducted by non-state actors reflect a substantial extension of their traditional authority. From a structural point of view, they suggest a shift in global regulation from state-centric forms of steering toward new non-territorial, multi-actor modes of governance (Scherer, Palazzo, and Baumann 2006, 506). In international relations and international law, states have long enjoyed (and continue to enjoy) conceptual and analytical preeminence apropos enacting and enforcing global rules (Bianchi 2011; Noortmann, Reinisch, and Ryngaert 2015). Among a select number of personae endowed with international legal personality, states have been considered the main bearers and creators of international rights and duties, and as a result have been ascribed key value allocation authority (Klabbers 2003, 55; Thirlway 2014). Positivist interpretations of international law maintain that international norm-making capabilities sit with states who lay down "shared boundaries of acceptable conduct in international [affairs]" (Mačák 2017, 2). However, in the context of cybersecurity, traditional conceptions of how norms and values come about and achieve legal status appear to be at odds with empirical realities.

With the intention of responding to the inadequacies posed by positivist interpretations of international law, a group of legal scholars has promoted the idea of *Global Administrative Law* (Krisch and Kingsbury 2006). Global administrative law offers a useful lens through which to contextualize the norm-stipulating activities of non-state actors and highlight their contributions.[4] Conceptually, it is closely related to notions of global governance.[5] Global administrative law refers to an emerging body of law which takes into account that a great number of global legal rules, principles, and institutional norms are shaped by administrative processes "that implicate more than purely intra-state structures of legal and political authority" (Kingsbury and Donaldson 2011, para. 1). It "acknowledges the informality of global administration, the diffusion of decision making in a multi-level system and the strong influence of private elements in global administration" (Andjelkovic 2006, 58).

According to Kingsbury, Krisch and Stewart, five different types of administrative processes can be distinguished, all of which can give rise to the emergence of global legal rules, principles, and institutional norms:

1. Administration by formal international organizations;
2. Administration based on collective action by transnational networks of cooperative arrangements between national regulatory officials;
3. Distributed administration conducted by national regulators under treaty, network, or other cooperative regimes;
4. Administration by hybrid intergovernmental–private arrangements;
5. Administration by private institutions with regulatory functions (Kingsbury, Krisch, and Stewart 2005, para. 20).

Of particular relevance for the purposes of this chapter are administrative processes conducted by private protagonists. Whether through company policies, dedicated normative initiatives or technical standard-setting, non-state actors have contributed substantially to global administrative processes pertaining to cybersecurity and have helped shape global practices and culture. The GCSC's institution-crossing policy efforts to enhance international security and stability and guide responsible state and non-state behavior in cyberspace or Siemens' and Microsoft's propagation of technical security standards are but a few examples in this regard (Global Commission on the Stability of Cyberspace 2018c; European Parliament 2018, para. 48). The same can be said about the interpretation and implementation guidelines issued by ICT-4Peace and Leiden University's Program for Cyber Norms apropos the norms contained in the 2015 UN GGE recommendations.

While contested in terms of legal status, these practices have the potential to constitute important determinants for the emergence of international custom pertaining to cybersecurity. According to traditional notions of customary international law, binding habitus requires the presence of two elements: (1) consistent state practice and (2) opinio juris (Wex Legal Dictionary 2018).[6] Although the practices advanced by non-state actors in the context of international peace and security in cyberspace fit only imperfectly into conventional frameworks of customary international law (as they are not state-driven), their law-like normative and custom-inspiring effects should not be discounted. Global administrative law helps acknowledge these custom and culture-shaping contributions of non-state actors as it lends credence to the idea of non-state actors possessing legislative qualities, that is, having international legal personality (Andjelkovic 2006).

Custom never emerges instantaneously or fully formed. Rather, it represents the product of repeated interactions and exchanges across different institutional contexts and among different entities over time (Finnemore and Hollis 2018). As many regulatory functions are increasingly constituted and performed outside formally public, governmental structures, the norm-advancing activities conducted by non-state actors as well as their political/diplomatic engagement, if sustained over time, have the capacity to act as mold shells for the emergence of customary red lines apropos responsible behavior in the digital realm. By lining out and verbally enforcing normative standards vis-à-vis acceptable conduct in cyberspace, non-state actors can curb the potential for malicious, norm-opposing behavior to become widely accepted, including among sovereign parties. Indeed, as sovereign entities continue to grapple with questions around the applicability of international law to the virtual sphere, the norm-stipulating practices of private protagonists can serve as important sources of input and incubators of customary principles ad interim.

The norm-promoting efforts of non-state actors can effectively be understood as signals of disapproval of certain malicious activities in cyberspace, for example, the targeting or deliberate destruction of critical (information) infrastructure. These signals, in turn, have the potential to incite counteractions among different parties (including states) and give rise to shared boundaries of acceptable conduct in cyberspace. Furthermore, the practices advanced by non-state actors may provide a model which other protagonists in global administration find persuasive to follow and/or cost-effective to emulate (Kingsbury and Donaldson 2011, para. 26).

CONCLUSION

A decade ago, the protection of critical systems and network infrastructures was considered a topic of low politics, one mainly concerning technical experts (Malcolm 2017). Today, cybersecurity has become a matter of high politics. It has become top of the agenda for a wide circle of stakeholders, including government officials, community leaders, and CEOs. The exorbitant increase in the number of users and processes relying on digital infrastructures since the 1990s has gone hand in hand with a surge in the number of vulnerabilities and insecurities. The rising tide of threats to the stability and future development of cyberspace has led many observers to call for rules and norms to secure the digital environment.

Against the background of progress-inhibiting contention at the intergovernmental level, this chapter has analyzed the contributions of non-state actors to projects of international cybersecurity norm-construction. It has argued that non-state actors have come to exert considerable influence, particularly as active stimulators of norms and shapers of customary standards of responsible behavior in the digital realm.

The normative efforts introduced as part of this chapter indicate that traditional conceptions wherein international standard-setting was seen as the exclusive purview of sovereign actors are fading.

The international societal body is changing at a rapid rate and new actors in international law are emerging and gaining prominence. Scholars and practitioners have to think fast to keep pace with global change. As a result, the theoretical discourse is sometimes lost in the attempt to provide a satisfactory explanation of legal processes in a changing and unpredictable world. (Bianchi 2009)

With the intention of better understanding and classifying the norm-stipulating activities of non-state actors in the context of international peace and security in cyberspace, this chapter turned to global administrative law. Global administrative law recognizes that "much administration is taking place in what might be thought of as a global administrative space, involving blurring of national and international, and public and private, dimensions" (Kingsbury and Donaldson 2011, para. 1). It also appreciates and helps conceptualize the law-like normative and custom-inspiring practices of non-state actors.

Irrespective of their ontological infancy and their loose connection among each other, the norm-promoting activities of non-state actors as well as their political commitment, if sustained over time, have the capacity to act as mold shells for the emergence of international custom pertaining to responsible behavior in cyberspace. Given the reluctance of states to actively present their views on where the thresholds are, non-state actor engagement is critical apropos effectuating responsible behavior in cyberspace (Vihul 2013). Although not endowed with formal law-making authority under positivist notions of international law, the work of non-state actors such as ICT4Peace Foundation, multinational technology firms, including Microsoft and Siemens, or the Global Commission on the Stability of Cyberspace is exceptionally important in terms of lining out and shaping the outer (non-legal) boundaries of acceptable conduct in cyberspace (Vihul 2013).

Furthermore, as non-state actors continue to be concerned about "the immediate and future threats to their critical services and infrastructures, [resulting] from the misuse of information and communications technologies," and seek diplomatic engagement, it is important to reconsider existing forms of interaction and cooperation among governmental and non-governmental entities (Melissa Hathaway in Hampson et al. 2017, 5). The norm-building activities of non-state actors point to a need for more collaborative forms of governance, in which the former participate in joint steering efforts and share responsibilities with sovereign authorities (Healey 2018, 1:1).

NOTES

1. "The main goals for agreeing on norms are believed to include increased predictability, trust and stability in the use of Information and Communication Technologies" (Osula and Rõigas 2016, 11).

2. Contrary to earlier communication technologies, and despite its emergence in a politically predicated context, sovereign actors initially displayed little inclination toward enacting measures of control over cyberspace. Operation and management of the infrastructure were, for the most part, left to the experts who had contributed to its development, including, among others, Barry M. Leiner, Vinton G. Cerf, David D. Clark, Robert E. Kahn, Leonard Kleinrock, Daniel C. Lynch, Jon Postel, Larry G. Roberts, and Stephen Wolff. Oversight was informal and reflected the academic context within which the digital realm had arisen.

3. According to Broeders the public core "does not comprise the whole of the internet or even enter into the content layer of the internet but is limited to the logical

and physical infrastructural layers of the core internet. It is deliberately a 'lowest common denominator approach' that aims to keep the concept of the public core as close as possible to the minimum that is needed to protect the functionality of the internet," see (Broeders 2017, 367).

4. "Underlying the emergence of global administrative law is the vast increase in the reach and forms of transgovernmental regulation and administration designed to address the consequences of globalised interdependence in such fields as security, . . . banking and financial regulation, law enforcement, telecommunications, . . . intellectual property" (Kingsbury, Krisch, and Stewart 2005, 16).

5. With regard to the governance of global networks, Drake considers global governance to be "the development and application of shared principles, norms, rules, decision-making procedures, and programs intended to shape actor's expectations and practices and to enhance their collective management capabilities in world affair," see (Drake 2008, 8–9).

6. "Opinio juris denotes a subjective obligation, a sense on behalf of a state that it is bound to the law in question. The International Court of Justice reflects this standard in ICJ Statute, Article 38(1)(b) by reflecting that the custom to be applied must be *accepted as law*" (Wex Legal Dictionary 2018).

BIBLIOGRAPHY

Adamson, Liisi. 2017. "Recommendation 13 (C)." In *Voluntary, Non-Binding Norms for Responsible State Behaviour in the Use Of Information and Communications Technology: A Commentary*, edited by Eneken Tikk. New York, NY: United Nations Office for Disarmament Affairs. https://www.un.org/disarmament/wp-c ontent/uploads/2018/04/Civil-Society-2017.pdf.

Andjelkovic, Maja. 2006. "Internet Governance: In the Footsteps of Global Administrative Law." University of Kent. https://www.iisd.org/pdf/2006/infosoc_int_gov _law.pdf.

Betz, Chris. 2015. "A Call for Better Coordinated Vulnerability Disclosure." Microsoft. 2015. https://blogs.technet.microsoft.com/msrc/2015/01/11/a-call-for-better-coordinated-vulnerability-disclosure/.

Bianchi, Andrea. 2009. "Non-State Actors and International Law." 2009. http://gra duateinstitute.ch/home/relations-publiques/news-at-the-institute/news-archives.h tml/_/news/corporate/2009/news_557.

———. 2011. "The Fight for Inclusion: Non-State Actors and International Law." In *From Bilateralism to Community Interest*, edited by Ulrich Fastenrath, Rudolf Geiger, Daniel-Erasmus Kahn, Andreas Paulus, Sabine von Schorlemer, and Christoph Vedder, 39–57. Oxford: Oxford University Press. https://doi.org/10.1093/acprof :oso/9780199588817.003.0006.

Broeders, Dennis. 2016. *The Public Core of the Internet: An International Agenda for Internet Governance*. Edited by The Netherlands Scientific Council for Government Policy. *The Public Core of the Internet: An International Agenda for Internet Governance*. Amsterdam University Press. https://doi.org/10.26530/ OAPEN_610631.

———. 2017. "Aligning the International Protection of "the Public Core of the Internet" with State Sovereignty and National Security." *Journal of Cyber Policy* 2 (3): 366–376. https://doi.org/10.1080/23738871.2017.1403640.

Charney, Scott, Erin English, Aaron Kleiner, Nemanja Malisevic, Angela McKay, Jan Neutze, and Paul Nicholas. 2016. "From Articulation to Implementation: Enabling Progress on Cybersecurity Norms." https://query.prod.cms.rt.microsoft.com/cms/api/am/binary/REVmc8.

Drake, William J. 2008. "Introduction: The Distributed Architecture of Network Global Governance." In *Governing Global Electronic Networks*, edited by William J. Drake and Ernest J. Wilson III, 1–80. The MIT Press. https://doi.org/10.7551/mitpress/9780262042512.003.0009.

European Parliament. 2018. "Report on Cyber Defence (2018/2004(INI))." http://www.europarl.europa.eu/sides/getDoc.do?pubRef=-//EP//NONSGML+REPORT+A8-2018-0189+0+DOC+PDF+V0//EN.

Finnemore, Martha, and Duncan B. Hollis. 2018. "Naming without Shaming? Accuzations and International Law in Global Cybersecurity."

Finnemore, Martha, and Kathryn Sikkink. 1998. "International Norm Dynamics and Political Change." *International Organization* 52 (4): 887–917. https://doi.org/10.1162/002081898550789.

Florini, Ann. 1996. "The Evolution of International Norms." *International Studies Quarterly*, 40: 363–389. http://www.jstor.org/stable/2600716.

Global Commission on the Stability of Cyberspace. 2017a. "Call to Protect the Public Core of the Internet." https://cyberstability.org/wp-content/uploads/2017/11/call-to-protect-the-public-core-of-the-internet.pdf.

———. 2017b. "Mission Statement." https://cyberstability.org/.

———. 2018a. "Call to Protect the Electoral Infrastructure." https://cyberstability.org/wp-content/uploads/2018/05/GCSC-Call-to-Protect-Electoral-Infrastructure.pdf.

———. 2018b. "Global Commission Introduces Six Critical Norms Towards Cyber Stability." News. https://cyberstability.org/research/singapore_norm_package/.

———. 2018c. "The European Parliament Supports the GCSC in Its Recent Report on Cyber Defence." News. https://cyberstability.org/news/the-european-parliament-supports-the-gcsc-in-its-recent-report-on-cyber-defence/.

———. 2019. "European Union Embeds Protection of the Public Core of the Internet in New EU Cybersecurity Act." News. https://cyberstability.org/news/european-union-embeds-protection-of-the-public-core-of-the-internet-in-new-eu-cybersecurity-act-2/.

Hall, Rodney Bruce, and Thomas J Biersteker. 2002. *The Emergence of Private Authority in the International System*. Cambridge: Cambridge University Press. https://doi.org/10.1017/CBO9780511491238.

Hathaway, Melissa. 2017. "When Violating the Agreement Becomes Customary Practice." In *Getting beyond Norms: New Approaches to International Cybersecurity Challenges*, edited by Fen Osler Hampson and Michael Sulmeyer, 5–12. Centre for International Governance Innovation. https://www.cigionline.org/sites/default/files/documents/Getting Beyond Norms.pdf.

Healey, Jason. 2018. "Innovation on Cyber Collaboration: Leverage at Scale." Vol. 1. http://www.atlanticcouncil.org/images/publications/Innovation-Cyber-WEB.pdf.

Hern, Alex. 2017. "WannaCry, Petya, NotPetya: How Ransomware Hit the Big Time in 2017." *The Guardian*. https://www.theguardian.com/technology/2017/dec/30/wannacry-petya-notpetya-ransomware.

Hinck, Garrett. 2018. "Private-Sector Initiatives for Cyber Norms: A Summary." Lawfare. https://www.lawfareblog.com/private-sector-initiatives-cyber-norms-summary.

Horenbeeck, Maarten Van. 2018. "Taking a Multi-Stakeholder Look at Cyber Norms." CircleID. http://www.circleid.com/posts/20180827_taking_a_multi_stakeholder_look_at_cyber_norms/.

Horenbeeck, Maarten Van, Sheetal Kumar, Global Partners Digital, Frans Van Aardt, Susan Mohr, Carina Birarda, Louise Marie Hurel, John Hering, Duncan Hollis, and Joanna Kulesza. 2019. "Cybersecurity Agreements." http://www.intgovforum.org/multilingual/filedepot_download/4904/1658.

ICT4Peace Foundation. 2017. "Call for Global Open Consultations on the United Nations Cybersecurity Norms Proposals." Activities. https://ict4peace.org/activities/call-for-global-open-consultations-on-the-united-nations-cybersecurity-norms-proposal/.

———. 2018. "ICT4Peace Sponsored First Global Commentary on Norms of Responsible State Behaviour in Cyberspace." https://ict4peace.org/activities/ict4peace-sponsored-first-global-commentary-on-norms-of-responsible-state-behaviour-in-cyberspace/.

———. 2019. "UN GGE and UN OEWG on Cybersecurity: ICT4Peace Supporting OAS Regional Consultations." Activities. https://ict4peace.org/activities/un-gge-and-un-oewg-on-cybersecurity-ict4peace-supporting-oas-regional-consultations/.

Kaeser, Joe. 2018. "Working Together for More Security in the Digital World." LinkedIn Pulse. https://www.linkedin.com/pulse/working-together-more-security-digital-world-joe-kaeser.

Keck, Margaret E., and Kathryn Sikkink. 1999. "Transnational Advocacy Networks in International and Regional Politics." *International Social Science Journal* 51 (159): 89–101. https://doi.org/10.1111/1468-2451.00179.

Kingsbury, Benedict, and Megan Donaldson. 2011. "Global Administrative Law." Max Planck Encyclopedia of Public International Law. http://iilj.org/wp-content/uploads/2016/08/EPIL_Global_Administrative_Law.pdf.

Kingsbury, Benedict, Nico Krisch, and Richard Stewart. 2005. "The Emergence of Global Administrative Law." *Law and Contemporary Problems* 68 (3): 48. http://heinonlinebackup.com/hol-cgi-bin/get_pdf.cgi?handle=hein.journals/lcp68&section=35.

Klabbers, Jan. 2003. "(I Can't Get No) Recognition: Subjects Doctrine and the Emergence of Non-State Actors." In *Nordic Cosmopolitanism*, edited by Martti Koskenniemi, Jarna Petman, and Jan Klabbers, 1813: 352–369. Leiden: Martinus Nijhoff Publishers.

Kleinwächter, Wolfgang. 2017. "The Kaljurand Commission: Building Bridges Over Troubled Cyber-Water." http://www.circleid.com/posts/20171202_kaljarund_commission_building_bridges_over_troubled_cyber_water/.

Krisch, Nico, and Benedict Kingsbury. 2006. "Introduction: Global Governance and Global Administrative Law in the International Legal Order." *European Journal of International Law* 17 (1): 1–13. https://doi.org/10.1093/ejil/chi170.

Mačák, Kubo. 2017. "From Cyber Norms to Cyber Rules: Re-Engaging States as Law-Makers." *Leiden Journal of International Law* 30 (4): 877–899.

Malcolm, Jeremy. 2017. "EFF at Cyberspace Events in Delhi: Protecting the Public Core of the Internet." Deeplinks Blog. https://www.eff.org/deeplinks/2017/11/ef f-cyberspace-events-delhi-protecting-public-core-internet.

Maurer, Tim, and Kathryn Taylor. 2018. "Outlook on International Cyber Norms: Three Avenues for Future Progress." Just Security. https://www.justsecurity.org/5 3329/outlook-international-cyber-norms-avenues-future-progress/.

McKay, Angela, Jan Neutze, Paul Nicholas, and Kevin Sullivan. 2014. "International Cybersecurity Norms." https://blogs.microsoft.com/cybertrust/2014/12/03/propo sed-cybersecurity-norms/.

Microsoft. 2013. "Five Principles for Shaping Cybersecurity Norms." https:// www.microsoft.com/en-us/cybersecurity/content-hub/five-principles-for-shaping -cybersecurity-norms.

Ministère de l'Europe et des Affaires Étrangères. 2018. "Cybersecurity: Paris Call of 12 November 2018 for Trust and Security in Cyberspace." French Foreign Policy. https://www.diplomatie.gouv.fr/en/french-foreign-policy/digital-diplomacy/france -and-cyber-security/article/cybersecurity-paris-call-of-12-november-2018-for-tru st-and-security-in.

Noortmann, Math, August Reinisch, and Cedric Ryngaert. 2015. *Non-State Actors in International Law*. Edited by Math Noortmann, August Reinisch, and Cedric Ryngaert. Studies in International Law. Oxford: Hart Publishing.

Nye, Joseph S. Jr. 2018. *"Normative Restraints on Cyber Conflict."* Cambridge, MA. https://www.belfercenter.org/sites/default/files/files/publication/Nye Normative Restraints Final.pdf.

Osula, Anna-Maria, and Henry Rõigas. 2016. *International Cyber Norms*. Edited by Anna-Maria Osula and Henry Rõigas. Tallinn: NATO Cooperative Cyber Defence Centre of Excellence. https://ccdcoe.org/sites/default/files/multimedia/pdf/Intern ationalCyberNorms_full_book.pdf.

Radu, Roxana. 2014. "Power Technology and Powerful Technologies: Global Governmentality and Security in the Cyberspace." In *Cyberspace and International Relations*, edited by Jan-Frederik Kremer and Benedikt Müller, 3–20. Berlin, Heidelberg: Springer Berlin Heidelberg. https://doi.org/10.1007/978-3-642-37481-4.

Ruggie, John Gerard. 2011. "Guiding Principles on Business and Human Rights: Implementing the United Nations "Protect, Respect and Remedy" Framework." Vol. HR/PUB/11/. New York, NY. https://www.ohchr.org/documents/publicat ions/guidingprinciplesbusinesshr_en.pdf.

Ruggie, John Gerard. 1993. "Territoriality and Beyond: Problematizing Modernity in International Relations." *International Organization* 47 (1): 139–174. http://www. jstor.org/stable/2706885.

———. 2004. "Reconstituting the Global Public Domain—Issues, Actors, and Practices." *European Journal of International Relations* 10 (4): 499–531. https://do i.org/10.1177/1354066104047847.

Sandholtz, Wayne. 2017. *International Norm Change. Oxford Research Encyclopedia of Politics*. Oxford: Oxford University Press. https://doi.org/10.1093/acrefo re/9780190228637.013.588.

Scherer, Andreas Georg, Guido Palazzo, and Dorothée Baumann. 2006. "Global Rules and Private Actors: Toward a New Role of the Transnational Corporation in Global Governance." *Business Ethics Quarterly* 16 (04): 505–532. https://doi. org/10.5840/beq200616446.

Siemens. 2018a. "Charter of Trust: For a Secure Digital World." https://www.sie mens.com/press/pool/de/feature/2018/corporate/2018-02-cybersecurity/charter -of-trust-e.pdf.

———. 2018b. "Time for Action: Building a Consensus for Cybersecurity." Cyber- security. https://www.siemens.com/innovation/en/home/pictures-of-the-future/digi talization-and-software/cybersecurity-charter-of-trust.html.

Sjöström, Emma. 2010. "Shareholders as Norm Entrepreneurs for Corporate Social Responsibility." *Journal of Business Ethics* 94 (2): 177–191. https://doi.org/10.1 007/s10551-009-0255-1.

Smith, Brad. 2017a. "A Digital Geneva Convention to Protect Cyberspace." https:// query.prod.cms.rt.microsoft.com/cms/api/am/binary/RW67QH.

———. 2017b. "The Need For a Digital Convention." Microsoft. https://blogs. microsoft.com/on-the-issues/2017/02/14/need-digital-geneva-convention/#sm.00 01hkfw5aob5evwum620jqwsabzv.

———. 2018. "34 Companies Stand Up for Cybersecurity with a Tech Accord." Microsoft. https://blogs.microsoft.com/on-the-issues/2018/04/17/34-companies -stand-up-for-cybersecurity-with-a-tech-accord/.

Stauffacher, Daniel, Ricardo Sibilia, and Barbara Weekes. 2011. "Getting Down to Business Realistic Goals for the Promotion of Peace in Cyberspace." Geneva.

Thirlway, Hugh. 2014. *The Sources of International Law*. Foundations of Public International Law. Oxford: Oxford University Press.

Tikk, Eneken. 2019. "UN GGE—Eneken Tikk's Cyber Norms Blogposts: Search for Cyber Norms—Where to Look? #4 The Norms Test: Existing Norms." ICT4Peace Foundation. https://ict4peace.org/activities/policy-research/policy-research-cs/un -gge-eneken-tikks-cyber-norms-blogposts-search-for-cyber-norms-where-to-loo k-4-the-norms-test-existing-norms/.

Tikk, Eneken, Zine Homburger, Mika Kerttunen, Liisi Adamson, Els DeBusser, Bar- rie Sander, Jason Jolley, Michael Berk, Caitriona Heinl, and Nicholas Tsagourias. 2017. *Voluntary, Non-Binding Norms for Responsible State Behaviour in the Use Of Information and Communications Technology: A Commentary*. Edited by Eneken Tikk. New York, NY: United Nations Office for Disarmament Affairs. https ://www.un.org/disarmament/wp-content/uploads/2018/04/Civil-Society-2017.pdf.

Väljataga, Ann. 2017. "Back to Square One? The Fifth UN GGE Fails to Submit a Conclusive Report at the UN General Assembly." NATO CCDCOE. https://cc dcoe.org/back-square-one-fifth-un-gge-fails-submit-conclusive-report-un-general- assembly.html.

Vihul, Liis. 2013. "The Tallinn Manual on the International Law Applicable to Cyber Warfare." Blog of the European Journal of International Law. https://www.ejiltalk .org/the-tallinn-manual-on-the-international-law-applicable-to-cyber-warfare/.

Wagner, Markus. 2009. "*Non-State Actors*." Edited by Rüdiger Wolfrum. Max Planck Encyclopedia of Public International Law. Oxford. https://ssrn.com/ abstract=2661832.

Wex Legal Dictionary. 2018. "Opinio Juris." Legal Information Institute. https://ww
w.law.cornell.edu/wex/opinio_juris_%28international_law%29.

Winston, Carla. 2017. "Norm Structure, Diffusion, and Evolution: A Conceptual
Approach." *European Journal of International Relations*, 135406611772079. https
://doi.org/10.1177/1354066117720794.

Wu, Timothy S. 1998. "Cyberspace Sovereignty? The Internet and the International
System." *Harvard Journal of Law & Technology* 10 (3): 647–666. https://doi.org
/10.3868/s050-004-015-0003-8.

Chapter 13

Big Tech Hits the Diplomatic Circuit

Norm Entrepreneurship, Policy Advocacy, and Microsoft's Cybersecurity Tech Accord

Robert Gorwa and Anton Peez

INTRODUCTION: MICROSOFT HITS THE DIPLOMATIC CIRCUIT[1]

The "existing and potential threats in the sphere of information security are among the most serious challenges of the twenty-first century," stated the United Nations Group of Governmental Experts on Developments in the Field of Information and Telecommunications in the Context of International Security (UN GGE) in its first report, published in 2010. Almost ten years later, it has become clear that the use of networked technologies to conduct espionage, sabotage, and subversion (Rid 2013) is a major feature of contemporary global politics (Kello 2017). How this behavior should be governed at the global level has been a major point of international contention, and efforts to develop "cyber norms" of conduct via established international institutions, bilateral summits, and other conventional forms of diplomacy have failed to resolve many fundamental disagreements between key states such as the United States, Russia, and China (Grigsby 2017; Segal 2017; Lantis and Bloomberg 2018; Henriksen 2019). How should the laws of war apply? What kinds of intrusions can be considered an armed attack? What type of networks are fair-play for military cyber commands and intelligence agencies, and what others are off limits?

Unsatisfied with the tenor of the government-led discussion on these issues, Microsoft president Brad Smith proposed a "Digital Geneva Convention" at the RSA Conference in March 2017, calling on states to renounce cyberattacks on the private sector (Smith 2017b, 10). Smith's speech also called upon tech firms to rally together in support of the cause by not collaborating with governments in cyberattacks, thereby acting as a neutral "Digital Switzerland" (Smith 2017b, 12). In a related initiative from April 2018 onwards, Microsoft has led a coalition of corporations proposing principles of responsible behavior in cyberspace for the private sector.[2] The Cybersecurity Tech Accord, which now has 110 industry members,[3] is a burgeoning industry alliance that appears to be exerting significant influence as a global policy entrepreneur on digital security issues.

In November 2018, the French government presented the "Paris Call for Trust and Security in Cyberspace" (France Diplomatie 2018), an multistakeholder initiative closely planned with Microsoft, but lacking the main cyber powers (Uchill 2018), "teeth" (Matsakis 2018), and ambition compared to the original Digital Geneva Convention proposal (Baker 2018). In this process, Brad Smith has become a global "cybersecurity statesman" of sorts, rubbing shoulders with world leaders, and earning valuable legitimacy as a policy advocate and trusted voice on digital security matters (Gorwa and Peez 2019a, 2019b).

Microsoft's multifaceted initiative—"unapologetically enter[ing] the political sphere" (Jeutner 2019, 170)—warrants a close examination as a novel exertion of corporate influence in international politics. To this end, this chapter will examine the emergence, guiding principles, and participants of Microsoft's various cybersecurity-related initiatives, with a particular focus on the Tech Accord. It will proceed as follows. First, we outline the accord's core normative scope and ambitions, its specific pre- and proscriptions, the involved actors, and norm addressees (Section 2). We then ask and answer three further questions. Why did Microsoft take this step, devoting resources and political capital to an apparent cyber norm-building campaign? Why has Microsoft chosen the "accord" design and employ the language of international humanitarian law throughout its campaign (Section 3)? Finally, why do certain firms choose to sign on to the accord, and who has joined (Sections 4 and 5)?

By answering these questions, this chapter contributes to the recent scholarship on the role of companies in shaping cyber norms (Hurel and Lobato 2020, 2018) in a number of ways. We examine Microsoft's potential motivations for setting up the accord, contextualizing it within the company's 2007–2013 involvement with the U.S. National Security Agency's (NSA) PRISM program and the subsequent PR and consumer trust fallout as one potential reading. Applying literature on international business in global politics, we further identify elements of a "levelling the playing field" strategy and trace Microsoft's actions using an amended "spiral model" of norm entrepreneurship. Next, we explain the accord's design as a nonbinding code of conduct through its flexible and performative benefits, and question the initiative's appropriation of the language of international humanitarian law.

Finally, we present the first descriptive analysis of the Tech Accord's 110 members, and examine the possible instrumental motivations of signatories by collecting and analyzing their public statements regarding accord membership. We argue that most firms—smaller ones, in particular—attempt to cast themselves as innovative "global players" and as impactful technology companies, "bandwagoning" alongside Microsoft.

WHAT IS THE CYBERSECURITY TECH ACCORD?

Microsoft president Brad Smith raised eyebrows in Silicon Valley and beyond when he delivered a keynote at the 2017 RSA security conference that called on states to sign a "Digital Geneva Convention" (DGC), renouncing cyberattacks on the private sector and users, and on companies to not be complicit in such attacks (Smith 2017b). This latter pledge was reformulated as the four-point Cybersecurity Tech Accord and launched in April 2018 by a group of thirty-four technology companies, including not only giants such as Microsoft and Facebook, but also a diverse group of international telecoms, hardware manufacturers, open-source software providers, and cybersecurity threat intelligence companies. The group has since grown in geographic and industry scope to a total of 110 countries, as Microsoft has embarked on a whirlwind global policy advocacy tour.

While Smith's original "Digital Geneva Convention"—certainly the centrepiece of the RSA speech—called for six commitments, the accord features four (see table 13.1). Smith's speech contained elements of what was later launched as the Cybersecurity Tech Accord, then under the heading of a "global tech sector accord" to supplement the DGC proposal (Smith 2017b). While Smith clearly envisioned the DGC to be a company-led process, the main target was still governments. The pledges were formulated as items governments would agree to, with commitments ranging from not "targeting tech companies, private sector, or critical infrastructure" to engaging in "nonproliferation activities [for] cyberweapons." Responding to the feasibility of the DGC in November 2018, Smith described it as a "long-term aspiration" (Smith 2018). The Tech Accord is more modest than the DGC and RSA speech proposal, extending four "core values" to be enacted by companies: no offense, stronger defence, capacity building, and collective action (Tech Accord 2018a). A notable feature is that accord members pledge not only to protect their own customers but also each other's.

Drawing upon Martha Finnemore and Kathryn Sikkink's seminal 1998 article, we define international norms as "standards of appropriate behaviour for actors with a given identity" (Finnemore and Sikkink 1998, 891;

Table 13.1 Commitments and "Common Values" as Proposed by Brad Smith in 2017, and Their Equivalents in the 2018 Tech Accord (Authors' Systematization, Numbers in Parentheses Correspond to the Numbering in the Original Documents)

	Digital Geneva Convention February 2017	"Global tech sector accord" February 2017 (within the DGC speech)	Cybersecurity Tech Accord April 2018
Addressee →	States	Tech firms	Tech firms
Defense		Collaborative and proactive defense (2); Support for intergovernmental defensive efforts (6)	*Stronger defense:* "Protect all customers globally regardless of the motivation for attacks online"
Capacity building	Assist private sector efforts to detect, contain, respond to, and recover from events (2)		*Capacity building:* "do more to empower developers and the people and businesses that use their technology"
Collaboration	Report vulnerabilities to vendors rather than stockpile, sell or exploit them (3)	Collaborative remediation after attacks (3); Software patches available to all (4); Coordinated disclosure practices for vulnerabilities (5)	*Collective action:* "establish new formal and informal partnerships (. . .) to improve technical collaboration, coordinate vulnerability disclosures, share threats"
Offense	No targeting of tech companies, private sector, or critical infrastructure (1); Exercise restraint in developing cyberweapons (4); Commit to nonproliferation activities to cyberweapons (5); Limit offensive operation to avoid a mass event (6);	No assistance in offensive actions (1)	*No offense:* "companies will not help governments launch cyberattacks against innocent citizens and enterprises"

see also Katzenstein 1996, 5). Early foundational work by Sikkink and Margaret Keck on non-state actors and norms focused primarily on grassroots, transnational advocacy networks (Keck and Sikkink 1998). The authors examined the tactics such networks employ in their attempts to affect domestic and international policy making. Traditionally, multinational corporations (MNCs) were discussed in the context of the adversarial role they took in relation to these grassroots networks (see also Wolf, Deitelhoff, and Engert 2007). The Tech Accord provides an interesting example of a reversal of this process, with MNCs engaging in their own transnational advocacy and norm-building, which—save for the Paris Call—has been largely separate from civil society and other non-state actors. As Hurel and Lobato (2020) have fruitfully explored for the Tech Accord case, a critical addition to this literature covers corporate entities as norm entrepreneurs (Wolf, Deitelhoff, and Engert 2007; Deitelhoff and Wolf 2013; see also Flohr et al. 2010).

Each accord principle consists of a brief one- or two-sentence explanation, but it is clear that the accord is aimed at companies, rather than at governments. Two of the four principles are relatively uncontroversial: *Collective action* calls for companies to "build on existing relationships and together establish new formal and informal partnerships with industry, civil society and security researchers to improve technical collaboration, coordinate vulnerability disclosures, share threats"—a practice which is already characteristic of the cybersecurity industry and is commonplace among certain vendors and firms (de Fuentes et al. 2017). *Capacity building* is even vaguer, and "may include joint work on new security practices and new features the companies can deploy in their individual products and services" alongside a pledge to help businesses protect themselves from digital threats (of course, many of the companies sell products marketed for this exact purpose). The two more compelling points are those which are more directly related to the original Digital Geneva Convention subject matter of cyberattacks: *no offense* and *stronger defence*.

According to *no offense*, accord signees "will not help governments launch cyberattacks against innocent citizens and enterprises, and will protect against tampering or exploitation of their products and services through every stage of technology development, design and distribution." One major story from the Snowden disclosures described how the U.S. National Security Agency was intercepting routers and other network infrastructure made by Cisco (a signee) mid-transit, reprogramming their firmware to record network traffic and report it back to NSA, and then repackaging them into their original boxes and sending them off to their final international destination (Schneier 2015). In this context, this point could be seen as a pushback against the U.S. national security apparatus, although it is unclear whether companies such as Cisco were aware of this practice (the business maintained it was not). But the language notably does not mention that these companies cannot help states engage in cyberattacks against other states (only against "innocent citizens and enterprises").

Stronger defence involves a commitment to "protect all customers globally regardless of the motivation for attacks online." It allows one to imagine an interesting hypothetical scenario where a cloud provider (such as Microsoft), based in the United States, has to protect servers rented by customers in a country that is a current U.S. adversary from an intrusion effort orchestrated by the NSA or another "Five Eyes" agency. It is exactly this scenario, in which the technology company would be caught between its interests in serving foreign customers as a global business and the national security or espionage-related interests of domestic intelligence agencies that seemed to underlie Smith's original desire to become a "neutral Digital Switzerland." Post-Snowden, it is no longer acceptable for technology companies to be seen publicly as working with intelligence agencies to provide behind-the-scenes access to data. The framing of the accord around "cyberattacks" seems to elide the reality that many of the same effects can be achieved completely legally via government access requests (via for instance, the U.S. Foreign Intelligence Surveillance Court, or FISA court), and in many cases, technology companies that host third-party user data comply with these requests. While an acknowledgment of these government access requests is missing from the Tech Accord, it is discussed by some of the 110 companies that signed on, 40 of whom published their own blog posts or statements discussing the accord and their reasons for joining (tables 13.2 and 13.4). The cybersecurity company Avast, for instance, noted that the accord was particularly important "at a time when world governments are frequently pushing hard for access to user data" (Avast 2018).

Table 13.2   Cybersecurity Tech Accord Members by Industry Sector and by Whether a Press Release Was Issued (as of July 25, 2019)

		Tech Accord members		Press releases	
Sector	Examples	Count	Share of Tech Accord members (N=110)	Count	Share within sector
Information security	FireEye, RSA	38	36%	19	50%
IT	Aliter, Cognizant	20	19%	7	35%
Software	Microsoft, Intuit	17	16%	4	24%
Cloud	Cloudflare, Oracle	8	8%	2	25%
Telecom	KPN, Orange	8	8%	2	25%
Hardware	Dell, HP	6	6%	2	33%
Platform	Facebook, GitHub	5	5%	2	40%
Misc.	WIPFLI, Nielsen	5	5%	2	40%
Industrial	Rockwell, Hitachi	3	3%	0	0%
Sum		**110**		**40**	**36%**

WHY DID MICROSOFT START THE ACCORD?

Why, of all companies, is Microsoft devoting substantial financial and political resources to the development of cyber norms? The Tech Accord has drawn significant media coverage, but little critical analysis to date. Recently, Hurel and Lobato argued that the efforts demonstrate an "an attempt to influence global public policies on cybersecurity" (Hurel and Lobato 2018, 61), and fruitfully applied the IR framework of corporate norm entrepreneurship to the Microsoft case (Hurel and Lobato 2020). Analyses of the Tech Accord have been primarily grounded in the international cybersecurity norms literature, which covers the narrow field of cyber conflict (e.g., Finnemore and Hollis 2016; Grigsby 2017), the broader field of Internet governance and architecture (e.g., Mueller 2010; DeNardis 2014), as well as the intermediary space of cybersecurity. This section applies further IR corporate norm entrepreneurship literature to the case of the Tech Accord, showing that Microsoft is indeed a paradigmatic case for such efforts.

We argue that past work on the Tech Accord has failed to account for Microsoft's recent past and possible readings thereof, and present one such reading. In 2007, ten years before Smith's keynote, Microsoft became the NSA's very first partner in the PRISM program, which involved close collaboration with the government agency to provide clandestine access to sensitive, encrypted user data (*The Guardian* 2013a; Landau 2014, 62–64). In 2013, PRISM came to public attention through the Edward Snowden disclosures. Within a few short years, Microsoft has switched from being engaged in the NSA's surveillance program to aggressively spearheading an initiative to "make the internet a safer place, (. . .) and [retain] the world's trust" (Smith 2017a). We argue that in order to fully understand Microsoft's remarkable current push and role as a corporate norm entrepreneur, this recent history must be considered in detail. The primary factor here is not the actual depth of NSA cooperation, but rather the perceived breach of consumer trust.

Annegret Flohr and colleagues hypothesize that the more vulnerable a company is to a loss of reputation, the more likely it is to engage in norm entrepreneurship initiatives (Flohr et al. 2010, 82). They show empirically that companies with business-to-consumer transactions (rather than business-to-business transactions) are far more likely to engage in norm entrepreneurship (Flohr et al. 2010, 85–94). Over 80 percent of all desktop computers use the Windows operating system (StatCounter 2018), a high rate of interaction with end users. By the firm's own account, two billion people use Microsoft products (Smith 2018). Microsoft representatives address this rationalist explanation by stating that "what is good" for shareholders in this case is also "what is right," by asserting a seamless overlap of Microsoft's business interests and the greater societal good in cyber-norms matters. This, coupled with the PR fallout from the Snowden revelations, and the waning position of Microsoft as a meaningful corporate player (relative to Google, Facebook, Amazon, and Apple) makes Microsoft a likely candidate for corporate norm entrepreneurship.

Nicole Deitelhoff and Klaus Dieter Wolf make three further particularly relevant points for the case of cyber norm entrepreneurship. First, they argue that corporate involvement in "governance in the post-national constellation" is generally strong (Deitelhoff and Wolf 2013, 222). The realm of cyberspace is emblematic of this setting. Therefore, Deitelhoff and Wolf's work provides a fitting theory to apply to the Microsoft-led case of norm entrepreneurship. Second, the authors amend Risse et al.'s five-phase "spiral model" of state norm socialization (Risse, Ropp, and Sikkink 1999) to fit the corporate context. The adjusted "spiral model" contains the following steps in which businesses deal with human rights norms: (1) denial and "quiet complicity," followed by typically unsuccessful (2) tactical concessions, leading to (3) growing norm acceptance and institutionalization, potentially followed by (4) corporate norm-setting in order to achieve a level-playing field with noncompliant competitors, and finally (5) ongoing rule-consistent behavior, norm-setting and norm development (Deitelhoff and Wolf 2013, 231–234). Third, and more broadly, the authors find that corporate norm entrepreneurship is often primarily driven by "rationalist calculations regarding the re-definition of fundamental business interests" (Deitelhoff and Wolf 2013, 237). In other words, when companies "proactively engage in norm-setting," they are mainly guided by the aim of minimizing losses by bringing competitors who are not adhering to the norm in question into the fold—"levelling the playing field" (Zadek 2004; Deitelhoff and Wolf 2013, 237). This assumption is particularly worth examining in the Microsoft and Tech Accord case.

The remainder of this section proceeds along these three steps. While Hurel and Lobato state that "governments usually look to the ICT industry to prevent, detect, respond to, and recover from cyber attacks" (Hurel and Lobato 2018, 62), governments have also long looked to tech corporations for access to private user data. In the following, we examine this interaction as a key mechanism in understanding Microsoft's ongoing Tech Accord efforts.

A critical element in the call for cyber norms is the difficulty of governing cyberspace in the first place. Cyberspace is today generally considered quasi-regulated space (Jakobi 2013; however, also see Jeutner 2019) and corporate entities are, therefore, crucial actors in this "area of limited statehood," a realm where "the state lacks governance capacities in different sectors or over certain periods" (Börzel and Deitelhoff 2018, 250). Where state governance is limited, corporations are both commonly normatively expected to get involved and empirically more likely to do so (Deitelhoff and Wolf 2013; Börzel and Deitelhoff 2018). The concept of "limited statehood" fits the online context in many ways—there are few binding rules and governance mechanisms in cyberspace, and the covert nature of cyber activities leads to great difficulties in enforcing any such rules (Kello 2017). The challenges faced by the state-driven and UN-based Group of Governmental Experts (UN GGE, see Grigsby 2017; Henriksen 2019) and the subsequent push by Microsoft and others to establish a loose set of rules for cybersecurity can, therefore, be seen as an attempt to introduce corporate-led norms into the relatively loosely governed area of cyberspace. This presents a difference in both norm entrepreneurs and norm addressees compared to the UN GGE, with corporations acting as both entrepreneurs and addressees. The relatively under-regulated nature of the Internet gives accord signees a—perhaps convincing and reasonable—claim to set cyber policy and standards (Hurel and Lobato 2020, 303–5).

Next, we apply Deitelhoff and Wolf's amended five-step explanatory spiral model for the business context to the case of Microsoft and the Tech Accord. This examination will seek to cover the ten years preceding the presentation of the accord. We argue that Microsoft's cooperation with the NSA on PRISM is a source of the company's norms initiative ten years later. As PRISM's first partner, Microsoft provided the U.S. government with access to U.S. and foreign nationals' data. While the NSA did not have blanket access to user data (as was reported at times, and has been widely misunderstood), the close cooperation between Microsoft and the NSA on FISA orders for foreign nationals' data was nonetheless a major revelation among the Snowden disclosures in July 2013 (*Washington Post* 2013). The fact that the number of Skype calls collected by the NSA tripled after Microsoft acquired the company in 2012 seems to indicate unusually close cooperation between the NSA and Microsoft (*The Guardian* 2013a; Der Spiegel 2013). Once the extent of the PRISM program had been revealed, many companies ardently denied any wrongdoing or responsibility (*New York Times* 2013). Deitelhoff and Wolf identify complicity in government human rights violations as a common point of departure of human rights socialization in the corporate sector. Microsoft's complicity in the broad targeting of foreign nationals' privacy with limited legal process fits this first step.

The second step on the way to norm entrepreneurship are "tactical concessions." Such concessions are driven by the strength of the newfound opposition to the company and its "social and material vulnerability" (Deitelhoff and Wolf 2013, 228, 231). At the time of the Snowden disclosures, the company's marketing campaign stated that "Your privacy is our priority" (*The Guardian* 2013a; Der Spiegel 2013). The PR fallout was swift, and the vulnerability of a corporation so intimately linked to its users' lives was high in the face of the perceived immense breach of trust. Consequently, many of the implicated firms turned to public norm entrepreneurship strategies. In December 2013, Microsoft, Apple, Google and others published an open letter to President

Barack Obama and the U.S. Congress, containing five "reform principles" to reign in government surveillance. They stated that "the balance in many countries has tipped too far in favor of the state and away from the rights of the individual." Brad Smith, then Microsoft's general counsel, put the responsibility for decreasing user trust squarely on the U.S. government's shoulders: "Governments have put this trust at risk, and governments need to help restore it" (*The Guardian* 2013c). In this way, Microsoft sought to highlight their compliance with civil liberty norms, a "regular instance of tactical concessions" (Deitelhoff and Wolf 2013, 230).

The third step—"norm acceptance and institutionalization"—is difficult to separate from concessions. The open letter was accompanied by an industry-wide push for stronger encryption and peer review of application code (*The Guardian* 2013b, 2013c). More antagonistically, Brad Smith compared government surveillance of its servers to "sophisticated malware or cyber attacks" in December 2013 (*The Guardian* 2013b). Microsoft had now accepted and firmly, publicly committed to higher standards, and to no longer providing broad access to user data. Thereby, the company had moved from long-term NSA cooperation to public support for civil liberties online to sharp public criticism of U.S. government practices (see also Hurel and Lobato 2020).

Fourth, this leads to what Deitelhoff and Wolf call "a curious and unexpected side effect"—the potential transformation of "norm-takers into norm-makers." Rather than using discursive tactics such as shaming, Deitelhoff and Wolf argue that companies often change their own behavior and lead by example, forging "collective self-commitments" (Deitelhoff and Wolf 2013, 231–232). The Digital Geneva Convention, Tech Accord, and Paris Call initiatives in 2017 and 2018 are examples of such commitments, as are the company's "Transparency Centres," the "Defending Democracy Program," and their "Digital Crimes Unit" (see Hurel and Lobato 2020). Through this lens and perhaps somewhat favorably, Microsoft's pushes can be interpreted as a genuine effort to drive and advance cyber norms as part of the "groundswell of private leadership" (Matsakis 2018) in this realm from 2014 onwards. In the absence of effective state-led international agreements and therefore the presence of "unregulated space," tech firms such as Microsoft may feel empowered to be more proactive and take the lead in norm and agenda setting, exemplified by the firm's activities as a "quasi-diplomatic actor" (Hurel and Lobato 2018) adopting the vocabulary of international relations.

Fifth, looking into the future, "companies often struggle to commit public actors (. . .) to comply with human rights," particularly in settings of "limited statehood more generally" (Deitelhoff and Wolf 2013, 235). This does not bode well for common cybersecurity norms, and may indeed be the reason why Microsoft toned down the "Digital Geneva Convention" language in the first place (see Smith 2018). The voluntary nature of the accord makes it increasingly open to interpretation and selective application, raising the question of whether there is any sort of perceived accountability for adhering to its principles at all (Deitelhoff and Wolf 2013, 238). Hurel and Lobato point out that these formal initiatives are only "the tip of the iceberg" (Hurel and Lobato 2020, 292), with Microsoft's norm-making also taking hold through its technical services and policy development, not only explicit public advocacy.

Finally, Deitelhoff and Wolf's observation of attempts to "level the playing field" are particularly apt for the Tech Accord. As this section has illustrated, Microsoft was prominently exposed as an early NSA collaborator in the wake of the Snowden revelations. Following this logic, as a particularly exposed global company (see above), Microsoft had little choice but to go on the offensive and enter the fray as a norm entrepreneur by "mak[ing] the case (. . .) to retain the world's trust" (Smith 2017a, 13)—though not explicitly in connection to the Snowden affair. Microsoft has attempted to do this through adhering to a self-written code of conduct, the Cybersecurity Tech Accord. This code comes alongside a somewhat more skeptical approach to cooperation with governments post-Snowden. Following the commercial necessity of minimizing losses, Microsoft has since attempted to bring tech sector competitors into the fold of also adhering to these higher standards of user protection. As an industry leader, Microsoft is well poised for such a push. This amounts to "levelling the playing field"—that is, bringing competitors up to Microsoft's voluntary standards regarding both governmental cooperation and general cyberattack prevention. Smith himself has chosen his words similarly, describing the Tech Accord in part as an attempt to "create a floor" to prevent a "race to the bottom" (Smith 2018) regarding offensive cooperation with states in cyber affairs.

In conclusion, owing to its early norm entrepreneurship efforts and the absence of major players from the accord (see Section 4), Microsoft has effectively assumed the role as a key spokesperson for tech firms in the cyber-norms debate, thereby creating part of the present-day cyber-norms environment. This, we argue, goes beyond merely carving out a place for themselves within the cybersecurity landscape (Hurel and Lobato 2020). Microsoft has not only aimed for a seat *at* the table, but for the seat at the *head* of the table as the cyber-norms effort grows with initiatives such as the Paris Call.

WHY ARE OTHERS JOINING THE ACCORD?

This section critically analyses the Cybersecurity Tech Accord itself, focusing on the benefits to corporate actors of (1) appropriating of the authoritative language of international humanitarian law without any of its commitment, and (2) a broad, nonbinding code of conduct open to PR "spin" on behalf of the signatories.

Smith's 2017 Digital Geneva Convention launch was part public relations pitch ("last year we added Advanced Threat Protection for Microsoft Exchange Online") and part plea ("those of us in the tech sector need to act collectively to better protect the internet and customers everywhere from nation-state attacks"). The heavy reliance on international humanitarian law analogies was a guiding theme throughout the original Digital Geneva Convention speech in particular (Smith 2017b). Smith seemed to be directly equating private, profit-maximizing technology firms with humanitarian organizations such as the Red Cross, arguing that just "as the Fourth Geneva Convention relies on the Red Cross to help protect civilians in wartime, protection against nation-state cyber attacks requires the active assistance of the tech sector" (Smith 2017b). Smith's 2017 proposal was critiqued for its sloppy use of the Geneva Convention metaphor: While perhaps a useful mental image, casting oneself in a similar mold as the International Committee of the Red Cross (ICRC), a three-time recipient of the Nobel Peace Prize, offers clear reputational benefits (see also Jeutner 2019, 168). The subsequent 2018 Tech Accord announcement backed away slightly from the Switzerland-related metaphors, as has the branding of the accord. Nonetheless, Microsoft continues to use the semantics of international politics in its broader policy initiatives (Hurel and Lobato 2018, 68), for example, through its "Digital Diplomacy" team (formerly "Global Security Strategy and Diplomacy").

Although consistently discussed as a matter of cyber norms, with norms generally defined as "shared understandings" (for a review, see Niemann and Schillinger 2017), the tenets of the accord seem to be neither particularly shared nor well-understood among the signatories. Given that the public-facing accord is short on detail (comprised of only four points and eight sentences total), it is unsurprising that company statements have varied significantly in how they interpreted the nature and purpose of the Tech Accord. A number of companies stated that they viewed the Tech Accord as an effort to "fight cybercrime" (ESET 2018; Gigamon 2018). Others viewed it as an "alliance" (Avast 2018), with some even invoking it as a tech-company equivalent of NATO's Article 5 collective defence provision (KoolSpan 2018). The accord's August 2018 endorsement of the "Mutually Agreed Norms for Routing Security," an initiative launched in 2014 by the Internet Society (ISOC), shows that the Tech Accord indeed does not only seem to be a set "Accord" but also a loose consortium or alliance that will continue to be involved in evolving Internet governance and technology initiatives.

Unlike the Global Network Initiative (GNI) for preventing censorship and protecting privacy online, or past efforts to bring together technology companies with an overarching human rights goal, there are no publicly accessible governance mechanisms or accountability frameworks which govern the accord (perhaps because this initiative does not feature any civil society or nonindustry stakeholders). Transparency is summarized in a single line, promising that "we will also report publicly on our progress in achieving these goals"—a far cry from the comprehensive GNI governance charter which details the GNI legal structure and board, along with the detailed requirements for the independent-third party assessments that are undertaken every two years to ensure compliance with the GNI principles (Global Network Initiative 2017). Because the accord is nonbinding, and does not have any clear governance mechanisms, it seems as if it can be, to modify Alexander Wendt's famous formulation, 'what companies make of it' (Wendt 1992).

WHO HAS JOINED THE ACCORD?

To further analyze the Tech Accord's membership, we compiled a list of all members by industry sector,[4] primary world region, date of joining, and whether they issued a press release upon joining.[5] In order to better assess why firms would opt to join the accord, we examined their public justification for doing so, compiling all public statements released by its members. The available blog posts, statements, and press releases were downloaded and assessed for major themes.

The list of signatories is diverse. It includes major platform companies (Facebook, LinkedIn), international telecoms (BT, Telefonica), cybersecurity threat intelligence companies (FireEye, F-Secure, TrendMicro), and PC manufacturers (Dell, Hewlett Packard). Other members include the online payments company Stripe, an enterprise technology company specializing in Tax software (Intuit), and the market research firm Nielsen. By July 2019, a total of 110 companies had pledged to "protect and empower civilians online and to improve the security, stability and resilience of cyberspace" (Tech Accord 2018a).

The tabulation of member statements by line of business and whether they issued a press release (table 13.2) shows that information security firms are most likely to have issued press releases regarding their joining the other firms. Fifty percent of all companies coded as information security firms have issued statements, compared to 29 percent of all remaining firms.

Examining the stated reasons for joining, it is immediately apparent that companies take advantage of the accord to "bandwagon"—proclaiming themselves as innovative, champions of security, and as impactful technology companies alongside Microsoft. This trend was most clear for smaller and less influential firms, eager to name themselves as part of a select group of globally recognized organizations (emphases added throughout). For instance, Avast, a Czech provider of antivirus software, "joined Microsoft, Facebook, Cisco, and thirty *other tech giants* in what is being considered a 'Digital Geneva Convention'" (Avast 2018); Spanish telecommunications provider Telefónica could brand itself *"among leading* tech companies which pledge to fight cyberattacks" (Telefónica 2018); the Romanian antivirus vendor Bitdefender could announce having joined the accord with "30 *other important players* who have shaped technology throughout the years" (Bitdefender 2018); and the Japanese threat intelligence company Trend Micro suggested that the accord "demonstrates a commitment by *key industry players like us"* (Trend Micro 2018).

Furthermore, the Tech Accord—steered by Microsoft—seems to have pursued a regional strategy of expansion in late 2018 and early 2019 (table 13.3). The two initial waves of membership primarily included firms from the United States and Western Europe. In September 2018, eight Eastern European firms signed on, followed by the first firms from the South America (Argentina and Chile) in November 2018 and January 2019. This finding could be a starting point for research on "how the company develops relations with Global South countries," broadly conceived (Hurel and Lobato 2020, 306; see also Tech Accord 2018b). Since March 2019, new members have once again mainly been from the United States and Western Europe. The complete absence of firms from states such as China, Russia, and Israel indicates that beyond norms for guiding corporate activity in the cyber realm, norms regarding public-private partnership and the relation of the state to its citizens are at stake.

Finally, combining the regional and publicity perspectives, European tech firms seem to be far more keen than their U.S. counterparts to publicly align themselves with the Tech Accord, Microsoft, and cybersecurity advocacy more broadly (table 13.4). While 62 percent of European members issued press releases, only 24 percent of U.S. firms did. This may be because the Microsoft brand might have greater currency in Europe than in the United States, or due to greater anticipated benefits of aligning oneself with user data protection in Europe compared to the United States.

Other than Microsoft, the leading organizer, none of the largest and potentially most impactful members—Facebook, Oracle, and Cisco—released a statement. The role of these major firms within the accord needs to be explored in further research, along with key unanswered questions about the lack of certain major firms that seemingly refused to join (most notably, Google). If the proscriptions of the accord are so flexible, *why not join*? Meanwhile, in the absence of other major players, Microsoft now appears to have taken up the role of spokesperson for the tech industry in this cyber-norms process.

The accord is both performative and flexible, allowing smaller firms to label themselves as meaningful changemakers and innovators, while also potentially allowing larger firms to point to the accord as a token of their goodwill without any meaningful commitments or enforcement mechanisms. If the goal of the Tech Accord is assembling a broad coalition of companies, it is worth pointing out that such flexibility certainly has advantages: It lowers the barriers for entry, perhaps setting the stage for an increasingly rigid process to come (for a policy maker perspective, see Lété and Chase 2018).

CONCLUSION: NEITHER SHARED NOR UNDERSTOOD?

With this chapter, we have sought to trace the evolution of Microsoft's norm entrepreneurship from 2013 Snowden revelations to the 2017 Digital Geneva Convention speech to the 2018 Cybersecurity Tech Accord initiative. We have explored the potential motives shaping Microsoft's behavior as the creator of the accord, unpacked the proscriptions of the accord itself, analyzed public statements issued by signatories to better understand why so many firms have joined, and tabulated its members along various characteristics. At 110 members, it is steadily growing and provides insightful precedent as an informal, potentially powerful coalition of non-state actors in the cyber-norms debate.

We show that Deitelhoff and Wolf's rationalist argument for why corporations may become norm entrepreneurs seems plausible for the Tech Accord and Microsoft case (Deitelhoff and Wolf 2013, 237). The accord may be an attempt to bolster user trust in the companies' data protection measures, a value that has been at the forefront of user demands since 2013. So will this lead to a catalogue of do's and don'ts, a cohesive alternative vision for responsible behavior in cyberspace? Under the commonly accepted definition of norms as "shared understandings" (see Niemann and Schillinger 2017), the accord's provisions and very organizational nature seem neither shared nor understood. Despite the apparent novelty of the initiative, and its ongoing endorsement by scholars frustrated with the current poor state of cybersecurity norms discourse (see, e.g., Tworek 2017; Korzak and Lin 2018), as it stands, the accord offers all the PR potential and heavyweight legitimacy and very little of the normative obligation of the international legal language Microsoft has emulated.

Nonetheless, the rationalist and instrumental accounts do not fully explain the accord, and the goal of profit maximizing "does not rule out the existence of underlying notions of appropriate business behaviour" (Deitelhoff

Table 13.3 Cybersecurity Tech Accord Membership by Date of Joining and by World Region (as of July 25, 2019)

	Wave 1 04/2018	Wave 2 06/2018	Wave 3 09/2018	Wave 4 11/2018	Wave 5 01/2019	Wave 6 03/2019	Wave 7 05/2019	Wave 8 07/2019	Sum	Share
US	21	7	4	5	1	8	14	3	63	57%
Western Europe	8	3	3	2	5	1	1	1	24	22%
Eastern Europe	2	1	8		3	1			15	14%
Asia	1		2			1			4	4%
South America				2	2				4	4%
Sum	**32**	**11**	**17**	**9**	**11**	**11**	**15**	**4**	**110**	

Table 13.4 Cybersecurity Tech Accord by World Region and by Whether a Press Release Was Issued (as of July 25, 2019)

	Tech Accord members	*Issued a press release*	*Share*
US	63	15	24%
Western Europe	24	15	63%
Eastern Europe	15	9	60%
Asia	4	1	25%
South America	4	0	0%
Sum	**110**	**40**	**36%**

and Wolf 2013, 237). Less than half of the accord's signees have issued statements on their joining (tables 13.2 and 13.4), and the biggest, most important members (Facebook, Cisco, LinkedIn, Hewlett Packard, Dell, and others) have been oddly silent regarding the accord, casting some doubt on the assumption of the accord as purely a PR exercise. If all firms are simply seeking to improve their public image through participation, why would they not issue a statement? The importance of individuals such as Brad Smith in driving change may come into play here and is worth exploring further— good-faith commitment to the principles of user privacy and data protection has been traced back to the idealism, ideology, and the institutional culture of the American technology industry (see, e.g., Turner 2008). Another major, unexplored question is why certain major industry players (such as Google) are missing, seemingly having refused to sign on to the accord.

Overall, the Tech Accord demonstrates several novel characteristics which provide a major departure from past norm-building efforts in the cyber realm. It is led by different stakeholders (i.e., tech companies rather than states), and seems to have virtually no external buy-in from civil society, nongovernmental organizations, or other key actors in international cyber governance. However, it seems to be positioning Microsoft as a responsible cyber actor, offering legitimacy for future endeavors, such as the November 2018 Paris Call, which does feature broader civil society participation. Microsoft's tactics can also be interpreted as an attempt to frame the company as a "quasi-diplomatic entity" (Hurel and Lobato 2018, 71), from their spearheading of the Tech Accord to the branding of a "Global Security Strategy and Diplomacy Team," and a way to exercise political influence in a potentially novel way. Watching how this process unfolds will be important for cybersecurity and international norms scholars, and those studying the role of technology and technology companies in politics more broadly.

Notwithstanding the general pessimism and in the cyber community regarding the future of common cyber norms, international norms often start as informal, loose standards and progress to more firm rules—both legally and socially.

NOTES

1. We thank Nicole Deitelhoff, Florian Egloff, Xenija Grusha, and the PRIF PhD colloquium for their helpful comments and suggestions. A previous version of this paper was presented at the inaugural the Hague Program for Cyber Norms Conference, November 5–7, 2018. Many thanks to Dennis Broeders, Corianne Oosterbaan, and the rest of the Hague Program's team for putting this collection together, and for their assistance in turning our initial paper into this book chapter.

2. Industrial manufacturer Siemens has initiated a cybersecurity "Charter of Trust," though with fewer members—16—and less public fanfare (as of July 25, 2019).

3. As of July 25, 2019, the Tech Accord website lists 111 members. Two companies originally announced as joining are now no longer listed, CA Technologies and Symantec (both joined in April 2018). One company currently listed was never announced in a press release, Sharp. For consistency, all three have been omitted from the data used in this paper, resulting in a final list of 110 members.

4. We assign one sector per company, opting for the most significant sector if a company is involved in multiple lines of business. For example, the Japanese conglomerate Hitachi is coded as "Industrial," though it also produces consumer electronics, and Microsoft is coded as "Software" while also offering cloud services. Sectors are defined as follows.

IT: general IT services, web/app development, call centers

Information security: vendors, threat intelligence, security solutions and software (e.g. antivirus)

Telecom: telecommunications firms, internet service providers

Platform: platform companies, social media, online marketplaces

Industrial: heavy machinery, industrial equipment

Software: content management software, tax software, operating systems, apps

Hardware: personal computers, routers, networking and computing hardware

Cloud: web hosting, data storage, cloud services

Misc.: residual category

5. Press releases were searched via online queries for *"Tech Accord" + [company name]*. We assume that there are no language or translation problems with this approach, as the query is not specific to the English language.

BIBLIOGRAPHY

Avast. 2018. "US & UK Issue Security Warning and Tech Giants Join Forces." April 20. https://blog.avast.com/us-uk-issue-security-warning-and-tech-giants-jo in-forces-avast.

Baker, Stewart. 2018. "If Paris Calls, Should We Hang Up? (11:55 Onwards)." The Cyberlaw Podcast. Episode 240. https://www.lawfareblog.com/cyberlaw-podcast-if-paris-calls-should-we-hang.

Bitdefender. 2018. "Your Protection Is Our Mission, and We're Serious About It." April 17. https://businessinsights.bitdefender.com/your-protection-is-our-missio n-and-were-serious-about-it.

Börzel, Tanja, and Nicole Deitelhoff. 2018. "Business." In *The Oxford Handbook of Governance and Limited Statehood*, edited by Thomas Risse, Tanja Börzel, and Anke Draude, 250–271. Oxford, UK: Oxford University Press.

Deitelhoff, Nicole, and Klaus Dieter Wolf. 2013. "Business and Human Rights: How Corporate Norm Violators Become Norm-Entrepreneurs." In *The Persistent Power of Human Rights: From Commitment to Compliance*, edited by Thomas Risse, Stephen C. Ropp, and Kathryn Sikkink, 222–238. Cambridge Studies in International Relations 126. Cambridge, UK: Cambridge University Press.

DeNardis, Laura. 2014. *The Global War for Internet Governance*. New Haven, CT: Yale University Press.

Der Spiegel. 2013. "Wie Microsoft Systematisch Den Geheimdiensten Hilft," July 12. http://www.spiegel.de/netzwelt/netzpolitik/wie-microsoft-mit-fbi-nsa-und-ci a-kooperiert-a-910863.html.

ESET. 2018. "ESET Joins Cybersecurity Tech Accord." June 20. https://www.ese t.com/int/about/newsroom/press-releases/announcements/eset-joins-cybersecur ity-tech-accord-1/.

Finnemore, Martha, and Duncan B. Hollis. 2016. "Constructing Norms for Global Cybersecurity." *American Journal of International Law* 110 (3): 425–479.

Finnemore, Martha, and Kathryn Sikkink. 1998. "International Norm Dynamics and Political Change." *International Organization* 52 (4): 887–917.

Flohr, Annegret, Lothar Rieth, Sandra Schwindenhammer, and Klaus Dieter Wolf. 2010. *The Role of Business in Global Governance*. Basingstoke, UK: Palgrave Macmillan.

France Diplomatie. 2018. "Paris Call for Trust and Security in Cyberspace." November 12, 2018. https://www.diplomatie.gouv.fr/IMG/pdf/paris_call_text_-_en_cle06 f918.pdf.

Fuentes, José M. de, Lorena González-Manzano, Juan Tapiador, and Pedro Peris-Lopez. 2017. "PRACIS: Privacy-Preserving and Aggregatable Cybersecurity Information Sharing." *Computers & Security* 69: 127–141.

Gigamon. 2018. "Gigamon Joins Cybersecurity Tech Accord." June 20. https://bl og.gigamon.com/2018/06/20/gigamon-joins-cybersecurity-tech-accord/.

Global Network Initiative. 2017. "Global Network Initiative Governance Charter." https://globalnetworkinitiative.org/gin_tnetnoc/uploads/2018/04/GNI-Governa nce-Charter.pdf.

Gorwa, Robert, and Anton Peez. 2019a. "Charmeoffensiven. Ist Das Schon Außenpolitik, Was Die Großen Technologiekonzerne Betreiben?" *Internationale Politik* 74 (4): 25–29.

Gorwa, Robert, and Anton Peez. 2019b. "Big Tech Hits the Diplomatic Circuit." Berlin Policy Journal/German Council on Foreign Relations (DGAP)). https://be rlinpolicyjournal.com/big-tech-hits-the-diplomatic-circuit/.

Grigsby, Alex. 2017. "The End of Cyber Norms." *Survival* 59 (6): 109–122. doi:10. 1080/00396338.2017.1399730.

Henriksen, Anders. 2019. "The End of the Road for the UN GGE Process: The Future Regulation of Cyberspace." *Journal of Cybersecurity* 5 (1). doi:10.1093/cybsec/ tyy009.

Hurel, Louise Marie, and Luisa Cruz Lobato. 2020. *"Cyber-Norms Entrepreneurship? Understanding Microsoft's Advocacy on Cybersecurity."* In *Governing Cyberspace: Behaviour, Power and Diplomacy*, edited by Dennis Broeders and Bibi van den Berg. London: Rowman & Littlefield.

Hurel, Louise Marie, and Luisa Cruz Lobato. 2018. "Unpacking Cyber Norms: Private Companies as Norm Entrepreneurs." *Journal of Cyber Policy* 3 (1): 61–76.

Jakobi, Anja P. 2013. "Non-State Actors All Around: The Governance of Cybercrime." In *The Transnational Governance of Violence and Crime*, edited by Anja P. Jakobi and Klaus Dieter Wolf, 129–148. London, UK: Palgrave Macmillan. doi:10.1057/9781137334428.

Jeutner, Valentin. 2019. "The Digital Geneva Convention. A Critical Appraisal of Microsoft's Proposal." *Journal of International Humanitarian Legal Studies* 10 (1): 158–170. doi:10.1163/18781527-01001009.

Katzenstein, Peter J. 1996. *The Culture of National Security: Norms and Identity in World Politics*. Columbia University Press.

Keck, Margaret E., and Kathryn Sikkink. 1998. *Activists Beyond Borders: Advocacy Networks in International Politics*. Ithaca, NY: Cornell University Press.

Kello, Lucas. 2017. *The Virtual Weapon and International Order*. New Haven, CT: Yale University Press.

KoolSpan. 2018. "An Enduring Principle: KoolSpan Joins Cybersecurity Tech Accord To Lead Industry Efforts For Collective Cyber-Defense." https://koolspa n.com/koolspan-joins-cybersecurity-tech-accord/.

Korzak, Elaine, and Herb Lin. 2018. "Proposal for a Cyber-International Committee of the Red Cross." *Lawfare*. October 17. https://www.lawfareblog.com/proposa l-cyber-international-committee-red-cross.

Landau, Susan. 2014. "Highlights from Making Sense of Snowden, Part II: What's Significant in the NSA Revelations." *IEEE Security & Privacy* 12 (1): 62–64.

Lantis, Jeffrey S., and Daniel J. Bloomberg. 2018. "Changing the Code? Norm Contestation and US Antipreneurism in Cyberspace." *International Relations* 32 (2): 149–172.

Lété, Bruno, and Peter Chase. 2018. "Shaping Responsible Behavior in Cyberspace. Workshop Briefing Paper." The German Marshall Fund of the United States. http: //www.gmfus.org/publications/shaping-responsible-state-behavior-cyberspace#.

Matsakis, Louise. 2018. "The US Sits Out an International Cybersecurity Agreement." *Wired*, November 12. https://www.wired.com/story/paris-call-cybersecuri ty-united-states-microsoft/.

Mueller, Milton. 2010. *Networks and States: The Global Politics of Internet Governance*. Information Revolution and Global Politics. Cambridge, MA: MIT Press.

New York Times. 2013. "Report Indicates More Extensive Cooperation by Microsoft on Surveillance," July 11. https://www.nytimes.com/2013/07/12/us/report-indic ates-more-extensive-cooperation-by-microsoft-on-surveillance.html.

Niemann, Holger, and Henrik Schillinger. 2017. "Contestation 'All the Way down'? The Grammar of Contestation in Norm Research." *Review of International Studies* 43 (01): 29–49. doi:10.1017/S0260210516000188.

Rid, Thomas. 2013. *Cyber War Will Not Take Place*. London: Hurst & Company.

Risse, Thomas, Stephen C. Ropp, and Kathryn Sikkink, eds. 1999. *The Power of Human Rights: International Norms and Domestic Change*. Cambridge, UK: Cambridge University Press. http://ebooks.cambridge.org/ref/id/CBO9780511598777.

Schneier, Bruce. 2015. "Cisco Shipping Equipment to Fake Addresses to Foil NSA Interception." March 20. https://www.schneier.com/blog/archives/2015/03/cisco_shipping_.html.

Segal, Adam. 2017. "The Development of Cyber Norms at the United Nations Ends in Deadlock. Now What?" *Council on Foreign Relations*. June 29. www.cfr.org/blog/development-cyber-norms-united-nations-ends-deadlock-now-what.

Smith, Brad. 2017a. "The Need for a Digital Geneva Convention. Blog Post." *Microsoft on the Issues*. February 14. https://blogs.microsoft.com/on-the-issues/2017/02/14/need-digital-geneva-convention/.

———. 2017b. "The Need for a Digital Geneva Convention. Transcript of Keynote Address at the RSA Conference 2017." https://blogs.microsoft.com/uploads/2017/03/Transcript-of-Brad-Smiths-Keynote-Address-at-the-RSA-Conference-2017.pdf.

———. 2018. "Digital Peace in an Age of Cyber Threats. Speech and Q&A at the Peace Palace, The Hague, the Netherlands." November 6, 2018.

StatCounter. 2018. "Desktop Operating System Market Share Worldwide. September 2017–September 2018." http://gs.statcounter.com/os-market-share/desktop/worldwide.

Tech Accord. 2018a. "Cybersecurity Tech Accord. Protecting Users and Customers Everywhere." https://cybertechaccord.org/accord/.

———. 2018b. "Cybersecurity Tech Accord Expands Rapidly; Announces Partnership with Global Forum on Cyber Expertise (GFCE)." https://cybertechaccord.org/gfce_partnership/.

Telefónica. 2018. "Telefónica among Leading Tech Companies Which Pledge to Fight Cyberattacks." April 17. https://www.telefonica.com/es/web/public-policy/blog/articulo/-/blogs/telefonica-amongst-leading-tech-companies-which-pledge-to-fight-cyberattacks.

The Guardian. 2013a. "Microsoft Handed the NSA Access to Encrypted Messages." July 12. https://www.theguardian.com/world/2013/jul/11/microsoft-nsa-collaboration-user-data.

———. 2013b. "Microsoft Likens Government Snooping to Cyber Attacks." December 5. https://www.theguardian.com/technology/2013/dec/05/microsoft-likens-government-snooping-cyber-attacks.

———. 2013c. "Twitter, Facebook and More Demand Sweeping Changes to US Surveillance." December 9. https://www.theguardian.com/world/2013/dec/09/nsa-surveillance-tech-companies-demand-sweeping-changes-to-us-laws.

Trend Micro. 2018. "The Cybersecurity Tech Accord: Time to Come Together to Combat Digital Threats." April 17. https://blog.trendmicro.com/the-cybersecurity-tech-accord-time-to-come-together-to-combat-digital-threats/.

Turner, Fred. 2008. *From Counterculture to Cyberculture: Stewart Brand, the Whole Earth Network, and the Rise of Digital Utopianism*. Chicago, IL: University of Chicago Press.

Tworek, Heidi. 2017. "Microsoft Is Right: We Need a Digital Geneva Convention." *Wired*, September 5. https://www.wired.com/2017/05/microsoft-right-need-digital-geneva-convention/.

Uchill, Joe. 2018. "U.S. Hasn't Signed Cyber Principles—yet. 13 November 2018." *Axios Codebook*. November 13. https://www.axios.com/newsletters/axios-codebook-66eb6017-f7ff-4f10-a0b5-1018a441cc43.html.

Washington Post. 2013. "Here's Everything We Know about PRISM to Date." June 12. https://www.washingtonpost.com/news/wonk/wp/2013/06/12/heres-everything-we-know-about-prism-to-date/.

Wendt, Alexander. 1992. "Anarchy Is What States Make of It: The Social Construction of Power Politics." *International Organization* 46 (2): 391–425.

Wolf, Klaus Dieter, Nicole Deitelhoff, and Stefan Engert. 2007. "Corporate Security Responsibility: Towards a Conceptual Framework for a Comparative Research Agenda." *Cooperation and Conflict* 42 (3): 294–320. doi:10.1177/0010836707079934.

Zadek, Simon. 2004. "The Path to Corporate Responsibility." *Harvard Business Review* 82 (12): 125–132, 150.

Chapter 14

Cyber-Norms Entrepreneurship?

Understanding Microsoft's Advocacy on Cybersecurity[1]

Louise Marie Hurel and Luisa Cruz Lobato

> In 2016, a mantra, "There's no national security without cybersecurity," took hold within Microsoft and started to seep into the public discussion. We were hardly alone with this recognition. As German conglomerate Siemens AG predicted succinctly, "Cybersecurity is going to be the most important security issue of the future." Clearly, any issue that would be fundamental to national security would propel the tech sector even more squarely into the world of international diplomacy. (Smith and Browne 2019, 110)

In February 2017, Microsoft called for the establishment of a Digital Geneva Convention, as a direct response to the expansion of state-sponsored cyberattacks. According to the company's president, Brad Smith (2017), such commitment should be of utmost importance for maintaining peace and stability in cyberspace, given that "nation-state hacking has evolved into attacks on civilians in times of peace." It is now common sense that most of the contemporary infrastructure that anchors the Internet is owned by private actors (Abbate 1999; Kitchin 2014; Musiani et al. 2016). This also means that potential targets include datacenters, servers, and devices; that is, the infrastructures owned by Microsoft and its industry peers as well as the data from its customers. While the Digital Geneva Convention was then met with different degrees of enthusiasm and skepticism by diplomats, scholars, and governments alike (Grigsby 2017; Interview, October 2019), as Brad Smith noted, "[a]t least we had succeeded in sparking a new conversation" (2019, 83).

The call for the Geneva Convention is not the first nor the last effort from the private sector to secure their infrastructure against state-sponsored attacks. Other Microsoft initiatives, such as the Tech Accord, the Paris

Call for Trust and Security, the CyberPeace Institute and engagement with governments—bilaterally or via international organizations—(Barrinha and Renard 2018), suggest that, at least, when it comes to cyberspace, companies have devised distinct regulatory and organizational strategies to build their legitimacy to negotiate with states. Of particular interest is the fact that their legitimacy as political actors is once again being debated.[2] What is more: Microsoft's involvement with the cyber norms-making has reanimated much of the talk on norms and private governance, as it becomes evident from the number of recent debates on this topic.[3]

We take the contestation over Microsoft's legitimacy as norm entrepreneur as an entry point to the discussion of how global cybersecurity governance unfolds in practice and how, instead of focusing on either the "public" or "private" aspects of it, cybersecurity governance happens in a grey zone of continuous contestation and negotiations over *who can engage in norms-making, how norms are made* and *what counts as norm*. In a previous study, we paid attention to the first question, looking at how private actors shape cybersecurity by means of public-private partnerships, lobbying, and self-regulation (Hurel and Lobato 2018). Now, we take a step further and look at how organizational complexity might highlight different modalities of exerting influence on public policy and engage in an interdisciplinary effort to portray the socio-technical arrangements (both intra-organizationally and internationally) as parts of a norms-making continuum. This exercise is relevant to the study of power, influence, agency, and authority in global cybersecurity governance, as it allows us to grasp the specific organizational, technical, and material arrangements that support the practices of stakeholders to negotiate their conditions of engagement in cybersecurity governance. Furthermore, these strategies allow us to deepen the critique of *who* produces norms so as to address the ontological problem of *what* it is to *produce* a norm.

In this chapter, we seek to provide two major contributions to the ongoing debate on cyber norms. The first contribution is with respect to how norms are usually conceived within this debate. Rather than being contained in the written text (law and regulation), norms extend to the processes (see Finnemore and Hollis 2016) of negotiation that happen until it reaches its "final" (written) and also to the agencies, resources, and organizational and technological structures that are mobilized in order for it to reach widespread public debate. The "expectations of behavior" that are a necessary component of norms also come in different forms, including through an infrastructure of access established to promote values such as transparency and trust (e.g., Transparency Centers). The second relates to the understanding of how global cybersecurity governance unfolds in practice and which agencies count as legitimate in the process of negotiating cyber norms. As we argue, the question of who's agency should count in cybersecurity norms development is also indissociable from the question of *how* norms-making processes are perceived and conceptualized.

We look specifically at Microsoft as a case composed by a plethora of dimensions, including a somewhat intriguing diplomatic engagement. In spite of its global reach, the company has consistently expanded the legal and policy engagement, developed an extensive list of cyber norms-specific documents, and invested in international cybersecurity initiatives (to name a few), all of which come together with promoting security of their services and products. These and other dynamics have raised important questions as to what kind of role the private sector plays in global cybersecurity governance. Some scholars have referred to these continuous efforts as "tech diplomacy" or "corporate foreign policy" (*Economist* 2019). We argue that such developments have resurfaced (see Hurel and Lobato 2018; Gorwa and Peez 2018) important discussions related to the different modalities of engagement of the tech sector in shaping and taking part in global/international cybersecurity.

We purposefully make use of the term "norms entrepreneurship" to engage with a more critical discussion of what constitutes as norms-making in cybersecurity governance while simultaneously proposing a different starting point to the discussion, that is, the formal and informal practices within the private sector. This task is guided by the questions of *how can we understand the role of private actors in cybersecurity governance* and *what it has to say about norms promotion*. Methodologically, we draw on an analysis of Microsoft's practices that could be traced from qualitative interviews conducted with company's representatives from different parts of the world, the analysis of policy documents published by its Diplomacy Team, information circulated in press releases and media headlines, and participant observation in different international and regional cybersecurity events. In the first section of this chapter, we assess different bodies of literature to conceptualize private governance and question whether there is something unique to be said about Microsoft's engagement in cybersecurity governance. Second, we provide an in-depth discussion on the role of technical mediation and organizational complexity as constitutive elements of corporate agency and norms-entrepreneurship in cybersecurity. Third, we engage with a more theoretical discussion on "how norms become norms," exploring the ways in which Microsoft engages in "diplomatic" practices. With this, we expect to provide a contribution to the existing IR literature on norms and private governance by showing how negotiations over who's a legitimate norm entrepreneur also depend on an overlap or blur in the line dividing the public/private, and to ongoing discussions on cyber norms, by raising the question of what counts as a norm and how norms are built-in practice.

FROM NORM TO NORMATIVE ARRANGEMENTS: PRIVATE GOVERNANCE AS A FRAMEWORK

Norms are fundamental international institutions that both describe and prescribe action in this world (Finnemore and Sikkink 1998; Onuf 1989; Wendt 1992; 1995). As such, norm advocacy is an important formal dimension of international governance in the most distinct spheres of international life—cybersecurity being no exception. It presents a way of compromising states and biding their behavior to particular technical, professional, and political agreements as to which actions to take to avoid, mitigate, and overcome threats and risks in cyberspace. There has been far less attention to this dimension of private governance in cybersecurity scholarship.[4] As we argued elsewhere (Hurel and Lobato 2018), IR literature on norms presents an important first step to approach this gap. But it is not enough, for it offers a far less nuanced perspective on how different kinds of private groups engage with shaping international norms of behavior for state actors.

In this chapter, we look at private governance as a way to emphasize the distinct normative arrangements that might come with corporations taking the stage in norms promotion. This requires us to revisit and question how norms promotion has been conceptualized thus far (sections two and three) so as to encompass a multiplicity of ways in which values are communicated with more established interlocutors in the field of norms-making. What follows is an exercise to first single out the ways in which corporate action has already been conceived in global governance, management, and media and communications studies, followed by a discussion on the relevance of looking at Microsoft as a case that is both *sui generis* when compared to what has been addressed by scholars across different disciplines and *unique* in its own organizational, situational, and contextual dynamics. Cases such as Microsoft call for an approach to cyber norms-making that is able to encompass the modularity, or perhaps, blurriness between its *sui generis/unique* character. Private governance allows us to approach this complex enmeshment between social, technical, material, and discursive arrangements that configure how the company influences and engages in cybersecurity governance.

Private governance is not typically recognized as a dimension of public policy making, despite the indisputable role of private actors in designing formal and informal rules for products, establishing sectoral regulation in tech, certifying professional competency and setting technical standards that impact society at large (Hall and Biersteker 2002; Rudder, Fritschler, and Jung Choi 2016). In cybersecurity, private actors have recognizably played a fundamental role in ensuring operational and technical security, as they help to set standards, determine authentication and trust mechanisms for both infrastructures and services, provide expertise, develop software, hardware, as well as hold considerable knowledge on cybersecurity risks and threats. However, their role in shaping formal and informal rules of behavior in cyberspace remains undertheorized.

Scholars in international relations[5] and management studies have long emphasized the role of private actors in a number of global governance fields (Strange 1998; Gilpin 1976; Avant 2005; Abrahamsen and Williams 2009; Leander 2010). Drawing from the end of the Cold War, many of the early IR literature on private governance focused on the effects of globalization and the need for new mechanisms and perspectives to cope with transnational challenges, jurisdiction, and international flows (Benz et al. 2007). This opened up an avenue for thinking "beyond the state" or what has been referred to as "governance without government" (Rosenau and Czempiel 1992) and a move from "government to governance" (Mayntz 2003). On the one hand, this perspective opens up the possibility for considering the agency and influence of actors other than states. On the other hand, it is important to note that this was also a period where the global market was opening up and with many countries, especially the United States, favoring competition and privatization of the public realm. Fuchs (2007) suggests that these were important enablers to the consolidation of, at least, three dimensions of business as an actor in global governance: instrumental power (lobbying, campaign, and party finance), structural power (capital flows as enablers to agenda-setting power, self-regulation, and PPPs), and discursive power (legitimation and political authority).

Management studies, on the other hand, has explored extensively the role of corporate governance and the development of further mechanisms of behavior, such as Corporate Social Responsibility (Bies et al. 2007; Mason and Simmons 2014). These mechanisms attempt to outline some of the political roles and responsibilities that companies should undertake. Literature on CSR also focuses on "how corporations facing governmental deficits can solve public problems independently or through multistakeholder initiatives to improve social welfare" (Westermann-Behaylo, Rehbein and Fort 2015, 389). This view resonates with a "governance without government" view that is rooted in self-regulation and privatization of different public services. It portrays the private sector as a necessary actor and as an intervenor that will ultimately produce positive outcomes in this exercise of "filling the gaps" *where* and *when* government fails to do so. This view holds the assumption that in a globalized world, business is better positioned to work as global interlocutors—combining the creation of value for their shareholders and for society (see Garriga and Melé 2004).

What is interesting in this particular approach to corporate governance within management studies is that, whereas it rightly points to an increase in private actors' competencies in a number of relevant governance themes, it misses the fact that they do not act only where and when governments fail. The 1980s opening of global markets also enabled an increase in the "spaces" in which companies could act by means of the delegation of a number of state competencies to the private sector (privatization) as well as the incorporation of market rationales into government functions (marketization), a number of new fields of intervention and competition opened to private companies (Bevir 2009; Crouch 2004). However, rather than meaning that corporations would "fill the gap" left by governments, this opening up provided for new spaces for *contested* and *negotiated* governance, that is to say, in which corporations and government actors had to, at all times, negotiate their own roles in it. What is more: with the so-called revolving door between public and private sectors (which was observable also from the professional backgrounds of part of our interviewees at Microsoft), part of the negotiations likely benefit from a shared understanding and grammar about what kinds of approaches and issues should be prioritized in public policy and how. Thus, rather than taking place in the absence of "public" governance, "private" governance is often deeply intertwined with it (Lobato 2016).

In this sense, contemporary private governance presents us with important challenges. First, it is difficult to define the boundaries of private groups' decisions that make it into public policy. Whereas private organizations make policies that affect the larger public, their rule-making functions often remain concealed by a variety of forms they take—which includes trade associations, not-for-profit organizations, and public policy teams within for-profit enterprises. Second, their operations can result in a lack of transparency, accountability, and legitimacy that is required of governments, despite the fact that private groups make and enforce rules that bind people to follow them, just like governments' laws and regulations (Rudder, Fritschler, and Jung Choi 2016).

Notwithstanding these challenges, this is a significant area of cybersecurity governance that deserves further scrutiny. Despite the often tacit recognition of private groups' role in shaping cybersecurity, there is scant empirical analysis on how this happens and through which venues.[6] This might possibly be due to a difficulty in accepting that companies' practices, such as lobbying, and principles-based action, including norms promotion, are not mutually excluding. Companies are very often analyzed under the terms of rational choice theory: they are usually seen as rational actors, acting on a cost-benefit based evaluation, rather than by any "common good" incentives. Claims of companies acting on moral or normative grounds are promptly criticized either because corporations cannot be morally distinguished from the human beings that constitute them (Rönnegard 2015) or because companies, even when acting on social ends, are seen to do so exclusively to maximize profits (Friedman 2007). And when companies are recognized as possibly acting on some kind of normative or social grounds, it is argued that, when doing so, they are not reduced to the actions and interests of their members. The challenge is, therefore, one of continuously attempting to locate agency amid a complex and evolving organizational structure in a context where perhaps that is not possible.

When it comes to cybersecurity, the increasing digitization of society and governments' reliance on informational infrastructures (cloud computing and data centers) provides a significant element to thinking about norms entrepreneurship and private governance, more generally. Business models are in constant development and this includes, but is not restricted to the (i) diversification of services and products, (ii) continuous organizational flexibility (new teams, posts) and (iii) key leadership influence. It plays a fundamental part in understanding the socio-technical dimension of private governance of actors *such as* Microsoft. The development of solutions and services requires careful consideration as it embeds specific protocols and functionalities that are selected to maintain a secure ecosystem. On the one hand, these arrangements prescribe what kind of security is "desirable" and "available" for consumers (public or private) (Hurel 2018) through technical architectures, protocol specifications, and security control mechanisms. Media and Communications scholars have drawn on science, technology and society studies to expose emerging dynamics of power of platforms and infrastructures (Kitchin 2014; Gillespie 2017; Plantin et al. 2017; Gorwa 2019). They consider protocols, algorithms, infrastructures, technical systems as an integral part of the governance *of* and *by* platforms. On the other hand, the development of products and services happens within a wider framework of overarching principles (trust and security), objectives and/or company strategies.

Understanding how corporate actors promote norms in cybersecurity, therefore, requires an integrated perspective between the socio-technical, organizational, and political arrangements. As the following sections show, the visibility of these configurations is indispensable and perhaps indissociable in understanding private influence in cybersecurity governance, in general, and norms-entrepreneurship, in particular. As one of our interviewees suggested, the global and diplomatic engagement is part of a continuum of what is done and advocated for on the enterprise side of the company. Though often-invisible to cyber-norms discussions, these arrangements provide the conditions of existence for the big tech companies to exert influence and maintain their engagement nationally, regionally, and globally with different stakeholder groups.

As this chapter seeks to illustrate, norms-making and entrepreneurship are not restricted to echoing or proposing new terms or international norms; rather, it encompasses a complex negotiation of the values and services and is enabled by continuous organizational flexibility and key leadership influence.

Therefore, delving into the practices of companies and showing how complex structures of governance work offers us a privileged take on how different kinds of norms are produced and negotiated. It also allows us to go deeper into the different practices adopted by the company so as to show that norms may come in a variety of shapes—the Tech Accord and the Digital Geneva Convention are but the tip of the iceberg; contemporary corporate entrepreneurship also comprises voluntary self-commitments in reaction to public expectations, rather than simply being a response to "delegated tasks" (Hurel and Lobato 2018, 67).

Unlike other big tech companies, Microsoft engages as much in platform governance[7]—by embedding compliance within their platform, for example, making sure that it is not being used to violate intellectual property, and so on—as they seek to establish room for themselves as both industry leaders *and* government interlocutors (Interview, September 2019). When asked about why would a company get involved with cyber norm promotion, an interviewee answered that global companies should be able to put governments to talk and that it is impossible for governments to do it all [the governance work in cyberspace] by themselves. At the same time, however, s/he emphasized that it is of fundamental importance that governments and companies act together in combating cybercrime, for example, and that corporations are unable to pursue this task by themselves (Interview, September 2019). Also part of Microsoft's business strategy (Interview, October 2019), norms become important meaning settlers and indicators of commitment between parties. In addition to engaging in lobbying with national governments, the company has for some time now raised interest for its explicit advocacy on norms of state behavior in cyberspace (Smith 2017). As we will explore in detail in section three, such engagement means that, despite obvious resistance and suspicion on the part of governments (and diplomats the most), the company is effectively *there* (in the meeting room) when it comes to discuss and negotiate action and norms with states.

Several times when conducting this research, we were met with the question of *why* we were looking at Microsoft, or if, due to its open advocacy and engagement with norms promotion, this would not be an exceptional case rather than a pattern, or even whether we could provide any valuable generalization from this case. Particularly interesting about Microsoft's case is that, because it is *sui generis* and not (yet) followed by its peers in the private sector when it comes to openly carving out a space for itself as a legitimate interlocutor in norms debate, it offers us with a yet underexplored perspective on potential new unfoldings of private practices in global governance. While they indeed embrace much of the patterns for private action that are identified by specialized literature—hybridization, revolving door, reliance on PPPs, increased participation in decentralized governance processes, for example, via platform governance, and so on—they also bring to the analysis a unique take on the way in which the organization's complexity—that is, the structures, people, technologies, and processes, that hold them together—makes it into the construction of this particular kind of legitimation that might be very similar and yet quite distinct from traditional corporate lobby, and what is more, substantially affect how we conceive norms. It is the curiosity with the kinds of practices that become part of cybersecurity governance by means of Microsoft's actions that moves us. Thus, rather than the question of why Microsoft is doing this, what interests us the most is the question of *how* they are doing it—and what it means for cybersecurity governance.

CYBER NORMS AND TECHNICAL/ TECHNOLOGICAL MEDIATION

An immediate consequence to the endeavor of singling out Microsoft yields an important question of whether there is something special about the company and how it operates. We argue that yes, there is. Not necessarily because Microsoft is a stand-alone case, but because perhaps the inquiry and study of norms and governance in cybersecurity requires more attention to particular socio-technical, organizational, and political arrangements and their role in shaping cybersecurity. We argue that unique dispositions within Microsoft (e.g., product, change in business model, organizational history and structure and leadership) provide an incrementally dynamic setting for specific modalities of influence, legitimacy-making and norms-setting to emerge. This arrangement includes a combination of practices—discourses, service provision, technical arrangements, knowledge and expertise—that support and configure norms-making and their capacity to engage in norms-entrepreneurship in cybersecurity.

It can be said that Microsoft's efforts to become a legitimate actor in cybersecurity norms-making depend on a double mobilization: the first is the assembling of an organizational structure that provides a seemingly comprehensive narrative not only to the task of engaging with governments (thus, including but not being restricted to government relations departments), but also to its "global" engagement with the topic of norms-making (e.g., Diplomacy Team). Of course, this coherence might be only apparent (e.g., it might be that most of the "diplomatic" work stems from the presidency). However, it matters that "public-facing" structures are able to hold within the broader attempt to fit the company's efforts on a coherent framework of action. This first mobilization has been and will continue to be explored continuously throughout the chapter.

The second mobilization, in turn, corresponds to the expectations over certain kinds of desired (state) behavior that are embedded in both their modes and infrastructures of engagement with governments (e.g., via Transparency Centers, its Digital Crimes Unit) and technological services—including the kinds of shifts in business strategies that have been adopted in the past years. Considering both these dimensions, we now turn to an examination of how technical, technological, and organizational affordances are productive of norms and advance the claim that norms are also embedded in the kinds of technical and technological mediations in place when the company interacts with states.

A Little Bit of Organizational Complexity

Microsoft works to socialize a common understanding of security concerns between tech companies (e.g., Business-to-Business security solutions) and governments—through activities that range from public-private partnerships (PPP) to a more direct engagement in proposing and influencing policy development. In what follows, we highlight three ways in which associations between the technical and organizational initiatives characterize Microsoft's normative influence on cybersecurity.

First, they do so by providing technical expertise and services. As a big tech company, Microsoft has developed a suite of services and products that aim at providing effective protection of infrastructures and data sets, promote the stability, resilience and security of systems, and facilitate logistics and data management. Concerns at the enterprise level seek to address issues related to authentication, trust, identity and access management, interoperability, and incident detection and mitigation. This perspective frames security as a service, as a set of techniques, and as expert knowledge about threats and vulnerabilities.

The provision of security services for governments takes the form of public-private partnerships and is contextualized in a customer-company relation. However, a "business-as-usual" approach to PPP has raised significant amounts of critique related to the expected role of governments as legitimate actors for providing security. Further concerns include the risk of incurring on a market-driven approach to cybersecurity (Carr 2016)—or "privatisation of security" (Avant 2005)—and the abdication of the state in protecting critical infrastructure (see Assaf 2009; Dunn Cavelty and Suter 2009). Notwithstanding, cooperation among both sectors is, as Dunn Cavelty and Suter note, "simply essential" when it comes to securing interconnected systems (2009, 180). On the one hand, PPPs refer to a particular way of outsourcing security services and expertise (also see Berndtsson and Kinsey 2016). On the other hand, this particular kind of expertise-driven engagement presents security as a feature—de-politicized, flattened, and technical in nature. Security is habitualized (see Berger and Luckman 1987) as an unquestioned set of assembled components (e.g., standards, packages, platforms, products) and exported as a ready-made product to governments (see Simos 2018). As McIntyre[8] suggests (2017), "we in the industry can better serve governments [. . .] by incentivizing migrations to newer platforms which offer more built-in security; and that are more securely developed." In a less visible manner, security is shaped through design—for example, through standards for hybrid cloud infrastructure, vulnerability management, security development life cycle, encryption and communication standards.

Technical PPPs are a fundamental form of engagement between Microsoft and local governments. These cooperation mechanisms allow them to socialize particular forms of security management and threat assessment, establish channels for information sharing, and create new avenues for trust-building. That is the case of the Government Security Program, their regional Transparency Centers (United States, Singapore, Belgium, Brazil, and China), and the Digital Crimes Unit (DCU) team, where Microsoft provides tailored security services and responds to cyberattacks—which includes source code sharing, information on malware, threats and vulnerabilities (Microsoft 2014; Government, n.d.). The DCU's Cybercrime Center gathers law enforcement, NGOs, academics, and industry in combating different modalities of crime—cloud crime and malware, misappropriation of Microsoft intellectual property, deterring nation-state actors, and online child exploitation—through networks of collaboration and by using (and promoting) secure technology deployment (e.g., cloud, PhotoDNA) (Digital, n.d.). Moreover, it took down six domains of the Russian hacking group accused of having launched a phishing campaign in the 2016 U.S. presidential election (Newman 2018). Cases such as the GSP and DCU provide a space where governments and industry can closely operate in taking down cybercriminal networks. Most importantly, the close collaboration between law enforcement and Microsoft DCU also relies on the recruitment of investigators and former prosecutors. The "revolving door" between both sectors in cases such as this provides a rather blurry distinction between public and private as the exchange between both (in terms of skills, expertise, and personnel) is a significant factor to coordinating responses.[9]

Second, they engage with policy to establish and/or reinforce specific values. This is not new. In 2005 Microsoft had advocated for a comprehensive privacy legislation in a speech to the Congressional Internet Caucus (see Microsoft 2005). Back then there was little response from the government, and concerns with privacy were only starting to emerge. Even so, the practice of prescribing specific principles for specific legislations on data privacy was the same then as it is now. In light of the diversification of services and products rooted in cloud computing and artificial intelligence, Microsoft's influence is also characterized by constant attempts at flagging new areas for public regulation (e.g., artificial intelligence and facial recognition) and greater corporate social responsibility (Smith 2018).[10] Though these suggestions are partly directed toward the construction of a narrative around common goods or shared values across society, government, and industry, there is an inherent "causal link" that "protecting consumers promotes commerce, and that's good for everyone" (Microsoft 2005). In the case of facial recognition, the company, as a leader in the development and application of such a technology, holds considerable knowledge and expertise over the technical and use-specific requirements—which also serves as leverage on claiming their say on how a technology-specific regulation should look like. Within this framing, it is not unlikely that this engagement with policy comes as a direct action from industry in seeking to influence the principles and legislation that will regulate the very technologies they work with.

Third, they advocate for international cooperation and cybersecurity norms. As previously mentioned, technical expertise and policy engagement at the national level highlight important dimensions of the association between the technical and organizational activities within the company. However, when it comes to international cyber norms, Microsoft faces a greater challenge in communicating the importance of including the private sector in a (originally conceived as) state-centric realm. Back in 2012, the consolidation of international debates on Internet governance was seen as a fruitful starting point for thinking about new PPP models for promoting international cybersecurity norms (see Hurel 2016).[11] As Matt Thomlinson (2012), former VP of Security at Microsoft noted, "global conversations on cybersecurity would also benefit from a private sector perspective that can help governments think through the technical challenges and priorities involved in securing billions of customers using the Internet around the world."

After having taken a proactive measure in advocating for a Digital Geneva Convention, the company explicitly positioned itself as a quasi-diplomatic actor (Hurel and Lobato 2018). Internally, it worked to develop whitepapers and policy documents aiming at broadcasting possible consensus areas for international cyber-norms development and established a Global Security Strategy and Diplomacy Team, which then gradually transformed into the Digital Diplomacy Team. States remain reluctant to the idea either because they deem private sector norms entrepreneurship illegitimate or due to the fact that if an initiative such as the Digital Geneva Convention is recognized, it might delegitimize previous government-led efforts to promote international norms for cyberspace—in particular, the UNGGE.

Having gone through an extensive list of documents, we were able to identify further forms of communication that perhaps set more clearly in the exercise of bringing coherence to the myriad of teams, programs and services—which we will explore in the last section. In publishing whitepapers and policy papers Microsoft publicizes their positions, provide an organized account of their strategy for policy engagement, and circulate their narrative for (i) cyber policy development and (ii) private sector inclusion (see Hurel and Lobato 2018). While this may be, at first, conceived as a "soft" approach to norms and policy making, documents range from general frameworks for cloud to frameworks for national cybersecurity strategy development, cyberpolicy toolkits or even "mandatory" incident disclosure models (Microsoft, n.d.).

Creating a Narrative: The First Clouds in the Sky

Against this backdrop, virtually every leading tech company found itself on the defensive in the summer of 2013. We conveyed our frustration to officials in Washington, DC. It was a watershed moment. It surfaced contrasts that have contributed to a chasm between governments and the tech sector to this day. Governments serve constituents who live in a defined geography, such as a state or nation. But tech has gone global, and we have customers virtually everywhere. The cloud has not only changed where and to whom we provide our services, it has redefined our relationship with customers. It has turned tech companies into institutions that in some ways resemble banks. People deposit their money in banks, and they store their most personal information—emails, photos, documents, and text messages—with tech companies. (Smith and Browne 2019, 22)

In 2014, as Satya Nadella took on the role as the CEO of Microsoft, he proposed a significant change in how the business operated. Back then he announced a new vision of what would promote a company-shift from a Windows-centric model to "mobile-first and cloud-first" model: "Microsoft is the productivity and platform company for the mobile-first, cloud-first world" (Nadella 2017, 54). Such a shift implied and enabled significant organizational, technological, and political changes—which spanned from diversifying cloud services to negotiating their public and private interests. One of the interviewees added that this change is, part and parcel, also a reflection of the need to innovate in a context where the company had gone from a global monopoly to sharing the stage with emerging technology companies. According to Nadella (2017), disputes such as the Microsoft versus United States, where the company challenged a warrant from the federal government to hand over e-mails that were originally stored in a server in Ireland, highlight the moral challenges that the company faced. Most importantly, it provides an interesting case for understanding the materiality of the services and infrastructures that not only support their operation as a platform and productivity company, but the social tensions and norms that are negotiated within and outside the company environment.

Interestingly, the company's narrative in cases such as this is one of exposing an inherent tension present in negotiating their role in the protection of individual "liberties of privacy and free speech and civil society requirements like public safety" (Nadella 2017, 112). However, it is also followed and informed by the development of strategies to further guide action. In Microsoft's case, this includes but is not restricted to the principle of designing trust in products and customers, partners, and governments. The "Redmond-based yet globally present" organizational structure is also an important feature to understanding how they claim legitimacy over their role in cybersecurity governance. As Brad Smith noted, "[t]he products and companies are far more global, and the pervasive nature of information and communications technology increasingly thrusts the tech sector into the center of foreign policy issues."

A second shift that followed from this "Windows-centric" to "cloud-first" model pertains to the relations of the company with governments. As one interviewee observed, for some time, some governments in Latin America were suspicious of the company for its monopoly on software services (and, accordingly, leveling up the pricing due to its comfortable position back then) and for its legal allegiance to the U.S. government, due to the fact that Microsoft is a U.S. company.[12] This has now changed, prompted by an increase in market competition, the loss of its monopoly of software production and distribution and by the attempts to carve out other market niches for the company (as the shift promoted by Mr. Nadella indicates). Not only did Microsoft need to "reinvent" themselves, they also had to convince governments that they could be *trusted* partners, which also depended on negotiating with their government interlocutors the need to establish transparency mechanisms and encode values, such as privacy, security, and trust, within their products.[13] This need becomes evident from one interview, held in October 2019, when it was said that if [Microsoft] could not show their clients and users (especially governments) that their products were safe, they would likely end up losing clients.

One such channel for building trust would be the company's transparency centers. Scattered in five different locations in Asia, Latin America, Europe, and the United States (there is no transparency center in the African continent to date), these centers allow governments access to source code and proprietary information from Microsoft's products and inspect them whenever there is suspicion about the products provided by the company. However, when we asked one of our interviewees about whether there was someone in the government of country A[14] that already requested access to the source code, the answer was negative (here, we could speculate whether this could be due to significant barriers in terms of availability of technical knowledge/skills to do this job within much of the already-short-of-resources branches of local and federal governments).

Transparency centers communicate one obvious expectation: that of trust, a value which is core to Microsoft's business model (Nadella 2017). Not only would these centers serve to expand dialogue with government interlocutors, they would also show the willingness of the company to open up itself to their scrutiny—of course, as long as certain requirements of confidentiality are met. Furthermore, in addition to being a channel of communication with government actors, Transparency Centers mobilize expectations around how "trust" with government actors should be practised (e.g., by means of granting access to—mostly illegible—proprietary information). For suspicious governments, in turn, "trust" becomes an important condition that will ultimately lead to either signing a contract or not. Since the shift to a cloud-based model and the resignification of its relationship with governments, not only is trust of fundamental importance to Microsoft's business model, its presence or absence is—at least, logically—core to the construction of spaces of negotiation.

As we have sought to show in this section, shared expectations of behavior are communicated through a multiplicity of channels—the legal text being only one of them, albeit the one that has received far more attention in specialized literature. In addition, we cannot detach the understanding of how these expectations come into being from the practical changes in business models and in the strategies that companies adopt to engage with governments. That is to say, we have emphasized here that through Microsoft's efforts to build themselves a legitimate space within norms-talk internationally, we can think of a different understanding of norm-building and cyber norms as part of a continuum in which the organizational and technological affordances in place matter as much as the negotiations undertaken to socialize the norm. In what follows, we will explore more of Microsoft's efforts to be seen as a "diplomatic" actor.

MICROSOFT, A DIPLOMATIC ACTOR?

As previously noted, private governance encompasses services and products, the maintenance of continuous organizational flexibility (new teams, posts) and key leadership influence. One dimension that has more recently gained considerable attention after the proposal for the Digital Geneva Convention is precisely how a global company such as Microsoft positions itself as a quasi-diplomatic actor. According to Brad Smith, his push toward diplomacy comes as one of the responses to the expansion of the company's global reach and rising concerns with cybersecurity: "The products and companies are far more global, and the pervasive nature of information and communication technology increasingly thrusts the tech sector into the center of foreign policy issues" (Smith and Browne 2019, 80). In order to advance their diplomatic engagement, the company works to influence global cybersecurity governance direct and indirectly. Engagement, in this front, relies mostly on the mobilization of staff within the company's Department of Corporate, External, and Legal Affairs (CELA)[15] and, most importantly, the Digital Diplomacy Team.

Microsoft works to advance multistakeholder and multilateral processes indirectly, whether through funding cybersecurity conferences,[16] participating in working groups,[17] attending international cybersecurity conferences or signaling support for norm entrepreneurship by others. When placed in a wider horizon on activities (indirect influence), the entrepreneurial efforts and cyber-norms documents of the company, the Digital Geneva convention is but one public-facing activity within a thread of continuous normative arrangements. Most notably, examples such as the Paris Call on Trust and Security and the Christchurch Call portray this cross-sector outward-facing norms engagement. However, members of the CELA Department also work continuously in providing inputs to specific multistakeholder cybersecurity processes. That is the case of the Internet Governance Forum,[18] where Microsoft has been continuously contributing to the work of the Best Practice Forum on Cybersecurity providing inputs to annual consultations. Within the Global Forum on Cyber Expertise, Microsoft has not only participated but also led—alongside government representatives—specific task forces on the implementation of cyber norms, Confidence-Building Measures and cyber diplomacy (see GFCE 2019).

Direct diplomatic engagement is equally central to the process of influencing the development of cyber norms as well as pushing for the broader participation within the private sector in cyber diplomacy. Even though from a tech sector standpoint, it might be indisputable that—as infrastructure providers and platform developers—a company such as Microsoft holds a considerable role in shaping and participating in global cybersecurity governance along with other tech giants, that is not necessarily the case when it comes to cyber-norms discussions. International processes such as the United Nations Group of Governmental Experts (UNGGE), whose main objective has been to discuss norms for responsible state behavior in cyberspace and, most recently, consider the applicability of international law in cyberspace. In light of fundamental immediate implications of any international negotiation such as the UNGGE, Microsoft has a direct interest mobilizing its resources to promoting norms to help mitigate and diminish cyberattacks and conflicts in an interdependent ecosystem such as cyberspace (see McKay et al. 2014; Charney et al. 2016; Nadella 2017; McKay 2018; Smith and Browne 2019).

Even though the company has maintained a long-standing relationship with different governments as part of their Government Security Programme, bilateral agreements or PPP, the international cyber-norms discussions presents a slightly different landscape (forums, initiatives) of interaction. Though bilateral and closed-meeting interactions are much more challenging to take into account in the study of how norms are built in practice, there is something to be said about how the company has expanded their engagement with governments. Be it on the "techplomacy" side, interacting with tech ambassadors from Denmark, Australia, and France, or creating a diplomatic cyber norms-oriented agenda to engage with governments bilaterally and multilaterally. One example worth noting was the Christchurch call, where Brad Smith narrates his encounter with New Zealand prime minister Jacinda Arden in March 2019, and how the Paris Call set a precedent back in December 2018 for thinking about a mechanism that could potentially bring governments, tech sector, and civil society together (Smith and Browne 2019). Cases such as this highlight an important feature of normative cascading effects of emerging cross-sector exchange—it also portrays how Microsoft diplomatic-focused interaction with governments has opened up avenues for their interaction with governments.[19]

Diplomatic efforts are not limited to strengthening ties with governments and/or socializing norms and principles in different multilateral fora, rather it entails circulating and developing norms *from* and *for* the private sector. That is the case of the Cybersecurity Tech Accord (CTA), a private sector-facing initiative launched in April 2018 that seeks to promote spaces for collective action, capacity building, and cooperation among global technology companies. The CTA also serves as a platform supporting other industry partners to onboard into cyber-norms discussions by (i) providing them the opportunity to attend consultations and conferences alongside governments and/or civil society and (ii) planning coordinated action and response to international processes (see Tech Accord 2019). Another example of peer-collaboration is the Global Internet Forum to Counter Terrorism (GIF-CT), an initiative established in early 2017 by Twitter, Facebook, Microsoft, and YouTube to deepen industry collaboration to combat terrorist abuse of platforms. Following the Christchurch Call, this group of companies has announced the creation of an independent initiative to work in a more structured setting with government and civil society organizations in preventing the exploitation of digital platforms by terrorists and violent extremist groups. Spaces such as this not only contribute as a coordination point, but serve as a knowledge and skills-sharing platform between sectors. However, such coordination and interaction contributes to the emergence of hybrid governance models that questions the differentiation between public and private roles and responsibilities.

The case of Microsoft's engagement with international cyber norms suggests that outcomes of corporate practices are not reducible either to the intentions of the individual human beings "behind it," nor do corporations act like independent beings with a life of their own. Instead, corporate action is more accurately seen as an aggregate of complex associations between internal policy and technical teams (which are more situated associations themselves), policy documents and initiatives, technologies and organizational infrastructures that support relations with governments and corporate customers, without which that what is called corporate action would look entirely otherwise (Latour 1994). This aggregate looks the way it does also because of the smaller associations that compose it and it is relevant to point out that each more complex association has an ontological status that is distinguishable from that of less complex ones.

Such a perspective over corporate norm entrepreneurship also allows us to bring in the commensurability of profit and rational action and normative and moral engagement. That is to say: when we look at how the company engages with governments, that is, through soft recommendations and attempts to influence policy making at either local, state, national, or international instances, or through mechanisms devised to "build trust" with state customers, we realize that, at once, companies can promote moral norms *and* seek profit. In Microsoft's case, what is pictured as norm promotion also has to do with what the company sees as an adequate use of for its products and services and may at times come as voluntary self-commitments with values—such as trust—deemed to be core to the reputation and afterlife of commercial and government solutions. As the relation between interests and moral values becomes more complex, it comes as no surprise then that the misuse of its software and hardware products, with attempts to exploit vulnerabilities in them, is among one of the company's primary concerns as it keeps advocating for some sort of accord among states.

Whereas there is a comprehensive assessment of how different private groups engage with international norms-making (Flohr et al. 2010; Rudder, Fritschler and Choi 2016; Strange 1992; Watkins 2007), this is a territory that still remains largely unknown to most studies on tech companies. Such a lack is nothing but problematic. Tech companies engage quite differently in regulating the behavior of its customers and users, and this has to do with the very nature of the services and products that are offered by them and how they work, are used, exploited, and transformed through practice. Indeed, some attention has been paid to how social media create community standards to bound what is an acceptable conduct on their platforms (Article 19, 2018) and regulate user behavior through technical (Musiani 2013) as well as legal (Belli and Venturini 2016) architectures. But these approaches remain mostly restricted to either self or individual regulation. Whereas they give us a hint on how companies—intentionally or not—develop sophisticated regulatory mechanisms through their products and services, they are less helpful once we try to make sense of the varied, sometimes conflicting or not-always-coherent-in-practice, organizational architectures underpinning such regulatory efforts. They are also not very helpful once we ask why and how companies engage with state actors to advocate for moral standards and common social codes of conduct to other actors beyond its peers in the private sector. Without in-depth discussion of why/how this happens, we foreclose our own understanding of how legitimacy is built through such efforts, as well as debates about how we should be dealing with these kinds of practices.

Adding to the burgeoning literature and policy initiatives to advance cyber norms (NATO 2013; McKay et al. 2014; Osula and Rõigas 2016; Finnemore and Hollis 2016; Charney et al. 2016; G7 2017; Nye 2018), Microsoft's call for a Digital Geneva Convention has drawn as much attention as suspicion to the company, as well as to its intentions and chances of succeeding. Whereas attention to corporate cyber-norms promotion and evaluations of its success or failure can be useful in assessing the efficacy (or not) of a situated initiative, both miss an important aspect of Microsoft's efforts: it is not—and, possibly, never was—about the Digital Geneva Convention. As our research on the company's organizational structure attempted to show, this is but one situated effort in the context of a diversified range of possibilities for political articulation undertaken by the company. As we sought to illustrate throughout this study, each particular relation begs the articulation of distinct policy strategies, infrastructures, and narratives that, in turn, constitute a multiplicity of associations in themselves—associations composed of people in policy teams, lobbying practices, technical systems, pieces of hardware, software, codes of conduct, different levels of government (local, state, national, and international), policy documents, physical installations, and so on. These associations point to the varied ways through which norms are articulated through corporate practice, some of them fairly straightforward, such as creating instruments of "soft influence," that is, policy papers and whitepapers, and producing advisory opinions, while some not so much—here, Transparency Centers are a case in point.

The empirical research suggests that such organizational complexity plays an important role in building legitimacy in private governance. This happens in—at least—three different ways. First, in devising strategies to deal with technical challenges to cyberspace security. As a platform and productivity technology company, Microsoft invests in the development of new technologies, software, and mitigation of incidents, such as the Conficker worm and the WannaCry ransomware, and also engages on combating cybercrime through its cybercrime unit.[20] This shaping of both the economic and technical dimensions of cybersecurity paves the way for private actors to be "recognized as legitimate by some larger public (that often includes states themselves) as authors of policies, of practices, of rules, and of norms" (Hall and Biersteker 2002, 4).

Second, in taking the lead in the proposal of a tech accord in the private sector and entering into cooperation with companies within and outside the tech sector, Microsoft has sought to establish itself as a moral leader among its peers. As Floh et al. (2010) note, establishing normative standards for its peers on the private sector is characteristic of corporate entrepreneurship. When engaging with norms promotion, corporations tend to work as meaning managers, establishing "new ways of talking about and understanding issues" (Finnemore and Sikkink 1998, 897). They may also support the setting or institutionalization of a new norm "by adopting a unilateral company code as best practice, by lobbying for it among its peers and by engaging in the creation of a collective self-regulatory initiative" (Flohr et al. 2010, 19) and play a role even after the norm has acquired some degree of institutionalization, by engaging with organizations supporting the norm and participation in revision processes (Flohr et al. 2010).

Third, by actively engaging with norms emergence beyond national borders, structuring public policy as well as diplomacy teams, regularly publishing policy documents aimed at state actors and getting involved in multilateral and multistakeholder policy processes, the company has clearly sought to stretch the boundaries of its legitimacy. Such stretching has less to do with the proposal of a Digital Geneva Convention in itself than with the company's aforementioned practices and organizational structure. That is to say, legitimacy building, at this stage, is better understood in terms of the complex associations and relations that follow from Microsoft's engagement with local, state, and national governments and its attempts to build legitimacy within the private sector and through its technical expertise.

The implications of this for the study of norms-making and power are manifold. The processual lenses hereto adopted suggest that power can be less straightforward than it seems: it can be distributed through internal teams, technical and policy considerations, expertise, "high-tech" centers, computational systems, soft-engagement. Consequently, what we call norms-making is equally distributed in these practices, stretching into every direction thanks to dynamic architecture of policy engagement. In this sense, norms-making cannot be understood as neither a state-only process, nor necessarily an actor-only process. By reintroducing private governance to the cyber-norms discussions—that is, looking at the strategies and associations involved in the establishing of a range of social codes of conduct—our goal was to provide an exercise of visualizing and further inquiring of what indeed, can pass as a norm. Initiatives such as a tech accord or a Digital Geneva Convention serve as important reminders that future cyber-norms and cybersecurity governance research needs requires careful unpacking.

CONCLUDING THOUGHTS ON CONTROVERSIES AND FURTHER RESEARCH

In this chapter, we sought to expand our previous research on private actor norm entrepreneurship in cybersecurity (Hurel and Lobato 2018) by undertaking an empirical analysis of the organizational structure of Microsoft. Through the analysis, we illustrated that not only questions of *who*—states? Nongovernmental organizations? Advocacy groups? Corporations?—produces norms matter, but also issues of *how* norms are made and *what* should be understood as norm-making processes in these analyses in the first place. This is a discreet albeit necessary step in the study of private governance in cybersecurity, as it opens up the field for entirely different and often extremely complex and messy ways of producing social codes of conduct—through technical means, soft influence, direct engagement with actors, and so on. Microsoft's case also shows that corporations can engage meaningfully and voluntarily with promoting and establishing socially accepted norms of conduct for both its peers and state actors at different levels of government—while also seeking to increase its profits and engaging with cost-benefits calculations. Thus, we can identify different dimensions stemming from the practices and associations constituted in and by corporate action, which include policy making, different degrees of advocacy (including lobbying), self-regulation and regulation through software and/or hardware.

By looking at the vast possibilities for associations—among documents, policies, teams, states, other corporations, high-tech infrastructures, techniques and technologies—we also highlighted three different dimensions of legitimacy building: technical/technological, among peers and multilateral/multistakeholder. Each form comes out of dynamic sets of associations, some more rigid, some more weak. What they tell us is that what is pictured as norm promotion is in fact a more complicated enterprise. By asking whether the Digital Geneva Convention proposal was actually novelty, we sought to illustrate that it is actually an actualization of these ever-changing associations. This is to say, it is a particular mode of producing norms, but not the only one, within Microsoft's organizational complexity.

One question that arises from the analysis is whether—despite the intense engagement with international norms promotion and the work of Transparency Centers as well as regional/national teams—the company still privileges its home country—the United States—as its main locus for policy making. Further research is still required about how the company develops relations with Global South countries and to what extent it is perceived by them as simply reproducing the interests of its "home country" or as something else. This could indicate whether the strength of particular associations at the expense of others might say something and potentially affect the company's advocacy. Distinctly, it could also shed a more clarifying light onto how local politics possibly shape long-term, global policies.

LIST OF INTERVIEWS

1. Interview, October 2019.
2. Interview, October 2019.
3. Interview, September 2019.
4. Interview, September 2019.

NOTES

1. The authors would like to thank Prof. Dennis Broeders, Prof. Duncan Hollis, and Prof. Anna Leader for their support and invaluable comments to the development of this chapter. The authors would also thank the panel discussion held on "(Re) assessing the role of private actors in cybersecurity governance" at the ISA Annual Conference 2019, Toronto.

2. In fact, the political role of companies has been widely debated within International Political Economy by means of discussions over multinational corporations. See: Strange (1991; 1996; 1998); Gill; Cutler (2014); Gilpin (1976); May (2015); Babic, Fichtner and Heemskerk (2017).

3. Such as the 2019 Brazil-EU Consultations on Preventing Conflict in Cyberspace, the 2018 Conference Responsible Behaviour in Cyberspace: Novel Horizons and the new European framework for Cyber Sanctions.

4. Notably, they are progressively becoming locus of attention. See, for example, Dunn Cavelty (2016) and Carr (2016).

5. In this work, we also consider as IR studies in Global Governance and International Political Economy.

6. This has also proven to be a challenge to the development of this chapter. In spite of having conducted interviews, analyzed public documentation, and engaged in participant observation across different events, the traceability of Microsoft's engagement and interests was an exercise in itself. The generativity and fast-paced change of the company's organizational structure allowed us to further understand that their engagement in diplomacy, policy and product development (enterprise side) is a continuous process of communication and internal negotiation. Norms are continuously challenged, reinforced, maintained, and transformed within complex arrangements

that do not necessarily imply in a clear-cut rational and objective response. Rather, they rely on internal alignments, leadership, and narrative-building.

7. However, in a far less explicit fashion than its peers (e.g., Facebook or Google) also due to different business models.

8. Executive security adviser at Microsoft Enterprise Cybersecurity Group.

9. See Smith and Browne (2019) chapter 5 note 2 for a detailed description of the development of the DCU since early 2000s.

10. The Cybersecurity Policy Framework, launched in 2018, holds together many of the previous documents directed to capacity building and development of national cybersecurity strategies. It serves as an interesting case for understanding how Microsoft gradually organized their agenda and positions on this particular area. Most importantly, they explicitly state the purpose of the document—and their aim in circulating it—that is, to provide "a high-level overview of concepts and priorities that must be top of mind when developing an effective and resilient cybersecurity policy environment" (McKay 2018).

11. Interestingly, in 2012, Microsoft developed an expected cybersecurity policy PPP timeline called "Cybersecurity Policy and Partnership Evolutionary Curve" that ranged from their early experiences in working with governments at the national level—risk management (2000) and resiliency (2005)—to new avenues for collaboration on cyber norms at the international level—starting from Internet governance (2010) to cybersecurity norms development (2015) and finally reaching harmonization (2020) (Thomlinson 2012).

12. Curiously, possibly in anticipation to this kind of criticism, one interviewee promptly emphasized the legal bond of the subsidiary in which s/he worked with the country in which it operated.

13. See Nadella (2017) and Smith (2019) for a detailed account of how both the president and CEO of the company portrayed the internal negotiations during the Snowden revelations and how they responded deciding to sue the U.S. government through the Foreign Intelligence Surveillance Court.

14. Where the subsidiary for which s/he works operates.

15. Regionally, the CELA Departments work to represent global principles and advocacy strategies in their respective countries.

16. Such as the Paris Peace Forum in 2018 (see Belin 2018), Global Commission on the Stability of Cyberspace, Global Conference on Cyberspace and others.

17. Such as the Best Practice Forum (BPF) on Cybersecurity within the Internet Governance Forum, or different Working Groups of the GFCE.

18. A global multistakeholder platform of the United Nations dedicated to facilitating the discussion of public policy issues related to the Internet.

19. In cyber norms-discussions (both internationally and regionally), Microsoft is perhaps the only industry representative participating in closed-door negotiations continuously. Though it is more challenging to generalize when it comes to interaction and influence in concealed environments, through participant observation the researchers were able to identify specific occasions where the company was the only industry partner represented either in multilateral negotiations or in closed multistakeholder environments. In early 2019, the EU Cyber Forum was followed by a closed civil society side meeting. Participants included civil society organizations, think

tanks, academics and Microsoft. Examples such as this illustrate not only the emerging spaces of interaction resulting from sustained engagement with global cybersecurity and cyber-norms community, but it creates an entry point for them to advocate, communicate and bring other industry sectors—such as those that are members of the CTA. All of which support the narrative echoed by Brad Smith of industry as technology providers and central to the promotion of peace and secure cyberspace.

20. The digital crime unit, in cooperation with academic experts and industry, successfully took down the Rustock botnet (Microsoft 2011) and further engaged in joint operations with the financial sector and law enforcement agencies—the most aggressive operation being Operation b54 (Boscovich 2013).

REFERENCES

Abbate, Janet. 1999. *Inventing the Internet.* Cambridge: MIT Press.

Abrahamsen, R., and M. Williams. 2009. "Security beyond the state: Global security assemblages in international politics". *International Political Sociology*, 3 (1): 7–17.

Article 19. 2018. *Facebook Community Standards: Legal Analysis*, June 2018. (Available at: https://www.article19.org/wp-content/uploads/2018/08/Facebook-Community-Standards-June-2018.pdf; accessed: Sept. 2, 2018.)

Assaf, D. 2009. "Conceptualising the use of public–private partnerships as a regulatory arrangement in critical information infrastructure protection". In: A. Peters, L. Koechlin, T. Förster, and G. Fenner Zinkernagel (eds.). *Non-State Actors as Standard Setters*, 61–83. Cambridge: Cambridge University Press.

Avant, Deborah D. 2005. *The Market Force: The Consequences of Privatizing Security.* Cambridge: Cambridge University Press.

Babic, Milan, Jan Fichtner, and Eelke M. Heemskerk. 2017. "States versus corporations: Rethinking the power of business in international politics". *The International Spectator*, 52 (4): 20–43.

Barrinha, André, and T. Renard. 2018. "Cyber-diplomacy: The making of an international society in the digital age". *Global Affairs*, 3 (4–5): 353–364.

Belin, Célia. "What the Paris Peace Forum tells us about France—and about the world". Brookings Institute. (Available at: https://www.brookings.edu/blog/order-from-chaos/2018/11/09/what-the-paris-peace-forum-tells-us-about-france-and-about-the-world; accessed: Oct. 21, 2018.)

Belli, Luca, and Jamila Venturini. 2016. "Private ordering and the rise of terms of service as cyber-regulation". *Internet Policy Review*, 5 (4). (Available at: http://policyreview.info/articles/analysis/private-ordering-and-rise-terms-service-cyber-regulation; accessed: 4 Sept. 2018.)

Berger, Peter L., and Thomas Luckmann. 1967. *The Social Construction of Reality: A Treatise in the Sociology of Knowledge.* Harmondsworth: Penguin.

Berndtsson, Joakim, and Christopher Kinsey. 2016. *The Routledge Research Companion to Security Outsourcing.* London: Routledge.

Bevir, Mark. 2009. *Key Concepts in Governance*, 128–132. New York: SAGE.

Bies, Robert J., Jean M. Bartunek, Timothy L. Fort, and Mayer N. Zald. 2007. "Corporations as social change agents: Individual, interpersonal, institutional, and environmental dynamics". *Academy of Management Review*, 32 (3): 788–793.

Boscovich, Richard Domingues. 2013. "Microsoft works with financial services industry leaders, law enforcement and others to disrupt massive financial cybercrime ring". *The Official Microsoft Blog*. (Available at: https://blogs.technet.microsoft.com/microsoft_blog/2013/06/05/microsoft-works-with-financial-services-industry-leaders-law-enforcement-and-others-to-disrupt-massive-financial-cybercrime-ring/; accessed: Sept. 3, 2018.)

Bouwen, Pieter. 2002. "Corporate lobbying in the European Union: The logic of access". *Journal of European Public Policy*, 9 (3): 365–390.

Burt, Tom. 2018a. "Announcing the defending democracy program". Microsoft. (Available at: https://blogs.microsoft.com/on-the-issues/2018/04/13/announcing-the-defending-democracy-program/; accessed: Sept. 10, 2018.)

Burt, Tom. 2018b. "Protecting democracy with Microsoft AccountGuard". Microsoft. (Available at: https://blogs.microsoft.com/on-the-issues/2018/08/20/protecting-democracy-with-microsoft-accountguard/; accessed: Sept. 10, 2018.)

Burt, Tom. 2018c. "Defending against disinformation in partnership with NewsGuard". Microsoft. Available at: https://blogs.microsoft.com/on-the-issues/2018/08/23/defending-against-disinformation-in-partnership-with-newsguard/; accessed: Sept. 10, 2018.

Carr, Madeline. 2016. "Public–private partnerships in national cyber-security strategies". *International Affairs*, 92 (1): 43–62.

Charney, Scott, Erin English, Aaron Kleiner, Nemanja Malisevic, Angela McKay, Jan Neutze, and Paul Nicholas. 2016. "From articulation to implementation: Enabling progress on cyber security norms". Microsoft, white paper, June 2016.

Crouch, Colin. 2004. "Markets and states". In: Nash, Kate, and Alan E. Scott (eds.). *The Blackwell Companion to Political Sociology*, 240–249. Oxford: Blackwell.

Digital. n.d. "Digital crimes unit: Leading the fight against cybercrime". Microsoft, policy paper.

Dunn Cavelty, Myriam. 2016. "Cyber-security and private actors". In: Rita Abrahamsen and Anna Leander (eds.). *Routledge Handbook of Private Security Studies*. New York: Routledge.

Dunn Cavelty, Myriam, and Manuel Suter. 2009. "Public-private partnerships are no silver bullet: An expanded governance model for Critical Infrastructure Protection". *International Journal of Critical Infrastructure Protection*, 2 (4): 179–187.

ENISA. 2017. *Public Private Partnerships (PPP): Cooperative Models*. ENISA. (Available at: https://www.enisa.europa.eu/publications/public-private-partnerships-ppp-cooperative-models; accessed: Sept. 6, 2018.)

FEC. 2018. "FEC approves advisory opinion and notification of availability". Federal Election Commission. (Available at: https://www.fec.gov/updates/fec-approves-advisory-opinion-and-notification-availability/; accessed: Sept. 6, 2018.)

Finnemore, Martha, and Duncan B. Hollis. 2016a. "Constructing norms for global cybersecurity". *Temple University Beasley School of Law. Legal Studies Research Paper* n. 52: 89–101.

Finnemore, M., and D.B. Hollis. 2016b. "Constructing norms for global cybersecurity". *American Journal of International Law*, 110 (3): 425–479.

Finnemore, Martha, and Kathryn Sikkink. 1998. "International norm dynamics and political change". *International Organization*, 52 (4): 887–917.

Flohr, Annegret, Lothar Rieth, and Sandra Schwindenhammer. 2010. *The Role of Business in Global Governance: Corporations as Norm-Entrepreneurs*. London: Palgrave.

Friedman, M. 2007. "The social responsibility of business is to increase its profits". In: W.C. Zimmerli, M. Holzinger, and K. Richter (eds.). *Corporate Ethics and Corporate Governance*. Berlin: Springer.

Fuchs, Doris. 2007. *Business Power in Global Governance*. Boulder, CO: Lynne Rienner.

G7. 2017. "On responsible states behavior in cyberspace". *Lucca*, 17 April 2017. (Available at: https://s3.amazonaws.com/ceipfiles/pdf/CyberNorms/Multilater al/G7+Declaration+on+Responsible+States+Behavior+in+Cyberspace+4-11-20 17.pdf; accessed: Sept. 4, 2018.)

Garriga, Elisabet, and Domènec Melé. 2004. "Corporate social responsibility theories: Mapping the territory". *Journal of Business Ethics*, 53 (51): 51–71.

GFCE. 2019. "Report GFCE WG A—Task Force on CBMs and norms implementation & Cyber diplomacy". Global Forum on Cyber Expertise. (Available at: https ://cdn.foleon.com/upload/17621/gfce_secretariat_wgm2019_wg_a_report.90f7333 bc1c3.pdf; accessed: Oct. 22, 2019.)

Gill, Stephen, and Claire A. Cutler. 2014. "New constitutionalism and world order: General introduction". In: S. Gill (ed.). *New Constitutionalism and World Order*, 1–22. Cambridge: Cambridge University Press.

Gilpin, Robert. 1976. "Review: The political economy of the multinational corporation: Three contrasting perspectives". *The American Political Science Review*, 70 (1): 184–191.

Gorwa, Robert. 2019. "What is platform governance?" *Information, Communication & Society*, 22 (6), 854–871.

Gorwa, Robert, and Anton Peez. 2018. "Tech companies as cybersecurity norm entrepreneurs: A critical analysis of microsoft's cybersecurity tech accord". SocArXiv, working paper, December 11, 2018. (Available at: https://doi.org/10.31235/osf.io/ g56c9.)

Government. n.d. "Government security program: An overview". Microsoft, policy paper.

Grigsby, Alex. 2017. "The end of cyber norms". *Survival: Global Politics and Strategy*, 56 (6): 109–122.

Hall, Rodney Bruce, and Thomas J. Biersteker. 2002. "The emergence of private authority in the international system". In: Rodney Bruce Hall and Thomas J. Biersteker (eds.). *The Emergence of Private Authority in Global Governance*, 3–22. Cambridge: Cambridge University Press.

Hurel, Louise Marie. 2016. "Cybersecurity and internet governance: Two competing fields?". *SSRN* (Available at: https://papers.ssrn.com/sol3/papers.cfm?abstract_id=3036855; accessed: Sept. 10, 2018.)

Hurel, Louise Marie. 2018. "Architectures of security and power: IoT platforms as technologies of government". MSc diss., London School of Economics and Political Science. (Available at: https://doi.org/10.13140/RG.2.2.28293.29920.)

Hurel, Louise Marie, and Luisa C. Lobato. 2018. "Unpacking cyber norms: Private companies as norms entrepreneurs". *Journal of Cyber Policy*, 3 (1): 61–76.

Kitchin, Robert. 2014. *The Data Revolution: Big Data, Open Data, Data Infrastructures and Their Consequences*. Thousand Oaks, CA: SAGE.

Lapowski, Issie. 2018. "Tech giants are becoming defenders of democracy. Now what?" *WIRED*, Aug. 22, 2018. (Available at: https://www.wired.com/story/microsoft-facebook-tech-giants-defending-democracy/; accessed: Sept. 10, 2018.)

Latour, Bruno. 1994. "On technical mediation: Philosophy, sociology, genealogy". *Common Knowledge*, 3 (2): 29–64.

Latour, Bruno. 2005. *Reassembling the Social: An Introduction to Actor-Network-Theory*. Oxford: Oxford University Press.

Leander, Anna. 2010. "Commercial Security Practices". In: P.J. Burgess (ed.). *Handbook of New Security Studies*. New York: Routledge.

Leigh Star, S., and K. Ruhleder. 1996. "Steps toward an ecology of infrastructure: Design and access for large information spaces". *Information Systems Research*, 7 (1): 111–134.

Lobato, Luisa. 2016. "Unravelling the cyber security market: The struggles among cyber security companies and the production of cyber (in)security". MSc diss., Pontifical Catholic University of Rio de Janeiro. (Available at: https://doi.org/10.17771/PUCRio.acad.27784.)

May, Christopher. 2015. "Who's in charge? Corporations as institutions of global governance". *Palgrave Communications*, 1: 1–10.

Mayntz, Renate. 2003. "New challenges to governance theory". In: Henrik P. Bang (ed.). *Governance as Social and Political Communication*, 27–40. Manchester: Manchester University Press.

McIntyre, Mark. 2017. "How public-private partnerships can combat cyber adversaries". Microsoft. (Available at: https://cloudblogs.microsoft.com/microsoftsecure/2017/12/13/how-public-private-partnerships-can-combat-cyber-adversaries/; accessed: Sept. 4, 2018.)

McKay, Angela. 2018. "Building on experience: A framework for cybersecurity policy". Microsoft, blog post. (Available at: https://cloudblogs.microsoft.com/microsoftsecure/2018/08/09/building-on-experience-a-framework-for-cybersecurity-policy/; accessed: Sept. 8, 2018.)

McKay, Angela, Paul Nicholas, Jan Neutze, and Kevin Sullivan. 2014. *International Cybersecurity Norms: Reducing Conflict in an Internet-Dependent World*. Microsoft.

Microsoft. 2005. "Microsoft advocates comprehensive federal privacy legislation". Microsoft. (Available at: https://news.microsoft.com/2005/11/03/microsoft-advocates-comprehensive-federal-privacy-legislation/; accessed: Oct. 21, 2019.)

Microsoft. 2011. "Taking down Botnets: Microsoft and the Rustock Botnet". Microsoft corporate blogs. (Available at: https://blogs.microsoft.com/on-the-issues/201

1/03/17/taking-down-botnets-microsoft-and-the-rustock-botnet/; accessed: Sept. 2, 2018.)

Microsoft. 2014. "Microsoft government security program: Helping address the unique security requirements of national governments". Microsoft.

Microsoft, n.d. "Cybersecurity policy toolkit: Mandatory incident disclosure models". Microsoft. (Available at: https://www.microsoft.com/en-us/cybersecurity /content-hub/cybersecurity-policy-toolkit-mandatory-incident-disclosure-models; accessed: Sept. 1, 2018.)

Musiani, Francesca. 2013. "Governance by algorithms". *Internet Policy Review*, 2 (3).

Musiani, Francesca, Derrick L. Cogburn, Laura DeNardis, and Nanette Levinson. 2016. *The Turn to Infrastructure in Internet Governance.* London: Palgrave Macmillan.

Onuf, Nicholas G. 1989. *World of Our Making: Rules and Rule in Social Theory and International Relations.* Columbia: University of South Carolina Press.

Nadella, Satya. 2017. *Hit Refresh: The Quest to Rediscover Microsoft's Soul and Imagine a Better Future for Everyone.* New York: Harper Business.

Newman, Lily Hay. 2018. "How Microsoft tackles Russian hackers—And why it's never enough". *WIRED*, August 21, 2018. (Available at: https://www.wired.com/ story/microsoft-russia-fancy-bear-hackers-sinkhole-phishing/; accessed: Sept. 4, 2018.)

Nye, Joseph. 2018. "How Will New Cybersecurity Norms Develop?" *The Strategist*, the Australian Strategic Policy Blog. (Available at: https://www.aspistrategist.org .au/how-will-cybersecurity-norms-develop/; accessed: Sept. 5, 2018.)

Osula, Anna-Maria, and Henry Roigas (eds.). 2016. *International Cyber Norms: Legal, Policy & Industry Perspectives.* Tallinn: NATO CCDCOE.

Plantin, Jean-Christophe, Carl Lagoze, Paul N. Edwards, and Christian Sandvig. 2016. "Infrastructure studies meet platform studies in the age of Google and Facebook". *New Media & Society*, 20 (1): 293–310.

Rönnegard, David (ed.). 2015. *The Fallacy of Corporate Moral Agency.* New York: Springer.

Rosenau, J. N., and E.-O. Czempiel (eds.). 1992. *Governance without Government: Order and Change in World Politics.* Cambridge, UK: Cambridge University Press.

Rudder, Catherine E., A. Lee Fritschler, and Yon J. Choi. 2016. *Public Policymaking by Private Organisations: The Challenges for Democratic Governance.* Washington: Brookings Institution.

Simos, Mark. 2018. "Cybersecurity reference architecture: Security for a hybrid enterprise". Microsoft. (Available at: https://cloudblogs.microsoft.com/microso ftsecure/2018/06/06/cybersecurity-reference-architecture-security-for-a-hybrid-e nterprise/; accessed: Sept. 7, 2018.)

Smith, Brad, and Carol Ann Browne. 2019. *Tools and Weapons: The Promise and the Peril of the Digital Age.* New York: Penguin.

Smith, Brad. 2018. "Facial recognition technology: The need for public regulation and corporate responsibility". Microsoft. (Available at: https://blogs.microsoft.c

om/on-the-issues/2018/07/13/facial-recognition-technology-the-need-for-public-re gulation-and-corporate-responsibility/; accessed: Sept. 9, 2018.)

Smith, Brad. 2017. "The need for a Digital Geneva Convention". Microsoft blogs. (Available at: https://blogs.microsoft.com/on-the-issues/2017/02/14/need-digital -geneva-convention/; accessed: Sept. 9, 2019.)

Strange, Susan. 1998. *States and Markets.* San Francisco: University of California Press.

Strange, Susan. 1996. *The Retreat of the State: The Diffusion of Power in the World Economy.* Cambridge: Cambridge University Press.

Strange, Susan. 1991. "Big business and the state". *Millennium Journal of International Studies*, 20 (2): 245–250.

Tech Accord. 2019. "The cybersecurity tech accord response to a call for contributions from best practice forum working group on 'Cybersecurity Culture, Norms and Values'". Tech Accord. (Available at: https://cybertechaccord.org/category/ policies-rfis/; accessed: Oct. 21, 2019.)

Thomlinson, Matt. 2012. "Cybersecurity norms and the public private partnership: Promoting trust and security in cyberspace". Microsoft. (Available at: https ://cloudblogs.microsoft.com/microsoftsecure/2012/10/05/cybersecurity-norms-and-the-public-private-partnership-promoting-trust-and-security-in-cyberspace/; accessed: Sept. 9, 2018.)

Van Dijck, J. 2013. *The Culture of Connectivity: A Critical History of Social Media.* Oxford: Oxford University Press.

Wendt, Alexander. 2004. "The state as person in international theory". *Review of International Studies*, 30 (2): 289–316.

Wendt, Alexander. 1992. "Anarchy is what states make of it: The social construction of power politics". *International Organization*, 46 (2): 391–425.

Wendt, Alexander. 1995. "Constructing international politics". *International Security*, 20 (1): 71–81.

Westermann-Behaylo, Michelle K., Kathleen Rehbein, and Timothy Fort. 2015. "Enhancing the concept of corporate diplomacy: Encompassing political corporate social responsibility, international relations, and peace through commerce". *Academy of Management Perspectives*, 29 (4): 389.

Index

About the Editors and Contributors

Liisi Adamson is a PhD researcher at the Hague Program for Cyber Norms. She has a background in international and comparative law as well as information technology law from University of Helsinki and University of Tartu, respectively. Prior to commencing her PhD studies, Liisi served as a research fellow at the Cyber Policy Institute in Estonia (2014–2017) and as an adviser to the Estonian delegation to the UN Group of Governmental Experts on Information Security (2016–2017). Her research at the Hague Program for Cyber Norms focuses on resilience in the context of cybersecurity.

Bibi van den Berg is full professor of Cybersecurity Governance at Leiden University, and the head of the Cybersecurity Governance research group at the Institute of Security and Global Affairs of this university. She is also a member of the Dutch Cyber Security Council, a Council that advises the Dutch cabinet on how to improve cybersecurity in The Netherlands.

Dennis Broeders is Associate Professor of Security and Technology and Senior Fellow of the Hague Program for Cyber Norms at the Institute of Security and Global Affairs of Leiden University, the Netherlands. His research and teaching broadly focuses on the interaction between security, technology, and policy, with a specific interest in international cyber security governance. He is the author of the book *The Public Core of the Internet* (2015). He currently also serves as a member of the Dutch delegation to the UN Group of Governmental Experts on international information security (2019–2021) as an academic adviser.

Rogier Creemers is an assistant professor in the Law and Governance of China at Leiden University, and an associate fellow of the Hague Program for Cyber Norms at the Institute of Security and Global Affairs. His research investigates China's domestic technology policies, as well as China's participation in global cyber affairs. His work has been published, among others, in *The China Journal* and the *Journal of Contemporary China*. He is also a founding member of DigiChina, a project run in cooperation with New America, as well as a frequent contributor to international news media.

Jacqueline Eggenschwiler is a doctoral researcher at the University of Oxford. Her research looks at the contributions of non-state actors to processes of global cybersecurity norm formation and corresponding governance implications. Jacqueline holds degrees in International Affairs and Governance, International Management, and Human Rights from the University of St. Gallen and the London School of Economics and Political Science.

Louk Faesen is a strategic analyst at the Cyber Policy and Resilience Program of the Hague Centre for Strategic Studies and project manager of the Global Commission on the Stability of Cyberspace. His research mainly focuses on international peace and security in cyberspace, norms of responsible state and non-state behavior, and confidence-building measures (CBMs) in cyberspace.

Ilina Georgieva is a PhD candidate of the Hague Program for Cyber Norms at Leiden University's Institute of Security and Global Affairs. Previously, Ilina served as a researcher on the Sweetie Project at eLaw, the Center for Law and Digital Technologies at Leiden University, and was an editor at the Utrecht *Journal of International and European Law*. She was also a part of Heidelberg University's Cluster of Excellence "Asia and Europe in a Global Context" and of the Austria Institute for European and Security Policy in her capacity as a research assistant. She also worked at the Max Planck Institute for Comparative Public Law and International Law in Heidelberg and served as a senior research associate and later on as a counsel for the Public International Law and Policy Group (PILPG).

Robert Gorwa is a doctoral candidate in the Department of Politics and International Relations at the University of Oxford. He is affiliated with the Centre for Technology and Global Affairs at Oxford, the Project on Internet and Democracy at Stanford University, and is a fellow at the Weizenbaum Institute for the Networked Society. He holds a BA from the University of British Columbia and an MSc from the Oxford Internet Institute.

Steven Hill is a legal adviser and director of the Office of Legal Affairs at NATO Headquarters in Brussels, Belgium. Mr. Hill came to NATO after serving as counselor for Legal Affairs at the U.S. Mission to the United Nations. Prior to his work in New York, Mr. Hill led the legal unit at the International Civilian Office in Kosovo. He previously worked in the Office of the Legal Adviser at the U.S. Department of State, where he advised on the law of armed conflict, human rights law, economic sanctions, and the law governing diplomatic premises. He was assigned to the U.S. Embassy in Baghdad from 2004 to 2005. He also served as counsel in proceedings before the International Court of Justice in 2003 and in several cases before the Inter-American Commission on Human Rights from 2006 to 2007. Mr. Hill also actively engages in teaching and research on international law and he has graduated from Yale Law School and Harvard College.

Geoffrey Hoffman is a doctoral student in political science and international affairs at the University of California, San Diego. He holds master's degrees from Columbia University and Tsinghua University.

Louise Marie Hurel is pursuing her PhD in Data, Networks, and Society at the London School of Economics and Political Science (LSE) working on technical security expertise, cybersecurity governance, and incident response. She also leads research and project development at Igarapé Institute's Cybersecurity and Digital Liberties Programme. Having concluded her MSc in Media and Communications (Data and Society) LSE and BA in International Relations at PUC-Rio, Louise Marie Hurel's work focuses on exploring interdisciplinary approaches to contemporary security challenges and the role of non-state actors in cybersecurity; having been awarded for her dissertation "Cybersecurity and Internet Governance: Two Competing Fields." Louise Marie has given lectures and presentations at King's College London, NATO, ICANN, and other organizations. Her previous experience includes consultancy for the UNESCO project on "What if we all governed the Internet," and research on Internet Governance, privacy, data protection, and security at the Center for Technology and Society at Getúlio Vargas Foundation (CTS-FGV).

Dr. Alexander Klimburg is director of the Cyber Policy and Resilience Program at the Hague Centre for Strategic Studies and Director of the Global Commission on the Stability of Cyberspace Initiative and Secretariat. Dr. Klimburg is an affiliate and former fellow of Harvard University, a nonresident senior fellow with the Atlantic Council, and an associate fellow at the Austrian Institute of European and Security Policy. He has worked on numerous topics within the wider field of international cybersecurity since 2007. He is the author and editor of numerous books, research papers, and commentaries—his most recent book *The Darkening Web: The War for Cyberspace* was published by Penguin Press.

Joanna Kulesza is a tenured professor of law at the University of Lodz, Poland, where she teaches International Law, Internet Governance and Media Law. Currently serving as a scientific committee member for the Fundamental Rights Agency of the European Union and for the At-Large Advisory Committee of the Internet Corporation for Assigned Names and Numbers, she combines academia with policy work. Professor Kulesza, aside from her primary academic involvement with the University of Lodz, has been serving as an expert on human rights online for the Council of Europe and European Commission. She has been a visiting professor with the Oxford Internet Institute, Oslo University, Justus-Liebig-Universität Gießen, and Westfälische Wilhelms Universität Münster. Kulesza was also a visiting researcher with the University of Cambridge and Ludwig-Maximilians-Universität München as well as a scholar of the Robert Bosch Stiftung, Polish Ministry of Foreign Affairs and the Foundation for Polish Science. She is a scientific committee member of the EUCyberDirect project and a member of the working group on international law and its application to cyberspace, set up by the CICIR and GCSP. She has also been involved with the Sino-European Cybersecurity Dialogue (SECD) and the Global Commission on the Stability of Cyberspace (GCSC) working on international cybersecurity and protecting Internet's core. Kulesza is currently working on various research projects on privacy and cybersecurity, including a fundamental rights review pilot project for the European Parliament, where she is responsible for the fundamental rights review of European agencies policies, including Europol and Eurojust. Since 2010 until 2018, she served as Membership Committee Chair for the Global Internet Governance Academic Network (GigaNet). She often engages with various NGOs working on cybersecurity and human rights.

Xymena Kurowska is an associate professor of International Relations at Central European University (CEU). She received her doctorate in political and social sciences from European University Institute in Florence, Italy. She has been a grantee of European Foreign and Security Policy Studies Programme, the CEU principal investigator in Global Norm Evolution and Responsibility to Protect project, a Marie Skłodowska-Curie senior research fellow at the Department of International Politics at Aberystwyth University, and serves as academic rapporteur for EU Cyber Direct. She works within International Political Sociology and publishes on European security, norms, Russian diplomacy and state-society relations, as well as reflexivity in the academic practice and interpretive methodologies.

Luisa Cruz Lobato is a PhD candidate in International Relations at the Pontifical Catholic University of Rio de Janeiro (IRI PUC-Rio) working on critical security studies, cybersecurity, global governance and Science and

Technology Studies. She is a visiting researcher at the Graduate Institute of International and Development Studies and researcher at the Igarapé Institute's Cyber Security and Digital Liberties Programme.

Nadia Marsan is a senior assistant legal adviser in the Office of Legal Affairs at NATO Headquarters in Brussels, Belgium. Nadia Marsan has been a member of NATO's International Staff since 2006.

Anton Peez is a doctoral researcher at Peace Research Institute Frankfurt (PRIF) and a PhD student at the University of Frankfurt. His research interests include norms, coercion, and compliance in international politics. He holds a BA from the University of Frankfurt and an MPhil from the University of Oxford.

Dr. Przemysław Roguski is a lecturer in Law at the Jagiellonian University in Kraków (Poland) and an expert on cybersecurity and international law at the Kościuszko Institute. His research focuses on the law of peacetime cyber operations and different aspects of international law relating to cybersecurity, ICT and Internet governance. Previously, Przemysław has worked in private practice and as a lecturer for the German Academic Exchange Service (DAAD). He holds law degrees from the University of Mainz (Germany), Trinity College Dublin (Ireland) and a PhD in international law from Jagiellonian University.

James Shires is an assistant professor at the Institute of Security and Global Affairs, Leiden University, and a nonresident research fellow with the Cyber Project at the Belfer Center for Science and International Affairs, Harvard Kennedy School. He is also a research affiliate with the Centre for Technology and Global Affairs at the Department of Politics and International Relations, University of Oxford. He holds a DPhil in International Relations from the University of Oxford, with a thesis on cybersecurity in Egypt and the Gulf states completed in August 2018. He holds an MSc in Global Governance and Public Policy from Birkbeck College, University of London, and a BA in Philosophy from the University of Cambridge. He has written many articles, policy papers, and blogs on cybersecurity in the Middle East, and has won awards for policy papers on cybersecurity from the Hague Program on Cyber Norms, the German Marshall Fund and the International Institute for Strategic Studies.

Nicholas Tsagourias is a professor of International Law at the University of Sheffield and director of the Sheffield Centre for International and European Law. He is also visiting professor at the Paris School of International Affairs.

Lightning Source UK Ltd.
Milton Keynes UK
UKHW012039150421
382057UK00001B/325